DATE DUE

~~NO 4'98~~		
~~NO 20 02~~		

DEMCO 38-296

The Gatekeepers

THE GATEKEEPERS

Federal District Courts in the Political Process

KEVIN L. LYLES

Westport, Connecticut
London

Library of Congress Cataloging-in-Publication Data

Lyles, Kevin L., 1959–
    The gatekeepers : federal district courts in the political process
/ Kevin L. Lyles.
      p. cm.
    Includes bibliographical references and index.
    ISBN 0–275–96082–X (alk. paper)
    1. District courts—United States. 2. Political questions and
judicial power—United States. 3. Judges—Selection and
appointment—United States. I. Title.
    KF8754.L95 1997
    347.73′22—dc21   97–25900

British Library Cataloguing in Publication Data is available.

Library of Congress Catalog Card Number: 97–25900
ISBN: 0–275–96082–X

First published in 1997

Praeger Publishers, 88 Post Road West, Westport, CT 06881
An imprint of Greenwood Publishing Group, Inc.

Printed in the United States of America

The paper used in this book complies with the
Permanent Paper Standard issued by the National
Information Standards Organization (Z39.48–1984).

10 9 8 7 6 5 4 3 2 1

For Pam, Dabney, Kelsey, and Ryan

Contents

Acknowledgments

The completion of this book required numerous and varied contributions and assistance from many people. This volume really developed in three stages. My special interest in the federal district courts had its genesis at Washington University at St. Louis. I must first then acknowledge the many contributions of my original advisors at Washington University, Liane Kosaki, Robert Salisbury, John Sprague, and especially Lucius Barker.

The second stage was during a very productive year as a Visiting Assistant Professor of Political Science and Post Doctoral Fellow in Law and Politics at Stanford University that I decided to undertake the National District Court Judge Survey (NDJS). The post-doctoral fellowship gave me the critical support needed to conduct the survey and my many interactions with so many "on the farm" helped to allay my early concerns and encouraged me to move forward. I especially appreciate the good advice and collegiality offered by Dave Brady, Dick Brody, Louis Fraga, and again, Lucius Barker. Lucius played an especially important role in the intellectual development of this project as well as in my overall training as a political scientist and student of the judiciary. As always, I am happy to count him as a friend as well as an intellectual mentor. Ora Hurd also helped to keep the business side of my stay at Stanford uncomplicated.

The Department of Political Science at the University of Illinois at Chicago provided a supportive environment for me while revising and polishing this book, the third stage. I must acknowledge the valuable assistance of my two research assistants: Marlene Rodriguez and Jennifer Rexroat. Marlene was instrumental in conducting the second wave of the district court judge survey and skillfully performed the tedious requirements of coding, re-coding, checking and re-checking the survey data. A special note of thanks is also due to John Gardiner, Director of the Office of Social Science Research (OSSR) at the University of Illinois at Chicago, who made office space available to house the second wave of the NDJS.

Jennifer Rexroat's contributions were also especially helpful: a doctoral student in political science with a concentration in American politics and women's studies, Jennifer was an uncommonly talented "sounding board" in reviewing the entire manuscript for final revisions.

Many others have offered words of support and made other significant contributions along the way. These include Twiley Barker, Michael Combs, Charles Franklin, Barbara Luck-Graham, Peter Leigh, Paula McClain, H. W. Perry, Andy McNitt, Debbie Melendez, Michael Preston, and Keith Yanner. Stephen Wasby also read a much earlier draft of the entire manuscript and his detailed comments were particularly helpful.

I must also acknowledge the assistance of those at Greenwood Publishing, including James Sabin and Marcia Goldstein. Especially do I appreciate the expertise of Terri Jennings and the work of others at the press who helped with production and promotion.

My final acknowledgments go to members of my family and closest friends, including Darla Brown, Donna Jones, and Michelle Paramore. I especially thank Pamela, my wife, and our children, Dabney, Kelsey, and Ryan. Their generosity of patience, support, and love was essential to the completion of this book. Finally I thank my parents, Marie and Leroy Lyles, whose support and encouragement have always made the difference. I owe so much to them all.

1   Introduction: Federal District Courts in the Political Process

Through his judicial appointments, a President has the opportunity to influence the course of national affairs for a quarter of a century after he leaves office. . . . [I]t is necessary to remember that the decision as to who will make the decisions affects what decisions will be made. . . . [T]he president [can] establish precise guidelines as to the type of man [sic] he wishes to appoint—his professional competence, his political disposition, his understanding of the judicial function—and establish a White House review procedure to assure that each prospective nominee recommended by the Attorney General meets his guidelines. . . . He [the president] may insist that some evidence exists as to the attitude of the prospective judge toward the role of the court. He may insist upon a man who has a passion for judicial restraint. . . . The criteria he can establish are as varied as the views held in different political, social, and legal circles today. But if he establishes his criteria and establishes his machinery for insuring that the criteria are met, the appointments he makes will be his, in fact, as in theory.[1]

INTRODUCTION

My focus on the role and function of the federal district courts is at bottom a study of the interaction of law and politics in our constitutional governing system. As so many have said regarding the institutional role and function of the U.S. Supreme Court, the federal district courts too are at once political *and* legal institutions. Both political scientists and lawyers alike would agree that given the dual nature of these lower federal courts, a better understanding of their operation and function in, as well as their impact on, the political system is appropriate. This is not an attempt to over-politicize the district courts. Clearly, as legal institutions the majority of their work is constrained by legal rules and procedures. Nonetheless, the frequency and salience of district court policymaking, their gatekeeping role in the federal judiciary, the characteristics and attitudes of the individual judges appointed to these courts, as well as the dynamics of the appointment process itself, suggest a political nature and function that should be rigorously analyzed.

To that end, this study first gives an overview of these lower federal trial courts in historical, institutional, and functional contexts and then addresses two principal lines of inquiry: (1) to what extent and with what success individual presidents have advanced particular policy objectives through their judicial appointments to the federal district courts; and (2) how the views of individual district court judges, on a variety of issues bring into sharp perspective the intimate interaction of law and politics generally. These views are also analyzed along the lines of race and gender.

The primary findings delineate more precisely the nature and effect of these various linkages between law and politics. Particularly do the findings shed light on the role and function of federal district courts in the judicial hierarchy and in the policy process generally. Specifically for example, my analysis indicates that presidents have been able to affect their policy agendas in areas where they have expressed clear policy preferences and actively recruited judges whom they believed shared these same views. Analysis supporting this conclusion is done on the basis of data yielded from a study of five issue areas over a thirty-six-year period, 1960–1996: namely, abortion rights, affirmative action, religious liberty, school desegregation, and voting rights.

The findings also suggest that practitioners themselves—federal district court judges—hold a wide variety of views and perspectives on matters that likewise reflect the basic interactive nature of law and politics in our governing system. This part of the analysis was achieved using data generated by the National District Court Judge Survey (NDJS).[2] These data illuminate a range of positions, attitudes, and perceptions among the judges relating to such matters as the nature and dynamics of judicial selection, the extent to which presidents are able to use judicial appointments to advance their policy positions, and the role and functions of lower court judges in policymaking.[3] By directly addressing how lower federal court judges themselves view such matters, this study helps to fill a void in which little systematic empirical data exist.

CONCEPTUAL AND CONTEXTUAL FRAMEWORKS

This study holds the view that courts and judges are in the political process and their "activity is interest activity not as a matter of choice but of function."[4] Thus, however particular judges view themselves—as conservatives or liberals, strict or broad constructionists, or interpretivists or noninterpretivists—the importance of courts and judges in American politics grows out of the nature and structure of our constitutional governing system. This is demonstrated clearly, for example, by the separation of powers among the three independent branches of government and the various checks and balances that affect their *interdependence on each other* rather than *independence from each other* in carrying out their respective functions. Thus, when viewed in the context of the American political system, the decisions made by judges advantage certain interests and disadvantage others. Thus, the positions taken by courts and judges can indeed prove crucial, even determinative, in particular policy conflicts.

Along these theoretical lines, for example, judicial policymaking may be viewed as the interaction of two major roles that courts may perform in the political process: (1) representing the unrepresented and underrepresented[5]; *and* (2) stimulating and legitimizing the policies of the dominant coalition.[6] However, whether judges decide to protect minority rights against majority tyranny or choose to stimulate or legitimate the policies that flow from the dominant coalition, the choices they make are policy choices that impact on interests conflicts. Indeed, the determination of who sits on the bench determines what and whose interests are represented.[7] At bottom, this volume demonstrates vividly three simple, yet still reluctantly acknowledged facts: (1) that judicial selection and appointments are an inextricable part of the political process; (2) that modern presidents have used and continue to use such appointments in their attempts to achieve particular policy objectives; and (3) that those who sit on the court determine what comes out of the court.

Accordingly, careful and resourceful analysis of the selection, nomination, and confirmation processes, as well as careful and resourceful analysis of the particular views of those so selected and those who now sit on these courts, bring into sharp focus the differential yet significant functions and roles that district courts perform in the formulation and implementation of public policy. This volume seeks to provide that careful and resourceful analysis.

WHY DISTRICT COURTS?

The importance of lower federal courts in the American political system generally as well as the congruence between presidential policies and judicial decisions are reflected in the recent growth of social science research.[8] District courts are often key determinants in deciding "who gets what, when, and how" from federal judicial policymaking. As the "workhorses of the federal judiciary," they are the only courts in the federal system where the litigants meet in open combat, where witnesses are heard, where the "facts" are determined, and where juries are used.

District courts not only interpret and apply Supreme Court decisions to the large numbers of cases that that Court cannot possibly address, but also implement the decisions made by the higher Court. In addition, given the broad formulations and resulting ambiguity that characterize most higher court rulings, especially those of the Supreme Court, the more numerous district court judges are given considerable leeway and opportunity to interpret and apply higher court decisions to many cases, most of which are disposed in these lower courts.

Nonetheless, most scholarly attention has focused on the Supreme Court, yet, the over 600 judges who now sit on the federal district courts also matter. As one federal district court judge aptly put it: "Justice stops in the district. They [the litigants] either get it here or they can't get it at all."[9] Empirical evidence offers strong support for this conclusion. The federal district courts decide some 230,000 civil cases annually and the decisions they reach in about 90 percent are final, with settlements being reached at this lower court level. Even the relatively few cases (about 10 percent) that are appealed are clearly influenced by the initial fact-finding proceedings that take place in the district courts. Consequently, these lower court judges not only influence the flow of information to the judicial hierarchy, but how they formulate questions also influences how higher courts, including the Supreme Court, answer such questions.[10] At times, for example, district courts exercise wide discretion when they receive cases back from the Supreme Court on remand for "further consideration." Thus, the district courts, by interpreting and applying the laws, may clearly promote, evade, or avoid the effects of Supreme Court decisions.

On balance, whatever our earlier preoccupations, increasing scholarly and popular attention suggests that we can no longer overlook the role and importance of district court judges in the formulation and implementation of public policy. These judges do indeed function at the heart of interest conflict in American politics. They desegregate school districts,[11] run mental institutions and prisons, break up monopolies (like AT&T)[12] and reapportion legislatures. How federal district courts handle these and other issues clearly effects the nature and quality of our everyday lives as well as our overall politics and society generally. It is quite understandable, then, that as trial judges, federal district court judges may be viewed as the "parish priests" of our legal order.[13]

A PREVIEW OF WHAT'S TO COME: CHAPTER ORGANIZATION

This volume utilizes multiple data sources, employs a number of straightforward methodological approaches, and provides a systematic analysis of the role and importance of federal district courts and judges in American politics and public policymaking.

Accordingly, this chapter briefly describes the conceptual and contextual framework of the study. The primary goal is to place the focus of the volume on district courts and judges as key participants in the policymaking process. Further, it suggests that this participation in the policymaking process is influenced by the structure and function of federal courts in our constitutional governing system, the nature and dynamics of judicial selection, as well as by the views and values held by individual judges so selected and who now sit on these courts. Theses matters will be discussed in subsequent chapters.

In Chapter 2, for example, I look at the federal district courts in institutional and functional perspectives by giving detailed attention to the history, operation, and function of the federal district courts. For the most part, this chapter is broadly descriptive; it utilizes various government documents, legal writings, historical essays, and so on, to trace the history and operation (e.g., jurisdiction, current workload, etc.) of these courts. Chapter 2 also introduces and utilizes NDJS data to assess how the district court judges themselves view the integral role and functions of their courts in public policymaking and in the political process generally.

Chapter 3 shifts attention from the role of the federal district courts as legal tribunals to a more specific focus on the general selection, nomination, and appointment processes for district court judges. The primary emphasis is to highlight the numerous actors, institutions, and unique procedures involved in the selection process for district court judges, including the president, the full Senate and the Senate Judiciary Committee, the attorney general and various other actors within the Department of Justice, state and local political officials (including senatorial courtesy), the American Bar Association, the FBI, and so on.

In short, Chapter 3 addresses the systemic and institutional processes and outcomes of how federal judges are selected and what observable impact groups and individuals, especially the president, have on those processes. Looking at the formal as well as informal politics of judicial selection provides perspectives and insights that might be overlooked in studies that focus primarily on doctrinal trends or judicial policymaking in particular issue areas. In this respect, the NDJS data prove especially informative in providing insights into the appointment and confirmation processes offered by the judges themselves that might not otherwise be discussed by simply reviewing public records, including Senate confirmation hearing transcripts. Overall, this chapter highlights the interactive and interdependent role of the executive, the Senate, and many relevant others in trying to control "who gets on the courts" so as to influence "what comes out of the courts."

This leads to a discussion of one of the primary issues addressed in this volume—in other words, the extent to which presidents might advance certain policy objectives through their judicial appointments to the federal district courts (chapters 4, 5, and 6). Given their sheer numbers and the importance of their roles in the federal court system, the extent to which district judges conform to presidential expectations holds enormous consequences regarding the role and influence presidents can play in shaping both judicial policies and public policies generally.

Because individual presidents have tailored the selection and nomination processes to promote their administration's legal philosophy it is necessary to provide some discrete analysis for each president in addition to the more general discussion in Chapter 3. To accomplish this task, using multiple data sources the analytical framework employed in Chapter 4 (1960–1975), Chapter 5 (1976–1987), and Chapter 6 (1988–1996) includes the creation of "presidential policy objective profiles" (PPOPs) that help to determine what policy areas were of special interest to particular presidents.[14] These profiles allow us to delineate policy concerns that a given president verifiably cared about. Based on these PPOPs, for example, five major policy areas were identified that were of special concern to particular presidents: abortion rights, affirmative action, religious liberty (e.g., school prayer), school desegregation, and voting rights.[15]

Next, the focus of Chapter 7 is directly on the extent to which presidents have successfully advanced certain policy objectives in these five areas through their judicial appointments to the district courts. Specifically, it analyzes the extent to which the judicial performance of district court judges, as measured by their decisions on "significant cases," reflects or comports with the overall presidential policy objective profiles developed in chapters 4, 5, and 6. "Significant cases" are defined as decisions involving issues of public policy that receive full written opinion and are "of general precedental value." Put directly, "significant cases" involve discretionary jurisprudence where influence and discretion may well guide the ability of judges to shape judicial policy, not merely to act with a mechanical jurisprudence. As such, the "significant case" approach complements—as well as provides a basis for comparison to—the "all case" and/or "published case" approaches utilized by existing works. For detailed discussion on the "significant district court case" data (SDCC) see Appendix B.[16] My primary findings, as indicated earlier, suggest that presidents have achieved much success in specific instances where they expressed clear policy preferences and actively recruited judges whom they believed shared these same views.

The following chapter, Chapter 8, utilizing the NDJS data, offers a comparative description and assessment of how African-American, Latino, and white federal district court judges view various aspects of their roles and functions as policy actors in the American political system generally.

Similarly, a comparative assessment of gender is the focus of Chapter 9. Again, I also utilize the NDJS data to offer a comparative description and assessment of how female federal district court judges view various aspects of their role and function as policy actors in comparison to male judges in the American political system generally.

A concluding chapter, Chapter 10, details the theoretical as well as practical implications of this research. Overall, the analysis provides additional insights into the nature, strengths, and effects of the various linkages between law and politics in our governing system. The findings particularly shed light on the role and function of federal district courts in the judicial system and in the policy process generally. They suggests clearly, for example, that judicial policymaking in our federal district courts may be influenced by the role of the president in the selection process. The findings also illuminate that federal district judges themselves hold a wide variety of views and perspectives on matters that likewise reflect the basic interactive nature of law and politics in our governing system.

This chapter and volume ends with a discussion of the value of research that combines the traditional approach and interests (in assessing doctrinal and significant case determinations) with the behaviorist's emphasis on systematic explanation (presidential expectation) and aggregate quantitative assessment (via the NDJS). Overall, the analysis suggests that a discussion of these matters yields theoretical as well as practical implications regarding the role of federal district court judges as policymakers in the American political system generally.

Next, I begin the study by taking a closer look at the historical, as well as the institutional and functional, contexts in which federal district courts and judges work.

NOTES

1. Memorandum written by Tom Charles Houston, a White House aide to President Nixon, on March 25, 1969, about two months after the start of the Nixon presidency. A copy of this memorandum was found by political scientist Sheldon Goldman in White House Central Files, FG 50, Box 1, Folder WHCF ExFG50, The Judicial Branch (1969–1970). Excerpts from the Nixon Presidential Materials Project, are published in Goldman's "The Bush Imprint on the Judiciary: Carrying on a Tradition," *Judicature* 74 (1991), p. 294. According to Goldman, the *original* copy of the memorandum, with written comments by President Nixon, was withdrawn from the president's papers at Nixon's direction.

2. See Appendix A.

3. Previous research on lower court judges' attitudes and perceptions has focused on issues such as district court judge socialization (e.g., see Robert A. Carp and Russell Wheeler, "Sink or Swim: The Socialization of a Federal District Judge," *Journal of Politics* 21 (1972), pp. 359–393; and Beverly B. Cook, "The Socialization of New Federal Judges: Impact on District Court Business," *Washington University Law Quarterly*, Spring (1971), pp. 253–279.); institutional perceptions using role analysis (e.g., William Kitchin, *Federal District Judges: An Analysis of Judicial Perceptions* [Baltimore: Collage Press, 1978]; selected three-judge district courts (e.g., Thomas G. Walker, "Judges in Concert: The Influence of the Group on Judicial Decision-Making," unpublished Ph.D. dissertation, University of Kentucky, 1970); race relations and trial judges (see, e.g., Kenneth N. Vines, "Federal District Judges and Race Relations Cases in the South," *Journal of Politics* 26 (1964), pp. 337–357, and Jack Peltason, *58 Lonely Men: Southern Federal Judges and School Desegregation* [Urbana, IL: University of Illinois Press, 1971]; rulings on police practices (Kenneth Dolbeare, "The Federal District Courts and Urban Public Policy: An Exploratory Study (1960–1967)," Joel B. Grossman and Joseph Tanenhaus, eds., *Frontiers of Judicial Research* [New York: Wiley, 1969], pp. 373–404); and sentencing behavior of district court judges (Susan Welch, with Michael Combs and John Gruhl, "Do Black Judges Make a Difference?" *American Journal of Political Science* 32 (1988), pp. 126–136, and Beverly B. Cook, "Sentencing Behavior of Federal Judges: Draft Cases, 1972," *University of Cincinnati Law Review* 42 (1973), pp. 597–633). Although the NDJS (1992–1996) revisits many of these issues, it differs from these previous works in that it is a national sample (as opposed to a nonrandom sample of twenty-one lengthy interviews covering only four circuits, i.e., Kitchin, 1978), and includes a broader range of inquiry with primary emphasis on the nomination and appointment process.

4. Jack Peltason, *Federal Courts in the Political Process* (New York: Random House, 1955).

5. See Martin Shapiro, *Law and Politics in the Supreme Court* (New York: The Free Press of Glencoe, 1964); and John Hart Ely, *Democracy and Distrust: A Theory of Judicial Review* (Cambridge: Harvard University Press, 1980).

6. Robert Dahl, "Decision-making in a Democracy: The Supreme Court as a National

Policy-Maker," *Journal of Public Law* 6 (1957), pp. 293–295. For a perceptive critique of Dahl, see Johnathon Casper, "The Supreme Court and National Policy Making," *American Political Science Review* 70 (1976), pp. 50–63.

7. See H. W. Perry, *Deciding to Decide* (Cambridge: Harvard University Press, 1991).

8. A case in point, for example, is the 1983 Carp and Rowland study where these authors conclude that, "to an impressive degree the voting patterns of district court judges do reflect the political values of their appointing presidents." See Robert Carp and C. K. Rowland, *Policymaking and Politics in the Federal District Courts* (Knoxville: The University of Tennessee Press, 1983), p. 53. See also, Craig R. Ducat and Robert L. Dudley "Federal District Judges and Presidential Power during the Postwar Era," *Journal of Politics* 51 (1989); Steve Alumbaugh and C. K. Rowland, "The Links Between Platform Based Appointment Criteria and Trial Judges' Abortion Judgments," *Judicature* 74 (1990); Rowland Songer, and Carp "Presidential Effects on Criminal Justice Policy in the Lower Federal Courts: The Reagan Judges," *Journal of Politics* 53 (1988), pp. 98–118; C. K. Rowland, Robert A. Carp and Ronald Stidham, "Patterns of Presidential Influence on the Federal District Courts: An Analysis of the Appointment Process," *Presidential Studies Quarterly* 14 (1984); Herbert M. Kritzer, "Political Correlates of the Behavior of Federal District Judges: A 'Best Case' Analysis," *Journal of Politics* 40 (1978), pp. 25–58; Sue Davis and Donald R. Songer, "The Changing Role for the United States Courts of Appeal: The Flow of Litigation Revisited," *Justice System Journal* 13 (1988–1989); and C. K. Rowland and Bridget Jeffery Todd, "Where You Stand Depends on Who Sits: Platform Promises and Judicial Gatekeeping in the Federal District Courts," *Journal of Politics* 53 (1991), pp. 175–185; and Ronald Stidham and Robert Carp, "Support for Labor and Economic Regulation among Reagan and Carter Appointees to the Federal Courts," *Social Science Journal* 26 (1989).

9. Robert A. Carp and Russell Wheeler, "Sink or Swim: The Socialization of a Federal District Judge," *Journal of Politics* 21 (1972), p. 359.

10. Walter F. Murphy, "Lower Court Checks on Supreme Court Power," *American Political Science Review* 53 (1959), pp. 1030–1034. See also, Tony Mauro, "High Stakes, Low Courts," *The Washington Monthly* 24, July-August, 1992.

11. However, decrees such as these and others, especially those upholding minority rights, are also among the most widely criticized manifestations of judicial intervention. See Abram Chayes, "The Role of the Judge in Public Law Litigation," *Harvard Law Review* 89 (1976), p. 1292.

12. *United States v. American Telephone & Telegraph Company*, 552 F. Supp. 131 (D.D.C. 1984. It was a Washington, DC district court that approved and continues to supervise the separation of local phone companies from AT&T, "thereby restructuring the entire American communications industry" (see Schwartz, *Packing the Courts*, p. 6.)

13. Harry Wilmer Jones, "The Trial Judge, Role Analysis and Profile," in *The Courts, the Public, and the Law Explosion*, Harry Jones, ed. (Englewood Cliffs, NJ: Prentice-Hall, 1965), p. 124.

14. These sources include, but are not limited to: (1) relevant materials and findings in scholarly and popular writing; (2) party platforms and campaign speeches by presidential nominees; (3) presidential addresses and news conferences; (4) statements and actions by the attorneys general, solicitors general, and other administration officials—especially those in the Justice Department; (5) Senate Judiciary Committee hearings on specific court nominations and related committee reports and Senate confirmation proceedings; and (6) briefs filed by the federal government.

15. It is important to note, however, that not all of the five issues were of equal con-

cern for each of the six presidents nor did they all openly express policy objectives regarding their district court appointments. The abortion issue, for example, was not a salient legal policy question in the early 1960s, and thus did not capture the attention of Kennedy and Johnson, as much as it did later presidents.

16. The significant case approach has been the widely accepted practice among political scientists and others in studying the role of the Supreme Court in politics and policymaking. For example, leading case books and treatises on constitutional law and civil liberties do not, and need not, include abstracts of every case the Supreme Court decides. For example, see Lucius J. Barker and Twiley W. Barker, *Civil Liberties and the Constitution* (Englewood Cliffs, NJ: Prentice-Hall, 1994) or David M. O'Brien, *Constitutional Law and Politics,* vols. I and II (New York: W. W. Norton and Company, 1995).

2 The Federal District Courts: Institutional and Functional Perspectives

By all odds, the workhorses of the federal judiciary . . .

—Henry Abraham[1]

This chapter looks directly at the district courts in both institutional and functional terms. First I look briefly at the nature and development of district courts as policy actors. Next, I look more closely at how these judges themselves view the operation and function of the district courts in both legal and political contexts. Throughout this discussion, relevant National District Court Judge Survey (NDJS) data are included where appropriate to fill the gaps between the institutional nature of the courts and the practical realities about what the judges actually believe about their role and institutional functions in the American political process.

THE FEDERAL DISTRICT COURTS: INSTITUTIONAL DEVELOPMENT, GROWTH, AND OPERATION

Article III of the Constitution vests judicial power in "one Supreme Court and in such inferior courts as Congress may from time to time ordain and establish" (Art. III, Sec. 1). However, soon after the ratification of the Constitution, Congress began to expand federal court organization by its passage of the First Judiciary Act of 1789.[2] By this Act, the First Congress established both federal circuit courts (a forerunner to the modern day Courts of Appeals)[3] as well as the district courts. A district court was established in each state and was presided over by a district judge.

Initially, the district courts were primarily federal misdemeanor courts with limited criminal and civil jurisdiction. As stipulated by the First Judiciary Act of

1789, the district courts had jurisdiction over crimes committed in the district or upon the high seas that were punishable by no more than thirty lashes, a fine of $100 or a term of imprisonment not exceeding six months. These courts had exclusive jurisdiction in all admiralty and maritime cases, suits for penalties and forfeitures, tort suits by aliens and suits by the United States.[4] However, the district courts had concurrent jurisdiction with the circuit courts when an alien sued for a tort in violation of the law on nations or treaty, or where the federal government itself sued and the amount equaled $100 or less, or suits against consuls.[5] The courts' civil jurisdiction in cases brought by the government was limited to matters exceeding $100. Although district courts were given jurisdiction over matters arising under patent laws in 1790,[6] and bankruptcy cases in 1800,[7] for the most part these new lower federal courts were considered primarily criminal courts during their first one-hundred years of existence.

One major institutional development, and perhaps the first major attempt to "pack" the district courts, was the Judiciary Act of 1801 (repealed in 1802). This 1801 act was spurred by the Federalists (associated with John Adams and Alexander Hamilton) who wanted to give outgoing President Adams the opportunity to appoint "deserving" Federalists to judiciary positions from which they could continue the battle with the incoming Republicans, especially Thomas Jefferson and James Madison. Following Jefferson's election, the lame duck Federalist Congress passed the 1801 statute, which created four new district courts, including a court for the District of Columbia and extended the jurisdiction of the federal courts to all cases arising under the Constitution or federal laws.[8] Although the newly empowered Jeffersonian Republicans repealed the law in 1802,[9] the majority of changes in the Judiciary Act of 1801 were more structural than procedural. Thus, as a result of the repeal, the jurisdiction of district courts remained as originally designated in the Judiciary Act of 1789.

Throughout the nineteenth century, a district court was established for each state when states were added to the union.[10] In the main, these district courts were considered primarily criminal trial courts. The perception of the district courts as primarily criminal courts results from the custom of the district court judge to try criminal cases in the district courts and most, if not all, of the civil cases in the circuit courts.[11] Indeed, one of the more colorful aspects of the history of the federal courts concerns the circuit riding by judges and lawyers as they traveled from one circuit to another. For example, beginning with the Judiciary Act of 1789, Supreme Court justices were required to travel the circuit to hold court with the district court judge of the district in which the circuit court was held. The district court judge would likewise travel throughout the state to hold court.[12]

While a number of minor intervening developments took place, legal historians suggest that the Judiciary Act of 1875 was the major turning point in the historical development of the federal district courts. The 1875 act conferred upon these lower federal courts enormous authority. As suggested by Justice Felix Frankfurter, the courts grew from "restricted tribunals of fair dealings between citizens of different states and became the primary and powerful reliances for vindicating every right given by the Constitution, the laws, and the treaties of the United States."[13] The fundamental effect of the 1875 statute was to afford individuals claiming rights under the Constitution or under state or federal law the ability to initially file suit in either federal or state court. Overall, the pattern of federal court development entailed reductions in the jurisdiction of the circuit courts, parallel increases in the jurisdiction of the district courts, and the establishment of the circuit courts of appeals[14] to take pressure off of the Supreme Court.[15] Eventually, the Judiciary Act of 1911 abolished the old "circuit courts," leaving the district courts as the only trial courts in the federal judicial system.

Expanding and Redefining Jurisdictions

Understanding the issue of jurisdiction is tantamount to understanding the distinctive role and function of the district courts in the political process. The broader the jurisdiction, the more types of interest conflicts that come before the courts for resolution. The jurisdiction of the district courts remains under the control of Congress, and, as evidenced in the preceding section, has changed dramatically over time. The district courts are currently the only trial courts in the federal judicial system with original jurisdiction that is in part exclusive and in part concurrent with that of state courts and that of the Supreme Court.[16] As of 1990, their original jurisdiction is over cases involving more than $50,000, where the parties are from different states or the case involves a *federal question*. "A federal question is one which involves the meaning and/or application of the Constitution, a statute, or a treaty of the United States."[17] The district courts have limited appellate jurisdiction in only a few classes of cases tried before U.S. magistrates (formerly U.S. commissioners).[18] The district courts dispose of cases and controversies under the plethora of federal law stemming from the Constitution, from laws made in pursuance of it, or from treaties of the United States. Also, for example, the U.S. District Court for the District of Columbia has a special responsibility in reviewing changes in local electoral practices in certain states by virtue of the Voting Rights Act. In sum, the district courts are exclusively controlled by Congress, which can expand or curtail their jurisdiction. These vast jurisdictional boundaries not only accent the courts' roles in the political process but also more or less determine the potential policy areas that presidents may hope to affect through judicial appointments.

And these policy areas cover a wide range of legal issues—including civil rights, civil liberties, criminal justice, environmental rights, Indian treaty rights, issues related to child care, and the exploration of the outer space. Overall these responses amplify the broad jurisdiction of the federal district courts as well as accent the potential of these courts to make policy in issue areas that presidents may hope to affect through judicial appointments.

Growth and Function

The number of federal district courts and judges has clearly increased over time. The Judiciary Act of 1789 provided for the creation of thirteen judgeships. By 1996, there were 94 U.S. District Courts, eighty-nine in the fifty states, and one each in the District of Columbia, Guam, Puerto Rico, the Virgin Islands, and the Northern Mariana Islands with some 649 judges presiding over roughly 400 localities. The district courts in the three territories are legislative courts having judges who serve ten-year terms, whereas the district courts in the District of Columbia and Puerto Rico, like those in the states, are established under Article III of the Constitution and have judges appointed for life.[19] Each of these 94 districts consists of an entire state or a portion thereof. No district encompasses more than one state and none cut across state boundaries to include parts of two or more states. However, there may be more than one district in a single state; for example, Texas, California, and New York each contain four districts. Nearly all districts have two or more judges and the Southern District of New York, which includes Manhattan and the Bronx, is the largest with twenty-eight judges. Nearly half of all litigation occurs in the twelve district courts that are located in the larger metropolitan areas. With the infrequent exception of three-judge district courts,[20] each federal district court is normally presided over by a single judge.[21]

In the main, there are basically three broad classes of cases, based on their respective importance, which routinely come before the federal district courts.[22] The most prolific class consist of *private* cases. These are adjudications in which the issues and laws do not involve broad public policy declarations. The second class is the *public* cases. These cases usually involve the public as prosecutor (as in all criminal cases) or as a defendant (as in a civil suit against the government).

The third category of cases—and least frequent—are those cases with the potential for far-reaching consequences regarding statutory interpretation or basic constitutional doctrines and varied public policies. This study is concerned primarily with cases growing out of categories two and three, for it is in these areas that the judges themselves may function as discretionary *political actors* in deciding cases that support, amplify, or oppose the policy preferences of the appointing president.

The Cases

Adjudicating both civil and criminal[23] cases, the district courts are indeed the "workhorses" of the national court system. Table 2.1 and 2.2 illustrate the increasingly heavy dockets of the district courts, what Richard Posner has termed the "caseload explosion."[24] Table 2.1 summarizes the rapid growth (with short periods of decline) in the civil cases workload in modern times, 1960–1996. As indicated, civil filings increased steadily to a total of 273,670 in 1985, decreased for several years to 210,890 in 1991,[25] but have since continued to grow steadily to 269,132 in 1996.

Similarly, as also indicated in Table 2.1, civil filings per authorized judgeship have followed a similar pattern, rising to 508 in 1984, declining 325 in 1991, before steadily increasing each year thereafter to a six-year high of 383 in 1995. Notice too, that the numbers of cases terminated and pending have followed similar patterns, both increasing in recent years to 229,820 and 242,274, respectively, in 1995. Lastly, the 13 percent increase, from 135,853 in 1994 to 153,849 in 1995, in civil cases filed on federal questions is consistent with the general trend of increase since 1960 (Table 2.1).

Table 2.1
Civil Cases Filed, Terminated, and Pending on Federal Questions, 1960–1996

Year	Authorized Judgeships	Total Civil Cases Filed	Cases per Judgeship	Civil Cases Terminated	Civil Cases Pending	Federal Questions
1960	245	59,284	242	61,829	61,251	—
1961	—	58,293	—	55,416	64,128	—
1962	289	61,836	185	57,996	67,968	—
1963	289	63,630	195	62,379	69,219	—
1964	294	66,930	207	63,954	72,195	—
1965	307	67,678	214	65,478	74,395	—
1966	318	70,906	200	66,184	79,117	—
1967	322	70,961	198	70,172	79,906	—
1968	323	71,449	207	68,873	82,482	—
1969	341	77,193	225	73,354	86,321	—
1970	401	87,321	213	80,435	93,207	—
1971	401	93,396	217	86,563	100,040	—
1972	400	96,173	253	95,181	101,032	—
1973	400	98,560	253	98,259	101,333	—
1974	400	03,530	268	97,633	107,230	—
1975	400	17,320	293	104,783	119,767	52,688
1976	399	30,597	327	110,175	140,189	56,823
1977	398	30,567	328	117,150	153,606	57,011
1978	399	38,770	348	125,914	166,462	59,271
1979	516	54,666	300	143,323	177,805	63,221
1980	516	168,789	327	160,481	186,113	64,928
1981	516	180,576	350	177,975	188,714	72,514
1982	515	206,193	400	189,473	205,434	79,197
1983	515	241,842	470	215,356	231,920	87,935
1984	515	261,485	508	243,113	250,292	92,062
1985	575	273,670	476	269,838	254,114	94,467
1986	575	254,828	443	266,765	242,177	98,747
1987	575	239,185	416	238,001	243,361	99,393
1988	575	239,634	417	238,753	244,123	101,710
1989	575	233,529	406	235,219	242,433	103,768
1990	575	217,879	379	213,922	242,346	103,938

Table 2.1 (continued)

Year	Author-ized Judge-ships	Total Civil Cases Filed	Cases per Judge-ship	Civil Cases Termi-nated	Civil Cases Pending	Federal Ques-tions
1991	649	210,890	325	220,262	226,234	*103,496*
1992	649	230,509	355	231,304	225,439	118,180
1993	649	229,850	354	226,165	218,041	126,271
1994	649	236,391	364	228,361	223,759	135,853
1995	649	248,335	383	229,820	242,274	153,849
1996	649	269,132	—	—	—	—
Percent Change 1995 over 1994	—	5.1	5.0	0.6	8.3	13.0

Source: Generated from the *Annual Reports of the Director of the Administrative Office of the United States Courts*, 1960; 1970; 1973; 1974; 1976; 1979; 1982; 1989; 1990; and the *Judicial Business of the United States Courts 1995 Report to the Director, Leonidas Ralph Mecham, 1995* (a reproduced report by the Statistics Division, Administrative Office of the United States Courts, microfiche). Beginning in 1992, these figures are reported according to fiscal years, not calendar years.

Overall, not only has increasing litigation opened up new channels for district court decision making, but the steadily increasing number of civil filings—particularly cases involving federal questions—also highlights the salient position of federal district judges to interpret and make the law, but also to impede or promote the policy positions of his/her appointing president. As one judicial scholar has noted: "Trial judges, because of the multitude of cases they hear which remain unheard or unchanged by appellate courts, as well as because of their fact—and issue—shaping powers, appear to play an independent and formidable part in the policy impact of the federal court system upon the larger political system."[26]

On the issue of caseload, consider the following 1996 report published in "The Third Branch," the monthly publication of the Administrative Office of the U.S. Courts.

"The Third Branch": July 1996

Federal judges today are faced with unprecedented levels of work. Their daily challenges are compounded by the fact that no new judgeships at any level of the federal courts have been created in nearly four years. "The demands placed on United States judges today are staggering," said Leonidas Ralph Mecham, Director of the Administrative Office. "Jurists at virtually every level of our federal system are facing a greater number of cases, which involve increasingly complex issues, explore novel areas of the law, and consume a larger portion of their time." The following are some examples.

There were nearly 48,000 more cases filed in the U.S. district courts in 1995 than in 1990. The number of civil rights cases filed in U.S. district courts jumped 86 percent in the last five years. During calendar year 1995 national filings for immigration-related offenses rose by 58 percent over the preceding year. In the U.S. District Court for the Southern District of California alone, immigration filings nearly tripled over the past 12 months. Due in part to breast implant litigation, the number of personal injury/product liability cases filed nationwide climbed 125 percent from the 12-month period ending March 31, 1995, compared to the corresponding period in 1996. . . . The AO recently studied trends in civil rights filings and criminal immigration filings in U.S. district courts.

Immigration

Criminal filings in federal district courts for immigration-related offenses such as re-entry after deportation, drug smuggling, documentation fraud, and immigration smuggling jumped 58 percent during calendar year 1995. Of this increase in filings, 97 percent occurred in nine districts: the District of Arizona, Central District of California, Eastern District of California, Northern District of California, Southern District of California, District of New Mexico, District of Oregon, Southern District of Texas, and Western District of Texas. In the Southern District of California, immigration filings nearly tripled from 441 in 1994 to 1,222 in 1995. This trend in growth is expected to continue as the Department of Justice and Congress place greater emphasis on aggressive immigration policies and add to the number of border patrol agents.

Civil Rights

The rapid increase in the number of civil rights cases filed started shortly after the last Article III judgeship bill was signed into law in December 1990. In the previous five years, civil rights filings were relatively stable with only small fluctuations. The recent increase was driven largely by cases related to employment civil rights, which rose 126 percent from 1991 to 1995. Recent civil rights legislation—in particular the Civil Rights Act of 1991 and the Americans with Disabilities Act of 1990—is largely responsible for this increase. When weighted for complexity, the increase in the number of civil rights filings equates to 55 district court judgeships and likely would have an impact also on the courts of appeals.[27]

More Cases: More Judges?

One necessary consequence of the caseload explosion has been the dramatic increase in the number of sitting judges.[28] Overall, fifty or more federal judicial vacancies become available annually.[29] The number of judges has increased notably in recent years. For example, while the number of district court judges doubled between 1900 and 1960 (an increase of 180 judges over sixty years), it more than doubled again between 1960 and 1990 (an increase of 404 judges over only thirty-five years). As summarized in Table 2.2, in 1961 there were only 245 district court judgeships; however, by 1990 this figure had dramatically increased more than 1.5 times to 649. The largest single increase was during the Carter administration when Congress passed the Omnibus Judgeship Act of 1978, which created 152 new judgeships and afforded President Carter significant opportunities to shape the bench during his final year in office. The Federal Judgeship Act of 1990 created seventy-four additional new district judgeships, bringing the current total to 649.

In addition to the increase in the number of judges, the primary method used to accommodate this caseload explosion has been the expansion in the number and function of supporting personnel, including United States magistrate judges, law clerks, staff attorneys, and interns. Consider, for example, the 385 U.S. magistrate judges who serve and function as a kind of "junior" district judge. Consider further the increase in the number of law clerks, the creation of a "floating law clerk" termed a staff attorney, and the utilization of "externs"— law students who work as junior law clerks for course credit.[30] At present, Congress has authorized two law clerks for each district court judge. Magistrate judges are authorized to have a clerical assistant and with special approval of the Magistrate Judges Committee on the Judicial Conference, a law clerk. And some district courts are allowed to hire staff law clerks who serve the entire court.

Table 2.2
Number of Authorized U.S. District Court Judges, 1789 through 1996*

Years	Authorized Judgeships
1789–1870	13–50
1871–1922	52–100
1923–1935	110–134
1936–1949	151–197
1950–1961	214–245
1962–1965	289–287
1966–1969	318–341
1970–1978	401–399
1979–1984	516–515
1985–1990	575
1990–1996	649

Source: Compiled and updated from numbers provided in Richard A. Posner, *The Federal Courts: Crisis and Reform* (Cambridge, MA: Harvard University Press, 1985), Table B.3, pp. 353–357, and, the *Annual Report of the Director of the Administrative Office of the United States Courts*, 1976, 1982, 1989, and 1993.

*Senior judges excluded for the years 1789 to 1959.

United States Magistrate Judges

In 1968, Congress passed the Federal Magistrates Act creating a "new echelon of judicial officers in the federal judicial system."[31] In 1990, Congress passed the Judicial Improvements Act changing their title to U.S. magistrate judge. Between 1970 and 1993, the number of full-time magistrate judges increased from sixty-one to 385.[32] Although new magistrate judges' positions are authorized by the Judicial Conference and subject to funding by Congress, they are formally selected and appointed by the district judge and serve either full-time (eight-year term) or part-time (four-year term) and function as a kind of "junior" district judge.[33] Moreover, within the guidelines set by the Federal Magistrates Acts of 1968, 1976, and 1979, it is the district court judges themselves who determine the duties and responsibilities of their magistrates, including permitting them [with the consent of the parties involved] to conduct all proceedings in a civil matter and enter a judgment in the case, and to conduct a trial of persons accused of misdemeanors committed within the district [with the defendants' consent]. In 1990, for example, U.S. magistrate judges disposed of 450,565 matters, an increase of 4 percent over 1989.[34]

The bottom line is that Congress has given federal district court judges the authority to delegate the magistrates' participation in the judicial process and that participation may vary among districts.[35] District court judges use magistrate judges in essentially one of three ways. They may be used as (1) additional judges who hear and decide their own civil cases; (2) as specialists who hear and make recommended action on some special aspect of law; or (3) as a "team player," i.e., the magistrate might hear all pretrial matters to determine whether the case is ready for the judge.[36]

As stated in the *Law Clerk Handbook*, "district court . . . clerks perform a wider variety of functions than do appellate clerks."[37] Overall, between 1970 and 1980, judicial personnel exploded by 111 percent and reached almost 15,000 in 1988.[38] And, according to the *Annual Report of the Director of the Administrative Office of the United States Courts*, by 1991 this figure had risen to 24,526—including more than 2,695 law clerks, over 1,891 secretaries, 196 staff attorneys, 129 district and circuit executives, and other staff supporting the 828 district and circuit judges.[39]

It would be misleading, however, to suggest that the federal court system has responded to this crisis of "demand" with a concurrent increase in the overall "supply" of judges. As one judicial scholar has stated, there is "perpetually an insufficient total" of district court judges.[40] Indeed, given the data presented in Table 2.1 under filing per judge, there has been only modest success in expanding the number of judges in proportion to the increase in civil caseload.[41]

FEDERAL COURTS IN POLICYMAKING

Overall, these increases in the jurisdiction, caseload, the number of sitting judges, and their supporting personnel all combine to suggest the key policymaking role and potential of our federal district courts. As discussed in this and other studies, these lower federal courts are clearly involved in the policy process and as such may be viewed as policymakers. But equally as clear, though not surprisingly, there remains division among judges themselves on such issues. Interestingly, however, there is considerable recognition among these judges in terms of their role and participation in the policy process.

That district court judges are *involved* in the policy process is a fairly strongly supported position, including support from the judges themselves. When responding, for example, to the NDJS question "[G]iven their role in judicial review and statutory interpretation, district court judges are *involved* in the policy process, regardless of their judicial philosophy," a significant majority, about 68 percent, agreed compared to only about 25 percent disagreeing (Table 2.3, Q14).[42] When the responding judges are placed in one of two presidential appointment cohorts, Democratic appointees and Republican appointees, about 75 percent of Democratic appointees agreed compared to about 65 percent of Republican appointees.

Moreover, when asked whether "while interpreting and applying the law, district court judges *make* policy," about 40 percent of the respondents agreed that they [district court judges] do in fact "make policy" (Table 2.3, Q10) compared to about 52 percent disagreeing. Clearly, these data suggest that there exists wide disagreement among the judges themselves as to their policy*making* role. This division is apparent among both Democratic appointees and Republican appointees and is well exemplified by the margin notes added to the survey by several judges. For example, Judge 264 wrote next to Q10, "I wish we could [make policy] in more instances." On the other hand, Judge 534 wrote in the margin "They should not be [on the bench] if they are [making policy]."

Table 2.3
District Court Judges and Institutional Perspectives on the Courts as Policymakers

	% Strongly Agree	% Agree	% No Opinion	% Disagree	% Strongly Disagree
Q14. Given their role in judicial review and statutory interpretation, district court judges are *involved* in the policy process, regardless of their judicial philosophy.					
All judges	1.8	66.2	5.5	24.2	1.4
Democratic appointees	3.0	71.7	7.2	16.3	.6
Republican appointees	1.2	63.4	4.7	28.3	1.9
Q10. While interpreting and applying the law, district court judges *make* policy.					
All judges	1.4	38.9	5.5	42.6	9.2
Democratic appointees	3.0	42.8	6.6	40.4	4.2
Republican appointees	.6	37.0	5.0	43.8	11.8
Q16. Most of the time, district court judges interpret the law; however, on occasion they *should* make the law.					
All judges	1.2	42.6	4.9	36.3	13.9
Democratic appointees	1.8	61.4	3.0	25.3	7.8
Republican appointees	.9	32.9	5.9	41.9	17.1

Table 2.3 (continued)

	% Strongly Agree	% Agree	% No Opinion	% Disagree	% Strongly Disagree
Q17. The Constitution is what the judges say it is.					
All judges	5.5	42.8	4.9	35.2	9.2
Democratic appointees	8.4	52.4	1.8	27.7	5.4
Republican appointees	4.0	37.9	6.5	39.1	11.2
Q13. Even if a district court judge strongly believes a particular Supreme Court decision is "wrong," the district court judge is nonetheless bound to follow such a ruling.					
All judges	48.8	48.4	.2	1.8	—
Democratic appointees	44.0	54.2	—	1.2	—
Republican appointees	51.2	45.3	.3	2.2	—
Q12. To a large extent, the decisional patterns of district court judges reflect the political values of their appointing presidents.					
All judges	1.0	27.3	9.6	55.7	6.1
Democratic appointees	2.4	27.7	6.0	59.0	4.2
Republican appointees	.3	27.0	11.5	54.0	7.1

	A Lot	Occasion-ally	Seldom	Never
Q15. To what extent do you *make* public policy.				
All judges	—	30.9	45.9	21.5
Democratic appointees	—	43.4	41.0	14.5
Republican appointees	—	24.5	48.4	25.2

	Often	Sometimes	Seldom	Never
Q27. Do you feel your personal attitudes and values affect your discretionary judgments on the court?				
All judges	6.6	51.0	34.6	5.9
Democratic appointees	8.4	59.6	27.1	4.8
Republican appointees	5.6	46.6	38.5	6.5
Q28. To what extent do you feel other district court judges allow their personal attitudes and values to affect their discretionary judgments on the court?				
All judges	9.2	64.1	23.0	.6
Democratic appointees	9.6	71.1	17.5	—
Republican appointees	9.0	60.6	25.8	.9

Percentages may not total 100 because "missing responses" are omitted.

The judges also remain divided when asked about their own—as opposed to other judges'—policymaking activity. When asked directly, "[T]o what extent do you *make* public policy," a considerable number of justices (31 percent) responded "occasionally"; however, about 22 percent responded "never" (See Table 2.3, Q15 and Figure 2.1). Nearly half, 46 percent, responded "seldom."

Figure 2.1
[T]o What Extent Do You *Make* Public Policy?"

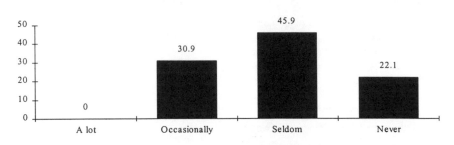

When the responding judges are placed in one of two presidential appointment cohorts, about 43 percent of Democratic appointees responded "a lot," compared to a significantly fewer 24.5 percent of Republican appointees. That is, while the majority of district court judges respond that they seldom make policy, Democratic appointees disproportionately make up those who admit to making policy "occasionally."

For the most part, the NDJS data suggest that district court judges not only acknowledge their role in the policy process but significant numbers recognize their role in *making* public policy. In addition, the NDJS also included a question designed to measure these judges' beliefs on whether or not they *should* be involved in the policy process. Consider, for instance, that when asked "most of the time district court judges interpret the law; however, on occasion they *should* make the law," almost half, 44 percent, of the judges agreed that they *should* make the law (Table 2.3, Q16). Further, a majority, 63.2 percent, of Democratic appointees "agreed" compared to far fewer, about 34 percent, of the Republican appointees. Consider the following comments that were written in the margins of the NDJS questionnaire by judges for this question:

Q16. "Most of the time district court judges interpret the law; however, on occasion they should make the law."

Judge 024   Disagree, "not 'should,' but they have no alternative if Congress has not made itself clear."

Judge 167   Disagree, "I don't believe in judicial activism—changing the law because Congress has failed to do, etc. On the other hand, every decision whether it is yes or no, 'makes the law'—and may change competing rights and values."

Judge 240	Disagree, "but it is an inevitable & necessary part of the job; but 'should' is inappropriate."
Judge 399	Disagree, "only when they must—i.e. for example—where the law is unclear."
Judge 691	Disagree, "On occasion, either way the law is interpreted it will have the effect of making law, trial judges should not attempt to make the law."
Judge 200	Agree, "Occasionally they do—it is inevitable."
Judge 483	Agree, "to decide a case on first impression you *must*."
Judge 636	Agree, "[They] have to."
Judge 741	Agree, "Where there is no binding precedent."

The stark division among district court judges' perceptions of their policy-making role is similarly revealed by their responses to other NDJS questions as well. By way of illustration, in response to NDJS Q17: "[T]he Constitution is what judges say it is," just about half, 48.4 percent agreed, compared to 44.4 percent disagreeing. With regard to appointing president, about 61 percent of all Democratic appointees agreed compared to about 42 percent of Republican appointees. Clearly, these judges are well aware of the interpretive role and function as nearly half agree that the Constitution is in fact "what the judges say it is." Unfortunately, though, the NDJS question was not worded specifically to determine whether the respondents who "agreed" included themselves (district court judges) in their assessment or were limiting their responses to Supreme Court justices. However, it appears from reviewing the comments in the margins by many judges that in fact at least some intended their "agree" response to be limited to Supreme Court justices, not district court judges.

Q17. "The Constitution is what the judges say it is."

Judge 84	Agree, "Supreme Court justices."
Judge 102	Agree, "The Constitution is what 'Supreme Court justices' say it is."
Judge 121	Agree, "Depends on what judges."
Judge 167	"I agree the Constitution is what judges say it is—but disagree that it is to be changed at the whim of the judiciary, or at the demand of the media."

Judge 189	Agree, "The Constitution is what 'Supreme Court' judges say it is."
Judge 286	"Justices."
Judge 327	Disagree, "Reason *not* will is the hallmark of American law."
Judge 506	Agree, "Supreme Court—yes!"
Judge 508	Agree, "The Constitution is what 'Supreme Court' judges say it is."
Judge 534	"*Not* what District Judges say it is unless there is no higher authority."
Judge 565	Agree, "Supreme Court only."
Judge 636	Agree, "Supreme Court only."
Judge 655	Disagree, "Not district judges."
Judge 657	"The Constitution is what 'the Supreme Court says' it is."
Judge 666	"Limited to the judges of the Supreme Court."
Judge 691	"Some of the phrases of the Constitution lend themselves to subjective analysis. Also, some justices have viewed the broad phrases as a license to support their view that the Constitution is whatever they want it to be."

Although the judges are greatly divided regarding their policymaking role in general, there is far less division among district court judges with regard to their status in the federal judicial system, especially with regard to the Supreme Court. When asked "[E]ven if a district court judge strongly believes a particular Supreme Court decision is 'wrong,' the district court judge is nonetheless bound to follow such a ruling," nearly all judges (97 percent) agreed, and of those about half strongly agreed (Table 2.3, Q13). In fact, only 12 (2.4 percent) of the 488 judges responding disagreed with the statement and there is no significant difference between Democratic appointees and Republican appointees. Judge 704 did however write in the margin of his/her survey that "I have always followed the appellate courts, but will not say, categorically, that I will *never* do otherwise." On balance, it appears that many judges, given the opportunity do recognize their participation in policymaking. In doing so, these judges can protect or retard individual and group interests. History, for example, shows us that at times the court has clearly acted to protect minority rights—the extent to which the judges themselves feel the protection of minority rights is the province of the judiciary is the focus of the next section.

Consider also, for example, that when the federal district court judges were asked whether "[T]o a large extent, the decisional patterns of district court judges reflect the political values of their appointing presidents." Although a majority of the judges disagreed (about 62 percent), nearly one-third (about 28 percent) agreed (Table 2.3, Q12); and, there is no significant difference between Democratic and Republican appointees. Clearly, a sizable number of district court judges themselves (about 28 percent) believe a pattern exists between presidential expectation and judicial performance. And there is some evidence to suggest that this perception may be increasing. For instance, Judge 691, a 1980 Carter appointee, wrote in the margin for Q12: "It seems that there is more effort in the past decade to assure that decisional patterns reflect the political values of the appointing president." However, when the "president" was removed from the NDJS question and judges were asked "Do you feel your personal attitudes and values affect your discretionary judgments on the court?," a majority, about 58 percent, responded that "often" or "sometimes" indeed their personal attitudes and values do affect their discretionary judgments (See Table 2.3, Q27). Democratic appointees were more likely to select "often" and "sometimes" (68 percent), than were Republican appointees (52 percent).

However, when asked whether "*other* district court judges allow their personal attitudes and values to affect their discretionary judgments," a higher overall percentage, nearly 75 percent, of all judges responded with often/sometimes compared to 58 percent in Q27. The difference between Democratic appointees and Republican appointees is small, but Democratic appointees were slightly more likely to respond "sometimes," 71 percent, than were Republican appointees, 60.6 percent (Table 2.3, Q28). Therefore, because a significant number of judges recognize that their—or others—personal attitudes and values affect their case decisions, coupled with these judges' perceptions (about 28 percent) that their decisions "to a large extent" reflect the political values of their appointing presidents, next I turn directly to a comparison of the judges' decisions and the appointing presidents' policy objectives.

More Policy More Rights?

There is widespread agreement among judicial scholars that federal courts operate within the context of the larger political system and thus engage in policymaking to some extent. Theoretically, there are commonly two major arguments concerning the role of the Supreme Court in the American political system, arguments that more or less attempt to relate the functioning of the Court to democratic theory. One view, often associated with Martin Shapiro, is that the Court's special function is the representation of potential or unorganized interests or values that are unlikely to be represented elsewhere in government; for example, the courts defend the underrepresented or the unrepresented.[43] In this role the Court might well serve as a protector of minority rights against majority tyranny.[44] This is the view articulated in Supreme Court Justice Harlan Stone's famous footnote four in *United States v. Carolene Products Co.*,[45] which suggests the Court should be concerned with what majorities do to minorities, especially regarding laws "directed at" religious, national, and racial "discrete and insular" minorities and those infected with prejudice against them.[46] In Justice Lewis Powell's words, the Court's mission is to afford "protection [to] . . . the constitutional rights and liberties of individual citizens and minority groups against oppressive or discriminatory government action."[47]

However, a second view suggests that court policymaking and interest representation most often mirror the views of the dominant lawmaking majorities. For example, Robert Dahl argued that the Supreme Court's main function is to confer legitimacy on the policies of the majority coalition in power.[48] Moreover, Dahl suggests that the role of the Court as a defender of minority rights is "rare and transitory" and that only during periods of upheaval or transition from one electoral coalition to another might we expect to find the Court in a position to block a particular policy.[49] Dahl concludes that the policy views dominant on the Court "are never far out of line with the policy views dominant among lawmaking majorities."[50] Although most scholarly works today view the Court's policymaking role as a combination of these two roles,[51] there is little extant research focusing on the judges' own views of their roles in protecting minority rights. To help fill this void, the NDJS asked the judges directly: "One of the special and unique functions of the federal judiciary is to protect minority rights against the majority," (see Table 2.4, Q31).

Table 2.4
Courts and Minority Rights

	% Strongly Agree	% Agree	% No Opinion	% Disagree	% Strongly Disagree
Q31. One of the special and unique functions of the federal judiciary is to protect minority rights against the majority.					
All judges	25.2	54.7	5.9	11.5	.6
Democratic appointees	33.1	50.6	2.4	12.0	—
Republican appointees	21.1	56.8	7.8	11.2	.9
Q30. Generally, it has been the judiciary, more so than the president or the Congress, that has led the fight for minority rights.					
All judges	10.5	46.9	13.9	25.0	2.0
Democratic appointees	16.9	52.4	6.0	19.9	3.0
Republican appointees	7.1	44.1	18.0	27.6	1.6

Percentages may not total 100 because "missing responses" are omitted.

In response, nearly 80 percent of judges agreed (including 25 percent strongly agreeing) that one of the of the special and unique functions of the federal judiciary is to protect minority rights against the majority. And there is little difference, about 5 percent, between Democratic appointees and Republican appointees that agreed. Thus a majority, but not all, modern-day district court judges seem to have adopted the philosophy of Justice Harlan Stone in his footnote with regard to the special role of the judiciary in American politics. By way of illustration, judges offered the numerous margin comments, including:

Q31. "[O]ne of the special and unique functions of the federal judiciary is to protect minority rights against the majority"

Judge 636	Agree, "One of the special and unique functions of the federal judiciary is to protect minority 'legal' rights against the majority."
Judge 662	Agree, "One of the special and unique functions of the federal judiciary is to protect minority rights against improper government action."
Judge 149	Agree, "Because the function is to protect all rights. In practice, this is mostly minority rights."
Judge 167	Agree, "I don't know that's our job—and it should not be. Congress and the executive should not dodge their responsibilities on the theory that the judges will legislate for them."
Judge 334	Agree, "It is my opinion that federal judges are protection against what I describe as the tyranny of business, whether it be big business, big labor unions or charitable organizations or whatever."
Judge 85	No opinion, "We should decide cases, not grind some ax for or against a class of person."
Judge 536	No opinion, "The court doesn't have an agenda of its own."
Judge 293	Disagree, "The law and the Constitution provide that protection. The judiciary applies the law."

However, when these same judges were asked whether the judiciary—"more so than the president or the Congress"—has "led the fight for minority rights," a less commanding majority than for the more general previous question of about 57 percent agreed. However, as indicated in Table 2.4 (Q30), nearly 70 percent of Democratic appointees agreed compared to about 51 percent of Republican appointees. Consider the following judges' unsolicited comments on this point.

Q30. "Generally, it has been the judiciary, more so than the president or the Congress, that has led the fight for minority rights."

Judge 84	Agree, "But it has varied greatly over time & administration."
Judge 172	Agree, "Generally, it has been the judiciary, more so than the president or the Congress, that 'has protected' minority rights."
Judge 200	Agree, "In the past; but not now."

Judge 240	Agree, "But each branch has played a role. The judiciary has played a leading role in certain areas at certain times such as *Brown*—but Congress & President have also led, i.e., Voting Rights Act [of] 1965."
Judge 327	Agree, "Minority rights—Individual rights or Politically Correct Class rights? President or the Congress—they pass repressive laws (IRS, forfeiture)."
Judge 398	Agree, "Since 1950."
Judge 521	Agree, "Up til recently."
Judge 662	No opinion, "Time is an important variable—In some periods one branch as been a "leader" while in other periods other branches have led."
Judge 13	Disagree, "Only to the extent of protecting minority rights."
Judge 744	Disagree, "In the 50's & 60's it was the courts who blazed the trail but since '64 most cases involving minority rights arise out of the Civil Rights Act of 1964, the Voting Rights Act of '65 et al. which are creatures of the congress & executive. All in all I think all 3 branches of government should get some credit or blame as the case may be!"
Judge 696	Strongly Disagree, "In the last decade."

In all, the NDJS data reveal that a strong majority (about 80 percent) of modern-day district court judges not only agree that the judiciary should protect minority rights against the majority, but also that the judiciary has indeed "led" the fight for minority rights.

Conservatives on the Court?

The preceding section examined the judge's views on the role of judiciary in the protection of minority rights. This section looks directly at the views of district court judges with regard to the philosophical makeup of the court. Much has been written during that last decade concerning a "new" conservative presence of appointed judges at all levels of the federal judiciary. President Reagan's unprecedented number of appointments to the district courts using philosophical litmus tests (see Chapter Five), his failed attempt to appoint Robert Bork to the Supreme Court, as well as President Bush's appointment of Clarence Thomas to replace retired Justice Thurgood Marshall illustrate the magnitude of these attempts.[52] While numerous studies, including the primary focus of several later chapters of this study, illustrate the increasing numbers of so-called "conservative decisions" of modern courts, the NDJS asks the judges directly the extent to which they feel the courts are indeed becoming more conservative and whether or not the courts *should* be more conservative. As a case in point, Q18 asked "Overall, the federal judiciary is *becoming more 'conservative'* than it was in the 1960s, 1970s, and early 1980s." In response, about 78 percent agreed that the federal judiciary is indeed *becoming more conservative* (see Table 2.5 and Figure 2.2).

It should be noted, however, that this view is somewhat more prevalent among Democratic appointees, 86 percent, compared to slightly fewer, 73 percent, for Republican appointees. That is, the perception that the judiciary is becoming more conservative is more prevalent among Democratic appointees; however, a good percentage of all judges agree that it in fact is more conservative.

Table 2.5
Conservatism and the Courts

	% Strongly Agree	% Agree	% No Opinion	% Disagree	% Strongly Disagree
Q18. Overall, the federal judiciary is *becoming more* 'conservative' than it was in the 1960s, 1970s, and early 1980s.					
All judges	16.6	61.1	11.1	9.8	.8
Democratic appointees	33.1	53.0	6.0	6.0	1.2
Republican appointees	8.1	65.2	13.7	11.8	.6
Q20. Overall, the federal judiciary *should be more* 'conservative' than it was in the 1960s, 1970s, and early 1980s.					
All judges	6.6	27.0	24.4	32.0	9.2
Democratic appointees	2.4	12.7	13.3	50.0	20.5
Republican appointees	8.7	34.5	30.1	22.7	3.4

Percentages may not total 100 because "missing responses" are omitted.

And, although a majority (78 percent) of the judges feel the judiciary *is becoming more* conservative, far fewer agree that it *should be more* conservative: 33.6 percent.[53] In fact, a somewhat higher percentage, 41.2 percent, of judges "disagreed" that it *should be more* conservative (See Figure 2.2). It is not surprising, however, that the NDJS data reveal that a higher percentage of Republican appointees, 43.2 percent agree that the judiciary *should be more* conservative compared to only 15 percent of Democratic appointees.

Finally, consider these judges' responses to a series of NDJS questions regarding the courts and minority rights. For example, when the judges were asked to indicate the extent to which they felt "[B]lacks have made considerable progress in securing civil rights," about 90 percent of all judges responding agreed—of these 10.5 percent responded "strongly agree" (Table 2.6, Q22).

Figure 2.2
Conservatives in Court

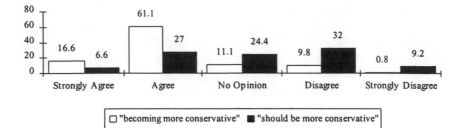

| | "becoming more conservative" | ■ "should be more conservative" |

Table 2.6
District Court Judges' Perceptions on Miscellaneous Issues

	% Strongly Agree	% Agree	% No Opinion	% Disagree	% Strongly Disagree
Q22. Blacks have made considerable progress in securing civil rights.					
All judges	10.5	77.5	1.6	7.4	1.4
Democratic appointees	6.0	73.5	1.8	13.9	3.0
Republican appointees	12.7	79.5	1.6	4.0	.6
Q23. Black litigants are treated fairly in the justice system.					
All judges	11.3	68.9	4.7	10.9	1.6
Democratic appointees	7.2	60.2	6.0	18.7	3.6
Republican appointees	13.4	73.3	4.0	6.8	.6
Q24. Poor litigants are treated fairly in the courts.					
All judges	8.8	69.5	4.5	14.5	1.0
Democratic appointees	6.6	60.8	4.2	24.7	2.4
Republican appointees	9.9	73.9	4.7	9.3	.3
Q25. More women and minority judges would *improve* the overall quality of the district courts.					
All judges	8.8	30.7	25.2	28.1	5.1
Democratic appointees	18.7	35.5	19.3	21.1	3.6
Republican appointees	3.7	28.3	28.3	31.7	5.9

Percentages may not total 100 because "missing responses" are omitted.

And, as indicated, Republican appointees were overwhelming in their agreement, 92 percent, compared to fewer, 80 percent, of Democratic appointees.
Consider also that when asked whether "[B]lack litigants are treated fairly in the

justice system," 80 percent of all judges agreed (Table 2.6, Q23). Again, however, a higher percentage of Republican appointees favor this statement than Democratic appointees, 87 percent to 67 percent, respectively.

Consider also that when judges were asked whether "[p]oor litigants are treated fairly in the courts," about 78 percent of all judges agreed (Table 2.6, Q24). Again, a higher percentage of Republican appointees, 84 percent, support this statement compared to a somewhat smaller percentage, 67 percent, of Democratic appointees.

Lastly, the NDJS asked the judges whether "more women and minority judges would *improve* the overall quality of the district courts." In response, about 40 percent of the judges agreed, however, only 32 percent of Republican appointees agreed with this statement compared to just over half, 54 percent, of Democratic appointees (Table 2.6, Q25).

CHAPTER SUMMARY

The basic focus of this chapter has been to examine the basic institutional and systemic role and functions of the federal district courts in the American federal judiciary. This profile emphasized, among other characteristics, the broad jurisdiction, increasing caseload, and the critical function of the courts as both visible trial courts and "gatekeepers" to the higher federal courts.

Overall, it follows that increases in the jurisdiction, caseload, the number of sitting judges, and their supporting personnel combine to illustrate the key policymaking role and potential of our federal district courts. In addition, relevant NDJS data were provided to fill the gaps between the institutional nature of the courts and the practical realities about what the judges actually believe about the courts' institutional functions in the American political process. These data reveal that majorities of district court judges agree that they are indeed involved in the policy process; large numbers of these judges do in fact make law; many feel that they *should* make law; and, many feel that one special and unique function of the federal judiciary is to protect minority rights against the majority.

On balance, the institutional nature of the district courts, combined with the judges' own attitudes about the function of these courts contribute to the increasing visibility and importance of district courts in the policy process. Thus, the focus on who these judges are and how they are appointed to serve on the district courts is increasing. These matters—the selection and confirmation processes for district court judges—are discussed in the next chapter.

NOTES

1. Henry J. Abraham, *The Judicial Process*, 6th. ed. (New York: Oxford University Press, 1993), p. 157.
2. This act has been mainly attributed to Oliver Ellsworth, who was later Chief Justice

of the Supreme Court. For a complete history of the passage of this bill, see the classic article by Charles Warren, "New Light on the History of the Federal Judiciary Act of 1789," *Harvard Law Review* 37 (1923), p. 49.

3. Circuit courts originally had the authority to review district court decisions by writ of error in matters exceeding $50 and by writ of appeal in admiralty and maritime cases involving more than $300.

4. Judiciary Act of 1789, Section 9.

5. Act of February 13, 1801, sec. 7 & 26, 2 STAT. 90, 97.

6. Act of April 10, 1790, sec. 5, 1 STAT. 111; Act of February 21, 1793, 1 STAT. 323.

7. Act of April 4, 1800, 2 STAT. 21.

8. Although the act was subsequently repealed, the power was granted again in the latter part of the century. This 1801 act, often referred to as the "midnight judges" act, also eliminated, for a time, circuit riding by the Supreme Court justices.

9. The Circuit Court Act of 1802 both expanded the number of circuits and restored circuit riding to Supreme Court justices. Additionally, the 1802 act provided for circuit courts to be presided over by a single district court judge. As noted by others, this change was of great importance because the district court judges assumed responsibility for both district and circuit courts; i.e., original and appellate jurisdiction were both in the hands of the district judges.

10. Erwin C. Surrency, *History of the Federal Courts* (New York: Oceana Publications, 1987), pp. 27–41.

11. The Judiciary Act of 1802 authorized the district court judge to preside in the circuit court in the absence of the justice—either of the two judges could preside in the circuit court alone.

12. Surrency, *History of the Federal Courts*, Chapter 5.

13. See Felix Frankfurter and James M. Landis, *The Business of the Supreme Court, A Study in the Federal Judicial System* (New York: The Macmillian Co., 1927), p. 65.

14. In March of 1891, Congress passed the "Evarts Act" that created these new courts known as the "circuit courts of appeals" to hear most of the appeals from the district courts. The old circuit courts (established in 1789) remained, however, until abolished by Congress in 1911. Thus, following the abolition of the old circuit courts in 1911, these new circuit courts of appeals took their place in the federal hierarchy as the intermediate appeals courts between the district courts and the Supreme Court. As a result of a name change implemented in the 1948 Judicial Code, these intermediate courts became known as courts of appeals.

15. For detailed information on these jurisdictional changes, see Richard J. Richardson and Kenneth N. Vines, *The Politics of the Federal Courts: Lower Courts in the United States* (Boston: Little, Brown and Company, 1970), Chapter 2.

16. "Original jurisdiction includes prosecutions arising under the postal laws and regulation, admiralty and maritime matters, patent and copyright laws, proceedings in bankruptcy, disputes growing out of the capture of prizes of war, and in general, all prosecutions based upon national law defining crimes against the United States." Stephen T. Early, *Constitutional Courts of the United States* (Totowa, NJ: Littlefield, Adams and Co., 1977), pp. 40–41.

17. Alpheus Thomas Mason and Donald Grier Stephenson, Jr. *American Constitutional Law*, 11th ed. (Upper Saddle River, NJ: Prentice-Hall, 1996), p. 28.

18. For a detailed treatment on this matter, see Christopher E. Smith, *United States Magistrates in the Federal Courts: Subordinate Judges* (New York: Praeger, 1990).

19. The "legislative" district courts—those in the Northern Mariana Islands, Guam, and the Virgin Islands—have jurisdiction over local cases as well as those arising under federal law. However, these judges are not protected against diminution of their salaries during their ten-year terms.

20. In 1903, Congress provided for special three-judge district courts to be created on an ad hoc basis to hear certain types of cases. Normally, two district court judges and one appellate judge make up a panel. These panels are disbanded when a case has been decided and appeals from three-judge district courts go directly to the Supreme Court. For example, the Civil Rights Act of 1964, the Voting Rights Act of 1965, and the Presidential Election Campaign Fund Act of 1974 all call for use of three-judge district courts. However, since 1976, and partially in response to complaints about caseload problems, Congress all but eliminated three-judge district courts except in cases concerning reapportionment and redistricting and in some cases under the civil rights acts. Accordingly, the number of cases heard by three-judge district courts declined dramatically. For yearly data on the numbers of cases heard by three-judge district courts, see *The Annual Report of the Director of the Administrative Office of the United States Courts* (Washington, DC: Government Printing Office). Nonetheless, it has been noted that the three-judge district court illustrates the use of the judicial structure to serve policy goals. See Charles Alan Wright, *The Law of Federal Courts*, 4th ed. (Saint Paul, MN: West Publishing, 1983), pp. 295–297.

21. In most instances, these lone district court judges sit with a jury unless that institution has been validly waived.

22. Early, *Constitutional Courts*, p. 59.

23. Between 1990 and 1995, criminal case filings in the district courts ranged between 49,000 and 45,000. For specific filings per year and discussion on criminal filing trends, see *Judicial Business of the United States Courts 1995 Report to the Director, Leonidas Ralph Mecham, 1995* (a reproduced report by the Statistics Division, Administrative Office of the United States Courts, microfiche), and *The Annual Report of the Director of the Administrative Office of the United States Courts* (Washington, DC: Government Printing Office, 1995).

24. Richard A. Posner, *The Federal Courts: Crisis and Reform* (Cambridge: Harvard University Press, 1985), especially Chapter 3, "Extent and Causes of the Caseload Explosion," pp. 59–93.

25. However, the numerical decline in the number of civil filings per year (between 1985 and 1991) does not suggest fewer opportunities for presidents to effect their policy choices via the district courts. In fact, closer examination of the categories of cases in reveals an altogether different picture. The Director of the Administrative Office of the United States Courts explains this query in the 1989 annual report: "Over the past decade, actions filed by the government for recovery of overpayment of veterans' benefits (VA cases) and defaulted student loans and claims for social security benefits have changed so dramatically that they have controlled the overall rate of change in civil filings. In 1979, these categories accounted for only 12 percent of all civil filings; by 1984, this figure had risen to 29 percent. Since then, filings in these categories have declined to the point where they represent only 11 percent of the civil workload." *Annual Report of the Director of the Administrative Office of the United States Courts 1988.* (Washington, DC: Government Printing Office, 1988), pp. 7–8. Therefore, exclusive of these two categories, civil filings have in fact risen consistently since 1982.

26. Kenneth Dolbeare, "The Federal District Courts and Urban Policy: An Exploratory Study (1960–1967)," in Joel B. Grossman and Joseph Tanenhaus, eds., *Frontiers of*

Judicial Research (New York: Wiley, 1969), p. 395.

27. "Record-setting Workloads Confront Federal Courts," *The Third Branch: The Newsletter of the Federal Courts* (Washington, DC: Office of Congressional, External and Public Affairs, July 1996), pp. 2–3.

28. Studies on the consequences of the caseload explosion include Posner, *The Federal Courts: Crisis and Reform*, Chapter 4, and, William P. McLauchlan, *Federal Court Caseloads* (New York: Praeger, 1984).

29. As quoted by David M. O'Brien, "The Reagan Judges: His Most Enduring Legacy?" in *The Reagan Legacy: Promise and Performance*, Charles O. Jones, ed. (Chatham, NJ: Chatham House Publishers, 1988), p. 64.

30. Posner, *The Federal Courts*, 97.

31. See Steven Puro, "United States Magistrates: A New Federal Judicial Officer," *Justice System Journal* 2 (Winter 1976), p. 141.

32. Carroll Seron, *The Roles of Magistrates in Federal District Courts* (Washington, DC: Federal Judicial Center, 1983), p. 8.

33. See Smith, *United States Magistrates in the Federal Courts.*

34 *Annual Report of the Director of the Administrative Office of the United States Courts* (Washington, DC: Government Printing Office, 1990), p. 24.

35. As noted by Carroll Seron, "[S]ome judges may, as a matter of common practice, request a magistrate's assistance in hearing all discovery motions, request a magistrate's assistance in scheduling . . . initial pretrial conferences, or request a magistrate's assistance in settlement conferences. In contrast, other judges may request a magistrate's assistance on a selective (i.e., case-by-case) basis for each of these types of matters. See Seron, *The Roles of Magistrates in the Federal District Courts*, p. 8.

36. Carroll Seron, *The Roles of Magistrates: Nine Case Studies* (Washington, DC: Federal Judicial Center, 1985).

37. Alvin B. Rubin and Laura B. Bartell, *Law Clerk Handbook* (Washington, DC: Federal Judicial Center, 1989), p. 1.

38. Clark, Davis S., "Adjudication to Administration: A Statistical Analysis of Federal District Courts in the Twentieth Century," *Southern California Law Review* 55 (1981), pp. 86–88.

39. *Annual Report of the Director of the Administrative Office of the United States Courts* (1991), p. 127.

40. Abraham, *The Judicial Process*, p. 158.

41. Posner, *The Federal Courts*, p. 97.

42. Judge 327 wrote in the margin, "I agree . . . given the Congress's passing indeterminate and inconsistent laws."

43. See Martin Shapiro, *Freedom of Speech: The Supreme Court and Judicial Review* (Englewood Cliffs, NJ: Prentice-Hall, 1966).

44. Martin Shapiro, *Law and Politics in the Supreme Court* (New York: The Free Press of Glencoe, 1964); and John Hart Ely, *Democracy and Distrust: A Theory of Judicial Review* (Cambridge: Harvard University Press, 1980), p. 135.

45. *United States v. Carolene Products Co.*, 304 U.S. 144 (1938). On its face, this case was merely one of numerous instances wherein the Supreme Court upheld federal economic policies. Its significance was generated from a footnote in which Justice Harlan Stone argued that the Court was justified in "tolerant" view of government economic policies, while it gave "more exacting judicial scrutiny" to policies that transgressed civil liberties.

46. John Hart Ely, *Democracy and Distrust*, p. 76.

47. Justice Powell's statement is in *United States v. Richardson*, 418 U.S. 166, 192 (1974).

48. Robert Dahl, "Decision-Making in a Democracy: The Supreme Court as a National Policy-Maker," *Journal of Public Law* 6, 1957, pp. 293–295.

49. Ibid. pp. 285, 294.

50. Dahl's view of the Supreme Court's role in the policy process has been broadly debated by judicial scholars. For example see David Adamany, "Legitimacy, Realigning Elections, and the Supreme Court," *Wisconsin Law Review* (1973), pp. 790–846; Richard Funston, "The Supreme Court in Critical Elections," *American Political Science Review* 69 (September 1975), pp. 795–811; Bradley C. Canon and S. Sidney Ulmer, "The Supreme Court and Critical Elections: A Dissent," *American Political Science Review* 70 (December 1976), pp. 1215–1218; Johnathon Casper, "The Supreme Court and National Policy Making," *American Political Science Review* 70 (March 1976), pp. 50–63; and Roger Handbag and Harold F. Hill, Jr., "Court Curbing, Court Reversals, and Judicial Review: The Supreme Court versus Congress," *Law and Society Review* 14 (Winter 1980), pp. 309–322.

51. "The Court may be a legitimator . . . but it is also a significant wielder of power." See Handbag and Hill, "Court Curbing."

52. For a detailed discussion of the failed Bork nomination, see Kevin L. Lyles, "The Bork Nomination and Black America: A Case Study," in Lucius J. Barker and Mack H. Jones. *African-Americans and the American Political System* (Englewood Cliffs, NJ: Prentice-Hall, 1994), pp. 133-172.

53. Q20. "Overall, the federal judiciary should be more 'conservative' than it was in the 1960s, 1970s, and early 1980s."

3 The Nomination and Appointment of Federal District Court Judges

The decision as to who will make the decisions affects what decisions will be made.[1]

This chapter looks more closely at how our federal district court judges are selected with particular emphasis on the nature of the process and the dynamics involved in their screening, nomination, and confirmation.[2] A better understanding of the procedures and dynamics leading to the selection of our district judges should enable us to develop more informed analyses both about their roles and functions, as well as about the linkages between individual presidential administrations and the performance of their judicial appointees. As in the previous chapter, relevant NDJS data are included throughout this discussion in an attempt to fill the gaps between the formal institutional processes of the selection, nomination, and confirmation of district court judges as compared to the practical realities of these processes as viewed by the judges themselves.

IN THE BEGINNING: THE ORIGINS OF JUDICIAL SELECTION

The essential constitutional provision regarding judicial selection is the "Appointments Clause" of Article II, par. 2, cl. 2: "[The President] shall nominate, and by and with the advice and consent of the Senate, shall appoint . . . judges of the Supreme Court, and all other officers of the United States . . . but the Congress may by law vest the appointment of such inferior Officers, as they think proper, in the President alone, in the Courts of Law, or in the Heads of Departments." However, as detailed in chapters 4 and 5, it is instructive to note here that these *general* procedures, guidelines, and practices that flow from this formal constitutional provision have been variously interpreted and tailored by presidential administrations, resulting in shifts of power, process, and product.

In any event, the selection of federal trial judges was included in the many matters debated and negotiated at the Constitutional Convention in 1787.[3] But of course, like many issues debated there, the delegates to the convention not only disagreed about how to appoint the justices of the Supreme Court, but also about the judges of other courts that might be established as well.

Briefly, this disagreement was polarized into two camps, each advocating a different method of judicial selection. In the first camp were those delegates who opposed the concentration of power in the executive branch and endorsed the appointment of justices and other judges by the Senate, the House, or both. Those who favored the legislative appointment of judges feared the potential of monarchical tyranny. They charged that the legislature was better positioned to know the pool of qualified nominees. Luther Martin argued that the Senate, "being from all the States . . . would be best informed of the characters and most capable of making a fit choice."[4] Roger Sherman echoed that the Senate "would have more wisdom. They would bring to their deliberation a more diffusive knowledge of characters. It would be less easy for candidates to intrigue with them than the Executive Magistrate."[5]

In the other camp were those delegates—notably James Wilson, Gouverneur Morris, Alexander Hamilton, and James Madison—who favored a strong executive branch and feared appointments by members of the legislature; they promoted the investment of the power to appoint in the executive branch alone. Early at the Constitutional Convention, James Wilson argued that "experience showed the impropriety of such appointments by numerous bodies. Intrigue, partiality and concealment were the necessary consequences. A principal reason for unity in the Executive was that officers might be appointed by a single responsible person."[6] One of the most persistent advocates of executive appointment during the Constitutional Convention was Nathanial Gorham of Massachusetts. Gorham challenged those in favor of legislative appointment:

As the executive will be responsible in point of character at least, for judicious and faithful discharge of his trust, he will be careful to look through all the states for the proper characters. The Senators will be as likely to form their attachments at the seat of government where they reside as the Executive. If they cannot get the man of the particular state to which they may respectively belong, they will be indifferent to the rest. Public bodies feel no personal responsibility, and give full pay to intrigue and cabal.[7]

Also defending the need for executive control of judicial appointments was Alexander Hamilton. Writing in *The Federalist Papers*:

One man of discernment is better fitted to analise and estimate the peculiar qualities adapted to particular offices, than a body of men of equal, perhaps even superior discernment.

The sole and undivided responsibility of one man will naturally beget a livelier sense of duty and a more exact regard to reputation. He will on this account feel himself under stronger obligations, and more interested to investigate with care and impartiality the persons who may have the fairest pretentions to them. He will have fewer personal attachments to gratify than a body of men.

Nonetheless, because neither group could muster the amount of support needed for their position, the delegates adopted a method of appointment proposed in part by James Madison. This compromise provided that the executive would nominate and appoint Supreme Court justices, among other officers, subject to the *advice and consent* of the Senate. One of the strongest and perhaps most noted defenses of the compromise appointment process was provided by Alexander Hamilton in *The Federalist Papers*, no. 66:

> It will be the office of the President to nominate and with the advice and consent of the Senate, to appoint. There will, of course, be no exertion of choice on the part of the Senate. They may defeat on choice of the Executive, *and oblige him to make another*; but they cannot themselves choose—they can only ratify or reject the choice of the President. They might even entertain a preference to some other person, at the very moment they are assenting to the one proposed, because there might be no positive ground of opposition to him; and they could not be sure, if they withheld their assent, that the subsequent nomination would fall upon their own favorite, or upon any other person in their estimation more meritorious than the one rejected. Thus it could hardly happen that the majority of the Senate would feel any other complacency toward the object of appointment than such as the appearances of merit might inspire, and the proofs of the want of it destroy (emphasis added).[8]

JUDICIAL SELECTION IN MODERN CONTEXT

Of course, one flaw in a modern application of Hamilton's argument is that presidents want to avoid being "obliged to make another," as the defeat of a nomination now signals a weakened administration. Most agree that modern presidents, for the most part, attempt to avoid these types of political battles and their consequences (e.g., President Reagan's failed nomination of Robert Bork to the Supreme Court) and seek instead a consensus before the nomination is formally voted on by the full Senate. In fact, in practice some argue that the Senate acts as merely a "rubber stamp" for most confirmations; especially at the lower court level.

In this respect, it is worthwhile to note how district court judges themselves view the Senate's role in the confirmation process. Consider, for example, how judges responded to the NDJS question: "In practice, the Senate *does* rubber stamp presidential nominations to the federal district courts." Here, about 28 percent of the judges agreed that the Senate acts as a rubber stamp (See Table 3.1, Q3). Those agreeing include 42 percent of all Democratic appointees but only 20.5 percent of all Republican appointees. However, significantly fewer judges, only about 5 percent, agreed that the senate "*should*," rubber stamp the nominees (Table 3.1, Q2) and there was no significant difference between Democratic appointees and Republican appointees. Of those agreeing, however, several judges qualified their responses in the margins. To cite an example,

Judge 492 wrote "[a]gree as to district courts appointments but disagree as to Circuit appointments." Judge 460 wrote "[a]gree, except regarding ethics." On the whole however, these data reveal that a majority of judges, about 93 percent, disagree that the Senate should rubber stamp the president's nominations. Unfortunately, the wording of the NDJS questions [Q2 and Q3] does not specify between the full Senate and the Senate Judiciary Committee; nonetheless, the findings do suggest that the judges disagree that the Senate's role should be pro forma. Evidence suggests, however, that Senate confirmation is more pro forma when the president's party controls the Senate. For the district courts, about 90 percent of the president's nominees have been confirmed when his party controls the Senate, while only 77 percent are confirmed when his party does not.[9]

Table 3.1
The Senate's Rubber Stamp

	% Strongly Agree	% Agree	% No Opinion	% Disagree	% Strongly Disagree
Q3. In practice, the Senate *does* "rubber stamp" presidential nominations to the federal district courts. (N = 487)					
All judges	1.4	26.2	5.9	58.0	7.0
Democratic appointees	3.0	38.6	6.0	45.8	6.0
Republican appointees	.6	19.9	5.9	64.3	7.5
Q2. The Senate *should* "rubber stamp" presidential nominees to the federal district courts. (N = 487)					
All judges	.4	4.5	1.8	66.6	26.2
Democratic appointees	.6	3.0	1.8	53.6	41.0
Republican appointees	.3	5.3	1.9	73.3	18.6

Percentages may not total 100 because "no response" answers are omitted.

Overall, although the parameters of the debate as to the role of the Senate were outlined in 1789, its central concern remains at the very root of this study—the power of the president to influence the policymaking role and function of the courts via the appointment process. Moreover, the informal and emerging participant players now actively involved in the selection, screening, and approval processes were not debated at the constitutional convention. The nature and dynamics of these processes become more clear as we compare the selection of federal district court judges with the more visible manner in which justices to the Supreme Court are selected.

Supreme Court Justices versus District Court Judges

It is widely agreed that modern presidents play an active and personal role in the selection of Supreme Court justices—giving the kind of focused attention paralleled only by cabinet appointments.[10] Clearly, the highly contentious and controversial Supreme Court nominations of Judge Robert Bork and Justice Clarence Thomas signal the direct and integral role presidents may play in Supreme Court nomination and confirmation battles.[11] It has only been in recent times, however, that presidents have given more systematic critical attention to the selection of lower court judges, particularly at the district level.

In general, many agree that presidents look to at least four criteria for the selection of judicial nominees: (1) similar personal policy preferences and party allegiance; (2) competence and ethical behavior; (3) a chance to reward friends or associates; and (4) coalition building.[12] Let us review briefly how these criteria have been variably used by presidents in selecting nominees at both the Supreme Court and district court levels.

Policy and/or Party. Presidents often attempt to appoint justices to the Supreme Court whom they believe share and will promote similar policy preferences and legal values to cultivate their own policy agenda—in other words, appointments that will match presidential policy objectives with judicial performance. Presidents have traditionally evaluated potential judicial nominees on the basis of their philosophy and accordingly, "have tried to 'pack' the bench to a greater or lesser extent."[13] And of course numerous presidents have openly expressed dismay when these attempts run afoul, as exemplified by President Dwight Eisenhower's reported comment that his appointment of Earl Warren as chief justice "the biggest damn fool mistake" of his presidency.[14]

Nevertheless, as discussed later (see Table 3.10), presidents nearly always select appointees from the same political party as their own. This results both from partisan pressures, including senatorial courtesy,[15] and from special efforts by some presidents to appoint judges with similar policy preferences as their own.

Clearly, there are consequences that flow from such activity. With respect to Supreme Court nominees, for example, empirical research indicates that the presidents' success in making such appointments is exemplified vividly by the strong and measurable agreement (some 75 percent) between presidential policy objectives and expectations and the subsequent performance of judges so appointed.[16] This confluence is strongly significant, suggesting that discretionary policy determinations and interest representation in large measure seem to be explainable and perhaps even predictable given the politics of the selection, nomination, and confirmation processes. Thus, inquiry into such matters is particularly salient since their observation suggests that the policymaking role of federal courts has become increasingly apparent, leading some to give increased attention to the ideological and particular policy positions of prospective nominees, at not only the Supreme Court level, but also at lower court levels.

The NDJS data indicate that judges' political ideology closely corresponds to the party affiliation of the presidents who appointed them. As evidenced in Table 3.2 below, most judges, about 60 percent, consider themselves to be "moderate"; however, as might be expected, Democratic appointees lean to the "liberal" side (20 percent compared to only 2.5 percent for Republican appointees) and Republican appointees lean to the conservative side (24 percent compared to 9 percent for Democratic appointees).

Table 3.2
Political Ideology

	% Liberal	% Moderate	% Conservative	% Other
Q26. How would you characterize your judicial beliefs?				
All judges	8.6	62.9	19.1	8.4
Democratic appointees	20.5	60.8	9.0	9.0
Republican appointees	2.5	64.0	24.2	8.1

Percentages may not total 100 because "no response" answers are omitted.

Competence and Ethics. It is usually assumed to be to the president's advantage to appoint judges of high competence and ethical behavior.[17] A nominee lacking these qualifications is likely to both embarrass the president as well as run afoul of standards imposed by other key participants in the nomination and selection process: namely the Senate Judiciary Committee; the ABA Committee on Federal Judiciary; and the Federal Bureau of Investigation (FBI). A highly competent and trustworthy Supreme Court justice who shares the president's policy goals, for example, may prove to be more effective in advancing those policies on the Court—"marshalling the Court"—than one whose competence and ethics raise questions.[18]

Even so, however, it has been suggested that such competence and ethics have not ranked high among the criteria used in the selection of judges to the lower federal courts. "Because of the perceived unimportance of the lower courts," as one commentator put it, "the Justice Department and relevant Senators often elevate other considerations over a candidate's merits." Understandably then, "the perceived quality of lower court nominees varies from very high to fairly low."[19]

Rewarding Associates and Friends. Research on judicial nominees for the Supreme Court also tells us that presidents have generally been inclined to select political associates or personal friends. Indeed, some 60 percent of the nominees to the Supreme Court personally knew their nominating president.[20] On the other hand, however, given the large number of district court appointments, with rare exceptions, it is less expected that direct presidential associations or friendships would play a crucial role in judicial selection at the lower court level. But the increasing salience and visibility of these lower court appointments may well lead to increased informal channels and networks that would allow at least the presidents' advisors to better know and scrutinize the "associates and friends" of those whom the president may wish to appoint.

Coalition Building. Judicial nominations and appointments also provide a means for presidents to accrue future political support—in other words, coalition building. By selecting judges with particular characteristics, especially at the highly visible Supreme Court level, presidents might gain support from voters who share those or similar characteristics. President Johnson's appointment of Thurgood Marshall, for example, undoubtedly helped to solidify Johnson's support among African-American voters. Similarly, former President Reagan's appointment of Sandra Day O'Connor might be viewed as an attempt to curry favor and support from women. And of course President Bush's appointment of African-American Justice Clarence Thomas clearly appealed to democratic symbols of freedom and equality, but it also stood to mute opposition to Bush's appointment of a conservative to replace the more liberal Justice Thurgood Marshall.

Overall, in making appointments to the Supreme Court, attentive presidents have for the most part broadly navigated that Court along the path of presidential policy objectives/expectations. This confluence of policy interests between the nominating president and the appointed judge—while having been studied at length focusing on the Supreme Court—remains much less visible at the lower court levels.[21] While the actual extent to which district court judges reflect the policy positions of their appointing presidents is analyzed in later chapters, nearly 90 percent of the district court judges responding to the NDJS agreed that "presidents have usually attempted to appoint district court judges who share their basic political values" (See Table 3.3, Q21), including 80 percent of Democratic appointees and 92 percent of Republican appointees.

Table 3.3
Packing the Lower Courts

	% Strongly Agree	% Agree	% No Opinion	% Disagree	% Strongly Disagree
Q21. In general, modern presidents have usually attempted to appoint district court judges who share their basic political values. (N = 486)					
All judges	9.4	79.3	6.4	4.3	.2
Democratic appointees	6.0	73.5	1.8	13.9	3.0
Republican appointees	12.7	79.5	1.6	4.0	.6
Q1. The president exercises too much control over district court appointments. (N = 487)					
All judges	3.1	9.0	7.8	57.4	22.3
Democratic appointees	6.0	16.9	6.0	53.6	16.3
Republican appointees	1.6	5.0	8.7	59.3	25.5

Percentages may not total 100 because "no response" answers are omitted.

Several judges did, however, comment upon their "agreement" response with regard to presidents Reagan and Bush. For example, Judge 619 wrote: "[R]eagan and Bush certainly!" Judge 741 wrote: "more recently, yes." Judge 130 responded: "strongly agree, assuming . . . Reagan and Bush." Furthermore, although a majority of judges believed that presidents do attempt to pack the lower courts, most of them (about 80 percent) do not believe that the "president exercises too much control over the district court appointments" (Table 3.3, Q1). Regarding those judges in disagreement, 85 percent of Republican appointees disagree that the "president exercises too much control over the district court appointments," compared to about 70 percent for Democratic appointees.

Emerging and Increasing Participants in Judicial Selection

All federal judges, including those on the district courts, must be nominated by the president and confirmed by a *simple majority* of the Senate. But the simple majority rule may not be so easy to meet, as exemplified by the 1991 confirmation of Justice Clarence Thomas to the Supreme Court—the narrowest confirmation vote margin (52–48) since 1888 when Lucius Lamar, a Cleveland appointee, was approved by a 32–28 vote. Thus, the chief executive does not enjoy unfettered choice in this selection. Although the formal methods of selection have not changed, the increase in the number of participants has resulted in "a shift in the locus of appointment power to new participants" who share in the president's appointment power.[22]

As Table 3.4 illustrates, in addition to the president and the full Senate, there are now many different paths that lead to, and actors who influence, appointments to the federal district courts. No single scenario controls all appointments. As indicated, a number of additional individuals as well as institutions participate in the recruitment and screening process of district court judges. Let us look at several more closely.

Senatorial Courtesy and State and Local Politics. Although related to another type of presidential appointment, the practice of senatorial courtesy developed soon after the Senate's power to advise and consent was expanded to include the confirmation of district court judges. In 1789, President George Washington nominated Benjamin Fishbourn to be Naval Officer of the Port of Savannah, Georgia. However, the Senate rejected Fishbourn in deference to their senatorial colleagues from Georgia who had selected another candidate for the position. On the following day, President Washington withdrew his nomination of Fishbourn and nominated the senators' candidate.[23] Summarized by Joseph P. Harris:

In one of the first confirmation cases, the Senate acted in a manner quite different from that envisioned by Hamilton, who had maintained that there would be no exertion of choice on the part of the Senate. In this early case, the senators from Georgia did exert a choice on the President, to which he eventually yielded. As a courtesy to the Georgia senators, the Senate rejected an exceptionally well-qualified nominee without regard to his qualifications, so that the senators could press for the nomination of their own candidate.[24]

Table 3.4
The General Selection Process for the District Courts

Initiation may be by: (singly or in combination)	Screening by: (usually all)	Affirmed by: (both)
Senator(s) of the presidential party President or his advisor Attorney General Nominating Committees Local party candidate him/herself Influential judge	Senators (s) of presidential party President Justice Department FBI investigation Committee on the Federal Judiciary of ABA Interests groups (usually bar groups) Internal Revenue Service	Senate Judiciary Committee Senate vote of majority

Source: Adopted and updated from Richard J. Richardson and Kenneth N. Vines, *The Politics of the Federal Courts: Lower Courts in the United States* (Boston: Little, Brown and Company, 1970), Table 1, p. 58.

This started the practice in which the Senate would condition confirmation upon the advice given by its colleagues from the particular state in which a presidential appointment was to be made.

And so it is perhaps more correct to suggest that the presidential power to appoint district court judges is actually shared with the Senate, who tends to rubber stamp nominees because of reciprocity. In practice this has often meant that it is the senators who make recommendations for filling district court vacancies that occur within their respective states.[25] In general, prior to President Carter, senators submitted only *one* name for each vacancy; however, Carter and subsequent presidents have requested three to five recommendations for each available judgeship (see discussion in chapters 4–6).

As it has evolved, senatorial courtesy in practice has come to mean that the president will at time defer to a senator's selection; even when the senator is from another political party, presidents have at times used judicial appointments to curry favor from the respective senator in other legislative matters. Overall, senatorial courtesy has played an integral role and function in the selection of district court nominees since about 1840, leading some researchers to suggest that "most" federal district court judges win appointment because of their connections with senators or other local party leaders.[26] The Senate's parliamentarian emeritus, Floyd M. Riddick, wrote in a 1981 book on Senate procedure, "Various nominations have been defeated on the grounds of senatorial courtesy, personal objections or that they were personally offensive." Regarding senatorial courtesy, Judge Patricia M. Wald, chief judge of the U.S. Court of Appeals for the District of Columbia, stated: "For a nominee, the difference between being unopposed or opposed is the difference between heaven and hell."[27] Judge Wald continued: "My point is simply to note how intensely political confirmation fights have become and how arbitrarily a candidate may be selected as a target."

On the other hand, however, in several exceptions senators in the president's party have on occasion refused to take part in district court selection. And, in instances where two senators from the state were of the president's party could not reach agreement on a nominee, president's have attempted to suggest nominees agreeable to both senators.[28]

For example, observers have described the selection and nomination process as follows:

The fact that inferior judgeships are treated as "party pie" is not the worst of it. Worst is the fact that these judgeships have become local "party pie." District and circuit judgeships have come to be regarded as jobs to be handed out at the behest of the local party chiefs.[29]

The influence of state and local pressures on the selection process led one writer to conclude in 1931: "The President has almost abdicated his power of selection."[30] Thirteen years later, another writer stated: "The net result is that . . . the Senate has expropriated the President's power of nomination so far as [it] concerns appointments of interest to senators of the party in power; the president has virtually surrendered his power directly to local party politics as to appointments in states where the senators are of the opposition."[31] And there is isolated evidence to support this theory. A 1988 study, for example, found that regional influences affect both the appointment and the subsequent decision making of federal district judges.[32] A case in point, yet another 1988 study, for example, indicated that "during the Kennedy-Johnson years, former Chicago mayor Richard J. Daley passed on every federal judgeship in Illinois."[33]

The overall interdependent roles and influences of the president, the senate, and partisan and local politics in the selection process is well captured in a comment by former Federal Judge (and Attorney General) Griffin Bell. Regarding his own appointment to the federal bench, Bell stated:

Becoming a federal judge wasn't very difficult. . . . I managed John F. Kennedy's presidential campaign in Georgia. Two of my oldest friends were the senators from Georgia. And I was campaign manager and special counsel for the governor.[34]

However, the influence of state and local politics on district court confirmations seems to be the exception, rather than the norm, according the NDJS. As an example, some 60 percent of the judges responding disagreed (almost 25 percent strongly disagreed) that "[s]tate and/or local government official[s] played an influential role in my Senate confirmation to the district court" (See Table 3.5, Q34).[35] There is no significant difference, however, between Democratic appointees and Republican appointees.

In addition to the participants discussed above, during the twentieth century yet still another participant, the attorney general, has come to share more of a key and determinative role in the selection of district court judges.[36]

The Attorney General and the Department of Justice. The attorney general plays a key role in judicial selection. Although some senators look to local party officials, and others have adopted the practice of employing nominating commissions that screen and recommend possible nominees for vacancies in lower federal courts (see discussion in Chapter 4), still others look directly to the Department of Justice and the attorney general:

Many senators, who find judicial patronage an embarrassment and a bother, approach the Justice Department privately and ask that they remove the onus by picking the judges for them. This leaves immense discretionary power in the hands of the Attorney General, who is, by tradition, a political arm of the President. Other senators tell the Attorney General what candidates they have chosen, but request that he publicize that the initiative for the appointment came from the Justice Department, not from them.[37]

Table 3.5
State and Local Politics

	% Strongly Agree	% Agree	% No Opinion	% Disagree	% Strongly Disagree
Q34. State and/or local government official[s] played an influential role in my Senate confirmation to the district court.					
All judges	5.3	20.9	13.1	35.9	23.6
Democratic appointees	4.8	22.9	13.9	35.5	22.3
Republican appointees	5.6	19.9	12.7	36.0	24.2

Percentages may not total 100 because "no response" answers are omitted.

The attorney general may select, and may also be charged with the primary responsibility to evaluate the credentials of, potential nominees. As Joel Grossman puts it: "In most cases the choice of a federal judge is the Attorney General's to make—provided only that he makes it within the framework of the relevant norms of behavior which operate on the selection process [including the president's criteria]. No President could devote the time needed to personally consider even all the *serious* candidates."[38]

Formally, this is accomplished primarily by way of the "U.S. Department of Justice Questionnaire for Judicial Candidates" used to assess the credentials of potential nominees to the federal judiciary.[39] However, it was President Hoover's Attorney General William D. Mitchell, for example, who announced in a national broadcast that the administration would appoint judges of high qualifications without regard or reward to political activity.[40] Further changes regarding the role of the attorney general developed during the Eisenhower administration, when Attorney General Herbert Brownell and his deputy and successor, William Rogers, convinced President Eisenhower to give the American Bar Association Standing Committee on Federal Judiciary an integral role in judicial selection. This prompted the committee's leadership to stop promoting candidates.[41]

However, it was during the Kennedy administration that the attorney general and his deputies began actively "spotting" and recruiting nominees. The Kennedy administration "was not content to accept candidates suggested by senators."[42] But their success was minimal. In spite of Kennedy's attempts his administration nevertheless endorsed the nomination and confirmation of at times hostile nominees (see Chapter 4).

Although playing a less active role during the Johnson administration, the attorney general became more involved in the selection process during the Nixon years and subsequent administrations.[43] The modern-day heightened role of the attorney general in the selection process began during the Carter administration, reached unprecedented significance during the first term of the Reagan presidency with William French Smith, and increased notably with Smith's successor, Edwin Meese.[44] Meese, acutely aware of the value of judgeships to secure a president's legacy, once stated regarding judicial appointments that the administration may "institutionalize the Reagan revolution so it can't be set aside no matter what happens in future presidential elections."[45] For example, Attorney General Meese openly initiated a public, and at times a rather sharp, debate over the role of judges in interpreting the Constitution.[46] Meese also appointed a special assistant to handle judicial selection and utilized personal interviews of prospective nominees to an unprecedented extent.

Consider, however, that with regard to the role of the Justice Department and lower court judicial selection, the NDJS indicates that district court judges are clearly divided. When asked whether the "Justice Department now plays *too active* a role in the selection and evaluation of district court nominees [Q6]," about one half, 48.6 percent, agree, compared to about 37 percent disagreeing (see Figure 3.1).

Figure 3.1
The Justice Department

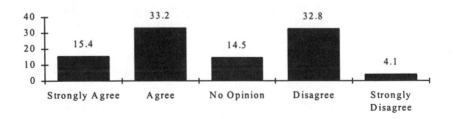

There is, however, greater difference between Republican and Democratic appointees on this issue. For example, about 62 percent of Democratic appointees agree that the "Justice Department now plays *too active* a role" compared to only about 42 percent of Republican appointees (see Table 3.6, Q6).

Overall, since the late 1940s the roles of the Justice Department and the attorney general in judicial selection have fluctuated over time. And so has the role of another major participant, the American Bar Association.

The American Bar Association Standing Committee on Federal Judiciary. The ABA participates in the selection and nomination process through its Standing Committee on Federal Judiciary.[47] Although other individuals and organizations have been formally (and informally) consulted with respect to individual nominees, the ABA became the first nongovernmental group to obtain a permanent consultant's position with regard to the nomination and appointment of federal judges.[48]

Table 3.6
The Justice Department

	% Strongly Agree	% Agree	% No Opinion	% Disagree	% Strongly Disagree
Q6. The Justice Department now plays too active a role in the selection and evaluation of district court nominees.					
All judges	15.4	33.2	14.5	32.8	4.1
Democratic appointees	25.3	36.7	13.3	24.7	—
Republican appointees	10.2	31.4	15.2	37.0	6.2

Percentages may not total 100 because "no response" answers are omitted.

This committee had been established previously in 1932 but was abolished in 1934. When reestablished in 1946 (during President Truman's first term) the committee was the Special Committee on Federal Judiciary, and was encouraged by the White House in 1947 to promote the nomination of competent persons for the judiciary and to oppose the unfit.[49] Two years later, in 1949, it became the Standing Committee on Federal Judiciary, charged with reviewing nominees' qualifications.

Recreated in 1946, the committee was assigned several tasks. Among these tasks were:

1. To promote the nomination and confirmation of such persons as the committee, after investigation, deems to be competent for appointment as federal judges.

2. To oppose the nomination and confirmation of such persons as the committee, after investigation, deems to be unfit or not sufficiently qualified for appointment as federal judges.[50]

Since 1991, the Standing Committee on Federal Judiciary consists of fifteen members: two members from the ninth circuit, because of its size, one member from each of the other twelve federal judicial circuits, and one member-at-large who serves as chairperson. These members are appointed for staggered once-renewable three-year terms by the president of the ABA. Thus, members are not allowed to serve more than two terms. Also, as a condition of appointment, each member agrees while on the committee and for at least one year thereafter not to seek or accept federal judicial appointment and agrees while on the committee not to participate in or contribute to any federal election campaign or political activity.[51]

In operation, the committee itself never "officially" proposes candidates for the federal judiciary, but rather considers prospective nominees referred to it by the attorney general and has restricted its review to issues bearing on professional qualifications—integrity, competence, and judicial temperament. In 1991, for example, during the Bush administration, the committee published revised guidelines. Significantly, these 1991 guidelines suggest that the committee may consider the political or ideological philosophy of a nominee "to the extent they may bear upon . . . the factors of judicial temperament." Further, in determining judicial temperament, the committee may consider among other factors "compassion, decisiveness, open-mindedness, sensitivity, courtesy, patience, freedom from bias and commitment to equal justice." Clearly, these revised guidelines do little to justify or explain the ABA's evaluative actions, or to silence the protests of the committee's critics. Essentially the ABA Standing Committee has wide discretion in determining whether or not a candidate's political philosophy of ideology bears upon his/her judicial temperament and also, whether the nominee's ideology fails to meet the committee's standards of "compassion," "sensitivity," and "commitment to equal justice," and so on. Indeed the Senate Judiciary Committee has requested the opinion of the ABA committee on every federal judicial nomination since 1948, and the ABA committee has been consulted by every president with respect to almost every federal judicial appointment since 1952.[52]

It could well be, however, as some have suggested, that ABA influence is perhaps best focused on the lower courts since the qualifications for these courts are of a more technical type that the committee is best suited to judge.[53]

Overall, the ABA committee's relations with different administrations have varied over time. For example, the committee maintained excellent relations and influence with the Department of Justice throughout the eight years of the Eisenhower administration, but its influence declined during the Kennedy and Johnson administrations. This decline was undoubtedly precipitated by the fact that during its first two years, eight of the judges nominated by the Kennedy administration were rated "not qualified" by the ABA.[54]

On the other hand, Nixon's deputy attorney general, Richard Kleindienst, announced in 1969 that the ABA "would have absolute veto over all lower-court nominations."[55] And although President Carter's attorney general Griffen Bell is reported to have "worked with the ABA," his successor Benjamin Civiletti endorsed several nominations of African-American judges whom the ABA had opposed in 1980.[56] The Reagan administration also enjoyed generally good relations with the ABA committee, considering the fact that Reagan put up many controversial nominees. Indeed, in support of the charges by numerous liberal organizations that the ABA bent to pressure by the Reagan administration, it is instructive to note that not a single Reagan district court appointee was rated "Not Qualified." (See Table 3.7 following this discussion.)

Between 1958 and 1988, lower court nominees have been given one of four ratings: "Exceptionally Well Qualified" (EWQ), "Well Qualified" (WQ), "Qualified" (Q), or "Not Qualified" (NQ). The ABA ratings of lower court nominees from the Eisenhower through the Clinton administrations are shown in Table 3.11, and, as this table indicates, few nominees are found "Exceptionally Well Qualified" or "Not Qualified." However, the fourth rating, "Exceptionally Well Qualified," was discontinued after 1988 (for discussion on this discontinuation, see Chapter 6, at "Bush and the ABA").

Ratings

The committee rates prospective nominees on the following scale:

Well Qualified: To merit *Well Qualified*, the prospective nominee must be at the top of the legal profession in his or her legal community, have outstanding legal ability, wide experience, the highest reputation for integrity and either have shown, or have exhibited the capacity for, judicial temperament, and have the committee's strongest affirmative endorsement.

Qualified: The evaluation of *Qualified* means that the prospective nominee meets the committee's very high standards with respect to integrity, professional competence and judicial temperament and that the committee believes that the prospective nominee will be able to perform satisfactorily all of the responsibilities required by the high office of a federal judge.

Not Qualified: When a prospective nominee is found *Not Qualified*, the committee's investigation has indicated that the prospective nominee does not meet the committee's standards with regard to integrity, professional competence, or judicial temperament.[57]

Overall, numerous studies have shown that the rating a judicial nominee receives from the ABA is one of the most important factors in determining both the "length" of the confirmation process as well as the conformation rate for federal judges.[58]

On balance, the ABA committee continues to engender both praise and criticism. The standing committee has been praised for helping to keep "unfit" nominees off the federal bench. But the standing committee has also been accused of representing only a small segment of the bar—"the predominantly white, male, high-income, corporate practice stratum—while purporting to represent all segments."[59]

As one commentator states: "[T]he chief defect in the ABA screening system is that the veto is not wielded by the 170,000-odd lawyers who are the membership, but by a tight committee of twelve men, appointed by the ABA president."[60] These challenges were directly put in 1979 by Massachusetts Senator Edward Kennedy, when he pondered whether the ABA "process assured an old boy network outcome, disadvantaged minority candidates because of the emphasis placed on judicial experience, or took into account a potential nominee's activity in public law concerns, such as poverty or environmental law."[61]

Similarly, Senator Howard Metzenbaum described his understanding of the ABA's procedures:

One person from each circuit . . . that person really does all of this investigation. . . . That one individual talks to everybody and then writes up the report. If that person has a preconceived idea, isn't there an element of subjectivity in that?[62]

Still others have observed that ABA evaluations of nominees' qualifications amount to "an expression of their standing in the legal profession."[63]

Some, however, have attacked the ABA and the input of legal organizations altogether. Conservative law professor Philip Kurland has criticized the "submission of names for approval to any segment of [the legal] profession, national, state, local, or individual, with duties of advice and consent. Since the bar is anything but a representative political body, it affords no legitimating function in this regard."[64]

For example, the conservative Washington Legal Foundation (WLF) initiated its first lawsuit against the ABA committee in December of 1985, alleging "the committee had expressly refused to comply with the WLF's repeated requests for information that the committee had shared with certain liberal activist groups."[65] Later, in 1986 while the aforementioned suit was still pending, the WLF complained that the ABA was providing names of judicial nominees to liberal groups that were trying to derail Reagan nominations.[66]

A few years later, in 1989, the Senate Judiciary Committee conducted a special hearing on the role of the ABA in judicial selection and members from *both* parties were highly critical of the ABA.[67] Chairman Joseph Biden (D-DE) charged "the ABA's Standing committee has become larger than life . . . its ratings have been viewed by all as nearly dispositive." Senator Orin Hatch (R-AZ) asserted: "I personally believe that is time to 'pull the plug' on the American Bar Association's preeminent role in judicial selection and reclaim for this Committee its full place in the advice and consent function." Senator Gordon Humphrey further articulated in very colorful terms his displeasure with the ABA:

I suggest that the decade-old arrangement under which the ABA enjoys the privileged status of a quasi-official advisory body to the executive and to the Senate, while operating in perfect secrecy and free of any of the processes of public accountability, is no longer good enough. This arrangement is a moldering, corrupted, malodorous old relic which should be given a quick burial for the sake of public health.

Accountability is the oxygen of good government. Choke off that oxygen . . . by conducting business in secret and beyond the range of elected officials, and just watch the ugly pathologies grow and multiply.

But is the Standing Committee, with this enormous power, in any way accountable to the public? No. . . . to the executive branch? No. . . . to the legislative branch? No. . . . [T]his kind of power without accountability is dreadfully dangerous and irresistibly inclined towards arbitrariness.[68]

The chairman of the ABA Standing Committee, Harold R. Tyler, responded to the senator's complaints with surprise: "I don't begrudge them saying, 'We would like you to do it a little differently.' That's fine. But what puzzles me is the argument that we are more powerful than we should be." Tyler continued, "We don't consider ideology or philosophy but we wouldn't overlook it if someone said 'I'm a member of the Ku Klux Klan, and don't intend to resign.' We look at any extremes."[69]

Challenges to the ABA's role arose yet again during the Clinton presidency following a *Washington Post* study that found that nine of the eleven members of the ABA Standing Committee on Federal Judiciary who had recently contributed to political campaigns supported Bill Clinton's or other Democratic campaigns (see Chapter 6).[70]

On balance, as the second Clinton administration begins, commentaries continue to frequently portray the ABA as "simply another political interest group," that "should be treated as such. They should have precisely the same role as other groups, but they should enjoy no special status, no veto power over judicial nominations."[71]

On the whole, many continue to share the position that the ABA Standing Committee's investigatory process is a Star-Chamberlike proceeding, using the criterion of "temperament" as a way to smuggle in committee members' biases against certain candidates.[72]

How the ABA Operates. Procedurally, when a vacancy arises, often the attorney general provides the chairperson of the ABA Committee with the name of a prospective nominee or a list of nominees. An investigation of the nominee is normally assigned to the circuit member of the committee in the judicial circuit where the vacancy exist. The attorney general's office also sends to each prospective nominee a comprehensive ABA-designed questionnaire (called the "ABA Personal Data Questionnaire") related to "fitness for judicial service."[73] For example, one of the questions, Q13, asks the candidate to describe the "ten most significant opinions" at constitutional law that they have written. These responses are sent to the U.S. Department of Justice, the ABA Committee chairperson, and the circuit member.

The circuit member then conducts the official investigation examining the nominees' legal writing and conducts extensive confidential interviews with those likely to have information "regarding the integrity, professional competence and temperament of the prospective nominee" including, where pertinent, "federal and state judges and their law clerks, practicing lawyers in both private and government service, law school professors and deans, legal services and public interest lawyers, representatives of professional organizations," and others who are in a position to evaluate the prospective nominee's "integrity, competence and temperament."[74] Following this investigation, a meeting is held between the circuit member, and in appropriate cases one or more other members of the committee, and the prospective nominee to allow the prospective nominee the opportunity to explain any adverse matters disclosed in the investigation and to provide any additional information. Additional investigation and interviews may be conducted to complete the investigation if necessary.

Next, the single committee member (the circuit designate) drafts a written informal report to the chairperson containing a description of the nominees' background, summaries of all interviews (including that of the prospective nominee), an overall evaluation, and a recommended rating. The chairperson then makes an informal report to the attorney general's office indicating the ABA rating. These data are discussed in more detail in chapters 4, 5, and 6 for each president.

Next the circuit member provides a formal and final report to all members of the ABA Committee and each member of the committee then sends a vote to the chairperson. Lastly, the chairperson confidentially reports the committee's rating to the attorney general and the president decides whether or not he will nominate the prospective nominee. In less than 1 percent of the nominations has a president opted to nominate a person found "Not Qualified" by the committee.[75] Notably, it was the Kennedy administration that chose to nominate a few persons who were rated unqualified by the ABA. For example, the hearing for Kennedy nominee Luther Bohanon for a district judgeship in Oklahoma lasted only fifteen minutes in spite of his unqualified rating. Researchers suggest that it was because of strong support for Bohanon by Senator Robert Kerr (D-OK) that no one at the hearing even questioned Bohanon about the ABA rating.[76] Should the president choose to nominate the prospective nominee, a public hearing is then held by the Senate Judiciary Committee. The Senate Judiciary Committee then requests that the ABA Committee submit its rating for the public record.

In perspective, some have argued that the ABA and its committee have continued to serve basically two purposes: "(1) to lend legitimacy to appointees while not altering the basic politics of appointments, and (2) to create a buffer between both the President and the Senate and the public for unqualified nominees."[77] Still others continue to view the committee's actions as both ad hoc and far from impartial.

Thus throughout this analysis one must keep in mind that the ABA has no constitutional or statutory standing in the politics of the judicial selection process; neither the president nor the Senate is obliged to abide by its recommendation or accept its evaluations. What is most instructive, however, is to note that the ABA Committee does play a crucial role in the evaluation process; a particularly powerful position for what many suggest amounts to basically a private interest group.[78]

In fact, as indicated by the NDJS, a majority, about 72 percent, of district court judges agree that "a district court nominee's rating by the American Bar Association Standing Committee on Federal Judiciary is a fair and generally accurate measure of his/her qualifications" (see Table 3.7). Little difference is revealed between Democratic and Republican appointees' responses. Of course, all those district court judges responding obviously survived the ABA committee's evaluation process. A quite intriguing comment was offered by Judge 327 in the margin. Judge 327 responded "disagree," and wrote "they [the ABA] gave me a unanimous 'well qualified,' occasionally it has its own agenda." Of course without asking Judge 327 directly about the comment, one can only speculate as to its intent and meaning.

Table 3.7
The ABA

	% Strongly Agree	% Agree	% No Opinion	% Disagree	% Strongly Disagree
Q11. A district court nominee's rating by the American Bar Association Standing Committee on Federal Judiciary is a fair and generally accurate measure of his/her qualifications.					
All judges	7.6	64.8	6.6	15.4	5.5
Democratic appointees	6.0	63.9	8.4	18.1	3.0
Republican appointees	8.4	65.2	5.6	14.0	6.8

Percentages may not total 100 because "no response" answers are omitted.

On balance, the role of the ABA is indeed part of both the interest conflict and the group struggle reflected in the overall judicial nomination and selection process.

The Senate Judiciary Committee. After having successfully navigated the screening and reviews of the Justice Department and the ABA Committee, the nominee's name is then sent to the Senate where it is the Judiciary Committee that plays a key, and at times determinative, role as to whether or not the nominee will be confirmed or rejected by the full Senate.[79] However, we must remain aware that in practice the overwhelming majority of lower federal court nominees—especially prior to the Bush and Clinton administrations (see discussion in Chapter 6)—received only nominal examination by the Senate Judiciary Committee before being *favorably* recommended to, and confirmed by, the Senate as a whole. This favorable confirmation usually came without debate or even roll-call votes. For example, of the ninety district and circuit nominations sent to the Senate in the 92nd Congress, forty-one went from hearings to full senate consideration in one day.[80] Indeed, with the exception of Edward Kennedy's chairmanship of the Senate Judiciary Committee, Table 3.8 indicates in recent times, most nominees have moved swiftly through the confirmation process with little to no independent inquiry and only brief hearings before a subcommittee of one or two senators.

Table 3.8
Nominations before the Senate Judiciary Committee (1965–1986), Average Number of Days between District Court Nominees' Referral and Hearings

Chairman	Congress	Average Number of Days
Eastland	89th	19.5
	90th	29.8
	91st	27.8
	92nd	18.9
	93rd	20.5
	94th	30.3
	95th	23.2
Kennedy	96th	55.5
Thurmond	97th	20.7
	98th	16.7
	99th	23.2

Source: Adopted as printed in David M. O'Brien, *Judicial Roulette: Report of the Twentieth Century Fund Task Force on Judicial Selection* (New York: Priority Press Publications, 1988), Table 4.2, p. 68.

During the two-year period 1985–1986, for example, the Senate Judiciary Committee considered a total of 136 Reagan nominations and only *six* were afforded more than one pro forma hearing.[81] Not only did the Senate fail to reject a single lower court nominee, but in only two cases did the Senate Judiciary Committee even file reports on the nominees with the full Senate.[82] One of the six that did not receive more than a pro forma hearing was Reagan's nomination of Sidney A. Fitzwater to be a U.S. district judge for the Northern District of Texas. Although five members of the Senate Judiciary Committee voted against Fitzwater, the committee did not provide the Senate with any report on his qualifications or on the allegations that he was "insensitive toward black voting rights." Senator Paul Sarbanes expressed his displeasure with the dearth of communication on the nominee during the floor debate:

Far be it for me really to intrude into the procedures of the Judiciary Committee, but it does seem to me that if we are going to have controversial nominations on the floor of the Senate—and this obviously is such a nomination, with a fairly close cloture vote, and I assume a fairly close vote on confirmation—we ought to have a report, or at a minimum that the hearings of the Committee should be printed so that the members of the Senate can have the opportunity to at least have the printed hearing record before them and be in a position to review it.[83]

Despite Sarbanes' disquiet, Fitzwater was nevertheless confirmed by a vote of 52–42, with Sarbanes voting to reject Fitzwater.

This perfunctory treatment of lower court confirmations was well captured by one commentator who observed that "the Senate as a whole ordinarily acknowledges [senatorial courtesy] by paying less attention to the confirmation process of a federal judge than to the price of bean soup in the Senate restaurants."[84] Similarly, a judiciary staff member commented that the Senate's consideration of nominees' qualifications and investigation into their backgrounds is "as *pro forma* as *pro forma* can be."[85]

Indeed, one of the principal findings of a 1988 task force on judicial selection was that the Senate too often gives "rubber stamp" approval to nominees to the district courts. The report concludes in part: "The Senate Judiciary Committee's confirmation hearings on lower-court judges are usually superficial, lasting five minutes or less, and the Senate's vote to confirm nominees is more often than not a mere formality. In short, the problem with the confirmation process for lower-court judges is a lack of accountability because the process lacks visibility."[86]

In the main, the political costs incurred by Senators who choose to oppose their colleagues in another state over a nomination seem to outweigh the desire. Thus, senatorial courtesy also directly enhances the Senate Judiciary Committee's ability to rubber stamp nominees. This situation is further aggravated by the absence of formal procedures and/or standards established for confirming nominees. There appear to be no clear or even observable fixed standards established or adhered to by the Senate Judiciary Committee for determining candidates' qualifications for confirmation. A 1986 Common Cause study reported that the Senate Judiciary Committee "has no affirmative standards for confirmation . . . [and] seems willing to endorse a nominee unless charges of criminal or flagrantly unethical behavior are proved."[87] And in view of charges of sexual harassment, the ethical morass surrounding the Senate confirmation of Justice Clarence Thomas to the Supreme Court clearly suggests the laxity of this requirement for "proved" unethical behavior.

For the most part, however, the operations, rules, and procedures of the committee are determined in large measure by the committee chairperson. What the chairperson does can enhance or retard a president's ability to win confirmation for judicial nominations. Indeed, the chair of the Senate Judiciary Committee can prove to be a powerful position with respect to judicial appointments—and may be used to influence and shape how the full Senate views a particular nomination. The chairperson determines in large measure both when nominees have hearings as well as the nature and amount of opposition a nominee might encounter. Since the 1940s, for example, it has been the chairperson of the Senate Judiciary Committee who receives the confidential FBI reports compiled on the nominees for the Department of Justice. And the handling, or mishandling, of these reports can bear serious consequences. One need only recall the *leaked* FBI Reports that disclosed the alleged sexual harassment of Professor Anita Hill by Supreme Court nominee Clarence Thomas and the ugly spectacle that followed. The chairperson also receives copies of the ABA rating as well as the personal questionnaire filled out by the nominee.

Let us review briefly the leadership and management style of the four persons who served as chairs of the Senate Judiciary Committee in recent times, 1960–1990.

The first, conservative Democratic Senator James Eastland (MS) chaired the committee from 1956 to 1979. Senator Eastland exercised tight control over judicial appointments and most hearings were brief and superficial. There was no special investigative staff, and, except for nominations to the Supreme Court, he did not utilize the full committee to consider nominations but instead appointed ad hoc subcommittees to consider all lower court nominees.[88] This was the setting inherited by the next chairperson, liberal Democrat Senator Edward Kennedy (MA).

Senator Kennedy chaired the Judiciary Committee from 1979 to 1981 and pushed for several significant changes in the committee's operations. In addition to requiring independent investigations of nominees by the committee's own investigative staff, during Kennedy's chairmanship the committee also developed a questionnaire that was sent to nominees along with those of the Department of Justice and the ABA. Moreover, the "blue slip" procedure was amended and notices of hearings were released to the press and put in the *Congressional Record*, and interest groups were sometimes invited to comment on nominees.[89] Two of these developments, the blue slip procedure and the personal questionnaire, deserve special focus.

The Blue Slip

The Senate Judiciary Committee formally institutionalized and extended the concept of senatorial courtesy through the blue slip procedure.[90] Originating in the mid-1940s, the committee began sending a one-page request (printed on a piece of blue paper) to senators from the state in which the vacancy existed. This blue slip requests the senators' "opinion and information" concerning a nomination. The blue slip states that if it is not returned to the committee chairman within a week, it is assumed that the Senator has no objections to the nomination. The blue slip reads as follows:

Dear Senator:
Will you kindly give me, for use of the Committee, your opinion and information concerning the nomination of (name, district, name of former judge.)
Under a rule of the Committee, unless a reply is received from you within a week from this date, it will be assumed that you have no objection to this nomination.
Respectfully,
Chairman's signature

Notwithstanding its actual wording, however, for many years the practice was that nonreturn of blue slips indicated the invocation of "courtesy" and thus allowed senators to delay indefinitely a judicial confirmation hearing. That is, if the blue slip was not returned, the assumption was made that the senator objected to the nomination and in fact no hearing was scheduled. Thus, in practice senatorial courtesy has been institutionalized through the blue slip as an automatic and mechanical one-member veto of nominees.[91] As President Nixon's attorney general John Mitchell said, "Those blue slips are the tickets to the ballgame."[92]

It is also important to note that blue slips are distributed to *all* home senators, regardless of party. Theoretically, the potential veto could be invoked by senators who *are not* members of the president's party and clearly were "never traditionally considered within the gambit of senatorial courtesy."[93]

As judiciary committee chairperson, Massachusetts Democratic Senator Edward Kennedy attacked the "silent courtesy" procedure and announced that failure to return the slip would no longer impede the committee from holding hearings or from sending the nomination to the Senate for confirmation. Indeed, at a committee hearing in 1979, Kennedy stated:

I will not unilaterally table a nomination simply because a blue slip is not returned by a colleague. If the blue slip is not returned within a reasonable time, rather than letting the nomination die, I will place before the committee a motion to determine whether it wishes to proceed to a hearing on the nomination, notwithstanding the absence of the blue slip. The committee and ultimately the Senate, can work its will.[94]

Kennedy's position was unanimously opposed by the seven Republicans on the seventeen-member committee[95] but was not tested since not a single confirmation arose during his chairmanship (1979–1981). Even so, when Senator Thurmond (R-SC) took over the chairmanship in 1981, he continued to subscribe to Kennedy's policy. And though during the remainder of this period of study, the blue slip has rarely been used to block nominees, it nonetheless remains a potential and valuable tool for "enhancing the [Senate's] negotiating position with the administration."

Personal Questionnaire. In addition to reforming the blue slip procedure, during Kennedy's term as chair of the Senate Judiciary Committee also institutionalized an in-depth personal questionnaire. This questionnaire requests information detailing financial data, including a full listing of assets and liabilities, a five-year income report, a list of businesses or enterprises with which the candidate has been connected during the past decade or has a continuing financial interest in, a list of deferred compensation agreements and stock options the candidate has entered into, and a list of potential contributions and contributions accepted.[96]

Additionally, the questionnaire requests copies of *every* speech the candidate has made over the last five years. Yet another question, and a potentially controversial request, is that the candidate is required to document "a commitment to equal justice under the law."[97] Thus, now the Senate Judiciary Committee's personal questionnaire is used to augment the information gathered by the ABA Standing Committee on the Federal Judiciary and information gathered by the

FBI.

Reagan's victory in 1980 brought with it Republican control of the Senate and thus chairmanship of the Judiciary Committee passed from Democratic Senator Kennedy to Republican Senator Strom Thurmond (SC). Thurmond, an influential ally of the Reagan administration, retained the position from 1981 to 1986, and once again aligned the committee more closely with the president. Thurmond reduced the size of the investigative staff and the committee was generally "less open to the concerns of outside groups—especially civil rights organizations."[98] He also clearly expedited the confirmation process. For example, as evidenced in Table 3.8, the average time between nomination and hearings under Chairman Kennedy was nearly two months; under Chairman Thurmond this period dropped to twenty days.[99] Moreover, committee votes on nominees were usually scheduled for only ten days later—twice as fast as under Kennedy.[100]

Thurmond's practice of rushing nominees through the process led Senator Paul Simon (D-IL) to complain that: "We have so many names coming at us so rapidly it becomes difficult for us to do the kind of intensive work that needs to be done."[101] Criticisms such as these led to several procedural changes in late 1985, including an agreement to wait a minimum of three weeks before voting on nominees. Additionally a limit of "six" was placed on the number of nominees who could be considered at any point and unlimited time was guaranteed for considering nominees who were viewed as controversial.

Thurmond's chairmanship ended when the Democrats recaptured control of the Senate in the 1986 elections. As a result, Senator Joseph Biden (D-DE) became chairman of the committee. Like Kennedy, Senator Biden sought to make the process more deliberative.[102] The committee was reduced (by agreement on committee assignments) from eighteen to fourteen members; thus removing three conservative Republicans from the judiciary panel—most notably Senator Jesse Helms (R-NC). The committee also slowed considerably the confirmation process during the final years of the Reagan administration. Senator Biden also created a four-member panel, headed by Senator Patrick Leahy (D-VT), that was charged with screening nominees. And clearly this change from Thurmond to Biden as committee chair proved significant, if not determinative, in the Senate's rejection of Robert Bork to replace Justice Powell on the Supreme Court in 1987.[103]

Thus, the Senate Judiciary Committee chairperson may play a key role in formulating and enforcing committee rules and procedures. And although most lower court nominations still receive only perfunctory treatment, in controversial nominations these rules and procedures may determine to a large measure the nominee's confirmation. As of this writing [1997] Senate Judiciary Committee rules require at least seven days between a hearing and a committee vote, and at least three days between a committee vote and a full Senate vote.[104]

The Media and Special Interests. Although the media and direct lobbying continue to play an increasing role in Supreme Court confirmations, nearly all district court confirmations remain relatively unnoticed. Indeed, most Senate Judiciary Committee confirmation hearings on lower court judges are perfunctory, many lasting five minutes or less, and the Senate's vote to confirm nominees is more often than not a mere formality. In general, these hearings take place without even minimal media coverage and even less lobbying by outside interests. With regard to the issue of the role of special interests, the NDJS data indicate that the judges are somewhat divided. For example, about 58 percent of the judges in all disagreed that "Special interests are too involved in the selection and evaluation of district court judges," with about 24 percent agreeing (see Table 3.9, Q8). On the other hand, about 34 percent of Democratic appointees agreed compared to about 19 percent of Republican appointees.

Table 3.9
Special Interests

	% Strongly Agree	% Agree	% No Opinion	% Disagree	% Strongly Disagree
Q8. Special interests are too involved in the selection and evaluation of district court judges.					
All judges	3.5	20.9	17.4	50.0	7.6
Democratic appointees	5.4	28.9	20.5	38.6	6.0
Republican appointees	2.5	16.8	15.8	55.9	8.4
Q35. Would you say that the government is pretty much run by a few big interests looking out for themselves or that it is run for the benefit of all the people?	A few big interests		All the people		Do not know/ not sure
All judges	18.4		44.3		28.1
Democratic appointees	29.5		32.5		27.1
Republican appointees	12.7		50.3		28.6

Percentages may not total 100 because "no response" answers are omitted.

The NDJS also asked these judges "Would you say that the government is pretty much run by a few big interests looking out for themselves or that it is run for the benefit of all the people?" On this question, 44 percent of the responding judges chose "all the people"; however, it is interesting to note that just over 18 percent did select "a few big interests" (Table 3.9, Q35). The "few big interests" response was also preferred by Democratic appointees, 29.5 percent, compared to only about 13 percent for Republican appointees. That is, Democratic appointees are more pessimistic about governmental leadership and representation.

Merit, Ideology, or Politics? Despite the evidence above that emphasizes the often highly politicized nature of the selection and confirmation process, only about 58 percent of the nearly 500 judges responding *disagreed* that the district court judge confirmations are "too political" (Table 3.10, Q5). Of these, about

48 percent of Democratic appointees disagreed compared to 62.5 percent of Republican appointees. However, one judge (Judge 534) who disagreed wrote in the margin: "The process *is* political!" Judge 691 wrote "inevitably they will be to a large extent political, hopefully in the political framework they will also have some merit." From these aggregate responses, again 58 percent, it appears that a significant number of district court judges recognize the politicized nature of the confirmation process but do not feel that it is "too political." Similarly, about 65 percent of judges responding agreed that "Partisan politics dominate and control district court appointments" (Table 3.10, Q7). It is worth noting also that nearly 84 percent of all Democratic appointees agreed, compared to a smaller majority, 56 percent, of Republican appointees.

Table 3.10
Merit, Ideology, or Politics

	% Strongly Agree	% Agree	% No Opinion	% Disagree	% Strongly Disagree
Q5. District court judges' confirma- tions are "way too political."					
All judges	3.3	29.5	8.8	53.3	4.3
Democratic appointees	4.2	41.0	5.4	44.6	3.6
Republican appointees	2.8	23.6	10.6	57.8	4.7
Q7. Partisan politics dominate and control district court appointments.					
All judges	9.0	56.4	6.4	25.6	1.2
Democratic appointees	16.3	67.5	2.4	11.4	.6
Republican appointees	5.3	50.6	8.4	32.9	1.6
Q4. All too often, a district court nominee's ideology is given more consideration than his/her merit quali- fication.					
All judges	7.8	43.0	11.5	33.2	3.5
Democratic appointees	13.9	52.4	12.0	19.3	1.2
Republican appointees	4.7	38.2	11.2	40.0	4.7

Q29. How much did politics play a role in *your* nomination and confirmation to the district courts?	A lot	Some	Very little	None
All judges	20.5	41.8	24.2	11.1
Democratic appointees	20.5	43.4	22.3	12.0
Republican appointees	20.5	41.0	25.2	10.6

Percentages may not total 100 because "no response" answers are omitted.

And when the judges were asked about their own personal confirmation experiences, in other words, "How much did politics play a role in *your* nomination and confirmation to the district courts [Q29]," again, nearly all judges admitted to political considerations (see Table 3.10 and Figure 3.2). In fact, the NDJS data reveal that just over 20 percent of the judges admitted that politics played "a lot" of a role in their confirmation. Very little difference is reported on this question between Democratic and Republican appointees.

Figure 3.2
How Much Did Politics Play a Role in Your Confirmation?

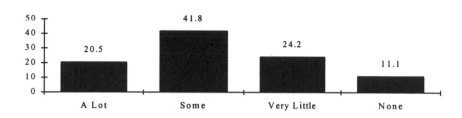

Lastly, in addition to issues of merit and politics—in fact, underlying many political considerations—remains ideology. The NDJS data indicate that half (50.8 percent) the district court judges responding agree that "All too often, a district court nominee's ideology is given more consideration than his/her merit qualification" (see Table 3.10, Q4). A majority of Democratic appointees agreed, 66 percent, compared to a minority, 43 percent, of Republican appointees.

Summary and Profile

Before showing how individual presidents have tailored the selection process and before outlining differences between presidents' appointees, a few generalizations can be made about who the federal district court judges are as a whole. Overall, as indicated Table 3.11, the selection process described above has produced a cadre of federal district court judges who are primarily wealthy white males. Although a detailed profile for each president's appointees is provided and discussed in greater detail in the following chapters (4, 5, and 6), Table 3.11 provides a general overview. As indicated, most have elite educations—about 50 percent attended ivy league or private schools for undergraduate and law degree. Most are not women or minorities. Most are rated as qualified by the ABA and nearly all are of the same political party as the president appointing them. And, in recent years, about 60 percent have records of active partisanship. The average age at appointment is forty-nine and over half are Protestants.

Overall, federal judges reflect a lack of diversity, often making it difficult to study issues of representation. As one analysis of the judicial selection process put it:

State jurists, like their counterparts on the federal bench are overwhelmingly older, white, male, and Protestant. They tend to be home-grown fellows who are moderately

Table 3.11
Background Characteristics of District Court Appointees by Administration, 1960–1994

Characteristic (%N)	Clinton	Bush	Reagan	Carter	Ford	Nixon	Johnson	Kennedy
Occupation								
Politics/gov.	10.7 (18)	10.8 (16)	12.8 (37)	4.4 (9)	21.2 (11)	10.6 (19)	21.3 (26)	10.7
Judiciary	44.4 (75)	41.9 (62)	37.2 (108)	44.6 (90)	34.6 (18)	28.5 (51)	31.1 (38)	5.8
Large law firm								
100+members	8.3 (14)	10.8 (16)	5.9 (17)	2.0 (4)	1.9 (1)	0.6 (1)	0.8 (1)	—
50–99	5.3 (9)	7.4 (11)	5.2 (15)	6.0 (12)	3.9 (2)	0.6 (1)	1.6 (2)	—
25–49	3.6 (6)	7.4 (11)	6.6 (19)	6.0 (12)	3.9 (2)	10.1 (18)	—	—
Moderate size firm								
10–24 members	8.3 (14)	8.8 (13)	10.3 (30)	9.4 (19)	7.7 (4)	8.9 (16)	12.3 (15)	—
5–9	8.3 (14)	6.1 (9)	9.0 (26)	10.4 (21)	17.3 (9)	19.0 (34)	6.6 (8)	—
Small firm								
2–4 members	5.3 (9)	3.4 (5)	7.6 (22)	11.4 (23)	7.7 (4)	14.5 (26)	11.5 (14)	—
Solo	2.4 (4)	1.4 (2)	2.8 (8)	25. (5)	1.9 (1)	4.5 (8)	11.5 (14)	—
Professor of Law	2.4 (4)	0.7 (1)	2.1 (6)	30. (6)	—	2.8 (5)	3.3 (4)	—
Other	1.2 (2)	1.4 (2)	0.7 (2)	05. (1)	—	—	—	—
Experience								
Judicial	49.7 (84)	46.6 (69)	46.6 (135)	54.5 (110)	42.3 (22)	35.2 (63)	34.4 (42)	33.0
Prosecutorial	37.9 (64)	39.2 (58)	44.1 (128)	38.6 (78)	50.0 (26)	41.9 (75)	45.9 (56)	—
Neither	31.4 (53)	31.8 (47)	28.3 (82)	28.2 (57)	30.8 (16)	36.3 (65)	33.6 (41)	—
Undergraduate education								
Public	44.4 (75)	44.6 (66)	35.5 (103)	57.4 (116)	48.1 (25)	41.3 (74)	38.5 (47)	44.6
Private	40.8 (69)	41.2 (61)	50.3 (146)	32.7 (66)	34.6 (18)	38.5 (69)	31.1 (38)	35.9
Ivy League	14.8 (25)	14.2 (21)	14.1 (41)	9.9 (20)	17.3 (9)	19.6 (35)	16.4 (20)	7.8
None indicated	—	—	—	—	—	0.6 (1)	13.9 (17)	11.7

Characteristic (%N)	Clinton	Bush	Reagan	Carter	Ford	Nixon	Johnson	Kennedy
Law school education								
Public	42.6 (72)	52.7 (78)	42.4 (123)	50.5 (102)	44.2 (23)	41.9 (75)	40.2 (49)	36.9
Private	37.3 (63)	33.1 (49)	45.5 (132)	32.2 (65)	38.5 (20)	36.9 (66)	36.9 (45)	41.8
Ivy League	20.1 (34)	14.2 (21)	12.1 (35)	17.3 (35)	17.3 (9)	21.2 (38)	21.3 (26)	18.4
None indicated					—		1.6 (2)	—
Gender								
Male	69.8 (118)	80.4 (119)	91.7 (266)	85.6 (173)	98.1 (51)	99.4 (178)	98.4 (120)	99
Female	30.2 (51)	19.6 (29)	8.3 (24)	14.4 (29)	1.9 (1)	0.6 (1)	1.6 (2)	.97
Ethnicity/race								
White	72.2 (122)	89.2 (132)	92.4 (268)	78.7 (159)	88.5 (46)	95.5 (171)	93.4 (114)	97
African-American	19.5 (33)	6.8 (10)	2.1 (6)	13.9 (28)	5.8 (3)	3.4 (6)	4.1 (5)	1.9
Hispanic	6.5 (11)	4.0 (6)	4.8 (14)	6.9 (14)	1.9 (1)	1.1 (2)	2.5 (3)	—
Asian	1.2 (2)	—	0.7 (2)	0.5 (1)	3.9 (2)	—	—	—
Native American	0.6 (1)	—	—	—	—	—	—	—
Percent white male	47.3 (80)	72.9 (108)	84.8 (246)	68.3 (138)	86.5 (45)	94.9 (170)	92.6 (113)	99.3
ABA rating								
Exceptionally well/ well qualified	63.9 (108)	57.4 (85)	54 (157)	51 (103)	46.1 (24)	45.3(81)	48.4 (59)	56.2
Qualified	34.3 (58)	42.6 (63)	45.9 (133)	47.5 (96)	53.8 (28)	54.8 (98)	49.2 (60)	31.5
Not Qualified	1.8 (3)	—	—	1.5 (3)	—	—	2.5 (3)	6.3
Party								
Democratic	90.5 (153)	5.4 (8)	4.8 (14)	90.6 (183)	21.2 (11)	7.3 (13)	94.3 (115)	90.3
Republican	2.4 (4)	88.5 (131)	91.7 (266)	4.5 (9)	78.8 (41)	92.7 (166)	5.7 (7)	9.7
Other	0.6 (1)	—	—	—	—	—	—	—
None	6.5 (11)	6.1 (9)	3.4 (10)	5.0 (10)	—	—	—	—
Past Party Activism	53.9 (91)	60.8 (90)	58.6 (170)	60.9 (123)	50.0 (26)	48.6 (87)	49.2 (60)	16.5

Table 3.11 (continued)

Characteristic (%N)	Clinton	Bush	Reagan	Carter	Ford	Nixon	Johnson	Kennedy
Religious origin/ affiliation								
Protestant	—	64.2 (95)	60.3 (175)	60.4 (122)	73.1 (38)	73.2 (131)	58.25 (71)	60.2
Catholic	—	28.4 (42)	30.0 (87)	27.7 (56)	17.3 (9)	18.4 (33)	31.15 (38)	28.1
Jewish	—	7.4 (11)	9.3 (27)	11.9 (24)	9.6 (5)	8.4 (15)	10.75 (13)	11.7
Net Worth								
Under $200,000	17.2 (29)	10.1 (15)	17.6 (15)	35.8 (53)	NA	NA	NA	NA
$200,000–499,999	22.5 (38)	31.1 (46)	37.6 (109)	41.2 (61)	NA	NA	NA	NA
$500,000–999,999	28.4 (48)	26.4 (39)	21.7 (63)	18.9 (28)	NA	NA	NA	NA
$1+ million	32.0 (54)	32.4 (48)	23.1 (67)	4.0 (6)	NA	NA	NA	NA
Average age at nomination	48.7	48.1	48.7	49.7	49.2	49.1	51.4	—
Total number of appointees	169*	148	290	202	52	179	122	103

Source: Compiled using Sheldon Goldman and Elliot Slotnick, "Clinton's First Term Judiciary: Many Bridges to Cross," *Judicature* 80 (May–June 1997), p. 261; Sheldon Goldman, "Bush's Judicial Legacy: The Final Imprint," *Judicature* 76 (April–May, 1993), p. 287, and Sheldon Goldman, "Characteristics of Eisenhower and Kennedy Appointees to the Lower Federal Bench," *The Western Political Quarterly* 18 (December 1965), pp. 755–762.

*Appointees confirmed as of the 104th Congress (1996).

conservative and staunchly committed to the status quo. They believe in the basic values and tradition of the legal and political communities from which they come . . . local boys who made it good.[105]

In general, Table 3.11 offers comparative background characteristics on recent presidents' appointments to the federal district courts.

CHAPTER SUMMARY

The purpose of this chapter has been to review the basic institutional and systemic parameters and primary participants in district court judicial selection, for example, the president, the senators of the party of the president (and those of the other party), the Senate Judiciary Committee, the Department of Justice and the attorney general, and the ABA Standing Committee on Federal Judiciary. It is important to note that in more recent times the president no longer solely initiates the process; it may also start in the Senate when the senators from the states involved send names to—or request names from—the Department of Justice.

In the main, there has been an increase in both the numbers of individuals and organizations involved in the process and an increasing independence of these participants, particularly the roles and influence of the attorneys general and Senate Judiciary Committee. Another principal finding, generated from the NDJS data, is that in most instances significant majorities of judges acknowledge, as well as support, the highly politicized nature of the appointment processes.

The next three chapters, Chapter 4 (1960–1975), Chapter 5 (1976–1987), and Chapter 6 (1988–1996), develop the presidential policy objective and expectation profiles for each president to better understand how and to what extent specific presidents tailored the selection, nomination, and confirmation processes.

NOTES

1. Jack Peltason, *Federal Courts in the Political Process* (New York: Random House, 1955), p. 29.

2. The classic study of the appointment process of lower court federal judges is Harold W. Chase, *Federal Judges: The Appointing Process* (Minneapolis: University of Minnesota Press, 1972).

3. For a well developed discussion of these debates see Joseph P. Harris, *The Advice and Consent of the Senate* (Berkeley: University of California Press, 1953), pp. 17-35, esp. chapter 2.

4. Eugene W. Hickok, Jr. "Judicial Selection: The Political Roots of Advice and Consent," in Henry J. Abraham, *Judicial Selection: Merit, Ideology, and Politics,* with Griffin B. Bell, Charles E. Grassley, Eugene W. Hickok, Jr., John W. Kern III, Stephen J. Markman, and William Bradford Reynolds, eds. (Washington, DC: National Legal Center for the Public Interest, 1990), p. 6. This source hereafter cited as Abraham, *Judicial Selection: Merit, Ideology, and Politics.*

5. Ibid.

6. Ibid.

7. Hickok, in Abraham, *Judicial Selection: Merit, Ideology, and Politics*, p. 8.

8. Alexander Hamilton, James Madison, and John Jay, *The Federalist Papers*, Clinton Rossiter, ed. (New York: New American Library, 1961), p. 401.

9. Garland W. Allison, "Delay in Senate Confirmation of Federal Judicial Nominees," *Judicature* 80 (1996), pp. 8–15, esp. Table 4 at p. 11.

10. See Lawrence Baum, *The Supreme Court* (Washington, DC: CQ Press, 1985), p. 37.

11. See Kevin L. Lyles, "The Bork Nomination and Black America: A Case Study," in Lucius J. Barker and Mack Jones, eds., *African-Americans and the American Political System*, 3rd ed. (Englewood Cliffs, NJ: Prentice-Hall, 1994), pp. 133–160.

12. Baum, *The Supreme Court*, pp. 38–44.

13. See, for example, Henry J. Abraham, *The Judicial Process* (New York: Oxford University Press, 1993); Laurence Tribe, *God Save This Honorable Court* (New York: Random House, 1985); and Herman Schwartz, *Packing the Courts: The Conservative Campaign to Rewrite the Constitution* (New York: Charles Scribner's Sons, 1988).

14. David M. O'Brien, *Storm Center*, 4th ed. (New York: W. W. Norton, 1996), pp. 93.

15. The influence of partisan pressures for judicial patronage intensify to the "point that few presidents can completely withstand." See Joel B. Grossman, *Lawyers and Judges: The ABA and the Politics of Judicial Selection* (New York: John Wiley and Sons, 1965), p. 34.

16. Robert Scigliano, *The Supreme Court and the Presidency* (New York: The Free Press, 1971), pp. 146–148. Clearly notable exceptions in the past would include Justice James McReynolds for President Wilson and Justice Harlan Stone for Coolidge, and in more recent years Chief Justice Earl Warren and Justice William Brennan for President Eisenhower and Harry Blackmun for President Nixon.

17. The confirmation battle of Justice Clarence Thomas amidst allegations of sexual harassment by law professor Anita Hill might call for additional analysis of this factor.

18. Walter F. Murphy, *Elements of Judicial Strategy* (Chicago: University of Chicago Press, 1964).

19. Baum, *The Supreme Court*, p. 38.

20. Scigliano, *The Supreme Court and the Presidency*, p. 95.

21. See Jack Peltason, *58 Lonely Men: Southern Federal Judges and School Desegregation* (Urbana: University of Illinois, 1961). Other researchers have suggested that local conditions, manners, and economic activity are parochial forces that operate around, on, and through the federal district courts. For example, in some civil rights cases in the South, even the Department of Justice was at times reluctant in jury trials to use lawyers from outside the area. When it was necessary to do so, the department was careful to use consul whose background and speech identified them with the locality. See Stephen T. Early, Jr., *Constitutional Courts of the United States* (Totowa, NJ: Littlefield, Adams and Co., 1977), p. 4.

22. Richard J. Richardson and Kenneth N. Vines, *The Politics of the Federal Courts: Lower Courts in the United States* (Boston: Little, Brown and Company, 1970), p. 58.

23. Alan Neff, *The United States District Judge Nominating Commissions: Their Members, Procedures and Candidates* (Chicago: American Judicature Society, 1981), p. 3.

24. Harris, *The Advice and Consent of the Senate*, p. 41.

25. As reported by Richardson and Vines, "until 1840, and before that time, all congressmen from the state where the appointment was to be made participated approximately equally." *The Politics of the Federal Courts*, p. 59.

26. Herbert Jacob, *Law and Politics in the United States* (Boston: Little, Brown and Company, 1986), p. 198.

27. Patricia M. Wald, "Random Thoughts on a Random Process: Selecting Appellate Judges," *Journal of Law and Politics* 6 (1989), pp. 15–23.

28. Chase, *Federal Judges*, pp. 36–37.

29. B. Shartel, "Federal Judges—Appointment, Supervision, Removal—Some Possibilities under the Constitution," *Michigan Law Review* 28 (1931), p. 485.

30. Ibid.

31. Evan Haynes, *Selection and Tenure of Judges* (Newark: National Conference of Judicial Councils, 1944), p. 23.

32. Ronald Stidham and Robert A. Carp, "Exploring Regionalism in the Federal District Courts," *Publius* 18 (1988), pp. 113–125.

33. Schwartz, *Packing the Courts*, p. 53.

34. See "Here Comes the Judges," *Time*, December 11, 1978, p. 112; and "Merit Selection Chances Improve," *Congressional Quarterly Weekly Report*, February 18, 1978, pp. 393–394.

35. Few additional comments were offered by judges in the margins to this question; however, two are worth mentioning. Judge 287 wrote in the margins, "Agree, The governor and both Senators wanted me to take the job." Judge 744 wrote: "Agree, I have known Sen. Nunn of GA for 23 years both as a lawyer and as a state legislator and Senator. He knew me well enough to convince the Democrats on the Judiciary Committee that I was a reasonable fellow who would follow the law."

36. Actually, as reported by Richardson and Vines, "shortly after 1840, the President delegated to the attorney general the formal authority to make recommendations for nominations." Previously, the secretary of state had handled nominations for the judiciary as well as for other offices in the national government (Richardson and Vines, *The Politics of Federal Courts*, p. 59.

37. Elaine Martin and Susan Tolchin. *To the Victor: Political Patronage from the Clubhouse to the White House* (New York: Random House, 1971), pp. 163–164.

38. Grossman, *Lawyers and Judges*, p. 25.

39. For a copy of the "U.S. Department of Justice Questionnaire for Judicial Candidates," see David M. O'Brien, rapporteur, *Judicial Roulette: Report of the Twentieth Century Fund Task Force on Judicial Selection* (New York: Priority Press, 1988), Appendix B, pp. 117–120.

40. Printed in the *Congressional Record*, 71st Congress, 1st Session (December, 17, 1929), p. 787.

41. Alan Neff, *Federal Judicial Selection during the Carter Administration: The United States District Judge Nominating Commissions, Their Members, Procedures and Candidates* (Chicago: American Judicature Society, 1981), p. 19.

42. Chase, *Federal Judges*, p. 88.

43. Neff, *Federal Judicial Selection during the Carter Administration*, p. 19.

44. While more detailed analysis of the critical role played by the attorney general during the Reagan administration is presented in the next chapter—where I develop Reagan's presidential expectation profile—brief attention here will help to illuminate its expanded role as a participant in the selection process.

45. Quoted in D. M. O'Brien, "Meese's Agenda for Ensuring the Reagan Legacy,"

Los Angeles Times, "Opinion," September 28, 1986, p. 3.

46. In addition to Chapter 5, see a discussion on the impact of Edwin Meese in the Reagan selection process in Sheldon Goldman, "Reagan and Meese Remake the Judiciary," in Sheldon Goldman and Austin Sarat, eds., *American Court Systems*, 2nd ed. (New York: Longman, 1989), p. 307.

47. For an in-depth and contemporary examination of the ABA's Standing Committee, see Henry J. Abraham, "Beneficial Advice or Presumptuous Veto? The ABA's Committee on Federal Judiciary Revisited," in Abraham, *Judicial Selection: Merit, Ideology, and Politics*, pp. 61–78. See also for example, the American Bar Association's publication *Standing Committee on Federal Judiciary: How It Is and How It Works* (Chicago: American Bar Association, 1991); Chase, *Federal Judges; Appointing Process;* Grossman, *Lawyers and Judges*; Joseph C. Goulden, *The Benchwarmers* (New York: Weybright and Tally, 1974); and Harris, *The Advice and Consent of the Senate*.

48. Grossman, *Lawyers and Judges*, p. 58.

49. Abraham "Beneficial Advice or Presumptuous Veto?" p. 63.

50. ABA Reports 72, 1947, p. 411 as quoted in Chase, *Federal Judges*, pp. 121–122; see also Neff, *Federal Judicial Selection*, p. 12.

51. American Bar Association, *Standing Committee on the Federal Judiciary*, p. 2.

52. Ibid.

53. Samuel Krislov, *The Supreme Court in the Political Process* (New York: Macmillan, 1965), p. 19.

54. O'Brien, *Judicial Roulette*, p. 85.

55. Ibid., p. 88.

56. See U.S. Congress, Senate, *Selection and Confirmation of Federal Judges: Hearings before the Committee on the Judiciary*, 1980, 99th Congress, 1st and 2nd sessions, pt. 6.

57. American Bar Association, *Standing Committee on the Federal Judiciary*, p. 7.

58. For the ABA's rating with regard to "length of time for confirmation," see Garland W. Allison, "Delay in Senate Confirmation of Federal Judicial Nominees," *Judicature* 80 (1996), p. 10, and note 10 on page 10. For "rate of confirmation," see, for example, Alan Neff, "Breaking with Tradition: A Study of the U.S. District Judge Nominating Commissions," *Judicature* 64 (1981), pp. 256, 258; Elliot Slotnick, "The ABA Standing Committee on Federal Judiciary: A Contemporary Assessment—Parts I and II," *Judicature* 66 (1983), pp. 348–362, 385–393; Elliot Slotnick, "Federal Judicial Recruitment and Selection Research: A Review Essay," *Judicature* 71 (1988), pp. 317–324; R. Townsend Davis, "The American Bar Association and Judicial Nominees: Advice without Consent?," *Columbia Law Review* 89 (1989), pp. 550–579.

59. Neff, *The United States District Judge Nominating Commissions*, p. 16.

60. Goulden, *The Benchwarmers*, p. 40. By 1989 the committee had fifteen members.

61. Testimony of Edward Kennedy, *Selection and Confirmation of Federal Judges, Hearing before the Senate Judiciary Committee*, January 25, 1979, 96th Congress, 1st session.

62. Senate Judiciary Committee, January 25, 1979, 96th Congress, 1st session.

63. See Glendon Schubert, *Judicial Policymaking: The Political Role of the Courts* (Glenview, IL: Scott, Foresman, 1974), pp. 15-16.

64. Schwartz, *Packing the Courts*, p. 99.

65. See *Washington Legal Foundation v. Department of Justice*, 691 F. Supp. 483, D.D.C. (1988); and *Washington Legal Foundation v. American Bar Association Standing Committee on Federal Judiciary*, 648 F. Supp. 1353, D.D.C. (1986). Both cases con-

sidered whether the ABA's Standing Committee on the Federal Judiciary falls under the open-record and open-meeting provisions of the Federal Advisory Committee Act (FACA).

66. See "ABA's Role under Scrutiny in High Court, Senate," *Congressional Quarterly Weekly Report,* April 22, 1989, pp. 896–898.

67. For comments from senators urging committee chairman Biden to hold hearings as well as excerpts from ABA Standing Committee on the Federal Judiciary Chairman Harold R. Tyler's response see "ABA's Role under Scrutiny in High Court, Senate," pp. 896–897.

68. Charles E. Grassley, "Reforming the Role of the ABA in Judicial Selection: Triumph of Hope over Experiment?" in Abraham, *Judicial Selection*, pp. 103–104.

69. See "ABA's Role Under Scrutiny in High Court, Senate," p. 897.

70. Press release by the NET: Political News Talk Network, "ABA Partisan, Evidence Shows," [http://net.fcref.org/press/release6.htm], April 29, 1996. See also the *Washington Post*, April 29, 1996.

71. For a discussion of the historical tendency of the ABA to endorse so-called liberal polices, e.g., abortion, repealing antisodomy laws, gun control, etc., see "Respectful Dissents: Tom's Dissent," for NET: Political News Talk Network, at [http://net.fcref.org /comm/LNcomm/1n042996.htm], April 29, 1996.

72. See Paul D. Kamenar, "The Role of the American Bar Association in the Judicial Selection Process," an article drawn from Mr. Kamenar's testimony of June 2, 1988 before the Senate Judiciary Committee and published in Abraham, *Judicial Selection*, p. 94.

73. For a copy of the "ABA Personal Data Questionnaire," see O'Brien, *Judicial Roulette,* Appendix B, pp. 113–117.

74. American Bar Association, *Standing Committee on the Federal Judiciary* (1988), p. 5.

75. American Bar Association. *Standing Committee on the Federal Judiciary* (1991), p 7.

76. Peter H. Schuck, Director, *The Judiciary Committees: A Study of the House and Senate Judiciary Committees.* The Ralph Nader Congress Project (New York: Grossman Publishers, 1975), p. 236.

77. Henry J. Abraham "Beneficial Advice or Presumptuous Veto? The ABA's Committee on Federal Judiciary Revisited," in Abraham, *Judicial Selection*, p. 71.

78. As Yale Professor Peter H. Schuck has noted, "If the ABA is to have the privilege of partnership in the nominating process—an extraordinary delegation of public power to a private organization—other interest groups should also be encouraged to participate." See Abraham, "Beneficial Advice or Presumptuous Veto?" in Abraham, *Judicial Selection*, p. 71.

79. Portions of this section are based on the "Report of the Twentieth Century Fund Task Force on Judicial Selection," in O'Brien, *Judicial Roulette.*

80. Schuck, *The Judiciary Committees*, p. 233. Laurence Tribe suggests that because presidents can and have "packed" the courts that the "spineless" Senate should therefore examine nominees more carefully. See Tribe, *God Save This Honorable Court*, pp. 77–92.

81. David M. O'Brien, "The Reagan Judges: His Most Enduring Legacy?" in Charles O. Jones, ed., *The Reagan Legacy* (Chatham, NJ: Chatham House, 1988), p. 72. One of the notable exceptions being Jefferson B. Sessions III for district judge. The committee voted 10–8 to reject Sessions and on a 9–9 tie vote prevented the committee from sending his name to the full Senate.

82. O'Brien, *Judicial Roulette*, p. 69. In the overwhelming majority of cases, not even a transcript of their hearings is available before a Senate vote.

83. Quoted in *Judicial Selection Project, Year End Report* (Washington, DC: Alliance for Justice, October 1986).

84. Philip Kurland, "Our Troubled Courts," *Nation's Business*, May 1971, p. 79.

85. M. Freedman, *Assembly-Line Approval: A Common Cause Study of Senate Confirmation of Federal Judges*, (Washington, DC: Common Cause, January 1986), p. 2.

86. O'Brien, *Judicial Roulette*, p. 6.

87. Freedman, *Assembly-Line Approval,* p. 3.

88. O'Brien, *Judicial Roulette*, p. 72.

89. For example, see "Kennedy and Rodino: How Two Very Different Chairman Run Their Panels," *Congressional Quarterly Weekly Report*, February 2, 1980, p. 267; and Elliot Slotnick, "The Changing Role of the Senate Judiciary Committee in Judicial Selection," *Judicature* 62 (1979), p. 502.

90. Slotnick, "The Changing Role," pp. 504–505.

91. Ibid. Memo from Senate Judiciary Committee Staff to Senator Kennedy, regarding Senatorial Courtesy, dated January 22, 1979, pp. 2, 505.

92. Nina Totenberg, "Will Judges Be Chosen Rationally?" *Judicature* 60 (1976), p. 94.

93. Slotnick, "The Changing Role," p. 505.

94. Testimony of Senator Edward Kennedy in *Hearings before the Committee on Judiciary, United States Senate, Ninety Sixth Congress, First Session, On the Selection and Confirmation of Federal Judges*, January 25, 1979, Serial No. 96–21, Part 1, p. 4.

95. *Congressional Quarterly Weekly Report* 190 (February 3, 1979) p. 192.

96. Slotnick, "The Changing Role," pp. 506–507.

97. Ibid., p. 507. These selection criteria are drawn from President Carter's executive order (November 8) outlining qualifications for the federal bench.

98. O'Brien, *Judicial Roulette*, p. 73.

99. This figure is based on data supplied to David M. O'Brien by the Senate Judiciary Committee and discussed in his "The Reagan Judges: His Most Enduring Legacy?" in *The Reagan Legacy*, p. 71.

100. O'Brien, *Judicial Roulette*, p. 75.

101. H. Kurtz, "Democrats Try to Slow Confirmation of Judges," *The Washington Post*, November 12, 1985, p. A3.

102. O'Brien, *Judicial Roulette*, p. 75.

103. Lyles, "The Bork Nomination."

104. See the *Judicial Selection Monitor*, December 1996/January 1997, [http://www.fcref.org/jsmp/monitor/dec_jan96_7.htm], p. 6.

105. Robert A. Carp and Ronald Stidham, *Judicial Process in America* (Washington, DC: CQ Press, 1996), p. 244.

4 Presidential Agendas and Judicial Appointments: From Kennedy Democrats to Nixon Republicans, 1960–1976

INTRODUCTION

To what extent might a president's judicial appointments reflect a president's policy agenda? This is the central focus to which I now turn. Indeed, it is instructive to remember that a given president's agenda is far more than an itemized list.[1] The issues (or choices between alternatives) a given president selects and may expect his judicial appointments to support are not arbitrary policies, but serve as signals to what the president considers to be the most important issues facing his administration.[2] Presidents concentrate on issues that match their personal and political goals.[3]

In addressing these matters, it is particularly useful to distinguish between a president's policy agenda and partisan agenda,[4] although both usually are interwoven and are played against the backdrop of party politics and group conflict. Essentially, insofar as it is possible to differentiate between the partisan agenda and the policy agenda, the policy agenda refers to the substantive policy goals or objectives of an administration and includes its legislative and administration program. The partisan agenda refers to the use of presidential power to shore up political support for the president and for the party.

Moreover, even though the policy agenda and the partisan agenda may be furthered at the same time, what distinguishes one from the other is the motivation behind the exercise of presidential power. For example, according to Sheldon Goldman, if the action is an attempt to "mend political fences, reward partisan supporters, provide incentives for party organizations, satisfy a constituency group within the party's coalition," and so on, the actions can "generally be considered to be *partisan agenda* actions." On the other hand, "if the concern is primarily to further the president's policy agenda, with partisan considerations of less concern, perhaps even to the point of the president willing to risk alienating one political ally or constituency group at the expense of another, or if the action has little partisan consequence, the action can be considered a *policy agenda* action." Thus, Goldman's theoretical framework suggests that motivation is the central characteristic distinguishing a policy agenda from a partisan agenda.

Additionally, we must also remember that both the policy agenda and the partisan agenda must be seen within the context of the political realities of pluralism and coalition politics. It is entirely possible that a given policy agenda is indeed driven in part by a partisan agenda. In other words, presidents may support and promote certain policy agendas to build and/or solidify partisan and/or coalition agendas. For example, as we shall see, presidents Johnson and Carter, not unlike presidents Nixon and Reagan, used judicial appointments both to promote policy agendas as well as enhance and engender particular constituencies.

Although Goldman admits that this duality in presidential motivation is "difficult to study systematically" it nevertheless remains an important, and not overlooked, contextual dynamic of judicial selection and confirmation. Still, however, it remains important to examine whether district court judges' policy performance comports with their appointing president's policy preferences. We are aware that intervening variables (e.g., senatorial courtesy) are partisan concerns. However, Goldman's theory is particularly useful to explain why in certain instances, some judicial appointments may *not* appear consistent with the president's articulated policy goals. For example, President Kennedy, perhaps more than any other president in this study, made appointments repeatedly for apparently partisan agenda reasons rather than in accord with his domestic policy preferences.[5]

In this and the succeeding chapter, we construct two important segments of our data base: (1) presidential policy objectives and expectation profiles so as to determine particular policy goals that given presidents sought to achieve; and (2) whether particular presidents have made attempts to translate these policy objectives through their judicial appointments in terms of the nature and type of person eventually nominated to a federal district judgeship.

The presidential policy objective profiles (PPOPs) are generated from various data sources. These sources include, but are not limited to: (1) relevant materials and findings in scholarly and popular writing; (2) party platforms and campaign speeches by presidential nominees; (3) presidential addresses and news conferences; (4) statements and actions by the attorneys general, solicitors general, and other administration officials, especially those in the Justice Department; (5) Senate Judiciary Committee hearings on specific court nominations and related reports and Senate confirmation proceedings; and (6) briefs filed by the federal government.

These PPOPs provide the context in which we discuss the other major concern of this and the next chapter: the nature and type of person eventually selected by the president to serve as a federal district court judge. Data for these judicial profiles are collected from various biographical collections and other relevant sources. Given these biographical data, we seek to determine whether those eventually appointed also share and promote certain policy and ideological positions in common with their appointing presidents.

The major time frame for this study—1960–1996—includes thorough examinations of the presidencies of John Kennedy, Lyndon Johnson, Richard Nixon, Gerald Ford, Jimmy Carter, Ronald Reagan, George Bush, and Bill Clinton. In this chapter I discuss the policy objectives, expectations, and the nature of judges appointed during the Kennedy, Johnson, Nixon, and Ford administrations (1960–1976). Because the Carter and Reagan administrations wrought significant procedural and ideological changes in the selection, screening, and nomination of federal judges, presidents Carter and Reagan are discussed in Chapter 5, and President Bush and President Clinton (first term) are the focus of Chapter 6. Let us now turn to how Kennedy, Johnson, Nixon, and Ford used their judicial appointments in relation to their policy objectives.

KENNEDY DEMOCRATS TO NIXON REPUBLICANS, 1960–1976

John F. Kennedy

I would hope that the paramount consideration in the appointment of a judge would not be his political party, but his qualifications for the office.[6]

John Kennedy's "New Frontier" represented a commitment to the legacy of the "New" and "Fair Deal(s)." He said the New Frontier was "not a set of promises," but a "set of challenges."[7] However, he was for the most part unable to garner the policy support required to implement much of his legislative agenda. This dilemma was equally reflected in Kennedy's selection of judicial appointments. In 1959, the early signs of the caseload explosion (discussed in the previous chapter) were beginning to materialize. Political leaders on both sides of the aisle, as well as social scientists, were also becoming increasingly aware of the value of district court appointments. Consider the following report in the 1959 *Congressional Quarterly Almanac:*

[In 1959] no one disputed the need to create additional federal judgeships to handle a rising volume of litigation (some of it backed up for years on overcrowded dockets), but for the third year in a row a Democratic Congress refused to give a Republican President the opportunity to fill these additional life-time jobs. On the basis of Administration assurances that the appointments would be split 50–50 between Democrats and Republicans, the House Judiciary Committee reported a bill June 15 [1959] to create 35 new judgeships—10 fewer than asked by Attorney General Rogers but 10 more than provided in a bill reported to the Senate late in 1959. Neither measure came to a vote, however. With all bets riding on the outcome of the 1960 election, Democrats rejected a half-loaf in hope of winning the whole loaf.[8]

Significantly, having narrowly won the presidency in 1960 with a sizable number of African-American votes,[9] Kennedy on February 10 requested fifty-nine additional federal judgeships—nine circuit and fifty district court judgeships. This request was increased to seventy-three by the Senate and passed March 33, 1961. The House version of this bill called for seventy new judgeships and passed 336–76 on April 19. The final bill, which passed both chambers on May 4, created ten circuit court and sixty-three district court judgeships—an addition amounting to 25 percent of the federal judiciary and the first increase since 1954 when Congress added thirty new positions.[10] By the end of 1961, as a consequence of resignations and deaths, the number of vacancies to be filled by Kennedy had risen to 115.[11] Next we consider President Kennedy's PPOPs in the five selected various issue areas. First we consider issues involving abortion rights and religious liberty.

Abortion Rights

In the 1960s, abortion loomed as a key issue in American law and politics. But it was the Burger Court, not the Warren Court, that decided the landmark *Roe v. Wade*[12] (on the woman's right to an abortion), and *Doe v. Bolton*[13] decisions in 1973. Until the late 1960s, federal policies dealing with many such issues including reproduction and even birth control were generally nonexistent. Although during the mid-to-late 1960s, and in part spurred by the Supreme Court's 1954 desegregation decision in *Brown*, these and other restrictive attitudes began to change.[14] In the main the abortion question was not directly on the policy nor the partisan agenda for Kennedy. This does not, however, mean that Kennedy and Johnson appointees did not (or do not) decide significant abortion decisions. Quite the contrary—again highlighting the significance of life tenure—these district court judges have participated in affecting the public policy debate and outcome regarding abortion rights long after their appointing presidents have left office (see Chapter 6).

For Kennedy, the reproduction issue focused more on birth control than abortion. As late as the 1950s, President Eisenhower had said, "This government will not . . . as long as I am here, have a positive political doctrine in its program that has to do with the problems of birth control. That's not our business."[15] But Kennedy, a Roman Catholic, was not totally against birth control. In an interview in 1959, Kennedy stated that it would not be "wise for the U.S. to refuse to grant assistance to a country like India, that had decided to encourage birth control as a policy it feels to be in its own best interest. To do so would be a kind of intervention in their national life."[16] It should also be noted that in 1963 Kennedy did support increasing research in human reproduction to improve fertility-control methods and make them available to other nations.[17]

Religious Liberty

For Kennedy, the first Catholic to be elected president, religion was an especially charged and controversial issue. Said Kennedy in 1960: "I believe in an America where the separation of church and state is absolute—where no Catholic prelate would tell the President (should he be Catholic) how to act and no Protestant minister would tell his parishioners for whom to vote."[18]

In Kennedy's first education message he asked for grants for public elementary and secondary schools, stating the "Constitution clearly prohibits such aid for 'constructing church schools or paying church school teachers' salaries'; for colleges, on the other hand, he asked for long-term, low interest Government loans that would be available for all colleges, public and private."[19] Similarly, in a March 8 press conference Kennedy said he believed across-the-board loans as well as grants to private elementary and secondary schools were forbidden by the Constitution.[20]

Kennedy also chose to address the religion issue more directly in an address to the Greater Houston Ministerial Association: "Whatever issue may come before me as President—on birth control, divorce, censorship, gambling or any other subject—I will make my decisions . . . in accordance with what my conscience tells me to be in the national interest, and without regard to outside religious pressure of dictates."[21]

Kennedy and Civil Rights Issues: An Overview

Next I review President Kennedy's policy positions relevant to our three remaining civil rights (racial policy) areas: affirmative action, school desegregation, and voting rights. However, given the often confusing nature of Kennedy's positions on these issues, it is instructive first here to preview these discussions with a brief overview of Kennedy's civil rights agenda generally.

The Kennedy stance on civil rights is not easily discerned. In the main, John Kennedy's presidential record on civil rights is a mixed one and assessments have fluctuated erratically since his death. Initially scholars wrote almost romantically of the age of Camelot.[22] Thus, on the one hand, he has been called the "second Emancipator President."[23] However, starting in the early 1970s, scholars began to more critically assess and even attack Kennedy and his administration with vigor.[24] As stated by one observer, "John Kennedy's record on civil rights contained failures that ran far deeper than his successes."[25] These studies now have given way to more balanced critiques assessing the strengths and weaknesses of Kennedy's leadership.[26]

Let us examine briefly Kennedy's civil rights campaign agenda. In August of 1960, Kennedy asked a campaign strategist (Harris Wofford): "Now, in five minutes tick off the ten things a President ought to do to clean up this god damn civil rights mess."[27] The Democratic platform adopted by the Democratic National Convention in Los Angeles on July 12, 1960 included unprecedented pledges for legislative as well as executive civil rights action. And most have read or heard of Kennedy's campaign pledge to abolish racial discrimination in federal housing projects "by a stroke of the Presidential pen." But, as it turned out, these and other promises were slow being brought to fruition, if at all.[28]

Well before his election, at a September 1, 1960 news conference, Kennedy announced that he had asked Senator Joseph Clark (D-PA) and Representative Emanuel Celler (D-NY), chairman of the House Judiciary Committee, to "prepare a comprehensive civil rights bill embodying our platform commitments, for introduction at the beginning of the next session [of Congress]."[29]

The platform's civil rights legislative planks included proposals to: eliminate literacy tests and poll taxes where they still existed as voting requirements; require segregated school districts to submit plans for at least first-step desegregation by 1963 and provide technical and financial assistance to school systems going through desegregation; authorize the attorney general to file suits seeking court injunctions against deprivation of any civil right; establish a federal Fair Employment Practices Commission; and strengthen and make permanent the Civil Rights Commission.[30] However, these pledges died almost immediately.

For example, Roy Wilkens, NAACP executive director recounts that "within ten days of his election came word that [Kennedy] was not going to advocate any new civil rights legislation because he did not want to split the party."[31] And, in his first state of the union address to Congress Kennedy included one "innocuous" sentence pertaining to civil rights: "The denial of constitutional rights to some of our fellow Americans on account of race—at the ballot box and elsewhere—disturbs the national conscience and subjects us to charge of the world opinion that our democracy is not equal to the high promise of our heritage."[32]

When the Clark-Celler bills were introduced on May 8, 1961, White House Press Secretary Pierre Salinger announced on May 9 that the Clark-Celler bills were "not Administration-backed bills." Salinger added, "The President does not consider it necessary at this time to enact new civil rights legislation."[33] Indeed, during Kennedy's first year as president, the only civil rights legislation to pass was a two-year extension for the Civil Rights Commission.

Consider also, that during the "Freedom Rides," Attorney General Robert Kennedy refrained from using federal marshals until the violence in Montgomery proved it imperative. And again, this hesitancy was a consistent pattern that would recur in the administration's overall handling of civil rights issues. The apparent strategy of the Kennedy administration was to use federal force to curb mob violence, but not to try to help integrate facilities. Moreover, Kennedy continually urged an end to the protests. The Kennedy administration did recognize, however, that the Freedom Riders had a right of safe passage in interstate commerce; but it was the protesters' right to travel, not *desegregated* travel, that the administration guarded during the Freedom Rides.[34]

Tactically, by intervening only to abrogate violence—and never endorsing the Freedom Rides—the Kennedy administration maintained widespread support in Congress. Thus, Kennedy was able to satisfy key congressional leaders in the South, whose support he needed, and still protect interstate commerce and the Riders from mob rule.

Civil rights issues were not totally abandoned, however. During 1961 the Department of Justice, while pursuing numerous court actions concerning voting rights, won an ICC ruling on September 22 barring segregation in bus termi- nals.[35] Also the Civil Rights Commission, including two Kennedy appointments, released reports condemning discrimination in voting and education. For exam- ple, several months earlier in 1961, on January 15, the Civil Rights Commission issued a report on higher education recommending that the Federal Government ensure that federal aid to higher education went to only nondiscriminatory in- stitutions.[36] This notion was also reflected in several amendments, none of which passed.

In the main, the core of Kennedy's early civil rights commitments were in the form of executive actions.[37] While some scholars have heralded these executive actions as "vanguards of new laws governing civil rights,"[38] some civil rights advocates suggest these executive actions provided little consolation. For exam- ple, Roy Wilkens of the NAACP likened Kennedy's calls for executive action to "an offering of a cactus bouquet to Negro parents and their children."[39]

Essentially, the Kennedy administration proved long on symbols but some- what short on substance. In sum, Kennedy was reluctant to incorporate his con- cerns on these social dilemmas into his legislative policy agenda despite his vo- cal opposition to racial segregation, especially in the South.

Affirmative Action

In March 1961 President Kennedy issued Executive Order No. 10926 com- bining the committees on Government Contracts and Government Employment Practices into the President's Committee on Equal Employment Opportunity.[40] By this order the vice president was appointed chairman of the committee and the secretary of labor was instructed to implement equal employment practices in hiring federal employees and government contractors.[41] Among other re- quirements, the order required contractors to publicize their antidiscrimination policies in their help-wanted ads and their requests to employment agencies; it also required contractors to "make every effort to obtain agreements with their unions that the unions would not practice discrimination."[42] Kennedy issued a statement accompanying Executive Order No. 10925, stating in part that imple- mentation of a government policy against discrimination had been hampered

by lack of personnel, by inadequate procedures and ineffective enforcement. As a result Americans who are members of minority groups have been unjustly denied the opportu- nity to work for the Government or for Government contractors. In this connection I have already directed all departments to take action to broaden the Government employ- ment opportunities for members of minority groups.[43]

Following the issuance of 10925, Kennedy encouraged all executive depart- ment and agency heads to take "positive measures [to ensure] equal opportunity for all qualified persons within the government."[44]

This order marked the first instance of an official requirement that contractors "*actively* pursue equal employment rather than settling simply for passive non- discrimination."[45] Significantly the order read in part: "The contractor will take *affirmative action* to ensure that participants are employed . . . without regard to their race, creed, color or national origin."[46] This order also contained penalties for imposing sanctions for violation, for example, contracts with noncomplying contractors could be terminated. Although the nature and effects of this order [and as amended later] included "broader enforcement powers, strong presidential backing, a larger budget, more stringent requirements for reporting," and resulted in "convincing several corporations to improve employment opportunities," these too were considered by some scholars as merely "token changes."[47] Nonetheless, although this action is considered by many to represent the basis of affirmative action, the real starch was not placed into the programs until President Johnson's executive orders in 1965 and 1967 (as discussed below).

School Desegregation

To varying degrees, most scholars agree that President Kennedy avoided pushing for school desegregation, fearing that such activity might jeopardize his other policy objectives.[48] According to Charles Hamilton, Kennedy spoke out on behalf of those seeking to implement school desegregation. But this, Hamilton admits, was primarily by way of private conversations between Attorney General Robert Kennedy and Southern governors. Consider the following *New York Times* report in 1961:

Robert Kennedy . . . has been doing a great deal on civil rights—most of it is unpublicized. It became known that he had telephoned lawyers and political leaders in Louisiana to try and get them to call off their war against desegregation in New Orleans. It is not generally known that he has called Governors and other leaders in almost every state in the South, for such purposes as obtaining voting records and getting the bail on Negro demonstrators lowered.[49]

The most often cited and celebrated examples of Kennedy's commitment to school desegregation include executive directives: (1) the use of federal marshals and the federalizing of Mississippi's National Guard in September 1962 to assist in registering James Meredith at the University of Mississippi[50]; and (2) the use of federal marshals and the Alabama National Guard to desegregate the University of Alabama in June 1963.[51] These actions by Kennedy were symbolic as well as substantive. They echoed a clearer message of support for school desegregation than had been heard from any president in history—including Eisenhower's reluctant actions in Little Rock.[52] As one October 1963 telecast reported during the Meredith confrontation, the president "was eyeball-to-eyeball with the segregationists and there was fire in his eye."[53]

Nonetheless, when Meredith finally entered the University of Mississippi on September 30, 1962, Kennedy still defined the issue as a legal issue and strove to defuse the violent hatred that Meredith's admission aroused.[54] Kennedy addressed the nation in a "law and order" speech that defined the entire civil rights issue as a legal issue requiring Americans to abide by the rulings of the court:

our nation is founded on the principle that observance of the law is the eternal safeguard of liberty and defiance of the law is the surest road to tyranny. The law which we obey includes the final rulings of the courts, as well as the enactments of our legislative bodies. Even among law-abiding men few laws are universally loved, but they are uniformly respected and not resisted.

Americans are free, in short to disagree with the law but not to disobey it. For in a government of laws and not of men, no man, however prominent, or powerful, and no mob rule, however unruly or boisterous, is entitled to defy a court of law.[55]

From this point in the address Kennedy went on to express "deep regret" for having to send federal troops into Mississippi and made a special plea to the University of Mississippi and the citizens of the state. "The eyes of the Nation and of all the world are upon you and upon all of us," said Kennedy, "and the honor of your University and State are in the balance." Nonetheless, even as Kennedy spoke, rioting raged at the university and two people were killed that same evening. In the main, in 1961, Kennedy chose to define the desegregation issue in the narrowest of legal terms and according to one scholar, "engaged in a rhetoric of supplication toward the white citizens of Mississippi."[56]

However, after the midterm elections there was a change in Kennedy's rhetoric. In contrast to the legal approach he adopted regarding the desegregation of the University of Mississippi, he began to speak more directly about the increasing "fires of frustration and discord" that surrounded the desegregation issue. Kennedy's rhetorical management of civil rights evolved from his regarding it as a "pragmatic political [or legal] issue" to raising it to the level of a moral crisis in American society.[57] For example, following the desegregation of the University of Alabama, in a speech on June 11, 1963, and approximately five months before his assassination, Kennedy defined desegregation as a moral issue. Kennedy posed controversial questions to the nation:

We are confronted primarily with a moral issue. It is as old as the Scriptures and is as clear as the American Constitution.

The heart of the question is whether all Americans are to be afforded equal rights and equal opportunities, whether we are going to treat our fellow Americans as we want to be treated. If an American, because his skin is dark, cannot eat lunch at a restaurant open to the public, if he cannot send his children to the best public school available, if he cannot vote for the public officials who represent him, if in short, he cannot enjoy the full and free life which all of us want, then who among us would be content to have the color of his skin changed and stand in his place? Who among us would be content with the counsels of patience and delay? We preach freedom around the world, and we mean it, and we cherish our freedom here at home, but are we to say to the world, and more importantly, to each other that this is a land of the free except for Negroes; that we have no class or caste system, no ghettoes, no master race except with respect to Negroes.[58]

In a sociopolitical context, although couched in the political rhetoric of the era, these statements indicate at a minimum Kennedy's growing concern for school desegregation and voting rights. Moreover, they signaled a turning point in the federal government's involvement in these issues.

Just eight days after Kennedy posed these questions to the nation, he proposed an omnibus civil rights bill, on June 19, 1963, in Congress calling for increased federal involvement in school desegregation, nondiscrimination in employment or in the use of federal funds, equal access to public facilities and accommodations, and, additional protection of voting rights.[59] In the main, this bill banned racial discrimination in public facilities and in public education, along with granting the Department of Justice broad enforcement powers. It should be noted, however, that the bill was still creeping through the deliberative legislative process at the time of President Kennedy's assassination.

Voting Rights

Although Kennedy's campaign manager, Robert Kennedy, did not view the final draft of the civil rights platform before it went to the convention floor, it is reported that he did give the nod of approval to an earlier draft. This platform called for "whatever action is necessary to eliminate literacy tests and the payments of poll taxes as requirements for voting" and committed the candidate to support legislation to "empower and direct" the attorney general "to file civil injunction suits in Federal Courts to prevent the denial of any civil right on grounds of race, creed, or color."[60]

Kennedy did, however, speak out directly against the intimidation of black voters. On February 28, 1963, in a special message to Congress, Kennedy charged:

Too often those who attempt to assert their constitutional rights are intimidated. Prospective registrants are fired. Registration workers are arrested. In some instances, churches in which registration meetings are held have been burned. Under these circumstances, continued delay in the granting of the franchise—particularly in counties where there is mass racial disfranchisement—permits the intent of the Congress to be openly floated [*sic*].

Federal executive action in such cases—no matter how speedy and how drastic—can never fully correct such abuses of power. It is necessary instead to free the forces of our democratic system within these areas by promptly insuring the franchise to all citizens, making it possible for their elected officials to be truly responsive to all their constituents.[61]

Further evidence of Kennedy's more direct and tangible support for voting rights is the Twenty-Fourth Amendment to the Constitution, which abolished the poll tax. This amendment was initiated by the Kennedy administration and was ratified in 1964.[62]

To sum up, overall religious liberty issues were of major concern to President Kennedy. In addition, Kennedy also issued Executive Order No. 10925—considered by most to be the basis for affirmative action. However, President Kennedy's positions on civil rights generally, especially regarding school desegregation and voting rights issues suggests a less than convincing commitment by

Kennedy for these more controversial and specific policy goals. In other words, Kennedy avoided pushing for school desegregation, as well as increased voting rights, fearing that such activity might jeopardize his other policy objectives. And, for Kennedy, the reproduction issue was more focused on birth control than abortion.

Let us now seek to determine whether Kennedy made attempts to translate these policy objectives and expectations into judicial appointments in terms of the nature and type of person he eventually nominated to a district court judgeship.

Selection, Screening, and Nomination under Kennedy

I agree with you, but I don't know if the government will.[63]

As described in Table 3.11 (Chapter 3), President Kennedy appointed 103 district court judges, including ten Republicans and the second woman ever to be appointed to the district courts. Kennedy also appointed the first African-American to a lifetime federal district court position (James Benton Parsons, District Court of Illinois), as well as two other African-Americans to the district courts.[64]

In general, the Kennedy appointees "tended to come from 'middle-class' backgrounds" and there "was little to support any claim of a class 'power elite' either by the schools attended or the occupations of the judges at the time of appointment."[65] However, as suggested above, perhaps more than any other president under consideration in this analysis, the Kennedy appointments create a special dilemma requiring distinctive understanding. The selection of district court judges under President Kennedy was largely a staff operation within the Justice Department wrought with dilemma. For example, the Kennedy administration's employment of a "spotter system" (i.e., young Democratic lawyers around the country who would look for nominees), proved ad hoc and unreliable.[66] And, in addition to generally greater difficulty appeasing the ABA (e.g., during its first two years the Kennedy administration nominated eight judges the ABA rated "not qualified"), the major difficulty for Kennedy arose with senators. One Kennedy staff member reported: "Everybody believes in democracy until he gets to the White House and then you begin to believe in dictatorship, because it's so hard to get things done."[67]

Accordingly, the Kennedy administration was unable to influence many senators to accept so-called "liberal" nominees, particularly those in the South, especially under the strong conservative leadership of Senate Judiciary Committee Chairman James Eastland. Instead the Kennedy administration adopted a defensive, rather than offensive posture. As reported by Kennedy's Deputy Attorney General Nicholas de B. Katzenbach, "play ball with the ABA, play ball with the Senate, do the best you can, don't let anyone through who has personally attacked the President."[68]

Although he repeatedly voiced opposition to segregation and other efforts to impede civil rights, President Kennedy nevertheless opted to reward lifetime judgeships to persons dedicated to impeding as well as attacking civil rights litigation. In fact, he appointed numerous southern judges who openly advocated racial segregation. This was due in large measure to various political pressures Kennedy faced, particularly from key congressional committee chairpersons from the South.

Evidence clearly suggests that the Justice Department did attempt to tailor its suggestions to make selections that would be acceptable to the senators involved—and this meant, for example, that African-Americans held no seats at all in Southern federal courts. Indeed, as late as 1964 when Robert Kennedy retired as attorney general, it was reported that "in the principal southern states there were no Negro circuit court judges (twelve white ones), no Negro district court judges (sixty-five whites), no Negro U.S. Commissioners (235 whites), no Negro jury commissioners (109 whites), and no Negro U.S. Marshals (twenty-nine whites). A Negro involved in a federal court action in the South could go from the beginning of the case to the end without seeing any black faces unless they were in the court audience."[69]

Although the Kennedys were certainly aware of this situation, they were not willing (and to some extent were unable) to promote and enforce affirmative remedies. As Kennedy's attorney general Katzenbach put it:

We do not expect to find or to be able to obtain confirmation for militant civil rights advocates in the South. What we seek is to assure ourselves that nominees will follow the law of the land. We are satisfied with that much.[70]

Basically, the Kennedys did not challenge Southern senators in this area since the overall strategy of the administration was to push for legislation to enhance the socioeconomic status of the poor, whose numbers contained a majority of whites but whose ranks also included a large and disproportionate number of blacks and minorities. Thus, President Kennedy's judicial nominations were tailored to fit this overall strategy. This led Attorney General Robert Kennedy to describe the judicial selection process as, "basically . . . senatorial appointment with the advice and consent of the Senate."[71]

One of the most noted and provocative studies on Kennedy's judicial selection is Victor S. Navasky's *Kennedy Justice*. Navasky, who served in the Department of Justice during the Kennedy administration, noted there was an "absence of any deep, abiding and overriding Kennedy commitment to the integrity and quality of the Southern Judiciary itself."[72] For example, one such judge, E. Gordon West of Louisiana, appointed in 1961, characterized the U.S. Supreme Court's landmark desegregation ruling in *Brown v. Board of Education*[73] as "one of the truly regrettable decisions of all time." Yet another 1961 Kennedy appointee, Judge W. Harold Cox of Jackson, Mississippi (a former college roommate and close friend of Senator Eastland), often made racist remarks in his courtroom. For example, in a literacy test case, Judge Cox responded "the intelligence of the colored people don't [sic] compare ratio-wise to white people."[74] In another voter registration case Judge Cox asked "Who is telling these niggers they can get in line to push people around, acting like a bunch of chimpanzees?"[75]

Indeed, one commentator has described Judge Cox as "a master of obstruction and delay, he may well have been the greatest single obstacle to equal justice in the South."[76] And Judge Robert Elliot of Georgia, also appointed by Kennedy in 1962, found against African-Americans in over 90 percent of the civil rights cases that came before his court while Robert Kennedy was attorney general.[77]

Overall, state and local, as well as federal pressures played a role in Kennedy's ability to fill judicial vacancies. Even outside of the South, for example, it is reported that "during the Kennedy-Johnson years, Chicago mayor Richard J. Daley passed on every federal judgeship appointment in Illinois."[78]

Kennedy and the ABA

During the Kennedy administration, the ABA's relations with the Justice Department were increasingly troubled. In its first two years, the Kennedy administration appointed eight judges whom the ABA rated not qualified (7.3 percent) of the judicial appointments made during this two-year period). Responding to criticisms on these appointments, Deputy Attorney General Nicholas de B. Katzenbach remarked at the 1962 ABA convention: "that the responsibility is the President's and the Senate's, and this Association does not have and would not wish to have veto power over the appointments to be made."[79] Katzenbach further challenged the import of the ABA's ratings:

I have no doubt that amidst these many appointments . . . there will be disappointments and some of the judges appointed will not come up to the standard which the Administration wishes for all judges. I would be very surprised if there were not judges appointed who will prove to have been unworthy and unqualified. I would be very surprised if this Committee were omniscient and infallible in that respect, and I do not think that they would claim that infallibility. I think that at least some of the Judges found by the Committee to be unqualified will . . . prove to have been good appointments. I think some of the Judges found to be qualified will, over a period of years, prove to have been bad appointments.[80]

A 1972 study by Harold Chase similarly reveals that a substantial percentage of the ABA's initial ratings of Kennedy's selections (nominees) were negative—though he also found a number were upgraded before the ABA's final evaluation and their nomination for appointment. As Chase reports: "in the give and take of discussions something happened in nearly 30 percent of the cases, usually resulting in an upgrading."[81]

To summarize, much evidence suggests that most of Kennedy's appointments were partisan-agenda rather than policy-agenda appointments.[82] Kennedy would acquiesce to Southern senators and appoint individuals known as racists to the federal bench.[83] But this was consistent with the Kennedy administration strategy not to irritate Southern Democrats by pressing for civil rights bills. In exchange the administration hoped Southerners would support its other bills.[84]

Thus, Kennedy's policy objectives, as well as expectations of his judicial appointments, on civil rights are tenuous at best. Though advocating civil rights, the president clearly experienced great difficulty in appointing such judges to the lower federal bench. To the contrary, he appointed a number of Southern judges who openly supported racial segregation. But we must also remember that in 1961, it was President Kennedy who appointed Thurgood Marshall to the Court of Appeals for the Second Circuit.

Indeed, as one writer observes:

[T]he contentious scholarly debate over John F. Kennedy's personal commitment to black civil rights misses an essential political reality. Whether he was for or against the issue in his heart was almost irrelevant to how he dealt with the issue as a politician. Kennedy's public position on civil rights was, almost always, simply a reflection of his perception of its strategic value to him in his pursuit of office.[85]

But the fact remains that Kennedy did appoint federal district court judges, and this is what makes his policy objectives and judicial expectations relevant in an overall attempt to analyze the subsequent performance of such judges in particular issue areas.

Lyndon B. Johnson

The Great Society rests on abundance and liberty for all. It demands an end to poverty and racial unjust.[86]

When Lyndon Johnson assumed the presidency in 1963 he also assumed the tasks begun in Kennedy's New Frontier, for example, civil rights, Medicare, voting rights, and so on. Just days after President Kennedy's death, on November 27, 1963, Johnson instructed the Congress:

No memorial oration or eulogy, could more eloquently honor President Kennedy's memory than the earliest possible passage of the civil rights bill for which he fought.

We have talked long enough in this country about equal rights. We have talked for one hundred years or more. It is now time to write the next chapter—and to write in the books of law.[87]

Johnson's commitment to civil rights was unequivocal and strong. Although two policy/issue areas (abortion rights and religious liberty) were not major policy concerns for the Johnson administration, consider his positions in the remaining three areas.

Affirmative Action

Many would agree that the 1964 Civil Rights Act, perhaps the most significant legislation to emerge from Lyndon Johnson's Great Society, "held the keys" to overcoming employment discrimination.[88] To be sure, Title VII of the act unmistakably prohibits employment discrimination in hiring, firing, and compensation terms due to race.

Overall, however, it was President Johnson's initiatives in the form of executive orders that put the teeth in affirmative action programs. Johnson's Executive Order No. 11197 (issued February 5, 1965) established the President's Council on Equal Opportunity charged with finding ways to "more effectively" implement the 1957 and 1964 Civil Rights Acts.[89] In September of the following year, Johnson issued the capstone of affirmative action, Executive Order No. 11246, requiring that all federal contracts include clauses agreeing "not to discriminate against any employee or applicant for employment because of race, color, religion or national origin."[90]

In sum, Executive Order No. 11246 strengthened Kennedy's earlier executive order requirement that government contractors with contracts over $10,000 take affirmative action an additional step forward. Additionally, Johnson's Executive Order No. 11246 also required that affirmative action be extended to all of a contractor's other operations as well, not merely to those government contracts. Moreover, it designated the secretary of labor to enforce the order and obligated the Civil Service Commission (CSC) to "supervise and provide guidance in the conduct of equal employment opportunity progress . . . within the executive departments and agencies."[91] Still further, the order also provided for the establishment of the Office of Federal Contract Compliance (OFCC). And Executive Order No. 11247, issued the same day, called on the attorney general to coordinate enforcement of the 1964 act.[92]

Two years later, in October 1968, Johnson issued Executive Order No. 11375. This order also included a ban on discrimination in employment on the basis of sex, for example, it prohibited "separate seniority rosters for men and women, discrimination based on a woman's marital or child bearing status, and, separate columns of help wanted advertisements in newspapers."[93] This order also included a requirement that contractors develop "written *affirmative action* plans to remedy the effects of past discrimination" (emphasis added).[94]

Though not always specifically mentioning affirmative action, Johnson's concern for equal opportunity employment was frequently addressed in his public speeches. For instance, in a 1969 speech at Howard University, the president stated boldly that African-Americans had been "twisted and battered by endless years of hatred and hopelessness" as a result of white racial prejudice. Said Johnson:

Freedom is not enough. You do not wipe away the scars of centuries by saying: Now you are free to go where you want, do as you desire, and choose the leaders you please. You do not take a man who for years has been hobbled by chains, liberate him, bring him to the starting line of a race, saying, "you are free to compete with all the others," and still justly believe you have been completely fair. Thus, it is not enough to open the gates of opportunity. . . .

Men are shaped by their world. When it is a world of decay, ringed by an invisible wall, when escape is arduous and uncertain, and the saving pressures of a more hopeful society are unknown, it can cripple the youth and it can desolate the man.

There is also the burden that a dark skin can add to the search for a productive place in society. Unemployment strikes most swiftly and broadly at the Negro, and this burden erodes hope. Blighted hope breeds despair. Despair brings indifference to the learning which brings a way out. And despair, coupled with indifference, is often the source of destructive rebellion against the fabric of society.

There is no single easy answer. . . . Jobs are part of the answer. They bring the income which permits a man to provide for his family. Decent homes in decent surroundings and a chance to learn—an equal chance to learn—are part of the answer. . . . And to all these fronts—and a dozen more—I will dedicate the expanding efforts of the Johnson Administration.[95]

Clearly, Johnson placed a clear and significant emphasis on increasing employment opportunities for African-Americans, including affirmative action programs and compliance. And so it will be well worth looking to see whether those district court judges he appointed pursued these same goals.

School Desegregation

As much of the published research record indicates, the judicial struggle for school desegregation prior to the Johnson administration had gained little ground. The majority of school districts were still completely segregated and "judges were still ordering plans calling for token integration of one grade a year to be carried out over a decade or more."[96] But all this changed with the passage of the Civil Rights Act of 1964 during the Johnson administration. That legislation began to put real teeth into the enforcement of school desegregation. Specifically, the 1964 Civil Rights Act:

1. Authorized the Justice Department to sue school districts on behalf of black students (Title IV)

2. Authorized the Justice Department to join school desegregation suits filed by private plaintiffs (Title IX)

3. Directed that institutions that segregated be denied federal funds (Title VI)[97]

In a "Letter to the Editor" of the *New York Times* in 1968, Jack Greenberg, former director of the Legal Defense Fund, captured well the importance of the 1964 act in regard to school desegregation. "Of thousands of school districts, there were but a few hundred cases . . . no formula could have desegregated these districts until civil rights lawyers became available to press cases there." Greenberg continued, "that was impossible until 1964 when the Civil Rights Act provided additional enforcement personnel through the Departments of Justice and Health, Education, and Welfare."[98] Thus, it was not until 1964 that the U.S. Congress, through the persistent efforts of President Johnson and civil rights leaders, fully endorsed school desegregation.

One of Johnson's initial actions in support of public school desegregation was to direct the U.S. Commission on Civil Rights in 1965 to conduct a nationwide study of segregated school systems. The commission's 1967 report, *Racial Isolation in the Public Schools*, called attention to increasing racial segregation in the nation's urban schools and recommended national legislation outlawing such practices.[99] The report also requested legislation providing increased financial aid to promote school segregation.

In sum, during the Johnson presidency, both the chief executive and the Congress were aligned with the Supreme Court in support of federal desegregation.[100]

Voting Rights

[W]e will not delay, we will not hesitate . . . until Americans of every race and color and origin in this country have the same rights as all others.
—Lyndon B. Johnson[101]

Voting rights were a special concern of the Johnson administration. The 1964 March on Selma provides a poignant example and commentary on Johnson's commitment to voting rights.[102] The Selma-to-Montgomery march was an Alabama statewide drive to register African-American voters. The drive began January 18, 1965 in Selma, a town considered the symbol of the Deep South's resistance to the civil rights movement. At the start of the march, Martin Luther King, Jr. stated "We are not asking, we are demanding the ballot."[103] And, President Johnson's early and personal support of the march was clearly expressed in a news conference on February 4: "All of us," said the President, "should be concerned with the efforts of our fellow Americans to register to vote in Alabama. . . . I intend to see [that the right to vote] is secured to all of our citizens."[104]

Just one week after the marchers were assaulted and brutally beaten on a bridge outside Selma, on March 15, 1965, Johnson proposed the enactment of the 1965 Voting Rights Act to a joint session of Congress in a speech that was broadcast to the entire country.[105] The spirit of Johnson's address was captured in two clearly stated passages: "It is wrong," said President Johnson, "deadly wrong to deny any of your fellow Americans the right to vote in this country. [I]t is not just Negroes, but really it is all of us, who must overcome the crippling legacy of bigotry and injustice. . . . And we shall overcome."[106]

Indeed, in personally addressing and proposing the voting rights act, Johnson actually invoked the words of the hymn of the civil rights movement, "We Shall Overcome." Thus, the president "inextricably linked the power of the federal government with the goals of King and others to civil rights."[107] The voting rights bill became one of Johnson's greatest crusades. Even during heated and protracted debates in the Congress, Johnson continued to give unprecedented support for the measure across the nation.

Although congressional opponents to this bill argued that the legislation was a usurpation of the "reserved powers to the states,"[108] because of the strong and relentless support by President Johnson, this opposition eventually waned.[109] Finally, on August 6, the 1965 Voting Rights Act (VRA) was signed by President Johnson at a ceremony in the Capitol rotunda. In signing the act, the president commented that the 1965 VRA was a "triumph for freedom as huge as any victory that has ever been won on any battlefield" and predicted that the law would "strike away the last major shackle of those fierce and ancient bonds" confining African-Americans to second-class citizenship.[110]

The act contained several key provisions for which President Johnson promised vigorous and immediate enforcement. For example, the law: (1) provided for federal examiners to register African-American voters who had been turned away by state officials; and (2) suspended all tests or devices found by the attorney general to deny the right to vote. As to enforcement of the act, the president said: "[W]e will not delay, we will not hesitate, or will not turn aside until Americans of every race and color and origin in this country have the same rights as all others to share in the process of democracy."[111]

Johnson followed through on his promise. He insisted that target areas be identified and federal examiners be sent to them without delay. And, just three days after the president signed the 1965 legislation, Attorney General Nicholas Katzenbach designated nine counties to receive federal examiners.[112] By this action, the president gave "clear signals to the Nation, especially the South, that the federal government was prepared to guarantee blacks the right to vote."[113] Let us now look at the nature and type of person Johnson appointed to the district courts—individuals who would be charged with promoting Johnson's legal philosophy.

Selection, Screening, and Nomination under Johnson

Lyndon Johnson appointed 122 federal district court judges, including seven Republicans, five African-Americans (two more than President Kennedy), three Latinos, and two women.[114] Overall, the majority of Johnson's appointees attended private or Ivy League schools (almost 60 percent); were Protestant (58 percent, 31 percent Catholic); and just under half had prosecutorial experience (about 46 percent).[115] See Table 3.11, Chapter 3.

Although some sources suggest that under Johnson senatorial preferences persisted in the Justice Department,[116] one close observer reports that "the Justice Department and the White House in the late Johnson Administration made independent judgments and were not bound by senatorial wishes."[117] Much of the available research suggests that to a much greater extent than realized during the Kennedy administration, the Johnson administration adopted an active and persuasive role in the process of judicial selection.[118]

More effort was given to assure that Johnson's judicial appointments shared the administration's legal-policy goals. Johnson's success in appointing "Great Society liberals" to the courts resulted from a selection process designed to "balance the politics of judicial selection with his own policy objectives."[119] Indeed it is suggested that Johnson, "to a greater degree than perhaps any president before him except William Taft, was concerned and personally involved in the selection of judges to all levels of the federal judiciary."[120]

The primary actor in the Johnson selection process was Deputy Attorney General Ramsey Clark. Clark, together with other White House officials, attempted to insure that judicial nominees were not only loyal to the president, but that they were also committed to his programs. The loyalty question was especially crucial, however, on the Vietnam War issue. According to special counsel to the president Harry C. McPherson, "what you felt about the war was more important than what you felt about anything else." McPherson continued, "I think you could even dislike Lyndon Johnson and support the war and that would be fine. You'd be on his 'A' list."[121] But this extended emphasis on the war issue was not at the exclusion of domestic issues: in particular civil rights and racial issues.

In this latter regard, Deputy Attorney General Clark required an extensive questionnaire that included evaluations of temperament, integrity, experience, and reputation, as well as the nominees' overall political philosophy and views on defendant's rights. As Clark stated in an interview: "I had a rule that a person with a history of neutrality on the race issue is not enough. We've been through so many times a person that had never done anything either way, turn[s] out to be a racist."[122] For example, in a letter from White House aide Lee C. White to Aaron F. Henry of the NAACP in 1965, White wrote: "Let me assure you of the importance attached to the attitude of any potential candidate on the extremely important subject of civil rights. This is one of the key factors considered in connection with any court vacancy."[123] It was also reported that when needed, Johnson might personally give a potential nominee a "good talking to on civil rights."[124]

Thus, the Johnson administration has been credited with having participated more fully in the selection processes than the Kennedy administration. For example, John Macy, the head of the Civil Service Commission, instituted a merit plan that included seeking out and reviewing the backgrounds of potential nominees.

Even so, Johnson's selections were not always easily confirmed—especially a few of his early attempts to go ahead with several left over Kennedy nominees.[125] Two of the most controversial of these nominations occurred in 1965. In the first instance, James P. Coleman, a staunch segregationist and former governor of Mississippi, had the backing of *both* Johnson and Senator Eastland. Nonetheless, civil rights advocates viciously fought the nomination but were defeated when Johnson sent Attorney General Nicholas Katzenbach to defend the nomination during the confirmation hearings. In the second instance, however, Johnson failed to win confirmation of Francis X. Morrissey—nominated as a personal favor to Joseph Kennedy—when Morrissey was rated "unqualified" by the ABA. Morrissey had attended an unaccredited law school and had failed the bar examination twice.[126]

Like the Kennedy administration, the Johnson administration, including the Justice Department, experienced problems with the ABA, particularly during the first years in office. A total of five nominations, including Morrissey, received unqualified ratings. But these difficulties diminished, and Johnson, unlike Kennedy, solidified his relationship with the ABA.[127]

In summary, when viewed in overall perspective, the record suggests that Johnson clearly had substantive policy concerns as they related to civil rights and the Great Society; and he wanted judges with similar policy views. As one major study of the Johnson administration's views in this regard stated, the president "was very much concerned about the policy views and personal inclinations of his judicial appointments."[128] The author of this study quotes from a handwritten note from President Johnson to White House aide Marvin Watson:

How is he on Civil Rights? Ask Ramsey [reference then to Deputy Attorney General Ramsey Clark] to thoroughly explore background—prior association in cases, etc., and give me memo before I act. I want this on every judge.[129]

In yet another instance, with regard to a recommendation for the Fifth Circuit, Johnson directed the Justice Department to "Check to be sure he is all right on the Civil Rights question. I'll approve him if he is."[130] And although judicial selection under Johnson has been labeled "unsystematic" and lacking organization[131] Johnson "sought those who shared the Johnson Great Society views, or who at least were not antagonistic to the basic thrust of his administration. Especially important was a progressive stand on civil rights and economic issues."[132]

On balance, we find that Johnson promoted both a policy and partisan agenda in the selection of judicial nominees, and he attempted to select judges with progressive civil rights views while simultaneously remaining sensitive to party considerations, especially those involving Democratic senators.

RICHARD M. NIXON

Fu-k the ABA!

—Richard Nixon[133]

Civil Rights and Civil Liberties: Nixon's Policy Objectives and Judicial Expectations

Nixon gained the presidency in 1968 at least partially because of his "Southern strategy," which was designed to reduce federal pressure on the South to comply with civil rights laws. Nixon "pledged to take a more cautious, slow approach to [civil rights laws] enforcement."[134] This included condemning busing, promising to terminate cutoffs of federal aid designed to impose desegregation, criticizing parts of the Voting Rights Act, and pledging to appoint "strict constructionists" to the Supreme Court.[135] Nixon's overall policy on civil rights was, in the words of Thomas and Mary Edsall, to develop "a strategy of staying within the letter of the law, while making abundantly clear wherever possible his reluctance to aggressively enforce it."[136]

Further evidence of President Nixon's position on civil rights was his administration's proposals to amend the 1965 Voting Rights Act when it expired in 1970. These proposed amendments included the elimination of the Section 5 (Preclearance) provision, which required the prior approval of changes in state or local election laws or procedures in covered states by the attorney general or the Federal District Court of Washington, DC.[137] Additionally, Nixon also proposed to remove exclusive jurisdiction over voting rights cases from the Federal District Court of Washington, DC and return it to the local federal district courts.[138] Of course, the concern of many African-Americans as well as liberal whites was that these cases would find little justice in localized Southern courts that were notorious for being unfriendly and unfair to African-Americans.

Overall, although the compromise bill that eventually passed the Congress was less damaging to the original 1965 act than Nixon's initial proposals,[139] the philosophy and ideology of the Nixon administration came to the fore and were clearly at odds with both desegregation and voting rights protections.[140]

Affirmative Action

Kennedy and Johnson were not the only presidents to issue executive orders promoting the affirmative hiring of minorities. Nixon not only attempted to enforce existing orders but also, in 1969, issued Executive Order No. 11478, which expanded both affirmative action policies and the authority of the Civil Service Commission (CSC). The CSC was charged with seeing that each department and agency "create and maintain an affirmative action program of equal employment."[141]

Indeed, in contrast to his desegregation stance, Nixon is often credited with promoting progress in black employment and demonstrated a willingness to push for change. But in the main, Nixon did not follow up on many of his early efforts.[142] Nixon also endorsed, in his 1972 State of the Union Address, legislation to amend Title VII of the 1964 Civil Rights Act to *expand* the enforcement powers of the Equal Employment Opportunity Commission (EEOC). Here Nixon sought to grant the commission authority to seek court enforcement against discrimination and to broaden its scope to ban discriminatory employment practices of state and local governments and educational institutions.[143] These proposals were made into law in March 1972 in the Equal Employment Opportunity Act of 1972.[144]

Nixon even personally supported some city affirmative action plans such as the Philadelphia Plan.[145] In essence, these city plans attempted to force construction industry contractors and labor unions to increase minority hiring. Although his support for the Philadelphia Plan is widely known, Nixon's enforcement efforts against discrimination overall were far from significant. In fact, under Nixon there were only limited improvements and overall the dearth of affirmative action hiring persisted.[146]

If we agree that Nixon only marginally supported affirmative action hiring early in his administration, we might further conclude that Nixon's position on affirmative action went from lukewarm to cold. For example, a plethora of stories criticizing Nixon's lack of support for affirmative action blanketed the *New York Times* during the early years of the Nixon administration.[147] Other examples include Nixon's 1972 statement that he was against quotas.[148]

School Desegregation

The general posture of President Nixon and the White House during his administration was to impede school desegregation efforts, again another component of his "Southern strategy" to maintain Southern support. But, he also opposed desegregating Northern urban areas. Although Nixon initially endorsed the *Brown* decision, his support for school desegregation was unconvincing. As one newspaper editorial put it: "[Nixon] opposed virtually every effort short of divine revelation for stepping up the desegregation process."[149] These efforts included pursuing anti-busing legislation; redirecting the enforcement efforts of the Department of Justice and the Department of Health, Education, and Welfare (HEW); and "making judicial appointments calculated to reduce what [Nixon] perceived to be excessive intrusions by federal courts into state and local matters."[150]

In 1969, for example, the Nixon Justice Department (Attorney General John Mitchell and Assistant Attorney General for Civil Rights Jerris Leonard) petitioned the Supreme Court in *Alexander v. Holmes County Board of Education* to impede the implementation of the requirements of the *Brown* cases.[151] But the Supreme Court rebuffed this effort. Nonetheless, this intervention, as one writer put it, marked the "first time in the memory of civil rights lawyers since those decisions that lawyers for the United States and lawyers for private plaintiffs were on the opposite side of a school desegregation case."[152]

Of course, Nixon's emphasis on litigation by the Justice Department rather than enforcement by HEW placed increased dependence on the Justice Department's decisions about the use of its authority.[153] Overall, these policy positions signaled a growing opposition of the Nixon administration to school desegregation generally.

For example, President Nixon's initial policy pronouncements led Gary Orfield, in his study *The Reconstruction of Southern Education*, to suggest that school desegregation was coming to an end. Orfield writes: "A clear electoral verdict against racial reconciliation [the election of Nixon] could mean that the episode of the school guidelines may recede into history as an interesting but futile experiment."[154] These sentiments were reported by many others as well.

Within a few months, concludes one study, "HEW had been stripped of its authority to cut off funds, and the Justice Department was siding with Mississippi districts that were requesting additional delays before desegregation. HEW employees who tried to secure busing plans from school districts were threatened with firing."[155]

Additionally, just after the Office for Civil Rights (OCR) had begun to enforce Title VI in higher education in 1969, the Nixon administration put the agency, in the words of one OCR official, "in a holding pattern."[156] By 1969 the agency had requested desegregation plans from ten states; but, congruent with Nixon's Southern strategy, Nixon fired OCR director Leon Panetta and OCR effectively stopped enforcing Title VI in higher education for three years.[157]

Nixon's calculated attack on slowing school desegregation was clearly evident in his policy statements. For example, in 1969 Nixon stated that:

It is not our purpose here to lay down a single arbitrary date by which the desegregation process should be completed in all districts, or to lay down a single arbitrary system by which it should be achieved.

A policy requiring all school districts . . . to complete desegregation by the same date is too rigid to be either workable or equitable.

In some districts there may be sound reasons for some limited delay.[158]

And in 1970, the president suggested in a nationally televised broadcast that the Court had only declared de jure segregation illegal and that matters of de facto segregation were "natural and not illegal."[159] Paul Rilling, HEW's (Office of Civil Rights) Atlanta regional compliance director, provided the following assessment of the Nixon administration's policy directions:

The result of this retreat has been the revival of active, increasingly well-organized segregationist opposition in the South. Many districts are backing away from voluntary or court-ordered desegregation plans. There has been one instance of mob violence against school children. The definitive policy statement of the President, finally issued on March 24, adopted much of the verbiage of the segregationist: we must preserve neighborhood schools; busing is bad; education is more important than integration; desegregation heightens racial tension; many Negroes don't want it, etc.[160]

In a policy statement about a year later (March 1970), Nixon further denounced what he termed "extreme" court orders, and warned that such judicial activity "raised widespread fears that the nation might face a massive disruption of public education: that wholesale compulsory busing may be ordered and the neighborhood school virtually doomed."[161]

In yet a later example, two days after the remedy hearings began in Detroit in *Swann v. Charlotte-Mecklenburg Board of Education*,[162] the president put forth his position in a televised address on the evening of March 16, 1972. In that address Nixon called for "Congress to enact a moratorium on busing remedies" and announced that he was "directing Justice Department attorneys to intervene in pending litigation to oppose further use of such remedies in the interim."[163] Additionally, following the *Swann* decision, President Nixon submitted two bills to Congress designed to abate school desegregation efforts. The first was the Student Transportation Moratorium Act of 1972. The primary thrust of this first proposal was to "freeze" the busing situation until the Congress could consider a more "long range solution to the problem of continuing segregation in public schools."[164] The second bill was the Equal Educational Opportunities Amendment.[165]

A primary thrust of this second proposal was to limit the court's jurisdiction and "autonomy" in formulating desegregation plans.[166] This bill, in addition to delaying existing court orders for desegregation, prohibited courts from further ordering or transferring pupils further than the "next closest school" to his or her own neighborhood or from increasing the busing in the school district. Additionally the proposed amendment would authorize school boards to reopen existing court orders, subsequently permitting the resegregation of many schools. Of course this bill was the source of intense debate and controversy. In fact, more than 500 law professors signed a letter expressing their belief that the bill was unconstitutional. It is also quite interesting that the Nixon administration was only able to produce one authority to testify to the contrary: Robert Bork, at the time a Yale Law School professor.[167] Although the bill was defeated by filibuster, Robert Bork later became solicitor general in the Nixon administration and later a failed Supreme Court nominee under President Ronald Reagan.

Voting Rights

Nixon's Southern strategy was also aimed at reducing federal pressure in that region, so in 1970 he sought to remove key features of the Voting Rights Act and accepted its extension only under considerable pressure.[168] In assessing Nixon's commitment to voting rights, one may look again to Charles Hamilton's 1973 study, *The Bench and the Ballot*. Hamilton considers three aspects of the Nixon administration's position with respect to enforcing the Voting Rights Act: "(1) the appointment of federal examiners; (2) response to state reregistration requirements; and (3) what is known as Section 5 procedures, that is, that part of the VRA requiring approval before a revised state or local election requirement could be instituted."[169] On all three of these measures, Hamilton's study concludes that under the Nixon administration, voting rights guarantees were not only "casually enforced," but were at times "under attack."[170]

Abortion and Religious Liberty

President Nixon said little regarding issues of religious liberty; however, Nixon's position regarding abortion was straightforward. Although the published record indicates that President Nixon supported affordable "family planning" in 1969,[171] he later expressed strong antiabortion sentiments as well as specific policy directives to that end. Initially we should remind ourselves that four members of the Court that decided *Roe v. Wade* in 1973 were Nixon appointees; and, that three of the four voted with the 7–2 majority. Moreover, there was "speculation" that the *Roe v. Wade* decision was "delayed" to avoid jeopardizing President Nixon's 1972 reelection bid.[172] Here is an example where a president's appointees clearly did not reflect the president's position in a given policy area. For example, Nixon had expressed visceral objection to the growing abortion question in 1972. As Tatalovich and Daynes have explained, Nixon's strong expressions in 1972 were part of his political strategy to lure Catholic voters from the Democratic standard-bearer.[173] Nixon also strongly rejected the findings of the 1972 President's Commission on Population Growth and endorsed Terrance Cardinal Cooke's position against abortion.[174]

From personal and religious beliefs I consider abortion an unacceptable form of population control. Further, unrestricted abortion policies, or abortion on demand, I cannot square with my personal belief of the sanctity of human life—including the life of the yet unborn. For surely the unborn have rights also, recognized in law, recognized even in principles expounded by the United Nations.[175]

On balance, given the above positions, next we explore whether and to what extent President Nixon attempted to translate these policy objectives and expectations into judicial appointments in terms of the type and nature of persons he appointed.

Selection, Screening, and Nomination under Nixon

Richard Nixon appointed 179 district court judges, fifty-seven more than Johnson and seventy-six more than Kennedy. Included in these appointments were thirteen Democrats (7.3 percent of his total appointments); two Latinos (1.9 percent); six African-Americans (3.4 percent); but only one woman (see Table 3.11).[176] And, although he was the "law and order" candidate, Nixon appointed fewer judges with prosecutorial experience than Kennedy, Johnson, Ford, or Reagan and also appointed the highest number of Protestant judges (73.2 percent).[177]

Nixon campaigned in 1968 against the courts (particularly the Supreme Court) on a platform of law and order. Nixon, a lawyer, took over the presidency with a well-defined and articulated judicial philosophy—in other words, a *legal policy agenda*. Nixon's 1968 presidential campaign set the stage for a transformation in the politics of judicial appointments. While campaigning, Nixon openly promised to appoint a "strict constructionist, law-and-order judge from the South" to the Supreme Court and the implication was that he would also seek conservatives and those committed to judicial self-restraint for the lower federal courts.[178]

Consider, for example the following memorandum written by Tom Charles Houston, a White House aide to President Nixon, on March 25, 1969, about two months after the start of the Nixon presidency:

Through his judicial appointments, a President has the opportunity to influence the course of national affairs for a quarter of a century after he leaves office. . . . [I]t is necessary to remember that the decision as to who will make the decisions affects what decisions will be made. . . . [T]he president [can] establish precise guidelines as to the type of man he wishes to appoint—his professional competence, his political disposition, his understanding of the judicial function—and establish a White House review procedure to assure that each prospective nominee recommended by the Attorney General meets his guidelines. . . . He [the president] may insist that some evidence exists as to the attitude of the prospective judge toward the role of the court. He may insist upon a man who has a passion for judicial restraint. . . . The criteria he can establish are a varied as the views held in different political, social, and legal circles today, But if he establishes *his* criteria and establishes his machinery for insuring that the criteria are met, the appointments he makes will be his, in fact, as in theory.[179]

Later, when running for reelection in 1972 Nixon boasted that his federal judicial appointments had made the Constitution "more secure" and he further promised to appoint more "strict constructionists."[180] Hence, Nixon also attempted to appoint judges with a *policy* agenda emphasis. We must recall again, however, that during Nixon's second term the Democratic party controlled both houses of Congress and this faction, when combined with the fallout from the Watergate scandal, forced Nixon to increasingly make *partisan* considerations in his appointments, as Nixon needed all the political support he could muster.

For example, others suggest that Nixon's "appointments of well-qualified blacks appeared to be partisanly motivated to make the Republican party more attractive to black voters."[181] However, it is somewhat questionable that the appointment of six African-American district court judges and zero African-American courts of appeals judges (out of forty-five) would engender significant support from the masses of the African-American electorate for the Republican party and Nixon's "Southern Strategy." Moreover, one would need to determine whether these "well-qualified blacks" shared and promoted the same policy objectives as did Nixon, or of the majority African-American electorate. But, of course, this is part of the burden of this analysis.

As a matter of fact, for the most part the Nixon administration was frequently unsuccessful in its attempts to appoint judges sharing Nixon's conservative judicial philosophy. Again, this lack of performance has been attributed to essentially two factors: first, Nixon was constrained by a Democratic-controlled Congress; second, the Watergate scandal eroded Nixon's power with the Senate.[182] The Nixon administration "failed to take a hard line" with Republican senators; unless the nominee was rated "not qualified" by the ABA the administration would acquiesce to the senators' selections.[183] Of course, our task remains to discover whether those appointments he did make promoted or retarded the policy areas under investigation.

Nixon and the ABA

Nixon was the first president in history to promise not to nominate district court judges found "not qualified" by the ABA. The president's deputy attorney general, Richard Kleindienst, announced at the outset in 1969 that the ABA would have an absolute veto over all lower court nominees found unqualified. But the Nixon administration's relationship with the ABA soured quickly and grew increasingly troubled following the Senate's rejection of Nixon's Supreme Court nomination of Court of Appeals Judge Clement Haynsworth. At first Haynsworth was rated "highly qualified" by a unanimous vote of the ABA Standing Committee, but on reconsideration, the committee split 8–4 on Haynsworth's nomination—a split that doomed the nomination. And when the ABA Committee rated Nixon's subsequent nominee, District Court Judge Harold Carswell, as "unqualified," relations between the administration and the ABA reached a breaking point. "Fu-k the ABA!" charged President Nixon, mandating in 1970 that future Supreme Court nominees would *not* be submitted to the ABA prior to formal selection.[184]

In the main, the Nixon administration drives home the hypothesis that "without presidential leadership, federal involvement becomes passive."[185] Overall, the primary thrust of Nixon's interests and activity concerning judicial appointments focused on nominations to the Supreme Court, winning the confirmation of Chief Justice Warren Burger, Lewis F. Powell (a former ABA president), and William Rehnquist (a Nixon administration assistant attorney general).[186] But, with regard to district court appointments, it is apparent that most often these judgeships were political rewards, "made in deference to senators or in recognition of a nominee's service to the Republican party."[187] As explained by Stephen J. Markman, assistant attorney general in charge of selection during Ronald Reagan's second presidential term: "While many Nixon appointees were more conservative judicially than judges selected under earlier administrations, the ability of the Nixon Administration to affect the overall philosophy of the federal bench was ultimately frustrated by the concessions the Administration was forced to make."[188] Moreover, it has also been suggested that Nixon's interests altogether focused more directly on foreign rather than domestic policy. Thus, Nixon's participation in the selection process is murky. According to political scientist James P. Pfiffner, Nixon "intended to concentrate his efforts as president on foreign affairs and delegate domestic policy to his cabinet."[189] "I've always thought this country could run itself domestically without a President," said Nixon, "[A]ll you need is a competent cabinet to run the country at home. You need a president for foreign policy."[190]

Gerald R. Ford

Judicial appointments on ideological grounds denigrates the nominee and the Court. The Court should not be benign nor a legislative court, but in between those extremes . . . moderate in between those lines.

—Gerald R. Ford[191]

President Gerald Ford inherited a political morass. The integrity and credibility of the executive branch, including the Department of Justice, was widely perceived as scorched following the Watergate scandal. "[N]owhere did Watergate leave more lasting scars than at the Department of Justice," said Ford. "In less than three years, it had three Attorneys General—Richard Kleindienst, Elliot Richardson, and William Saxbe."[192] Consequently, as many scholars have noted, the Ford civil rights record was "not notable."[193] With the exception of exacerbating President Nixon's assault on busing, President Ford continued along the paths cut by the Nixon administration, providing little or no new policy initiatives in one direction or the other. With regard to the five policy areas discussed in this analysis, President Ford said little about affirmative action, and, like Nixon before him, President Ford similarly said little about religious liberty. Consider Ford's other policy positions below.

Abortion

During the 1976 presidential campaign, Gerald Ford gave less than a resounding endorsement to a constitutional amendment to ban abortion. In fact, he said he would "support but not seek" a "states'-rights" amendment. But the Republican party platform was much more direct: it called for an amendment "to restore the protection of the right to life for unborn children."[194]

The 1976 Republican party platform addressed abortion in two separate instances. First, under the section on "The American Family": "Because of our concern for family values, we affirm our beliefs, stated elsewhere in this Platform, in many elements that will make our country a more hospitable environment for family life . . . a position on abortion that values human life."[195] And a following section of the 1976 Republican party platform read:

The question of abortion is one of the most difficult and controversial of our time. It is undoubtedly a moral and personal issue but it also involves complex questions relating to medical science and criminal justice. There are those in our Party who favor complete support for the Supreme Court decision which permits abortion on demand. There are others who share sincere convictions that the Supreme Court's decision must be changed by a constitutional amendment prohibiting all abortions. Others have yet to take a position, or have assumed a stance somewhere in between polar positions. . . . The Republican Party favors a continuance of the public dialogue on abortion and supports the efforts of those who seek enactment of a constitutional amendment to restore protection of the right to life for unborn children.[196]

But Ford was uncomfortable with the Republican party platform and preferred that the solution to the abortion controversy be found somewhere other than in a constitutional amendment. Therefore Ford let it be known that he preferred an amendment that would allow each state to determine its own position on abortion.[197] And the president stated his position on abortion quite clearly when he vetoed a 1976 Labor-HEW appropriations bill (HR 14232) with an attached antiabortion amendment: "I agree with the restriction on the use of

Federal funds for abortion. My objection to this legislation is based purely and simply on fiscal integrity."[198] Overall, Ford's position on abortion differed little from the previous Nixon stance. His position was to thwart existing abortion policy and one might assume he also expected this from his judicial appointees.

School Desegregation

Like President Nixon before him, President Ford also strongly opposed school desegregation through busing. During the 1976 presidential election campaign, President Ford was adamant in his condemnation of busing in numerous speeches.[199] The 1976 GOP platform also endorsed an antibusing amendment. And although Ford never submitted an amendment, he had strongly supported President Nixon's attempt (discussed above) made as GOP House minority leader.[200]

President Ford did, however, attempt to curb busing through the Congress. In 1976, after an eight-month study by the Justice Department, President Ford directed the department to draft a legislative proposal captioned as the School Desegregation Standards and Assistance Act, primarily an antibusing bill.[201] The proposal stood to practically nullify the implementation of the busing remedy by barring it in cases of de facto segregation. Although Ford's proposal received no action in the Congress (it died in committee), his policy position remained relatively clear. Furthermore, a later proposal (often called the Byrd amendment) restricting busing as a means of administrative enforcement by HEW was signed into law by President Ford.[202]

In the same year that President Ford proposed antibusing legislation (1976), he also directed the attorney general to actively search for a test case to generate a review of the current case law on school busing that might overturn that judicial decree.

Voting Rights

The extension of the Voting Rights Act of 1965 for seven years was the only major voting rights legislation enacted during the Ford administration.[203] This legislation, enacted in 1975, included for the first time provisions for protecting the voting rights of language-minority citizens. But Ford did not make "vigorous enforcement [of the act] one of his highest priorities."[204] In the main, with regard to voting rights, Ford followed the precedents established by Nixon as discussed above. Moreover, there is little evidence to suggest that President Ford attempted to promote his policy positions via judicial appointments.

Selection, Screening, and Nomination under Ford

Ford came to the presidency in 1974 unelected, and was faced with a Democratic-controlled Congress. As a "moderate Republican," he was faced with the overwhelming goal of restoring the reputation of the American presidency and the Justice Department following the Watergate debacle. Watergate, stated Ford:

had a devastating impact on the record and morale of the Department of Justice. Allegations of partisan politics were rampant. Relations with Congress were at a low ebb. The Federal Bureau of Investigation had gone through a disturbing era. United States intelligence and counterintelligence activities were being seriously challenged by Congress, the news media, and the public.[205]

Even so, Ford was generally viewed as a lame-duck president. And during the past century, the Congress on occasion has sought to keep lame-duck presidents from making judicial appointments so as to prevent them from attempting to change the ideological complexion of the Court. In fact, this was precisely the case in 1960 and, again, in 1975 in order to prevent presidents Eisenhower and Ford the opportunity to make large numbers of lower court judicial appointments.[206]

But Ford did make some appointments. And the president understood well the importance of judicial nominations, especially to the Supreme Court.[207] "Few appointments a President makes," stated Ford, "can have as much impact on the future of the country as those to the Supreme Court."[208] However, Ford considered it "improper" and "a mistake [for presidents] to appoint people to the Court on ideological grounds."[209] Judicial appointments on "ideological grounds," said Ford, "denigrates the nominee and the Court." "The Court," stated Ford, "should not be benign nor a legislative court, but in between those extremes . . . moderate in between those lines."[210]

Ford appointed fifty-two district court judges, and eleven—an unprecedented 21.2 percent—went to the opposing party (Democrats); three to African-Americans. He appointed one Latino, and, like Nixon, President Ford appointed only one woman (see Table 3.11). Overall, judicial selection under President Ford was routine. Numerous chroniclers report that President Ford placed a higher premium on the "professional qualifications of nominees, to the exclusion of ideological considerations and occasionally even partisan politics."[211] There was not an overt attempt to "infuse a sharp conservative judicial philosophy into the federal bench."[212] As one observer has noted, "the Ford Administration did not make significant changes in the judicial selection process" and "the weakness of the Ford Administration may be seen in the statistic that a record 21 percent of its district appointments went to members of the opposing party."[213] Again, looking back on Table 3.11, Ford did make more of his fifty-two district court appointments to members of the opposite party—a higher percentage than any other president in history. Nevertheless, the operative question remains whether on key policy issues these appointees decided cases congruent with the Ford administration's *policy agenda.*

In sum, Ford considered the selection of district court judges basically a routine staff operation for the Justice Department. Initially, he delegated virtually all responsibility for handling lower court judgeships to his attorney general, Edward H. Levi, who personally handled these nominations. However, after several months, Attorney General Levi delegated these "routine" matters to Deputy U.S. Attorney General Harold R. Tyler, a former federal judge (and future ABA committee chairman), who was assisted by two career attorneys. Reports indicate that Tyler enjoyed a "virtually free hand," in other words, conferring with Levi only after conducting his own investigations of nominees.[214] Tyler also worked to rebuild stronger relations with the ABA.

In conclusion, for the most part Ford was a chief executive fighting for not only his own political career, but also to restore the credibility of the office of the president and the integrity of the Department of Justice. If Ford's civil rights agenda, as well as his involvement in judicial selection and nomination was less developed than those of his immediate predecessors, they were almost nonexistent compared to his immediate successors, Jimmy Carter and Ronald Reagan. As we shall see, during the Carter and Reagan administrations, the processes for selecting federal district court judges underwent overwhelming changes and developments. These matters are discussed in the next chapter.

NOTES

1. As explained by E. E. Schattschneider, some two decades ago, "The definition of the alternatives is the supreme instrument of power. . . . He who determines what politics is about runs the country, because the definition of alternatives is the choice of conflict, and the choice of conflict allocates power." See E. E. Schattschneider, *The Semisovereign People*, 2nd ed. (Hinsdale, IL: The Dryden Press, 1975), p. 66.

2. See Paul Charles Light, *The Presidential Agenda* (Baltimore: The Johns Hopkins University Press, 1982), pp. 2–3.

3. Ibid., p. 62.

4. Sheldon Goldman, "Judicial Appointments and the Presidential Agenda," in Paul Brace, Christine B. Harrington, and Gary King, eds., *The Presidency in American Politics* (New York: New York University Press, 1989), pp. 20–21.

5. Symbolism and substance in American law and politics are inextricably linked, and this linkage makes symbols and symbolic forms a salient feature in the allocation of goods and services, i.e., the resolution of group interest conflict. And so, we must bear in mind that presidents also at times promote symbolic signals that may or may not be realized or even shared by their judicial appointments. See Murray Edelman, *The Symbolic Uses of Politics* (Urbana: University of Illinois Press, 1967).

6. Presidential Candidate John Kennedy in a speech before the American Bar Association on August 30, 1960. *Congressional Quarterly Almanac*, 1961, p. 375.

7. Theodore Otto Windt, Jr., *Presidents and Protesters: Political Rhetoric in the 1960s* (Tuscaloosa: The University of Alabama Press, 1990), p. 19.

8. *Congressional Quarterly Almanac*, 1960, p. 84.

9. Theodore White pointed out that in Illinois, which Kennedy carried by 9,000 votes, 250,000 blacks were estimated to have voted for Kennedy. And in Michigan, which Kennedy carried by 67,000 votes, another 250,000 blacks were estimated to have voted for him. See Theodore H. White, *The Making of the President 1960* (New York: Atheneum, 1961), p. 323. It is reported that President Eisenhower claimed that Kennedy won the presidency because of a single phone call. When Martin Luther King, Jr. was jailed in Atlanta and sentenced to a four-month term at hard labor at a rural Georgia prison, Democratic candidate Kennedy telephoned Mrs. King to offer support. However, further investigation provided by Mark Stern suggests that the decision to call Mrs. King

was not his own. As clarified by Mark Stern, it was Sargent Shriver, head of the Catholic Interracial Council of Chicago and Kennedy in-law, that approached candidate Kennedy at O'Hare Airport in Chicago and informed him of King's arrest. "Why don't you call Mrs. King and give her your sympathy," said Shriver to Kennedy. "Negroes don't expect everything will change tomorrow no matter who's elected. But they do want to know whether you care. If you telephone Mrs. King they will know you understand and will help. You will reach their hearts and give support to a pregnant woman who is afraid her husband will be killed." Kennedy's spur-of-the-moment response was "That's a damn good idea. Get her on the phone." See also Mark Stern, "John F. Kennedy and Civil Rights: From Congress to the Presidency," *Presidential Studies Quarterly* 19 (1989), pp. 797–823. One interesting result of Kennedy's intervention was that Dr. King's father, who had previously supported Richard Nixon, publicly switched to Kennedy, saying: "I've got a whole suitcase of votes and I'm going to take them to Mr. Kennedy and dump them in his lap." See White, *The Making of the President,* p. 323. Also see Charles V. Hamilton, *The Bench and the Ballot: Southern Federal Judges and Black Voters* (New York: Oxford University Press, 1973), p. 79.

10. *Congressional Quarterly Almanac,* 1961, p. 81.

11. By September 27, Kennedy had appointed seventy-eight Democrats, three Republicans and one Liberal. Three of these nominees were African-Americans. For discussion of the House and Senate action and debate see the *Congressional Quarterly Almanac,* 1961, p. 373, "Congress Creates 73 New Judgeships."

12. *Roe v. Wade,* 410 U.S. 113 (1973).

13. *Doe v. Bolton,* 410 U.S. 179 (1973).

14. For instance, in 1965 President Johnson stated he would "seek new ways to use our knowledge to help deal with the explosion in world population and the growing scarcity in world resources." See Rodney Hyman, Betty Sarvis, and Joy Walker Bonar, *The Abortion Question* (New York: Columbia University Press, 1987), p. 16.

15. Ibid.

16. Interview with James Reston reported in *The New York Times,* November 28, 1959, as quoted in Frederick S. Jaffe, Barbara L. Lindheim, and Philip R. Lee, *Abortion Politics: Private Morality and Public Policy* (New York: McGraw-Hill, 1981), pp. 169–170.

17. Press conference statement reported in the *New York Times,* April 25, 1963, as quoted in Jaffe, 1981, p. 170.

18. Excerpt from presidential candidate John F. Kennedy's speech to the Greater Houston Ministerial Association in Houston Texas, on September 12, 1960, as reprinted in "Legal, Historical Background on Private Schools Issue," *Congressional Quarterly Almanac,* 1961, p. 229.

19. Ibid., p. 229.

20. Ibid., pp. 226–229.

21. Speech to the Greater Houston Ministerial Association, September 12, 1960, reprinted in the *Speeches of Senator John F. Kennedy—Presidential Campaign of 1960* (Washington, DC: Government Printing Office, 1961), p. 210.

22. For example, See Arthur M. Schlesinger, Jr., *A Thousand Days, John F. Kennedy in the White House* (New York: Fawcett Crest, 1965), esp. pp. 843–892; Theodore C. Sorensen, *Kennedy* (New York: Bantam Books, 1965), pp. 528–569.

23. Harry Golden, *Mr. Kennedy and the Negroes* (New York: World Publishing, 1964), p. 269.

24. Victor Lasky, *JFK: The Man and the Myth* (New York: Macmillian, 1963); Nancy

Cager Clinch, *The Kennedy Neurosis* (New York: Grosset and Dunlop, 1973); Bruce Miroff, *Pragmatic Illusions, The Presidential Politics of John F. Kennedy* (New York: David McKay, 1976); Gary Wills, *The Kennedy Imprisonment, A Meditation on Power* (New York: Little, Brown and Company, 1981); Peter Collier and David Horowitz, eds., *The Kennedys: An American Drama* (New York: Summit Books, 1984).

25. Miroff, *Pragmatic Illusions*, p. 269.

26. For example, see J. Richard Snyder, ed., *John Kennedy: Person, Policy, Presidency* (Wilmington, DE: Scholarly Resources Inc., 1988); or, Herbert S. Parmet, *JFK: The Presidency of John Fitzgerald Kennedy* (Baltimore: Penguin, 1982). Political scientist Mark Stern has summarized many of the competing theories on the perceptions of Kennedy's commitment to civil rights. Stern examines views ranging from Kennedy as not only an advocate but as a leader in civil rights to the notion that Kennedy was a "reluctant participant in an inevitable movement." (Stern, "John F. Kennedy and Civil Rights," pp. 797–823). Others, most notably Theodore Sorensen and Arthur M. Schlesinger, Jr., argue that "John Kennedy was a friend of civil rights who needed to wait until the time was ripe." See Schlesinger, *A Thousand Days*, pp. 843–892; Sorensen, *Kennedy*, pp. 528–569. Schlesinger writes: "While [Kennedy] did not doubt the depth of the injustice or the need for remedy, he had read the arithmetic of the new Congress and concluded that there was no possible chance of passing a civil rights bill" (Schlesinger, 1965), pp. 849–850; Carl M. Bauer argues that "Kennedy both encouraged and responded to black aspirations and led the nation into its Second Reconstruction." (Bauer, *John F. Kennedy and the Second Reconstruction* [New York: Columbia University Press, 1977], p. 320); Herbert Parmet posits that Kennedy "had to be pressed too hard, but when the time came he provided the leadership that the struggle for equality had always needed in the White House." (Parmet, *JFK*, pp. 299, 354–355; Harvard Sitkoff concludes that "the Kennedy's saw the struggle against racism as a conundrum to be managed, not a cause to be championed" (Sitkoff, *The Struggle for Black Equality* [New York: Hill and Wang, 1981], p. 106); Bruce Miroff suggests that "Kennedy policy led to civil rights advocates having their hopes raised and dashed repeatedly as deeds failed to follow the word of administrative encouragement: 'Pragmatic illusions' of control and response became betrayal to those who believed in ideals." (Miroff, *Pragmatic Illusions*, pp. 227–228); Gary Wills found that Kennedy's "encouragement of the civil rights issue was largely inadvertent." (Wills, *The Kennedy Imprisonment*, p. 209); and still other scholars of the American presidency have labeled Kennedy's congressional record on civil rights almost "nonexistent" (Berman, *The New American Presidency*, p. 241); and, even those close to him have since claimed that "John Kennedy . . . did not know much about black civil rights or black problems in general." See Harris Wofford, oral history interview by Berl Bernhard, November 29, 1965, in JFKL, as quoted as oral history interview by Mark Stern, February 20, 1988, 1, in Stern, "John F. Kennedy and Civil Rights," p. 805.

27. Harris Wofford, Jr., *Of Kennedys and Kings, Making Sense of the Sixties* (New York: Farrar, Straus and Giroux, 1980), pp. 37–38.

28. For example, it was not until eighteen months later that Kennedy effected a "timid executive order covering very little of the country's housing." See Jeff Fishel, *Presidents and Promises: From Campaign Pledge to Presidential Performance* (Washington, DC: CQ Press, 1985), p. 2. Kennedy also issued executive orders that prohibited discrimination in federally aided libraries and hospitals, in the armed forces, in the training of civil defense workers, and in the off-base treatment of military personnel. See Berman, *The New American Presidency*, p. 242.

29. U.S. Senate Committee on Commerce, *Speeches, Remarks, Press Conferences and*

Statements of Senator John F. Kennedy (Washington, DC: Government Printing Office, 1961), p. 69. See also, Press Release, "From the Offices of Senator Joseph F. Clark (D-PA) and Representative Emanuel Celler (D-NY)" September 16, 1960, Papers of Emanuel Celler, Box 272, LOC, quoted in Stern, "John F. Kennedy and Civil Rights," p. 811.

30. See *Congressional Quarterly Almanac*, 1961, p. 392. For the complete text see "Complete Text of 1960 Democratic Platform" (*Congressional Quarterly Almanac*, 1960), pp. 776–788).

31. Stern. "John F. Kennedy and Civil Rights," p. 815.

32. *Public Papers of the Presidents: John F. Kennedy*, 1960 (Washington, DC: Government Printing Office, 1962), p. 22.

33. *Congressional Quarterly Almanac*, 1961, p. 392

34. Catherine Barnes, *Journey from Jim Crow: The Desegregation of Southern Transit* (New York: Columbia University Press, 1983), p. 184.

35. *Congressional Quarterly Almanac*, 1961, p. 81.

36. See "Civil Rights Issue," under "Senate Passes Aid-to-Education Bill, 49–34, on May 25," in *Congressional Quarterly Almanac*, 1961, p. 220. Also see "President's Requests," under "General School Aid Again Blocked," *Congressional Quarterly Almanac*, 1961, p. 215.

37. In addition to executive orders regarding employment and nondiscriminatory grants-in-aid policies, the Kennedy administration also sought changes through executive action in the areas of housing and transportation. As reported in the *Congressional Quarterly Almanac* (1961, p. 393), early in his administration Kennedy was credited with "considering" issuing an executive order designed to give "Negroes" equal opportunity to live in houses constructed with federal aid. Indeed, during his presidential campaign he boldly stated that the "next president must issue an executive order putting and end to racial discrimination in federally assisted housing." This he said could be accomplished "by a stroke of pen." The Civil Rights Commission had recommended just such a order in 1959 and 1961. Nevertheless, because a housing bill was one of the main priorities of his administration in 1961, and under the leadership of Southern sponsors, the housing order was delayed for fear that its issuance would damage the housing bill's chances (*Congressional Quarterly Almanac*, 1961, p. 393). On November 20, 1962, Kennedy issued Executive Order No. 11063, marking the beginning of the executive effort to ban desegregation in housing (Norman C. Amaker, *Civil Rights and the Reagan Administration* (Washington DC: The Urban Institute Press, 1988), p. 17. This order created the President's Committee on Equal Opportunity and directed federal agencies and departments to take steps to prevent discrimination in housing owned in part or in whole by the federal government or built with federal loans, grants, or other assistance. With regard to transportation, the Department of Justice, under Kennedy's leadership, emphasized the desegregation of facilities in interstate travel. Via Attorney General Robert Kennedy, the DOJ petitioned the ICC on May 29, 1960 to issue regulations banning segregation in bus terminals. The Justice Department also brought suits against several airports charging that the Federal Airport Act barred any "unjust discrimination" in interstate air transportation (*Congressional Quarterly Almanac*, 1961, p. 393). These actions served to augment and perhaps in part were even generated by the Freedom Rides and the Supreme Court's December 5, 1960, ruling in *Boynton v. Virginia* (364 U. S. 454, 1960) that a bus terminal restaurant may not segregate passengers traveling across state lines and providing that the restaurant is an "integral" part of an interstate bus service (See *Congressional Quarterly Almanac*, 1961, p. 393).

38. Ruth P. Morgan, *The President and Civil Rights: Policymaking by Executive Order* (New York: St. Martin's Press, 1970), p. 3.

39. *The New York Times*, May 11, 1961.

40. It was President Roosevelt who issued the first executive order that dealt with equal opportunity in employment. This order forbade employment discrimination on the basis of race, creed, color, or national origin by employers who held Defense Department contracts. However, as explained by political scientist Michael B. Preston, it was not until twenty years after Roosevelt's 1941 order that "the idea of affirmative action became interwoven with the discrimination ban." See Michael B. Preston, "Affirmative Action Policy: Can It Survive the Reaganites?," in Michael W. Combs and John Gruhl, eds., *Affirmative Action: Theory, Analysis, and Prospects* (Jefferson, NC: McFarland, 1986), p. 167. Under presidents Truman and Eisenhower, further executive orders were issued, extending the ban on discrimination by government contractors and setting up various bodies to oversee and enforce it. See Nathan Glazer, *Affirmative Discrimination* (New York: Basic Books, 1975), pp. 44–46.

41. Executive Order No. 10925, 3 C.F.R. 86 (Supp. 1961), 6 R.R.L.R. 9 (1961).

42. *Congressional Quarterly Almanac*, 1961, p. 392.

43. For the complete text of the March 6 statement by President Kennedy accompanying his Executive Order No. 10925 establishing the President's Committee on Equal Employment Opportunity. See the *Congressional Quarterly Almanac*, 1961, p. 860.

44. Amaker, *Civil Rights and the Reagan Administration*, p. 16.

45. See also Nijole V. Benokraitis and Joe R. Feagin, *Affirmative Action and Equal Opportunity: Action, Inaction, Reaction* (Boulder, CO: Westview Press, 1978), pp. 9–10.

46. 26 *Fed. Reg.* 1977, 3 C.F.R., 1959–63 comp. 448, pt. 3, 301(1).

47. Benokraitis and Feagin, *Affirmative Action and Equal Opportunity*, p. 10. These authors consider Kennedy's Executive Order No. 10925 to be "A first tentative step."

48. See Charles S. Bullock III and Charles M. Lamb, eds., *Implementation of Civil Rights Policy* (Monterey, CA: Brooks/Cole Publishing, 1984). p. 57.

49. *The New York Times*, March 12, 1961, and as quoted and discussed in Hamilton, *The Bench and the Ballot*, pp. 81–82.

50. For a thorough account of the integration of the University of Mississippi, see James Meredith's *Three Years in Mississippi* (Bloomington: Indiana University Press, 1966); also see Harold Fleming, "The Federal Executive and Civil Rights: 1961–1965," *Daedalus* 94 (Fall 1965).

51. John F. Kennedy, Proclamation No. 3497, September 30, 1962; Code of Federal Regulations, 1959–1963 Compilation, 225. Also for an informative yet condensed summary of the Meredith case, see Richard Bardolph, *The Civil Rights Record: Black Americans and the Law, 1849–1970* (New York: Thomas Y. Crowell Co., 1970), pp. 473–491; Amaker, *Civil Rights and the Reagan Administration*, p. 17.

52. Perhaps one measure of Kennedy's personal commitment to civil rights (school desegregation and voting rights) may be found in the reaction of Martin Luther King, Jr., after a private breakfast meeting between the two in May of 1960. "I was very impressed by the forthright and honest manner in which he discussed the civil rights question. I have no doubt that he would do the right thing on this issue if he were elected President." King further elaborated that when he "specifically mentioned the need for strong civil rights legislation to guarantee the right to vote and to speed up school segregation" that Kennedy "agreed with all of these things." Letter from Martin Luther King, Jr., to Chester Bowles, June 24, 1960, King Papers, Box 3. BUL, as quoted in Stern, "John F. Kennedy and Civil Rights," p. 807.

53. National Broadcasting Company telecast (October, 1962) as quoted in Amaker, *Civil Rights and the Reagan Administration*, p. 18.

54. Windt, *Presidents and Protestors*, p. 22.

55. Quotation taken from Beth Ingold and Theodore Windt, eds., "Desegregation at the University of Mississippi: A Legal Issue," televised report to the nation, September 30, 1962, in *Essays in Presidential Rhetoric* (Dubuque, IA: Kendall/Hunt, 1983), p. 34.

56. Windt, *Presidents and Protestors*, p. 80.

57. Ibid., p. 22.

58. Speech on June 11, 1963. As quoted by Beth Ingold and Theodore Windt, eds., "Civil Rights: A Moral Issue," report to the nation, June 11, 1963, in *Essays in Presidential Rhetoric*, pp. 46–47; see also Berman, *The New American Presidency*, p. 243; and Sorensen, *Kennedy*, pp. 556–557.

59. Amaker, *Civil Rights and the Reagan Administration*, p. 18.

60. Donald B. Johnson, compiler, *National Party Platforms, Volume II, 1960–76* (Urbana: University of Illinois Press, 1978), p. 599.

61. Special message to Congress from the president, 1963, as quoted in Hamilton, *The Bench and the Ballot*, pp. 178, 228. Hamilton asserts that this was a "relatively mild" message.

62. For discussion, see Harrell R. Rodgers, Jr., and Charles S. Bullock, *Law and Social Change: Civil Rights Laws and Their Consequences* (New York: McGraw-Hill, 1972), pp. 36–37.

63. John F. Kennedy, quoted in Larry Berman, *The New American Presidency* (Boston: Little, Brown and Company, 1987), p. 99.

64. Kennedy's remaining three African-American federal court appointees were Wade H. McCree, Michigan; Spottswood W. Robinson, District of Columbia; and A. Leon Higginbotham, Jr., Pennsylvania.

65. For an in-depth study of the socioeconomic, political, and other characteristics of Kennedy's appointees see Sheldon Goldman, "Characteristics of Eisenhower and Kennedy Appointees to the Lower Federal Bench," *Western Political Quarterly* 18 (December 1965), pp. 755–762.

66. David M. O'Brien, rapporteur, *Judicial Roulette: Report of the Twentieth Century Fund Task Force on Judicial Selection* (New York: Priority Press, 1988), pp. 52–53.

67. Quoted by Thomas Cronin, *The State of the Presidency* (New York: Little, Brown and Company, 1980), p. 223.

68. Donald Dale Jackson, *Judges* (New York: Atheneum, 1974), p. 244.

69. Victor S. Navasky, *Kennedy Justice* (New York: Atheneum, 1971), p. 243.

70. Navasky, *Kennedy Justice*, p. 244.

71. Robert Kennedy oral interview, John F. Kennedy Presidential Library, Waltham, Massachusetts, p. 603, or as quoted in O'Brien, *Judicial Roulette*, p. 33.

72. For a discussion of the contradictions in the Kennedy's civil rights positions and judicial appointments, see Navasky, *Kennedy Justice*, Chapter 5, "Southern Justice: The Judges and the General," pp. 243–276.

73. *Brown v. Board of Education* 347 U.S. 483 (1954)

74. Charles V. Hamilton, "Southern Judges and Negro Voting Rights: The Judicial Approach to the Solution of Controversial Social Problems," *Wisconsin Law Review* 65 (Winter 1965), pp. 86–87.

75. Quoted in "Judge in Rights Case: William Harold Cox," *New York Times*, February 26, 1965. Indeed, Judge Harold Cox's hostility to African-Americans and civil rights issues generally is legendary. See also, Neil R. McMillian, "Black Enfranchisement in

Mississippi: Federal Enforcement and Black Protest in the 1960's," *Journal of Southern History* 43 (1977), pp. 351–372, esp. pp. 357–358; Gerald M. Stern "Judge William Harold Cox and the Right to Vote in Clarke County, Mississippi," Leon Friedman, ed., *Southern Justice* (New York: Random House, 1965), pp. 165–186.

76. McMillian, "Black Enfranchisement in Mississippi," p. 357.

77. Navasky, *Kennedy Justice*, pp. 243–276.

78. Herman Schwartz, *Packing the Courts: The Conservative Campaign to Rewrite the Constitution* (New York: Charles Scribner's Sons, 1988), p. 53.

79. "Oral Reply of Nicholas de B. Katzenbach to house of Delegates," Annual Meeting of the American Bar Association, San Francisco, 1962 (mimeo), p. 3, as reprinted in Joel B. Grossman, *Lawyers and Judges: The ABA and the Politics of Judicial Selection* (New York: John Wiley and Sons, 1965), p. 79.

80. Grossman, *Lawyers and Judges*, p. 79.

81. Harold W. Chase, *Federal Judges: The Appointing Process* (Minneapolis: University of Minnesota Press, 1972), p. 135.

82. Sheldon Goldman, "Judicial Appointments and the Presidential Agenda," in Paul Brace, Christine B. Harrington, and Gary King, eds., *The Presidency in American Politics* (New York: New York University Press, 1989), p. 33.

83. Navasky, *Kennedy Justice*, pp. 243–276.

84. For discussion on this point see *Congressional Quarterly Almanac*, 1961, p. 392.

85. Mark Stern, "John F. Kennedy and Civil Rights: From Congress to the Presidency," *Presidential Studies Quarterly* (Fall 1989), pp. 817–818.

86. A speech by Lyndon Johnson at the University of Michigan in 1964. As quoted in Berman, *The New American Presidency*, p. 251.

87. *The New York Times*, November 27, 1963; see also, Steven F. Lawson, *Black Ballots: Voting Rights in the South, 1944–1969* (New York: Columbia University Press, 1976), p. 298.

88. See Tom Rice and Kenneth Whitby, "Racial Inequality in Unemployment: The Effectiveness of the Civil Rights Act of 1964," in Michael W. Combs and John Gruhl, eds., *Affirmative Action: Theory, Analysis, and Prospects* (Jefferson, NC: McFarland, 1986), p. 69.

89. Executive Order No. 1197, 3 C.F.R. 278 (1964–65 comp.) revoked by Executive Order No. 11247.

90. Benokraitis and Feagin, *Affirmative Action and Equal Opportunity*, pp. 11–12. See also, Glazer, *Affirmative Discrimination*, p. 46.

91. U.S. Commission on Civil Rights, *Federal Civil Rights Enforcement Effort* (Washington, DC: Government Printing Office 1970), p. 64; see also discussion in Rodgers and Bullock, *Law and Social Change*, pp. 117–118. As Rodgers and Bullock summarize, despite these measures discrimination in federal employment continued unabated primarily because "CSC's role under E.O. 11246 was characterized more by passivity than by 'leadership'; more by neutrality than by 'guidance.'" A 1967 study by the U.S. Commission on Civil Rights, *Federal Civil Rights Enforcement Effort* (supra, p. 70) revealed that "15 percent of all Federal employees were black but almost all of them were concentrated in the lowest-paying jobs. Only 1.8 percent of the higher paying (GS 12 through 18) jobs were held by blacks."

92. 10 R.R.L.R. 1848 (1965), superseded by Executive Order No. 11764.

93. Benokraitis and Feagin, *Affirmative Action and Equal Opportunity*, p. 12.

94. Ibid.

95. Congressional Quarterly, *Congress and the Nation, Vol. II, 1965–1968* (Wash-

ington, DC: Congressional Quarterly, Inc., 1969), p. 325 and as discussed and reprinted in Gary Orfield, "Race and the Liberal Agenda: The Loss of the Integrationist Dream, 1965–1974," in Margaret Weir, Ann Shola Orloff, and Theda Skocpol, eds., *The Politics of Social Policy in the United States* (Princeton, NJ: Princeton University Press, 1988), p. 317.

96. Gary Orfield, *Must We Bus?: Segregated Schools and National Policy* (Washington, DC: The Brookings Institution, 1978), p. 362. Also see Jack Peltason, *Fifty-Eight Lonely Men: Southern Federal Judges and School Desegregation* (New York: Harcourt, Brace and World, 1961); and Reed Sarratt, *The Ordeal of Desegregation* (Harper and Row, 1966), pp. 209–220.

97. Bullock and Lamb, *Implementation of Civil Rights Policy*, p. 57.

98. Jack Greenberg, "Letter to the Editor," *New York Times Magazine* (November 3, 1968), p. 16.

99. U.S. Commission on Civil Rights, *Racial Isolation in the Public Schools* (Washington, DC: Government Printing Office, 1967).

100. Michael Warren Combs, "Courts, Minorities, and the Dominant Coalition: Racial Policies in Modern America," Ph.D. dissertation, Washington University, 1978.

101. Public Papers of the Presidents, Lyndon B. Johnson, 1965, II, p. 843, as quoted and cited in Steven F. Lawson, *Black Ballots: Voting Rights in the South, 1944–1969,* (New York: Columbia University Press, 1976), p. 329.

102. For a well-developed discussion of the relationship between the Selma-Montgomery March and the eventual passage of the 1965 Voting Rights Act, see David L. Garrow, *Protest at Selma: Martin Luther King Jr. and the Voting Rights Act of 1965* (New Haven: Yale University Press, 1978).

103. Although the initial march was blocked several times by state law enforcement personnel and marred by fatalities perpetuated by violent white mobs, the fifty-four-mile march finally began on March 21 and ended in front of the state Capitol in Montgomery on March 25. For example, shortly after the first of several unsuccessful attempts to start (March 7 and March 9), a "vanguard of about 525 marchers were attacked by 200 state troopers and sheriff's deputies, some on horses, using tear gas, nightsticks and whips." On the first day, Reverend James J. Reeb, a Unitarian minister who participated in the march, was beaten to death by a group of whites on a Selma street corner. For discussion see Lester A. Sobel, *Civil Rights, 1960–66* (New York: Facts on File, 1967), pp. 292–296; see also David J. Garrow, *Bearing the Cross: Martin Luther King, Jr., and the Southern Christian Leadership Conference* (New York, William Morrow, 1986), pp. 405–408, 419; and, *Life Magazine*, March 19, 1965.

104. Sobel, *Civil Rights, 1960–66*, pp. 293–294.

105. President Johnson, "State of the Union Message," Public Papers of the Presidents of the United States. (Washington, DC: Government Printing Office, 1965), pp. 1–9.

106. Amaker, *Civil Rights and the Reagan Administration,* p. 20.

107. Bullock and Lamb, *Implementation of Civil Rights Policy*, p. 25.

108. U.S., *Congressional Record*, 1965, 89th Congress, 1st session, CXI, p. 8359.

109. Combs, "Courts, Minorities, and the Dominant Coalition: Racial Policies in Modern America, " pp. 112–114.

110. Congressional Quarterly Service, *Congress and the Nation*, vol. II, 1965–1968 (Washington, DC: Government Printing Office, 1969), p. 32.

111. Public Papers of the Presidents, Lyndon B. Johnson, 1965, II, p. 843.

112. For discussion, see Lawson, *Black Ballots*, pp. 329–352.

113. See Bullock and Lamb, *Implementation of Civil Rights Policy*, p. 49.

114. For an in-depth study of the socioeconomic, political, and other characteristics of the Johnson appointees, see Sheldon Goldman, "Johnson and Nixon Appointees to the Lower Federal Courts: Some Socio-Political Perspectives," *Journal of Politics* 34 (1972), pp. 934–943.

115. Although 46 percent is not a majority, as indicated in Table 3.11 (Chapter 3), it is the second highest rating among all six presidents except Ford at 50 percent. Significantly, despite Nixon's "law and order" policy, at 41.9 percent, Nixon's appointment of judges with prosecutorial experience falls behind Kennedy, Johnson, Ford, and Reagan; i.e., all but Carter.

116. O'Brien reports that Johnson, as a former Senate majority leader, was "sensitive to demands of senatorial courtesy, as he himself had held up 13 of Eisenhower's nominees in order to win a judgeship for one of his friends in Texas" (O'Brien, *Judicial Roulette*, p. 53). See also Chase, *Federal Judges*; Harold Chase, "The Johnson Administration-Judicial Appointments 1963–66," *Minnesota Law Review* 52 (1968), p. 965; and, Alan Neff, *The United states District Judge Nominating Commissions: Their Members, Procedures and Candidates* (Chicago: American Judicature Society, 1981), p. 19.

117. This was of course after Attorney General Robert Kennedy resigned in 1964 and Katzenbach took over as head of the Justice Department with Ramsey Clark serving as the new deputy attorney general.

118. At the outset of any discussion of judicial selection during the Johnson administration must be the acknowledgment of Neil D. McFeeley's 1987 work, *Appointment of Judges: The Johnson Presidency* (Austin: The University of Texas Press, 1987). McFeeley offers such an altogether thorough and well developed discussion that the most one can hope for is to adequately and briefly summarize the highlights of that work.

119. McFeeley, *Appointment of Judges*, p. 138.

120. Ibid., pp. 51–52. See also, Walter F. Murphy, "Chief Justice Taft and the Lower Court Bureaucracy," *Journal of Politics* 24 (1962), p. 453.

121. Transcript, Harry C. McPherson Oral History Interview, undated, tape 9, p.4, LBJ Library, as quoted in McFeeley, *Appointment of Judges*, p 86.

122. Clark Interview, LBJ School of Public Affairs Project, p. 34, as reprinted in McFeeley, *Appointment of Judges*, p. 86.

123. Letter, White to Aaron Henry, 18 May 1965, Gen FG 505, WHCF, LBJ Library, as reprinted in McFeeley, *Appointment of Judges*, p. 87.

124. McFeeley, *Appointment of Judges*, p. 88.

125. For example, David Rabinovitz from Wisconsin was withdrawn due to opposition over his qualifications from the ABA and his two home-state senators (O'Brien, *Judicial Roulette*, p. 54).

126. Ibid., p. 54.

127. Although this volume is primarily concerned with the district courts, it is instructive to note here that Johnson's biggest judicial defeat was his attempt to elevate Supreme Court Justice Abe Fortas in 1968 to replace retiring Chief Justice Earl Warren.

128. McFeeley, *Appointment of Judges*, pp. 87–88.

129. Memo, Watson to president, 23 June 1966, Ex FG 500, WHCF, LBJ Library.

130. Memo from president, 14 August 1966, Ex FG 505/5/A, WHCF, LBJ Library.

131. O'Brien, *Judicial Roulette*, p. 55; McFeeley, *Appointment of Judges*, pp. 38–41.

132. McFeeley, *Appointment of Judges*, p. 136.

133. Henry J. Abraham, "Beneficial Advice or Presumptuous Veto?" The ABA's Committee on Federal Judiciary Revisited," Henry J. Abraham with Griffin B. Bell, Charles E. Grassley, Eugene W. Hickok, Jr., John W. Kern III, Stephen J. Markman, and

William Bradford Reynolds, eds., *Judicial Selection: Merit, Ideology, and Politics,* (Washington, DC: National Legal Center for the Public Interest, 1990), p. 65.

134. Bullock and Lamb, *Implementation of Civil Rights Policy,* p. 27.

135. See Gary Orfield, "Nixon and the Assault on Civil Rights," in *The Politics of Social Policy in the United States,* pp. 347–351.

136. Thomas Edsall and Mary Edsall, *Chain Reaction: The Impact of Race, Rights and Taxes on American Politics* (New York: Norton, 1991), p. 81.

137. See the *Congressional Quarterly Almanac,* (Washington, DC: Government Printing Office, 1970), p. 193; and Bullock and Lamb, *Implementation of Civil Rights Policy,* pp. 27–28, 33–37. For a well developed discussion on the development of Section 5 Preclearance see Mack Jones, "The Voting Rights Act as an Intervention Strategy for Social Change: Symbolism or Substance?" in Franklin D. Jones and Michael Adams, eds., *Readings in American Political Issues* (Dubuque, IA: Kendall/Hunt, 1987), pp. 141–160. It should also be noted that this discretionary preclearance power afforded the Attorney General had been recognized and defended by the Supreme Court in *South Carolina v. Katzenbach* (383 U. S 301, 1966).

138. Congressional Quarterly Service, *Congressional Quarterly Almanac,* vol. 26. (Washington, DC: Government Printing Office, 1970), p. 193.

139. For a summary of the significant revisions in the compromise bill, see Bullock and Lamb, *Implementation of Civil Rights Policy,* p. 28.

140. It is also instructive to note that by the middle of the first Nixon administration, civil rights as a national issue had declined drastically (almost completely) from its preeminent position in the mid-1960s. This information is based on Gallup Polls, 1963–1971 and compiled by Gary Orfield, "Race and the Liberal Agenda: The Loss of the Integrationist Dream, 1965–1974," in *The Politics of Social Policy in the United States,* p. 335. See Table 9.1.

141. For a more detailed discussion on Executive Order No. 11478, see Rodgers and Bullock, *Law and Social Change,* pp. 118–119.

142. Ibid., pp. 126–127.

143. Amaker, *Civil Rights and the Reagan Administration,* p. 22.

144. P.L. 92–261, 86 Stat. 103.

145. Rodgers and Bullock, *Law and Social Change,* pp. 126–127.

146. Ibid.

147. Glazer, *Affirmative Discrimination,* p. 36.

148. Ibid., p. 211.

149. *Charlotte Observer,* September 15, 1968.

150. See for example Phillip J. Cooper, *Hard Judicial Choices: Federal District Court Judges and State and Local Officials* (New York: Oxford University Press, 1988), p. 100.

151. *Alexander v. Holmes County Board of Education,* 396 U.S. 19 (1969).

152. Amaker, *Civil Rights and the Reagan Administration,* p. 23.

153. As Gary Orfield reminds us, until 1964 the DOJ did not have the power to initiate cases. It could only participate by filing *amicus* briefs. However, the 1964 CRA empowered the Civil Rights Division to file new cases and to intervene in cases filed by others. See Orfield, *Must We Bus?,* p. 319; the *Washington Post,* July 4, 1969; and the *New York Times,* July 4, 1969.

154. Gary Orfield, *The Reconstruction of Southern Education: The Schools and the 1964 Civil Rights Act* (New York: Wiley, 1969), p. 1

155. See Bullock and Lamb, *Implementation of Civil Rights Policy,* p. 80; *Congres-*

sional Quarterly Weekly Report (August 28, 1971), p. 1829; Orfield, *Must We Bus?*, Chapter 9; and Leon Panetta and Peter Gall, *Bring Us Together* (Philadelphia: Lippincott, 1971).

156. Claire Guthrie, interview with Office for Civil Rights official, June 23, 1976 as quoted in Bullock an Lamb, *Implementation of Civil Rights Policy*, pp. 131–132.

157. Ibid. Also, for a excellent discussion on Title VI, see generally, Augustus J. Jones, *Law, Bureaucracy, and Politics: The Implementation of Title VI of the Civil Rights Act of 1964* (Washington, DC: University Press of America, 1982).

158. *New York Times*, July 4, 1969.

159. Rodgers and Bullock, *Law and Social Change*, p. 92.

160. See Paul M. Rilling, "Desegregation: The South Is Different," *New Republic* (May 16, 1970), pp. 17–18; and Orfield, *Must We Bus?*, p. 288.

161. "Statement about Desegregation of Elementary and Secondary Schools, March 24, 1970, *"Public Papers of the Presidents: Richard Nixon, 1970* (Washington, DC: Government Printing Office, 1971), p. 305.

162. *Swann v. Charlotte-Mecklenburg Board of Education* 402 U.S. 1 (1971).

163. The text of the speech is reprinted in the *New York Times*, March 17, 1972, p. 22. See also Cooper, *Hard Judicial Choices*, p. 112.

164. For further discussion, see Gary McDowell, *Curbing the Courts: The Constitution and the Limits of Judicial Power* (Baton Rouge: Louisiana State University Press, 1988), p. 160 and Cooper, *Hard Judicial Choices*, p. 112.

165. Failed Supreme Court nominee Judge Robert H. Bork has written in detail on the constitutionality of President Nixon's two proposals. See Robert H. Bork, *The Tempting of America: The Political Seduction of the Law* (New York: The Free Press, 1990), p. 325, especially note 15 referencing a 1972 monograph written by Bork titled *"Constitutionality of the President's Busing Proposals."*

166. See Orfield, *Must We Bus?*, p. 254.

167. Robert Bork's testimony appears in *Equal Educational Opportunities Act of 1972*, Hearings before the Subcommittee on Education of the Senate Committee on Labor and Public Welfare 92:2 (Washington DC: Government Printing Office, 1972), pp. 1312–1320; see also *Congressional Quarterly*, December 16, 1972, p. 3135; March 10, 1973, p. 513. Bork replaced Erwin Griswold in 1972 as solicitor general. Griswold had argued for "less desegregation" in numerous cases; See Orfield, *Must We Bus?*, p. 333.

168. Bullock and Lamb, *Implementation of Civil Rights Policy*, p. 49.

169. Hamilton, *Bench and the Ballot*, p. 241.

170. Ibid., pp. 241–244.

171. In 1969 President Nixon proposed to Congress that "we should establish as a national goal the provision of adequate family planning services within the next five years to all those who want them but cannot afford them." See Hyman et al., *The Abortion Question*, p. 16.

172. See Eva R. Rubin, *Abortion, Politics and the Courts: Roe v. Wade and Its Aftermath* (Westport, CT: Greenwood Press, 1982), p. 63; and Bob Woodward and Scott Armstrong, *The Brethren* (New York: Simon and Schuster, 1979), p. 230ff.

173. See Raymond Tatalovich and Byron W. Daynes, *The Politics of Abortion* (New York: Praeger, 1981), p. 196.

174. Ibid. Also, see "Population and the Growth of the American Future," the report of the Commission on Population Growth and the American Future, March 27, 1972 (Washington, DC: Government Printing Office, 1972); and Robert D. McFadden, "President Supports Repeal of State Law on Abortion," *New York Times*, May 7, 1972, p.

1.

175. "Miscellaneous Issues," *Congressional Quarterly Weekly Report*, September 2, 1972, p. 2,222.

176. See Table 3.11 (Chapter 3). For an in-depth and comparative study of the socio-economic, political, and other characteristics of the Johnson and Nixon appointees, see Sheldon Goldman, "Johnson and Nixon Appointees to the Lower Federal Courts: Some Socio-Political Perspectives," in *The Journal of Politics* 34 (1972), pp. 934–942.

177. This number is not however significantly different than Ford's equally high percentage of Protestants; i.e., both Nixon and Ford appointed significantly more Protestants than their counterparts.

178. See for example, the *New York Times*, November 3, 1968, p. II, as discussed in Sheldon Goldman's, "Judicial Appointments and the Presidential Agenda," in *The Presidency in American Politics*, p. 35; and Berman, *The New American Presidency*, p. 259; and, O'Brien, *Judicial Roulette*, pp. 20, 55.

179. Memorandum written by Tom Charles Houston a White House aide to President Nixon, on March 25, 1969, about two months after the start of the Nixon presidency. A copy of this memorandum was found by political scientist Sheldon Goldman in White House Central Files, FG 50, Box 1, Folder WHCF ExFG50, The Judicial Branch (1969–1970). Excerpts from the Nixon Presidential Materials Project are published in Goldman's "The Bush Imprint on the Judiciary: Carrying on a Tradition," *Judicature* 74 (1991), p. 294. According to Goldman, the *original* copy of the memorandum, with written comments by President Nixon, was withdrawn from the president's papers at Nixon's direction.

180. *New York Times*, October 16, 1972, p. I.

181. For example, see Sheldon Goldman, "Judicial Appointments and the Presidential Agenda," in *The Presidency in American Politics*, p. 36.

182. O'Brien, *Judicial Roulette*, p. 55.

183. Ibid.

184. Abraham, "Beneficial Advice or Presumptuous Veto?," p. 65.

185. Charles M. Lamb, "New Federalism and Civil Rights," *University of Toledo Law Review* 9 (1978), pp. 841–845.

186. But again, recall that Nixon did suffer major defeats in his Supreme Court nominations. Although he experienced little difficulty winning confirmation for Warren Burger as chief justice in 1969, he was defeated in both the Clement F. Haynsworth (a Southerner who had ruled against school desegregation and for segregated hospitals to receive federal funds) and G. Harold Carswell (also attacked by civil rights groups) nominations.

187. O'Brien, *Judicial Roulette*, p. 57.

188. Ibid.

189. James P. Pfiffner, "White House Staff versus the Cabinet: Centripetal and Centrifugal Roles," *Presidential Studies Quarterly* 16 (Fall 1986), p. 677.

190. Rowland Evans, Jr., and Robert D. Novak, *Nixon in the White House* (New York: Random House, 1971), p. 11.

191. David M. O'Brien, "The Politics of Professionalism: President Gerald R. Ford's Appointment of Justice John Paul Stevens," *Presidential Studies Quarterly* 21 (1991), pp. 103–126.

192. Gerald R. Ford, *A Time to Heal* (New York: Harper and Row, 1979), p. 235.

193. Amaker, *Civil Rights and the Reagan Administration*, pp. 24–25.

194. See the *New York Times*, excerpt, September 29, 1975, p. 21; and Jaffe, *Abortion*

Politics, p. 118.

195. Originally quoted in "Text of the 1976 Republican Platform," *Congressional Quarterly Almanac*, 1976, p. 909.

196. Ibid., p. 907.

197. Bob Rankin, "Candidates on the Issues: Abortion," *Congressional Quarterly Weekly Report*, February 28, 1976, p. 464.

198. "Labor-HEW Veto," *Congressional Quarterly Almanac*, 1976, p. 25-A. The veto was eventually overridden by both houses.

199. *New York Times*, August 20, 1975; *Education Daily*, August 21, 1975; *Washington Post*, September 17, 1975.

200. *New York Times*, February 16 and 17, 1972.

201. McDowell, *Curbing the Courts*, p. 161; and, Orfield, *Must We Bus?*, p. 267.

202. P.L. 94–206, par. 209 (1976), (amending 42 U.S.C. par. 2000d, 90 Stat. 22).

203. Amaker, *Civil Rights and the Reagan Administration*, p. 25.

204. Ibid., pp. 24–25; Bullock and Lamb, *Implementation of Civil Rights Policy*, p 49.

205. Gerald R. Ford, "Attorney General Edward H. Levi," *University of Chicago Law Review* 52 (1985), p. 284.

206. O'Brien, *Judicial Roulette*, pp. 34–35.

207. For a well developed discussion on Ford's involvement in the selection and appointment of Justice John Paul Stevens, see David M. O'Brien, "The Politics of Professionalism: President Gerald R. Ford's Appointment of Justice John Paul Stevens," *Presidential Studies Quarterly* 21 (1991), pp. 103–126.

208. See Ford, *A Time to Heal*, p. 334.

209. Interview with President Gerald R. Ford (16 February 1989) by David M. O'Brien and reported in O'Brien, "The Politics of Professionalism: President Gerald R. Ford's Appointment of Justice John Paul Stevens," p. 104.

210. Ibid.

211. Ibid., p. 108.

212. Ibid.

213. This opinion is offered by Stephen Markman, the assistant attorney general in charge of judicial selection during President Reagan's second term. See O'Brien, *Judicial Roulette*, p. 57.

214. Ibid., p. 58.

5 Presidential Agendas and Judicial Appointments: From Carter Democrats to Reagan Republicans, 1976–1988

INTRODUCTION

In contrast to their immediate predecessors, the Carter and Reagan administrations wrought significant procedural and ideological changes in the selection, screening, and nomination of federal judges. Presidents Kennedy, Johnson, Nixon, and Ford, as the previous chapter suggests, generally worked within the traditional norms and procedures of judicial selection, for example, the Justice Department, the ABA, senatorial courtesy, local political pressures, and so forth.

But, as we shall see, presidents Carter and Reagan both became much more directly involved in the selection and nomination processes, and this involvement brought about dramatic and significant changes in the nature and character of the federal judiciary.

JAMES EARL CARTER

Because I knew the power and importance of judges, I was determined to get the very best people possible to serve on the federal bench. I was also determined that women and minorities, whose destinies have so often depended upon the kind of justice our courts provided, should be included in those judgeships.
—President Carter speaking to the National Association of Women Judges, October 1980.[1]

The election of Jimmy Carter in 1976 signaled the beginning of some of the most fundamental and historic changes in the selection, screening, and nomination of federal judges in the twentieth century. While campaigning in 1976, Carter pledged that if elected he would select all federal judges on the basis of professional competence, rather than for personal or political loyalty to him, or as a reward for assistance to his personal campaign.[2] Perhaps more importantly,

Carter pledged to make the federal bench "more representative" by seeking out and by appointing women, African-Americans, and other minorities to the federal bench. Said Carter, in a December 7, 1978 press conference: "If I didn't have to get Senate confirmation of appointees, I could tell you flatly that 12 percent of my appointees would be Blacks and 3 percent would be Spanish-speaking and 40 percent would be women and so forth."[3] Carter's position was affirmed by his attorney general, Griffen Bell, who said that "Carter was prepared to appoint to the federal bench a Black, Hispanic, or a woman lawyer who was found less qualified than a White male so long as the appointee was found qualified."[4]

Let us now review President Carter's positions with respect to the key policy issues with which this study is concerned.

Abortion

On the question of abortion, the policy preference and/or expectations of the Carter presidency are the most unclear of any recent administration. Consider Carter's vacillating positions:

In 1976 [Carter] took a position supporting pro-life advocates. But . . . while Governor of Georgia, Carter had written statements in the foreword to a pro-abortion book, *Women in Need*, that have been viewed as favoring abortions. [I]n Ohio in 1976 he said he felt government should do nothing to encourage abortion, and he opposed a constitutional amendment to overturn the *Wade* decision.[5]

The 1976 Democratic National Committee platform provides a clearer indication as to that party's stance, a position that was not totally in sync with Carter's later pronouncements. The platform read: "We fully recognize the religious and ethical concerns which many Americans have on the subject of abortion. We feel, however, that it is undesirable to attempt to amend the U.S. Constitution to overturn the Supreme Court decision in this area."[6]

In an attempt to clarify his increasingly muddled position, Carter stated:

I do not support Constitutional amendments to overturn the Supreme Court ruling on abortion. However, I personally disapprove of abortion. I do not believe government should encourage abortion. The efforts of government should be directed towards minimizing abortions. If within the confines of the Supreme Court ruling, we can work out legislation to minimize abortions with better family planning, adopting procedures, and contraception for those who desire it, I would favor such a law.[7]

On the other hand, however, Carter's official "Campaign Promises Book," released by the White House in late February 1977, was conspicuous in its absence of any mention of abortion. [8] Carter was also opposed to a constitutional amendment prohibiting abortion but also opposed federal payments for abortion under Medicaid.

President Carter reiterated his opposition to federal funding ("government should do nothing to encourage abortion") for abortions against charges of "unfairness" to the poor following the Supreme Court's Medicaid cases in June 1977. In these cases, *Beal v. Doe*[9] and *Maher v. Roe*,[10] the Supreme Court ruled that neither the Constitution nor the federal Medicaid statute prevented a state from refusing to pay for "elective" abortions. President Carter responded to these decisions just weeks later, in July 1977: "Well, as you know, there are many things in life that are not fair, that wealthy people can afford and poor people can't. But I don't believe that the federal government should take action to try to make those opportunities exactly equal, particularly when there is a moral factor involved."[11]

Another of Carter's repeated concerns involved the possible misuse, or reuse, of abortion as a contraceptive measure. At a press conference in Yazoo City, Mississippi, on July 21, 1977, President Carter told reporters: "I'm afraid that to take a very permissive stand on abortions, paying for them—which puts them in the same category, roughly, as other contraceptive means—will be an encouragement to depend on abortions to prevent pregnancy." Later, at the same conference, Carter charged that "it is very disturbing how many of the recipients of Federal payments for abortion in the past have been repeaters!"[12]

During Carter's unsuccessful bid for a second term, the 1980 Democratic party platform provided little clarification of Carter's vacillating abortion views. In fact, the 1980 Democratic platform was as strong in support for abortion as the Republican platform was in opposition to it. The Democratic platform stated in part:

We fully recognize the religious and ethical concerns which many Americans have about abortion. We also recognize the belief of many Americans that a woman has a right to choose whether and when to have a child.

The Democratic Party supports the 1973 Supreme Court decision on abortion rights as the law of the land and opposes any constitutional amendment to restrict or overturn that decision.[13]

On balance, it appears that Carter's policy positions were designed for a broad appeal. That is, it would appear that Carter was trying to please both pro-choice and pro-life advocates. Next we look at Carter's policy objectives and expectations on key civil rights issues.[14]

Civil Rights: An Overview of Carter's Policy Objectives and Expectations

The fundamental thrust of the Carter administration's developments in the area of civil rights was in making enforcement mechanisms more effective, particularly for enforcing equal opportunity laws and regulations, and in prohibiting discrimination in federally assisted programs.[15] An essential element of this enforcement emphasis, as indicated above, included the appointment of women,

African-Americans, and other minorities to positions where they might aggressively promote and enforce such laws. In January 1980, Carter stated in his final state of the union address that "the goal of the effort was to restructure the civil rights enforcement machinery to allow the government to focus on large-scale enforcement of the civil rights laws."[16]

In addition to promising unprecedented numbers of African-American and female judges, Carter's actions included the total reorganization of the equal opportunity programs under his 1978 Reorganization Plan No. 1. Under this plan, the Equal Employment Opportunity Commission (EEOC) became primarily responsible for nearly all federal efforts combating employment discrimination. In keeping with Carter's efforts to diversify the enforcement authority, for the first time since the commission was established in 1964, it was chaired by an African-American woman, Eleanor Holmes Norton.

Carter also attempted to diversify enforcement authority personnel within the Justice Department. A case in point was the appointment of Drew Days III, an African-American, as assistant attorney general for civil rights, in other words, head of the civil rights division. Days' presence, although only accompanied by the "halfhearted" support of Griffin Bell, has been credited with seizing the "leadership reins" with "innovative lawsuits designed to carry out the affirmative action goals of federal law in housing, . . . voting, . . . employment, . . . and education."[17] Thus, overall, Carter attempted to increase civil rights enforcement, in part by diversifying the enforcement authority, including the federal judiciary.[18]

Affirmative Action

To gain yet an additional understanding of President Carter's commitment to affirmative action, it is instructive to look to the 1980 Democratic party platform:

An effective affirmative action program is an essential component of our commitment to expanding civil rights protections. The federal government must be a model for private employers, making special efforts in recruitment, training, and promotion to aid minority Americans in overcoming both historic patterns and the historic burdens of discrimination.

We call on the public and private sectors to live up to and enforce . . . affirmative action requirements.[19]

Nonetheless, some did question Carter's overall commitment to such civil rights, particularly in regard to the Supreme Court's 1978 *Bakke* decision.[20] As former HEW Secretary Joseph A. Califano put it: "I never heard Carter speak privately with the burning conviction, much less the passion, of Lyndon Johnson about civil rights or race in America."[21] Califano was specifically critical of Carter's "noncommittal" stance during the debates of the *Bakke* case within the administration. Califano observed, "Perhaps speaking out on civil rights was just not his style."[22] In Carter's defense, this challenge is addressed and put into perspective by historian Edward R. Kantowicz. Kantowicz explains that the *Bakke* case during Carter's administration was "not amenable to the 'fire in the belly' [of Lyndon Johnson]; and that the last thing it needed was a president shouting slogans from the barricades. It is far easier to champion a social revolution than to administer its consequences."[23]

Overall, however, it is important to note that civil rights enforcement was strengthened during the Carter administration through expanding the powers of the EEOC. Indeed, as a result of a major reorganization in 1978, the Carter administration created a "Super-EEOC" with both new leadership and new policies, including jurisdiction over the federal government.[24]

School Desegregation

The issue of school desegregation was not an administrative priority for the Carter leadership. Further, the desegregation issue—like the abortion issue—received confusing and at times unclear direction from the Carter administration. This confusion was equally prevalent in the 1976 Democratic platform, which glowingly endorsed integrated education but was less than enthusiastic about the use of busing to achieve that end. The platform read in part:

Mandatory transportation of students beyond their neighborhoods for the purpose of desegregation remains a tool of last resort. . . . The Democratic Party will be an active ally of those communities which seek to enhance the quality as well as the integration of educational opportunities. We encourage a variety of other measures, including the redrawing of attendance lines, pairing of schools, use of the "magnet" school concept, strong fair housing enforcement, and other techniques for the achievement of racial and economic integration.[25]

During the whole of Carter's administration, the future of school desegregation was quite uncertain. This was somewhat reflective of the president's position itself. Political scientist Gary Orfield, for example, reports that Carter "sent Congress neither negative nor positive proposals; he said nothing about the issue."[26] Orfield summarizes that Carter: (1) strongly supported integrated education, at times referring to HEW's enforcement of the 1964 CRA as the "best thing that ever happened to the South"; (2) repeatedly stressed his personal opposition to court-ordered busing; but (3) pledged to oppose any antibusing amendments to the Constitution and to support the desegregation orders of federal courts.[27]

These sentiments were also spelled out in the 1980 Democratic party platform, which stressed a commitment to "support programs aimed at achieving communities integrated both in terms of race and economic class through constitutional means." The platform stated: "We oppose efforts to undermine the Supreme Court's historic mandate of school desegregation, and we support affirmative action goals to overturn patterns of discrimination in education and employment."[28] More specifically: "We encourage redrawing of attendance lines, pairing of schools, utilizing the "magnet school concept" as much as possible, and enforcing fair housing standards. Mandatory transportation of students beyond their neighborhoods for the purpose of desegregation remains a judicial tool of last resort."[29]

But these positions were somewhat incongruous with Carter's immediate and sharply criticized selection of both Griffin Bell as attorney general and Peter Flaherty as deputy attorney general. Indeed, perhaps it is advantageous to look briefly at these nominees' views on school desegregation as an index to Carter's policy objectives as well as his expectations from his appointed Justice Department officials.

In the first instance, Griffin Bell's previous record on school integration was negative, to say the least. For example, one cannot overlook the fact that Bell had helped to develop Georgia's "massive resistance" laws to resist racial integration in public schools—laws that permitted the closing of public schools to avoid integration. Bell had also served on a state commission that "denounced" the Supreme Court's 1954 *Brown* decision."[30] Carter's nomination of Bell as attorney general engendered criticism and controversy. For example, Senator William Proxmire charged that he saw "nothing in [Bell's] record to show that he would be the kind of champion of civil rights that the principal law-enforcement official . . . must become."[31]

This situation was not helped at all by Carter's selection of Pittsburgh mayor, Peter Flaherty, as deputy attorney general. Like Bell's nomination, the Flaherty nomination also generated criticism from civil rights advocates as his record, particularly on school desegregation, was similarly negative. For example, after school desegregation was ordered by the Human Rights Commission in Pittsburgh in 1971, Flaherty responded: "this community is against it" and it "cannot be enforced." Later, addressing the Pittsburgh school board on a busing order, Flaherty commented: "The people of this City have made it clear that they want their neighborhood schools preserved . . . the safety and well-being of their children cannot be overcome by any social reform."[32] Flaherty's, as well as Bell's, positions were however placed in perspective by White House Press Secretary Jody Powell's defense of the Flaherty nomination. Speaking about the criticisms of Flaherty made by civil rights groups, Powell explained: "The President is aware of those feelings. And as I understand it, that opposition is based on Flaherty's opposition to busing, a position the President shares and made very clear during the campaign."[33]

Indeed, during the Carter administration, numerous legislative proposals were introduced to curb the use of busing. For example, in 1977 Congress prohibited HEW from requiring schools to use busing to promote racial balance. However in 1980 a busing prohibition directed at the Department of Justice passed both houses of Congress but was removed when President Carter threatened to veto it.[34] This position, of course, was consistent with Carter's vacillating stance on other controversial issues as well, including abortion rights.

Altogether, given President Carter's mixed and at times unclear views on these issues, let us now examine whether and/or to what extent he attempted to translate these policy objectives into judicial appointments in terms of the nature and type of person eventually appointed to a district court judgeship during his administration.

The Setting: Carter's Opportunity

When Jimmy Carter came to the presidency, there were 400 authorized federal district judgeships (see Table 2.5). However, in 1978 Congress passed the Omnibus Judgeship Act of 1978, which created 152 new judgeships and required the president to establish a "comprehensive plan for selecting judges."[35] As a result, Carter issued Executive Order No. 12097 which encouraged—but did not require—Senators to establish nominating commissions on the appointment of federal judges. For the most part, it was the responsibility of the attorney general to supervise and assure minority representation among the nominees.[36]

Carter appointed more minority and women judges than all previous presidents combined.[37] As indicated in Table 3.11, Carter appointed 202 federal district court judges. Of this number, twenty-nine were women (women comprised over 14 percent of his total appointments and included six African-American women); twenty-eight African-Americans (close to 14 percent of his total appointments), and fourteen Latinos (close to 7 percent of his total appointments). Still, Carter's appointees were overwhelmingly white and male.

Further data in Table 3.11 on the socioeconomic characteristics of Carter's judicial appointments indicate that nine were Republican (4.5 percent); six were Independents; twenty-four were Jewish (the largest proportion of any president);[38] and over half (57.4 percent) attended state-supported colleges or universities. Relatively few of Carter's appointees held political or governmental posts at the time of appointment. However, there was a larger proportion of Carter appointees with previous party activism (60.9 percent) than for each of the preceding three administrations *and* the succeeding Reagan administration.

Overall, by the end of Carter's term, the proportion of female judges on the federal bench had risen from 1 percent to nearly 7 percent; for African-Americans, this figure rose from 4 percent to nearly 9 percent.[39] Of course these proportions were still well below these groups' representation in the general population; but even so, it is clear that Carter's appointments significantly increased the representation of women and African-Americans in the federal judiciary.

SELECTION, SCREENING, AND NOMINATION UNDER CARTER

Jimmy Carter campaigned as a reformer and was viewed by many as a "new broom" that would sweep Washington clean.[40] Part of this new broom approach included changing both the racial and gender composition of the federal judiciary. To realize a more representative judiciary, Carter worked in conjunction with the National Bar Association—a national organization of African-American lawyers—and the Federation of Women Lawyers.[41]

Carter's unprecedented success in diversifying the federal judiciary was apparent in the 1980 Democratic party platform:

More women, Blacks and Hispanics have been appointed to federal judgeships during the Carter Administration than during all previous Administrations in history.

Of the 39 women federal judges, 35 have been Carter appointees; of the 38 Black federal judges, 19 have been Carter appointees; of the 14 Hispanic judges, 5 have been Carter appointees.

This record must be continued. The Democratic Party is committed to continue and strengthen the policy of appointing more women and minorities to federal positions at all levels including the Supreme Court.[42]

In addition to Carter's attempt to diversify the judiciary, a significant innovation of his administration with respect to the selection of federal judges was the institution of "merit" or nominating commissions.

The District Judge Nominating Commissions

At the outset, following Carter's Executive Order No. 12079, only about half of the states (twenty-two) created commissions; by 1979 this number increased to thirty-three. In the end, it is reported that every state with one or more Democratic senators, except one, did establish commissions.[43] In those states with Republican senators, in every instance they agreed to a commission system.[44]

Although the nature and operation of the merit commissions have been thoroughly discussed at length in numerous studies[45] and need not be repeated here, it may prove useful to discuss the political consequences that flowed from the use of such commissions; in other words, the extent to which these commissions influenced the role and function of courts in the interest conflict and how they changed the politics of judicial selection.

Overall, the commissions relied heavily on lengthy and detailed questionnaires.[46] In general, these nominating commissions were widely criticized and remained the focus of intense debate throughout the Carter administration years.[47] For example, the commissions were criticized for being highly partisan—an estimated 85 percent of their members were active Democrats. Senator Edward Kennedy, for example, exercised sole authority in choosing his nine member commission and senators Nunn and Talmadge (both of Georgia) chose their entire seventeen-member panel jointly.[48] Thus, many charged that these commissions neither established "merit" selection nor depoliticized the process. Members of the circuit judge commissions, for example, were generally selected by the White House staff; these were individuals who had worked in Carter's campaign and were familiar with the judicial philosophy Carter wanted. Yet other members were selected from lists that were developed at the Department of Justice.

Most criticisms of the merit commissions centered around two primary issues. *First* was the criticism that the character of the commissions among the various states varied widely. In those "states with Republican senators, commissions were more bipartisan; in states with Democratic senators, the commissions sometimes exercised considerable independence, sometimes they were simply a facade for nominating the choices of the senators."[49] Given how deeply individual senators cherish the "right" of senatorial courtesy, we can readily imagine the difficulties one might encounter from the home-state senator. Attorney General Griffin Bell recalls this dilemma: "We set out to convince the senators who were Democrats, and who were expecting the district court patronage, to establish commissions of their own on a state level to open up the process and consider more applicants than would ordinarily be considered. This was difficult because many of the senators had lists of their own and in some instances had been waiting for a long time to make appointments of friends and supporters to district judgeships."[50]

Yet a *second* major criticism of the commissions was that potential appointees were routinely asked about their views regarding controversial and hotly debated legal issues. In a 1980 study (though focusing on circuit judge nominating commissions) for the American Judicature Society, researchers found that: "Both panel members and candidates reported that applicants were questioned about nine contemporary social issues. . . . The four areas which received the most attention were the Equal Rights Amendment, affirmative action, first amendment freedoms and defendant's rights."[51] Other social policy issues that judicial candidates were questioned on included abortion, forced busing, economic regulation, capital punishment, and pending U.S. Supreme Court decisions.[52]

Criticisms about such questioning procedures came from both sides of the aisle. For example, Attorney General Griffin Bell (a conservative Democrat), Deputy Attorney General Michael Egan (a registered Republican), and Assistant Attorney General Daniel Meador, all voiced opposition to such questioning. In Bell's words, it "politicized the process badly. I don't believe that you should ask a judge his views [on specific issues] because he is likely to have to rule on that."[53] As Judge Rees (when he was a law professor) cautioned in 1983: "Indeed, the very reason that future promises of judicial votes are improper—that each case has its own facts, that litigants have a right to expect the Court to consider the briefs and arguments of counsel, that new arguments can be made and old arguments become more persuasive in the light of experience—make it most unlikely that a reasonable person would mistake a statement of present opinion for a promise."[54]

In addition to opposing philosophical questioning, Bell similarly opposed actively recruiting more African-Americans and women to the bench and as a result confronted opposition from the White House staff seeking to influence the selection of judges.[55] But nevertheless, and as described earlier, perhaps the most significant change in the composition of the federal bench was produced by the Carter administration's affirmative action policies.

To be sure, during the Carter administration the proportion of women judges on the federal bench rose from about 1 percent to 7 percent and African-Americans from about 4 percent to 9 percent. But it was not easy finding women and minorities using traditional procedures. As one scholar studying Carter's appointments to the lower federal court put it:

White male candidates were generally recruited for judgeships after having traveled a well worn path established by a time honored selection process. They enjoyed long years of legal experience, prestigious courtroom admissions and, for the most part, highly successful practices. Such prominent and successful private practices were not likely to be fertile grounds for locating viable non-traditional judgeship candidates. Non-whites, however, were recruited from sitting judgeships or, more generally, from among those who had gained some public prominence in their legal careers through their judicial experience. Non-whites, particularly males, were most likely to have had legal aid backgrounds and to have served in predominantly criminal practices. . . . In seeking women for the bench, recruitment authorities turned disproportionately to the law schools where several women attorneys had gained prominence as academicians.[56]

Additionally, in an effort to confront senatorial courtesy, Carter requested three to five recommendations for each vacancy. But this request was not always respected. As former Judiciary Committee chairman, James Eastland, told Carter's attorney general, Griffin Bell: "I'll hand you a slip of paper with one name on it, and that'll be the judge."[57]

Carter, the Attorney General, and Judicial Selection

Attorney General Bell assumed a more active role in judicial selection than most of his immediate predecessors; particularly he was more active than former Attorney General Edward Levi. Attorney General Griffin Bell recalls that early on, Carter held a group meeting with several prominent black leaders from the South, including Dr. Martin Luther King, Sr. and Mrs. Coretta Scott King, at the White House. At this meeting, said Bell, Carter told the group that he was "instructing me [Bell] to immediately set out to find at least one black federal judge for each of the states of the old Confederacy." "This goal," concluded Bell, "was eventually reached except for Mississippi and Virginia."[58]

By executive order (No. 12097)[59] President Carter enhanced the role and influence of the office of the Attorney General by directing him to "make available" suggested guidelines for establishing the nominating commissions, and to recommend to the president persons who were "qualified" to be district judges.[60]

Associate Attorney General Mike Egan was primarily responsible for gathering the data on each nominee. Egan and his staff read the FBI file[61] and the Internal Revenue Service investigation report for each nominee. After Egan,

Bell, who himself was a former federal judge, is reported to have personally read *each* candidate's file including reports from the FBI and ABA. Apparently, Bell also gave the National Bar Association (the African-American lawyers organization) the opportunity to respond to each nominee.[62]

Following the attorney general's review, Bell would then submit the names to a committee consisting of the White House counsel, Robert Lipshutz, the congressional liaison staff member, Frank Moore, the White House press secretary, Jody Powell, and Hamilton Jordon (chief of staff).[63] Bell would then submit the recommendation to the president along with views of the committee. A final requirement under Carter was that all candidates had to undergo a physical examination before their names could be passed on to the Senate by the president.

Carter and the ABA

To an extent, the influence of the ABA was diminished because of Carter's circuit nominating commissions; however, ABA representatives contend that as a whole they still maintained "most favored status."[64] Yet, obviously, some changes did occur. In the final analysis, it seems clear that the ABA must bend to administrations in order to preserve its role in the selection process. This acquiescent posture was realized even more evident during the Carter years. In response to Carter's affirmative action policy, for example, the ABA changed its requirement that nominees have fifteen years of prior legal experience.

Attorney General Griffin Bell also convinced the ABA to reduce its standard to twelve years so that the administration "could name more blacks and women, who, because of professional career opportunities, tended to have less legal experience than the traditional white nominee."[65] But even this revised ABA requirement was flexible. For example, eleven out of thirteen Carter nominees with less than twelve years of legal experience were given qualified or better ratings. And these eleven included four females (one of whom was African-American), two African-American males, and three Latino males.[66]

A member of the ABA Standing Committee during the Carter administration stated:

We were quite concerned about the criteria not having been met by women and/or minorities because of the realities of professional discrimination. There were a number of women and minority candidates that we found "qualified" despite the lack of twelve years at the bar. Less experience was sufficient in some women, but not in some white males.[67]

ABA ratings themselves were at times flexible. For example, Carter's Attorney General Griffin Bell noted that "in over 250 judicial appointments . . . the ABA initially found only ten or twelve unqualified and subsequently gave five or six of them qualified ratings."[68] For instance, in response to a controversy that resulted from a not qualified rating being given to two African-American Alabama attorneys nominated for the district courts, the ABA in 1980 modified its procedures again. Consequently, since 1980, when a committee member determines that a nominee is not qualified, a second circuit representative is assigned to investigate that nominee.

Elliot Slotnick has suggested that "one could argue that the nominating panels cut at the heart of the ABA committee's credibility if it opposed a nominee the panels had approved."[69] To the ABA's defense, Brooksley Born, the first woman to serve on the ABA Standing Committee (1977–1980) and the first female chair (1981–83), concluded that:

In the past, we were used more often as a screening commission. Now the nominating commissions do that. We are now a post-selection check. We continue to play a significant role in the in-depth investigations that the nominating commissions cannot do.[70]

On balance, clearly the ABA Standing Committee experienced a fundamental shift in power as a result of Carter's nominating commissions. However, it still retained "most favored status" among outside interests participating in the politics of the screening and confirmation process.

Carter and Judicial Selection: A Summation

Overall, judicial selection under Carter was more concerned with appointing more women and minorities as judges rather than focusing on the policy views of the individual nominees put forward. As explained by Deputy Attorney General Michael Egan, "we never talked about whether this guy would support the policies of the president; there was no going into ideological or thought processes."[71]

Indeed, at times Carter seemed to exhibit tunnel-vision with regard to diversifying the federal bench, largely at the expense of ideological concerns. For example, one of Carter's African-American female appointees, Court of Appeals Judge Cornelia Kennedy (Michigan) had a "startling" and "uniform" record of refusal to rule in favor of civil rights. [72] But perhaps this was part of Carter's leadership style. Political scientist Robert Strong writes that Carter was "inclined to deal with issues on their merits without drawing connections to broad themes or political symbols. He was a non-ideological politician."[73] Even so, as Table 3.11 clearly reveals, the Carter administration—like all others—rewarded the party faithful.

In general, however, it is difficult to pigeonhole Carter's judicial appointments to the district courts as motivated by partisan or policy agendas. Clearly they were a combination of both. Others have reached similar conclusions. "[T]he Carter Administration looked at lower court appointments as furthering the partisan agenda, which for a Deep South Democrat in the White House meant aggressive recruitment of blacks, women, and Hispanics regardless of their philosophical or ideological orientation."[74] This suggests that for practical political reasons Carter at times was willing to roll the dice on appointments, assuming that his judicial nominees would also perform along the same policy lines as those he promoted. The extent to which Carter's judicial appointments did perform along the lines of Carter's policy agenda is discussed in Chapter 7.

At this point, however, we can say that Carter's direct involvement and concern with district court appointments set a precedent that was both followed and enhanced by his successor, Ronald Reagan. Indeed, as we shall see, Reagan openly and intentionally sought to utilize judicial appointments to promote his legal philosophy and policy agenda.

RONALD REAGAN

> Reagan's regime wanted judges to undo much of the constitutional jurisprudence of the last half-century affecting civil rights.[75]

"No administration" said one Reagan official, "has thought longer and more deeply about the law since that of FDR, and we have thought [about it] more deeply than that administration."[76] This view has been reflected in a number of significant studies. For example, Walter F. Murphy, reflecting on Reagan's judicial strategy, concluded that the Reagan presidency sought judges who would "undo much of the constitutional jurisprudence of the last half-century affecting civil rights."[77] Similarly, others have written that during the Reagan administrations, the "courts were seen as centers of policy-making activity on social issues important to the administration—abortion, prayer in the public schools, busing for the purpose of school desegregation, affirmative action at the workplace, the rights of criminal defendants, [and] sexual privacy."[78] Indeed, President Reagan is on record favoring amendments to overturn the Court's school prayer and abortion decisions.[79]

Along this line, Murphy also suggests that the Reagan administration favored a judicial philosophy that came close to being a parody on legal positivism; that is, "where individual rights were concerned, judges should follow the narrowest possible interpretation of the constitutional document's plain words as modified—usually restricted by what the judges imagined to be the original intent."[80] More specifically, Murphy writes that the Reagan White House "adamantly opposed earlier decisions of the Court that: recognized constitutional rights to privacy and abortion; broadly construed rights of the criminally accused; read the Constitution and federal statutes as mandating and/or permitting affirmative action . . . construed the antiestablishment clause to forbid prayers in public schools."[81]

In the main, scholars agree that President Reagan turned to the courts as a way of achieving his policy objectives during his second term. This shift resulted from his first term failures to get Congress to totally dismantle existing rulings on abortion and school desegregation, or to pass a proposal for a school prayer amendment. As one former Reagan official said: "It became evident after the first term that there was no way to make legislative gains in many areas of social and civil rights. The President has to do it by changing the jurisprudence."[82] Similarly, the *National Journal* reported in 1985 that: "Conservatives are gearing up to battle over what many of them hope will be President Reagan's most lasting legacy: reshaping the federal judiciary. . . . [G]rowing congressional opposition to the conservatives' agenda has increased pressure for 'friendly' judges to promote the Reagan Revolution in the legal sphere."[83] And just months afterward, *Congressional Quarterly* reported that "conservative groups are pressing the administration to populate the federal bench with judges who share their ideology."[84]

But some thought that President Reagan was "straying from the campaign path."[85] One conservative spokesman, Richard Viguerie, charged that the administration "was being pushed toward the political center by the Bush factions."[86] It seems apparent that Reagan's strategy could lead to various interpretations. For example, Samuel Kernell stated that President Reagan opted to "go public." In other words, "[I]nstead of pushing Congress on constitutional amendments to ban abortion and permit school prayer, during the first term [Reagan] did little more than periodically pay lip service to these causes with well-staged speeches at conservative gatherings."[87] Still other scholars suggested that Republican issues such as school prayer, crime, and abortion were neglected so as to avoid the Carter mistake of sending Congress too much too soon."[88]

Thus, Reagan chose to attack these issues via judicial appointments.[89] Why? It was because Reagan, more than any of his immediate predecessors understood that the function of the judiciary is to resolve the interest conflict. And what better way to influence those decisions than placing on the court individuals who shared and would promote his legal policy views? Let us now look directly at President Reagan's policy positions on the various interests with which this study is concerned.

Abortion

I don't think that womanhood should be considering murder a privilege.

—Ronald Reagan[90]

The Reagan administration declared war on both the method and result of the Supreme Court's *Roe v. Wade* decision. In stark contrast to Carter, Reagan's position on abortion was strikingly clear.[91] Reagan referred explicitly to the Supreme Court's landmark *Roe v. Wade* decision as "an abuse of power as bad as the transgressions of Watergate and the bribery on Capitol Hill."[92] To emphasize Reagan's opposition to abortion, the Reagan campaign staff developed and circulated policy position handouts to the press under the committee's imprimatur, *Reagan for President*. One of these press releases read:

I personally believe that interrupting a pregnancy is the taking of human life and can be justified only in self-defense—that is when a mother's life is in danger. . . . I support enactment of a constitutional amendment to restore protection of the unborn child's right to life. . . . In the meantime, I am opposed to using federal tax money to pay for abortions in cases where the life of the mother is in no danger.[93]

These sentiments were later set forth in the 1980 Republican party platform:

There can be no doubt that the question of abortion, despite the complex nature of its various issues, is ultimately concerned with equality of rights under the law. While we recognize differing views on this question among Americans in general—and in our own Party—we affirm our support of a constitutional amendment to restore protection of the right to life for unborn children. We also support the Congressional efforts to restrict the use of taxpayers' dollars for abortion. We protest the Supreme Court's intrusion into the family structure through its denial of the parents' obligation and right to guide their minor children.[94]

These antiabortion sentiments were repeatedly supported in both the 1980 and later 1984 Republican party platforms, which both pledged to appoint those "whose judicial philosophy is characterized by the highest regard for protecting the rights of law-abiding citizens. [This] is consistent with the belief in the decentralization of the federal government and efforts to return decision-making power to state and local elected officials [and those] who respect traditional family values and the sanctity of innocent human life."[95]

Many of Reagan's other comments were also very direct, rather than cloaked in the traditional political rhetoric of the Carter years. Reagan expressed his antiabortion sentiments frequently and explicitly promised to appoint only antiabortion federal judges.[96] For example, regarding his opposition to the *Roe v. Wade* decision, Reagan commented, "I don't feel that I'm trying to do something that is taking a privilege away from womanhood, because I don't think that womanhood should be considering murder a privilege."[97]

In another example, at a 1982 convention of the Knights of Columbus, Reagan stated directly that "the national tragedy of abortion on demand must end."[98] Reagan also made use of opportunities to speak at the 1985 and 1986 annual public protest demonstrations against the Supreme Court's *Roe v. Wade* decision. More concretely, various federal agencies during the Reagan years reduced their backing for abortion programs.[99]

President Reagan's desire to dismantle standing abortion policies via judicial action was well known. In 1986, an antiabortionist minister publicly recommended prayers for Supreme Court Justice William Brennan's death so that President Reagan could replace him with a pro-life judge.[100] Although Reagan's articulated strategies were not this perverse, he did attempt to quash abortion rights by intervening in litigation as amicus curiae. In 1985, for example, the Reagan administration—through the Justice Department—filed an amicus curiae brief in *Thornburgh v. American College of Obstetricians and Gynecologists*.[101] This brief supported the unsuccessful statutory attempts of Illinois and

Pennsylvania to restrict abortion as well as petition the Supreme Court to reconsider and overturn *Roe v. Wade*.[102] Indeed, in this brief, acting Solicitor General Charles Fried asked the Supreme Court to reconsider the *Roe* decision "and on reconsideration abandon it."[103] Yet another part of the solicitor general's brief included the following language: "The courts of appeals betrayed unabashed hostility to state regulation of abortion and ill-disguised suspicion of state legislators' motives," and *Roe v. Wade* had "no moorings in the text of our Constitution or in familiar constitutional doctrine."[104]

Moreover, it is clear that the Reagan administration attempted to follow up on this policy and partisan stance when screening nominees. Dennis Mullins, a Reagan Justice Department official indicated: "we ask [potential judges] whether they thought Justice Blackmun's analysis was sound in [*Roe v. Wade*]. If they said yes, that would give us real concern about their judicial philosophy."[105]

Religious Liberty

I will support a constitutional amendment restoring the right to hold voluntary prayer in our public schools.

—Ronald Reagan[106]

From the commencement of the 1980 presidential election, Reagan's position on school prayer was also clear and forthright. In 1980, Reagan stated directly: "I will support a constitutional amendment restoring the right to hold voluntary prayer in our public schools."[107] In a separate speech during the 1980 campaign, Reagan promised that he would ask the Congress to pass tuition tax credit legislation to aid parents who send their children to nonpublic elementary, secondary, and postsecondary schools. Reagan also declared that he had "a great many questions about evolution" and thought "that the biblical story of creation should be taught as well as Darwinian theory."[108]

These promises were not idle campaign rhetoric. For example, on May 17, 1982, Reagan did present to Congress a proposed constitutional amendment to permit voluntary and vocal school prayer in the nation's public schools. However, despite Reagan's staunch support, the first attempt to bring the issue of school prayer to the Senate floor was defeated.[109]

Nevertheless, the Reagan administration continued to express a desire to influence the courts to adopt a softer line on questions of church and state. For example, in 1984, Attorney General William French Smith made clear the Reagan Administration's unwavering position. Said Attorney General Smith: "We would like to see the Court re-assess the consequences of its own establishment clause precedents and the lower courts' increasing tendency to be hostile toward religion. If not soon, at some later point, the Court may wish to decide that a subtler analysis of the establishment clause is in order, one that encourages the state to take an attitude of—in the Court's own words—benevolent neutrality toward religion."[110]

Affirmative Action

President Reagan firmly opposed affirmative action. More directly, Reagan criticized and attacked affirmative action geared toward achieving racial balance in the workplace. This retrenchment of affirmative action could be seen in several areas; for example, policy guidelines in the bureaucracy, legislation, and legal challenges.

The signals of affirmative action retrenchment were sounded by Reagan clearly during the 1980 campaign. Yet another of the Reagan campaign press releases provided the following: "We must not allow this noble concept . . . of equal opportunity to be distorted into federal guidelines or quotas which require race, ethnicity or sex—rather than ability and qualifications—to be the principal factor in *hiring and education*. Instead, we should make a bold commitment to economic growth, to increase jobs and education for all Americans" (emphasis added).[111]

Examples of Reagan's attacks on affirmative action run the gamut. In August 1981, for example, Reagan's secretary of labor, Raymond Donovan, issued new guidelines for the Office of Federal Contract Compliance (OFCCP) programs, effectively limiting its jurisdiction to government contractors with 250 or more employees and a federal contract of one million dollars or more.[112] Donovan himself admitted that these new guidelines would exempt almost 75 percent of all federal contractors from affirmative action requirements.[113] And, later that month on August 20, William Bradford Reynolds, head of the Justice Department's Civil Rights Division, announced that "in the area of civil rights he would restrict remedies to the aggrieved party, rather than impose remedies to benefit an entire class of persons."[114]

Consistent with Reagan's personal opposition to affirmative action, the Reagan administration argued that courts should strictly scrutinize all race-based laws or policies. In fact, acting through William Bradford Reynolds, the Reagan administration attacked affirmative action repeatedly. A case in point, following the Supreme Court's 1984 attack on racial quotas in *Firefighters v. Stotts*,[115] which Reagan's first solicitor general Rex E. Lee called "one of the greatest victories of all time,"[116] Reynolds affirmed that he would "order the review and assess the validity of hundreds of court-ordered affirmative action programs where the courts had employed racial quotas and goals in hiring to effectuate appropriate relief."[117] Earlier, in 1981, Reynolds had made known his intention to attempt to persuade the Supreme Court to overrule *United Steel Workers of America v. Weber* (1979),[118] which effectively upheld Kaiser's voluntary affirmative action plan.[119]

There is also evidence to support the argument that Reynolds at times was responsible for *initiating* action against affirmative action in line with Reagan's broad suggestions, despite the fact that the president himself was generally unaware of many specifics. For instance, in a December 17, 1981 press conference, Reagan admitted his lack of knowledge about the *Weber* case. When asked by the press about the case, the president replied, "If it is something that simply allows the training and bringing up so that more opportunities are there for them in voluntary agreements between the union and management, I can't see any fault with that. I'm for that." But the president was clearly off base, particularly since the president's response followed Reynolds' admission to the press that the Justice Department was actively looking for a case to overturn *Weber*. Immediately following this blunder, the White House issued a "clarification," explaining that the president did not "disagree" with the Justice Department on the case and that both found "this racial quota unacceptable."[120]

Nonetheless, these actions clearly reflected the administration's hostility to affirmative action generally. The administration's posture could also be seen in other actions, including the appointments of two antiaffirmative action African-Americans: Clarence Pendleton to the head the Civil Rights Commission, and Clarence Thomas, now Justice Thomas, to head the Equal Employment Opportunities Commission (EEOC). Pendleton's appointment, for example, was clearly strategic and altogether supportive of the president's position. Indeed Pendleton stated directly that "affirmative action with its goals and preferences is a bankrupt policy because it often leads to an emphasis on statistical parity rather than equal opportunity."[121]

In general, as political scientist Michael Preston put it, "No administration since the inception of the affirmative action program . . . has reacted more negatively to it [affirmative action] than has the Reagan Administration."[122]

School Desegregation

Those bastards just want to bring in the busing issue. . . . They're probably entitled to intervene, but let's make them jump through every hoop.
—William Bradford Reynolds[123]

Ronald Reagan's opposition to school busing and school desegregation generally has been well chronicled. For example, Reagan's position on school desegregation during his 1976 campaign against Ford for the GOP nomination included a constitutional amendment and antibusing legislation. These sentiments were also reflected in Republican party platforms[124] and subsequent presidential campaigns. For example, during the 1980 presidential campaign, Reagan and the Republican party leadership attacked the Carter administration and Democratically controlled Congress for launching "one fad after another" with respect to education. "The result has been a shocking drop in student performance, lack of basics in the classroom, forced busing, teacher strikes . . . amoral indoctrination."[125] In regard to forced busing to achieve school desegregation, another of the 1980 "Reagan for President" press releases made Reagan's position equally very clear: "It is time we removed control of our schools from the courts and federal government and returned it to local school

boards where it belongs. I [oppose] court-ordered compulsory busing."[126]
Similarly, the 1980 Republican party platform stated:

We condemn the forced busing of school children to achieve arbitrary racial quotas. Busing has been a prescription for disaster, blighting whole communities across the land with its divisive impact. It has failed to improve the quality of education, while diverting funds from programs that could make a difference between success and failure for the poor, the disabled, and minority children.

We must halt forced busing and get on with the education of all our children.[127]

These issues were in fact eventually acted upon in 1982. For example, the Department of Justice sent a letter through Attorney General William French Smith in support of a bill, sponsored by Senator Jesse Helms (R-NC), and Senator J. Bennett Johnston (D-LA), that sought to remove federal court jurisdiction over busing.[128] Indeed, with the support of the Reagan administration, conservatives in the Senate did approve—although the House of Representatives failed to enact—legislation that would (1) ban the Justice Department from asking judges to require busing, (2) prohibit federal judges from using busing as a remedy, and (3) allow districts that were then implementing court-ordered busing to have a rehearing on that issue.[129]

As with Reagan's assault on affirmative action, a good amount of Reagan's attack on school desegregation was spearheaded by William Bradford Reynolds, head of the Civil Rights Division at the Justice Department. In addition to criticizing nearly every significant Supreme Court decision in favor of school desegregation,[130] Reynolds also promoted tactics and plans that called for lengthy delays. For example, when African-American parents in Charleston, South Carolina, asked the NAACP Legal Defense Fund to enter their desegregation litigation, Reynolds instructed his staff to oppose the intervention, saying, "Those bastards just want to bring in the busing issue. . . . They're probably entitled to intervene, but let's make them jump through every hoop."[131]

Reynolds is frequently reported to have summed up his position on school desegregation with the promise that "future enforcement policies will be aimed" at remedying "substantial disparities in the tangible components of education" between minority and white children, a statement that one writer has called a "latter day restatement of separate but equal."[132]

In addition, the Reagan administration also sought to stifle desegregation cases initiated prior to Reagan's presidency. The strategy was explained as follows: knowing that the government wins most of the cases in which it takes a "friend of the Court" position,[133] the Reagan administration opted to settle out of court most of the desegregation suits against Southern state higher education systems that Carter had initiated.[134]

Voting/Elections

We support the repeal of those restrictive campaign spending limitations that tend to create obstacles to local grassroots participation in federal elections.[135]

President Reagan's position on voting rights, as indicated below, was consistent with his overall assault on civil rights. For example, during the debate over the extension of the Voting Rights Act in 1982, his first attorney general, William French Smith, endorsed a discriminatory "intent" version provision that would have severely weakened the act's enforcement. However, it must be noted that Reagan did sign the 1982 extension of the 1965 Voting Rights Act—endorsing the Senate version—but, he did so with "considerable reluctance."[136] The president signed the bill with great exhibition, proclaiming that "this legislation proves our unbending commitment to civil rights." But the president's claims of having supported the bill were "unjustified," in that "he abandoned his opposition only when it became clear that the amendments would be passed despite his opposition."[137]

And again, as in several civil rights issues discussed above, Reagan's William Bradford Reynolds was there to carry the torch against civil rights. Reynolds repeatedly gave approval to discriminatory voting procedures. In two separate instances, in Louisiana and Alabama, Reynolds certified plans diluting African-American voting strength that even his own staff found discriminatory.[138]

Altogether, given President Reagan's clear and direct views on these issues, let us now examine whether and/or to what extent he attempted to translate these policy objectives into judicial appointments in terms of the nature and type of person eventually appointed to a district court judgeship.

SELECTION, SCREENING, AND NOMINATION UNDER REAGAN

Ideology is the primary qualification.[139]

Throughout history, Congress has on occasion created a large number of new judgeships all at one time, thus affording a president enormous opportunity to reshape the federal bench and therefore the potential to determine the interest conflict in his favor. The Omnibus Judgeship Act of 1978, which created 152 new judgeships, and the Federal Judgeship Act of 1984, P.L. 98-353, which created twenty-four appellate and sixty-one district court judgeships, afforded Reagan just such an opportunity. In 1987 alone, Reagan had the opportunity to make between fifty and seventy-five new appointments, and overall had the opportunity to appoint nearly 50 percent of the lower federal bench.[140]

By December 31, 1987, Ronald Reagan had appointed an unprecedented 290 federal district court judges out of the 575 authorized. As indicated in Table 3.11, only twenty-four (8.3 percent), of these appointments went to women, only six (2.1 percent) to African-Americans, and fourteen (4.8 percent) to Latinos.[141] If it had been Carter who opened the door for judges from underrepresented groups, clearly Reagan slammed the door shut for these groups (e.g., African-Americans) and left only a side window open for women.[142] For example, as a proportion of total appointments, African-Americans dropped dramatically from nearly 14 percent (Carter) to 2.1 percent (Reagan), and women dropped from 14.4 percent (Carter) to 8.3 percent under Reagan. Notably, Reagan's appointment record for African-Americans was the worst since the Eisenhower administrations—when some have argued the "pool of qualified blacks was much smaller" than it was during Reagan's time.[143]

By contrast, however, Reagan appointed the highest number of Catholics ever appointed by a Republican president—higher than Carter and nearly the same as Johnson. And, as indicated in Table 3.11, Reagan's judges were generally wealthy; over one in four appointees were millionaires at the time of appointment. Subsequent studies reveal that 22 percent of Reagan's district court nominees were millionaires versus only 4 percent for Carter.[144] The Reagan administration, perhaps more so than any other administration in recent history, clearly understood the crucial role and function of courts and judges in the American policy process. Bruce Fein, a former associate deputy attorney general who assisted in judicial selection under Reagan, stated the matter quite simply: "the judiciary is a primary player in the formulation of pubic policy"; consequently "it would be silly for an administration not to try to affect the direction of legal policy" through appointments.[145]

Ronald Reagan came to the presidency believing that he possessed a national mandate on several key social issues. As these issues related to judicial selection, Bruce Fein stated that Reagan wanted judges who supported: (1) a constitutional amendment to ban abortion; (2) the restoration of voluntary prayer in public schools; (3) an end to the use of mandatory busing for racial balance in schools; (4) the abandonment of quotas and ratios as a remedy for racial injustice (in employment);[146] and (5) the curbing of the strict one-person, one-vote standards for political apportionment.[147] Of course it is not a coincidence that these five policy areas mirror those selected for the presidential policy objective/expectation profiles in this analysis. Indeed, as indicated earlier, the POPPs tell us the issues in which particular presidents are interested.

Judicial selection processes used by Carter and Reagan differ not only in methodology but also intent. For example, even the 1980 Republican party platform included a passage condemning judicial selection under Carter and espoused a clear intention to appoint antiabortion judges.

Under Mr. Carter, many appointments to federal judgeships have been particularly disappointing. By his partisan nominations, he has violated his explicit campaign promise of 1976 and has blatantly disregarded the public interest. We pledge to reverse that deplorable trend, through the appointment of women and men who respect and reflect the values of the American people, and whose judicial philosophy is characterized by the highest regard for protecting the rights of law abiding citizens, and is consistent with the belief in the decentralization of the federal government and efforts to return decision-making power to state and local elected officials.

We will work for the appointment of judges at all levels of the judiciary who respect traditional family values and the sanctity of innocent human life.[148]

While Carter sought to make the judiciary more "representative" of the population, and therefore perhaps more representative of his own views, Reagan likewise sought openly to make the judiciary more directly representative of his own views. For example, political scientist Sheldon Goldman maintains that the "Reagan Administration [was] the most determined since the first [Franklin D.] Roosevelt Administration to mold a judiciary to its liking."[149]

Unlike the Carter administration, selection under Reagan was more centralized and openly political. As one study on judicial selection concludes, "the [Reagan] Administration [had] a more coherent and ambitious legal-policy agenda that [has] been more systematically, meticulously, and effectively imposed than that of any prior Administration."[150]

From the very start, the Reagan administration operated under a "simple set of priorities." "Personal and ideological loyalty were the primary criteria for [cabinet] appointees."[151] Similarly, it appears that such ideological litmus tests were also a guide for judicial appointments; that is, the Reagan administration used *policy agenda* considerations for its judicial appointments for the expressed purpose of directing judicial policymaking and the resolution of the interest conflict.

To achieve this objective, one of the first operations of the Reagan administration was to eliminate the nominating commissions. One commentator put it this way: "[F]or those in Reagan's Justice Department, Jimmy Carter's 'affirmative action' program was irrelevant and sacrificed 'judicial merit' for the political symbolism of a more 'representative' federal bench."[152] A former member of the Reagan Justice Department explained that "greater control was necessary if the administration was to reverse past trends that were pushing toward the selection of moderate to liberal judges."[153]

The Reagan administration took concrete steps to implement its plan. For one thing, Reagan required that senators submit three to five names for each district court vacancy.[154] Further, he discontinued altogether Carter's policy of working with the National Bar Association (African-Americans) and various women's organizations in finding judicial nominees. Instead Reagan placed increased emphasis on concentrating judicial selection in the White House, seeking to institutionalize the White House role. There is some evidence, however, to suggest that these types of groups were at times consulted, or at least contacted, by the ABA.[155]

Reagan also transferred the primary responsibility for judicial selection from the Deputy Attorney General's Office to the Office of Legal Policy and he established the President's Committee on Federal Judicial Selection. The president's committee consisted of key members of both the White House and the Justice Department, to screen judicial nominees and allow the administration to apply a consistent ideological measure. This selection committee met weekly, was chaired by Counsel to the President Fred Fielding, and included the chief of staff and other White House advisors, including: one or more other presidential counselors; the presidential assistant for legislative affairs; the attorney general;

the deputy attorney general; the associate attorney general; and the assistant attorneys general for the Office of Legal Policy, Personnel, and Legislation.[156]

The effect of this committee was to both institutionalize and centralize the role of the White House in the politics of the selection process, thus better positioning the administration to more effectively combat or bargain with Republican senators (senatorial courtesy).[157] Never before had any administration so systematically considered issues of patronage, legislative relations, and public policy and the interest conflict. The President's Committee on Federal Judicial Selection enabled "consistent ideological or policy orientation screening of all appointments."[158] Administration officials stated quite openly that the committee facilitated the selection of "people of a certain judicial philosophy."[159]

In addition to institutionalizing the White House in the selection procedure, Reagan instituted rigid screening procedures. The candidate's records were scrutinized and compared with those of others using computer data banks that contained published speeches, articles, and opinions of hundreds of potential nominees. Reagan's nominees routinely underwent several day-long interviews with Justice Department officials.[160] For example, in 1987, Stephen Markman, assistant attorney general in charge of judicial selection during Reagan's second term, suggested that in the process of selecting over 300 judges, "over 1,000 individuals had been interviewed."[161]

The advent and extent of these interviews were the continuing subject of debate and controversy from varying camps. Bruce Fein and other Reagan administration officials defended the interviews, arguing that "a president who fails to scrutinize the legal philosophy of federal judicial nominees courts frustration on his own policy agenda." They also criticized former Republican administrations (most often the Nixon administration) for merely taking into account a candidate's "reputation and standing" and not judicial philosophy.[162]

On the other hand, many were strongly and openly critical of the ideological screening. In addition to many "liberal" senators and others, even some Republicans voiced concern. For example, conservative Chicago Law School professor Philip Kurland charged: "judges are being appointed in the expectation that they will rewrite laws and the Constitution to the administration's liking. Reagan's judges are activist in support of conservative dogma—what some people would call hanging judges in criminal law and anti-regulation judges in civil law."[163]

Highlighting the depth of this process was the resignation of Philip Lacovara, a former official in Nixon's Justice Department, as Reagan's representative on the nominating committee for the District of Columbia. According to Lacovara, when he himself wished to be considered for a judgeship, he was told by officials that he was "too liberal," "not politically reliable," and that he failed the "litmus test for philosophical orthodoxy."[164] In a 1986 New York Times interview, Lacovara, who considered himself a "conservative Republican,"[165] charged that:

political affiliation has provided a source of recognition, not a litmus test, for philosophical orthodoxy. Over time, this pattern created a federal judiciary rich in diversity and perspective.

Today the message is quite different: ideology is the primary qualification, and it is a candidate's demonstrated orthodoxy that brings his name before the President and ultimately before the Senate. Unique in our nation's history, the current Justice Department has been processing any judicial candidate through a series of officials whose primary duty is to assess the candidate's ideological purity.[166]

Despite these charges, other Reagan administration officials steadfastly denied any ideological "litmus test." For example, during Reagan's second term, Attorney General Edwin Meese protested:

we do discuss the law with judicial candidates. . . . In discussing the law with lawyers there is really no way not to bring up cases—past cases—and engage in a dialogue over the reasoning and merits of particular decisions. But even here, our primary interest is how someone's mind works, whether they have powers of discernment and the scholarly grounding required of a good judge.[167]

At the end of Reagan's first term, former Justice Department official Jonathan Rose stated that the administration was "tremendously pleased" with those judges who had "fully met our expectations of being people committed to the President's judicial philosophy."[168]

Reagan's commitment to affect judicial policy extended into his second presidential term of office with equal if not increased determination. Indeed, the 1984 Republican party platform included in part that:

Judicial power must be exercised with deference towards state and local officials. It is not a judicial function to reorder the economic, political, and social priorities of our nation. We commend the President for appointing federal judges committed to the rights of law-abiding citizens and traditional family values. In his second term, President Reagan will continue to appoint Supreme Court and other federal judges who share our commitment to judicial restraint.[169]

Two years later in a 1986 speech, Reagan assessed his administration's success in remaking the federal bench: "In many areas—abortion, crime, pornography, and others—progress will take place when the federal judiciary is made up of the judges who believe in law and order and a strict interpretation of the Constitution. I am pleased to be able to tell you that I've already appointed 284 federal judges, men and women who share the fundamental values that you and I so cherish, and that by the time we leave office, our administration will have appointed some 45 percent of all federal judges."[170]

Again, Assistant Attorney General Stephen Markman assessed the president's performance: "[T]he Reagan administration has in place what is probably the most thorough and comprehensive system for recruiting and screening federal judicial candidates of any administration ever." Markman continued, "this administration has, moreover, attempted to assert the President's prerogatives over judicial selection more consistently than many of its predecessors."[171]

Accordingly, in 1986 Attorney General Edwin Meese was compelled to boast, regarding the administration's judicial appointments, that the administration would "institutionalize the Reagan revolution so it can't be set aside no matter what happens in future presidential elections."[172] Initial evidence published in a 1984 study indicates that Meese's comments were not too far off the mark. Looking primarily at the appellate level, the study by the conservative Center for Judicial Studies concluded in part that "during 1981–1982 Reagan appointees had *fulfilled* the Administration's expectations, especially at the appellate level" (emphasis added).[173]

On balance, whether litmus tests were rigidly employed or not, selection during the first term varied little from the second; if anything, the second term was perhaps even more politicized. Reagan was nearly unanimously successful in his lower court nominations—excepting the nomination of Jefferson B. Sessions, Sidney Fitzwater, and a few others.[174] Of course, the Senate rejection of Supreme Court nominee Robert Bork remains Reagan's most significant defeat.[175]

To summarize, under the Reagan administration, once potential candidates for a vacancy were identified, there was an initial screening conducted by the Office of Legal Policy of the Department of Justice. Given the results of a preliminary evaluation, including a candidate's written work, comments of local bar leaders, recommendations of members of Congress, and others, a decision was then made whether or not to invite potential candidates for interviews. At these interviews, coordinated by the Office of Legal Policy, the candidates would be questioned by attorneys, both from the Office of Legal Policy and from the Department of Justice. Each of these interviews often lasted from thirty minutes to an hour and candidates generally averaged between four and five hours of interviews during their visit to the department.[176]

Following these interviews, coupled with additional consideration of a candidate's background and telephone inquiries made by officials in the Office of Legal Policy to public officials, bar leaders, sitting judges, and others in a candidate's home state, the Office of Legal Policy would then prepare a summary of each candidate's qualifications for the attorney general. Then the attorney general would meet with other Department of Justice officials to review these summaries and to select one candidate to recommend to the President's Committee on Federal Judicial Selection. This committee was chaired by the counsel to the president, and included among others the attorney general, the deputy attorney general, and the assistant attorney general for the Office of Legal Policy. When a consensus was reached on the Justice Department recommendation, the candidate's name was then submitted to the FBI as well as the ABA Standing Committee on Federal Judiciary. Finally, given no adverse information revealed in the FBI and ABA background investigations, the attorney general and the counsel to the president would then recommend him/her to the president for formal nomination.

Reagan, the Attorneys General, and the Department of Justice

Similar to the responses of Democratic senators to Carter's insistence on more than one nominee for each vacancy, Reagan also requested multiple names for nomination and was also met with negative response. For example, one report suggested that even from the very beginning

> there was considerable tension from the outset between the Justice Department under Attorney General William French Smith and Republican Senators. . . . Attorney General Smith moved quickly to establish a process whereby Republican Senators would be asked to submit to the Justice Department three to five names for each judicial vacancy at the district court level. The Attorney General also made it clear that the preferred names would be subject to extensive analysis, and that if none of the names submitted was acceptable, the Administration reserved the right to ask for more names from the Senator— or simply to nominate the Administration's own choice.[177]

As in the Carter administration, this practice was intended to provide flexibility and bargaining power to allow the president a greater chance to fill vacant positions with nominees who shared his judicial philosophy. And also, as under Carter, there were varying responses to the request. For example, one anonymous high-ranking official in the Reagan administration said that some senators accepted the practice well while others accepted it only in part; in other words, at times "insisting in some cases involving close friends or political allies on submitting only one name, but agreeing more generally to submit a number of candidates."[178] This anonymous official recounts that some senators would in fact publicly submit several names but then privately indicate to the Justice Department or the White House that "only one would see the light of day on the Senate floor."[179] Others just flatly rejected this perceived attack on senatorial prerogatives. On balance, as one anonymous high-ranking official in the Reagan White House has written, the president was often involved in "pitched and protracted battles over particular nominees; many hard feelings resulted on both sides . . . it was frequently hand-to-hand political combat."[180] And these battles were even more prevalent for district court appointments. As our anonymous Reagan official concluded: "Senators generally seemed substantially more determined to get 'their' district court nominees confirmed by the Senate, rather than spending their time on courts of appeals nominees or district court candidates with whom the Senator had no very close connection or political agenda."[181]

Reagan and the ABA

The Reagan administration's relationship with the ABA went from bad to worse during his eight-year term. The attitude toward the ABA within the Justice Department was at times hostile; in former Reagan official Bruce Fein's words, "we didn't think one second about ABA ratings."[182] Significantly, the Reagan administration was the first Republican administration in thirty years in which the ABA was not actively used and consulted in the *pre*-nomination stage.[183] In fact, the ABA Committee on the Federal Judiciary no longer received a short list of candidates to evaluate—only the final selection.

Just as during the Carter administration, the ABA again relaxed various rules to accommodate the wishes of the incumbent administration. Because Reagan called for young white male conservatives who shared the administration's legal-policy objectives, the ABA again bent its standard of twelve years of prior legal experience for several appointments. The extent to which the ABA was willing to accommodate the administration is realized in the number of appellate judges who were appointed at ages under forty. For example, studies indicate that while less than 2 percent of those appointed under Eisenhower, Kennedy, or Johnson were under forty; 10 percent of Reagan's appellate judges were under forty.[184]

Nonetheless, age differences between Carter and Reagan appointees do not differ appreciably. As evidenced in Table 3.11, the average age at the time of appointment of the Carter's appointees was 50.4 years. The average age, at the time of appointment, of Reagan appointees was 49.2.[185] This difference of approximately one year clearly does not represent a significant difference between Carter and Reagan appointees; indeed, neither Carter's nor Reagan's appointments were significantly younger than those of previous administrations. (See Table 3.11.)

Overall, the Reagan administration encountered difficulties with the ABA in less than "one out of 20 nominees."[186] Of course, one of the most notable exceptions to this claim would be the split vote by the ABA on Reagan's failed nomination of Judge Robert Bork to the Supreme Court. More than once was the ABA's assessment of Judge Bork's qualifications used against him during the confirmation battle.[187]

In sum, looking back to Table 3.11, we see that the Reagan administration named few women, African-Americans, or other minorities to the bench and instead concentrated on younger, upper-middle class white males.[188] According to Gary McDowell, associate director of public affairs at the U.S. Department of Justice from 1985 to 1987 and chief speech writer to Attorney General Edwin Meese, "[M]ore than anything else, Reagan's nominees personified the President's own belief in judicial restraint and deference to legislative power."[189] "You won't see Reagan's appointees taking over school systems and jails or ordering forced busing," confirmed University of Virginia Law School professor A. E. Dick Howard.[190] Others have been more critical in their assessment. For example, American University law professor Herman Schwartz (testifying before Congress in 1985) characterized the Reagan administration as "turning the federal courts away from their historic role of protecting individual rights," predicting that "this effort will politicize the courts and deprive them of both the substance and appearance of that fairness on which so much of their legitimacy depends."[191]

On balance, perhaps Reagan's PPOPs were best summarized in a 1983 interview with Jonathan C. Rose, then head of the Office of Legal Policy in the Reagan Justice Department, stating that "philosophy certainly has been a factor with regard to our appointments." Rose added that the Reagan administration was attempting to "correct the imbalance created by Carter's appointment of so many liberals to the lower federal courts."[192] Reagan appointed judges who "share[d] his opposition to busing, racial hiring quotas and elaborate procedural protections for criminal defendants, and his disagreement with Supreme Court decisions on the death penalty, abortion, and school prayer."[193]

Finally, as summarized by Fred Fielding, former counselor to Reagan, younger judges with a conservative track record of aggressive conservatism are "Ronald Reagan's best legacy."[194] Quite appropriately, it is just a suggestion such as Fielding's and others[195]— the suggestion of a legacy that requires further analyses. More specifically, what is the success of this legacy and how does it compare to others, and to what extent have presidents been able to effect their policy objectives through district court appointments.

CHAPTER SUMMARY

The essential purpose of this and the preceding chapters (4 and 5), has been to determine the presidents' policy positions on the five selected policy issue areas (PPOPs). The most obvious feature of the above discussions is that whether for *policy* or *partisan* agenda reasons, judicial appointments are linked to a *presidential* agenda. It is clear, for example, that presidents, via the selection and appointment process, may attempt to promote their policy agendas, shore up partisan coalitions, and reward the party faithful.

All told, partisan goals sometimes coincide with policy goals and vice versa. This chapter suggests that both Carter and Reagan gave considerable weight to their own agenda and goals when assessing the professional qualifications of their nominees. Both persuaded the ABA to bend its established standards to accommodate their nominees. The Carter administration made a calculated effort to appoint more women, African-Americans, and Latinos. By comparison, few from these groups were named by President Reagan. Reagan's major focus was to appoint those who shared his philosophy of judicial conservatism and his social agenda. In the next chapter, Chapter 6, similar analysis is provided for presidential policy objectives and judicial selection during the Bush and Clinton administrations.

NOTES

1. At their second annual meeting held in Washington in October 1980, the National Association of Women Judges was invited as a group to the White House and addressed by President Carter. See Beverly B. Cook in the *Feminist Connection*, October 1981.

2. *The Presidential Campaign*, 1976. Vol. part 1. Prepared for the Committee on House Administration, 95 Congress, 2nd session, 1978, p. 494 and reprinted in Alan Neff, *The United States District Judge Nominating Commissions: Their Members, Procedures and Candidates* (Chicago: American Judicature Society, 1981), p. 31.

3. The White House, Washington, DC. Carter's words were later mocked and quoted directly by Stephen Markman, assistant attorney general, Office of Legal Policy, for the Reagan administration. See "The Performance of the Reagan Administration in Nominating Women and Minorities to the Federal Bench," Hearing before the Committee on the Judiciary, United States Senate, 100th Congress, Second Session, February 2, 1988 (Washington, DC: Government Printing Office, 1990), pp. 14, 29.

4. Henry J. Abraham, *The Judicial Process*, 6th ed. (New York: Oxford University Press, 1993), p. 30. Carter was also the most aggressive of recent presidents (before Clinton) in appointing African-Americans to cabinet-or subcabinet-level positions. See Office of Louis Martin, The White House, *Fact Sheet 115, Revised Appointees List* (Washington, DC: The White House, August, 1980).

5. Raymond Tatalovich and Byron W. Daynes, *The Politics of Abortion* (New York: Praeger, 1981), pp. 198–199.

6. "Democratic Platform: 'A Contract with the People,'" *Congressional Quarterly Almanac*, 1976, p. 860.

7. Bob Rankin, "Candidates on the Issues: Abortion," *Congressional Quarterly Weekly Report*, February 28, 1976, p. 465.

8. See Jeff Fishel, *Presidents and Promises: From Campaign Pledge to Presidential Performance* (Washington, DC: CQ Press, 1985), pp. 67–68.

9. *Beal v. Doe*, 432 U.S. 438 (1977).

10. *Maher v. Roe*, 432 U.S. 464 (1977).

11. Office of the White House Press Secretary, press conference no. 11, July 12, 1977, pp. 8–9; and as quoted in Frederick S. Jaffe, Barbara L. Lindheim, and Philip R. Lee, *Abortion Politics: Private Morality and Public Policy* (New York: McGraw-Hill, 1981), p. 132. See also Carl Tucker, "Carter on Abortion," *Saturday Review* (September 17, 1977), p. 64.

12. Office of the White House Press Secretary, Press Conference, Yazoo City, Mississippi, July 21, 1977, p. 14; as quoted in Jaffe, *Abortion Politics*, pp. 8, 12.

13. Donald Johnson, *National Party Platforms of 1980* (Urbana: University of Illinois Press, 1982), p. 47.

14. Because religious liberty was a "non-issue" in both Carter's policy statements as well as his selection politics, there is no religious liberty expectation profile provided here. Nonetheless, however, as discussed in Chapter 7, Carter appointees rendered more significant opinions concerning issues of religious liberty than in any one of the other four policy areas under review.

15. See Norman C. Amaker, *Civil Rights and the Reagan Administration* (Washington, DC: The Urban Institute Press, 1988), pp. 25–28.

16. Ibid.

17. Ibid.

18. The Voting Rights Act of 1965 provides for the Justice Department to send observers to polling places to ensure that local officials permitted blacks to vote. The numbers of these observers dropped noticeably during the Nixon years, but increased during the Carter administration. See "GAO Report," 1978, p. 182; U.S. Commission of Civil Rights, 1981, pp. 101–102.

19. Johnson, *National Party Platforms of 1980*, p. 60.

20. *Regents of the University of California v. Bakke*, 438 U.S. 265 (1978).

21. Joseph A. Califano, Jr., *Governing America: An Insider's Report from the White House and the Cabinet* (New York: Simon and Schuster, 1981), p. 230.

22. Ibid.

23. Edward R. Kantowicz, "Reminiscences of a Fated Presidency: Themes from the Carter Memoirs," *Presidential Studies Quarterly* 16 (1986), p. 662.

24. Charles Bullock III and Charles M. Lamb, eds., *Implementation of Civil Rights Policy* (Monterey, CA: Brooks/Cole Publishing, 1984), p. 110.

25. Democratic Platform as reprinted in *Congressional Record* (daily edition), July 2, 1976, p. S11580.

26. Gary Orfield, *Must We Bus? Segregated Schools and National Policy* (Washington, DC: The Brookings Institution, 1978), p. 278.

27. Ibid., p. 275.

28. Johnson, *National Party Platforms of 1980*, p. 60.

29. Ibid., p. 53.

30. Additionally, Bell had helped to formulate the Atlanta "compromise" following the 1971 *Swann* decision, which provided for the hiring of additional Black administrators in lieu of desegregating the schools. This compromise was heralded by then Governor of Georgia Jimmy Carter as a "model solution" (Orfield, *Must We Bus?*, pp. 25, 106, 354–355, 369–370). See also "What Carter Believes: Interview on the Issues," *U.S. News and World Report* (May 24, 1976), pp. 22–23; and *Congressional Record* (daily edition), January 25, 1977, pp. S1301–S1306.

31. For additional comments by Proxmire and others opposing Bell's nomination, see the *Congressional Record* (daily edition), January 25, 1977, pp. S1296, S1308, S1312, S1321, S1328.

32. Orfield, *Must We Bus?*, p. 356.

33. *New York Times*, March 10, 1977.

34. For further discussion, see Bullock and Lamb, *Implementation of Civil Rights Policies*, p. 60.

35. Previously, in 1977, by Executive Order No. 11972, Carter created a "United States Circuit Court Judge Nomination Commission" with a separate panel for each circuit.

36. As governor of Georgia, Carter instituted a commission form of selecting judges on all levels. Initially, Carter allowed the state bar Association to constitute the selection commission but later reconstituted the commission by appointing a majority of the commission by one and allowing the state bar to appoint the others. See Griffin B. Bell, "Federal Judicial Selection: The Carter Years," in Henry J. Abraham with Griffin B. Bell, Charles E. Grassley, Eugene W. Hickok, Jr., John W. Kern III, Stephen J. Markman, and William Bradford Reynolds, eds., *Judicial Selection: Merit, Ideology, and Politics* (Washington, DC: National Legal Center for the Public Interest, 1990), p. 25.

37. Stuart Taylor, Jr., "Carter Judge Selections Praised, but Critics Discern Partisanship," *New York Times*, 3 October 1980, pp. A1, A20.

38. Reagan appointed twenty-seven Jewish judges—three more than Carter—but these represented only 9.3 percent proportionally.

39. See Sheldon Goldman, "Carter's Judicial Appointments: A Lasting Legacy," *Judicature* 64 (1981), p. 349.

40. James L. Sundquist, "Jimmy Carter as Public Administrator: An Appraisal at Midterm," *Public Administration Review* 39 (January/February 1979), p. 3. See also Nolan J. Argyle and Ryan J. Barilleaux, "Past Failures and Future Prescriptions for Presidential

Management Reform," *Presidential Studies Quarterly* 16 (1986), p. 724.

41. For discussion on the involvement of the National Bar Association and the Federation of Women Lawyers, see Neff, *The United States District Judge Nominating Commissions*, p. 45.

42. Donald Bruce Johnson, compiler, *National Party Platforms of 1980* (Urbana, Illinois: University of Illinois Press, 1982), p. 62.

43. The two senators from West Virginia never did create a commission but did however "come forth jointly with good candidates for appointment for their state." See Griffin B. Bell, "Federal Judicial Selection: The Carter Years," in Abraham, *Judicial Selection: Merit, Ideology, and Politics*, p. 27.

44. In the main, these Republican senators did appoint the members of the commissions but were not instrumental (if involved at all) in selecting those from the list comprised by the commission.

45. For a state-by-state breakdown of the procedures used by each commission see Neff, *The United States District Judge Nominating Commissions*, pp. 78–81, esp. Table 5.3.

46. A complete copy of "United States District Judge Nominating Commission Candidate Questionnaire," is reprinted in Neff, *The United States District Judge Nominating Commissions*, Appendix D, pp. 179–182.

47. For example, again see Neff, *The United States District Judge Nominating Commissions*; or Larry Berkson and Susan Carbon, *The United States Circuit Judge Nominating Commissions: Its Members, Procedures and Candidates* (Chicago: American Judicature Society, 1980); Joseph W. Tydings, "Merit Selection for District Judges," *Judicature* 61 (1977), p. 113; Judith Rosenbaum, "Implementing Federal Merit Selection," *Judicature* 61 (1977), p. 125; S. Levinson, "U.S. Judges: The Case for Politics," *The Nation*, March 4, 1978, p. 228; Peter Fish, "Merit Selection and Politics," *Wake Forest Law Review* 15 (1979), p. 635; Elliot Slotnick, "The U.S. Circuit Judge Nominating Commissions," *Law and Society Quarterly* 1 (1979), p. 464; and Elliot Slotnick, "Overview: Judicial Selection. Lowering the Federal Bench or Raising it Higher?: Affirmative Action and Judicial Selection during the Carter Administration," *Yale Law and Policy Review* 1 (1983), p. 270.

48. See Joseph W. Tydings, "Merit Selection for District Judges," pp. 112–118.

49. David M. O'Brien, rapporteur, *Judicial Roulette: Report of the Twentieth Century Fund Task Force on Judicial Selection* (New York: Priority Press, 1988), p. 59.

50. Bell, "Federal Judicial Selection: The Carter Years," in *Judicial Selection: Merit, Ideology, and Politics*, p. 27.

51. Larry Berkson and Susan Carbon, *Federal Judicial Selection during the Carter Administration—The United States Circuit Judge Nominating Commission: Its Members, Procedures and Candidates* (Chicago: American Judicature Society, 1980), pp. 96–101; see also, Peter Fish, "Questioning Judicial Candidates," *Judicature* 61 (1978), p. 9.

52. Ibid. In this American Judicature Society study, one panel member was quoted as saying that some of his colleagues "asked every applicant . . . if they supported ERA."

53. Telephone interview with Griffin Bell, December 11, 1986, as quoted in O'Brien, *Judicial Roulette*, p. 59.

54. Rees, "Questions for Supreme Court Nominees at Confirmation Hearings: Excluding the Constitution," *Georgia Law Review* 17 (1983), pp. 913, 961.

55. Telephone interviews with Judge Bell (December 11, 1986), Michael Egan (December 8, 1986), Philip Modlin (December 9, 1986), and Drew Days (December 8, 1986) as quoted in O'Brien, *Judicial Roulette*, p. 59. See also Judge Bell's testimony in

U.S. Congress, Senate, *Nomination of Sherman E. Unger: Hearings before the Committee on the Judiciary*, 1984, 98th Congress, 1st session, pt. 1, pp. 777–781. See also, G. Bell and R. Ostow, *Taking Care of the Law* (New York: William Morrow, 1982), pp. 39–42.

56. Elliot Slotnick, "The Paths to the Federal Bench: Gender, Race, and Judicial Recruitment," *Judicature* 67 (1984), pp. 371, 387. See also, E. Martin, "Women on the Federal Bench: A Comparative Profile," *Judicature* 65 (1982), p. 306.

57. Memorandum on Senatorial Courtesy, January 22, 1979, reprinted in U.S. Congress, Senate, *Selection and Confirmation of Federal Judges: Hearings before the Committee on the Judiciary*, 1980, 96th Congress, 1st session, pp. 118–122. Also see "Here Come the Judges," *Time*, December 11, 1978, p. 112.

58. Griffin B. Bell, "Federal Judicial Selection: The Carter Years," in Abraham, *Judicial Selection: Merit, Ideology, and Politics*, p. 28.

59. Executive Order No. 12097 (November 8, 1978, 43 F. R. 52455). For the complete text of Carter's executive order, see "Executive Order: Standards and Guidelines for the Merit Selection of United States District Judges," in Neff, *The United States District Judge Nominating Commissions*, Appendix I, pp. 192–193.

60. A complete copy of the "Suggested Guidelines for U.S. District Judge Nominating Commission[s]," is reprinted in Neff, *The United States District Judge Nominating Commissions*, Appendix L, pp. 196–199.

61. The FBI investigation consisted of contacting a *minimum* of 125 people in order to get the background of the candidates. This included assigning several agents to interview the candidate's professional and personal references: state and federal judges before whom the candidate had appeared or with whom he or she had sat on the bench, fellow practitioners, family, friends, former teachers and others (Neff, *The United States District Judge Nominating Commissions*, pp. 29–30).

62. O'Brien, *Judicial Roulette*, p. 60.

63. Actually, Jordon was never officially Chief of Staff. According to James Pfiffner, "Carter wanted to be his own chief of staff on the Kennedy and Roosevelt model and refused to designate a chief of staff." See James Pfiffner, "White House Staff versus the Cabinet: Centripetal and Centrifugal Roles," *Presidential Studies Quarterly* (Fall 1986), p. 679.

64. Elliot Slotnick, "The ABA Standing Committee on the Federal Judiciary: A Contemporary Assessment—Part I," *Judicature* 66 (March 1983), p. 355.

65. O'Brien, *Judicial Roulette*, p. 89.

66. Ibid.

67. Quote by Brooksley Born who thereafter became the Chairmen of the Committee. See Slotnick, "The ABA Standing Committee on the Federal Judiciary," pp. 355, 360.

68. See Henry J. Abraham, "Beneficial Advice or Presumptuous Veto? The ABA's Committee on Federal Judiciary Revisited," in Abraham, *Judicial Selection: Merit, Ideology, and Politics*, p. 68.

69. Quoted in Slotnick, "The ABA Standing Committee on the Federal Judiciary," p. 353.

70. Ibid.

71. As quoted in R. Friedman and S. Wermiel, "Reagan Appointments to the Federal Bench Worry U.S. Liberals," *The Wall Street Journal*, September 6, 1985, p. A1.

72. This analysis of Judge Kennedy is offered by Herman Schwartz, *Packing the Courts: The Conservative Campaign to Rewrite the Constitution* (New York: Charles Scribner's Sons, 1988), pp. 58–59.

73. Robert A. Strong, "Recapturing Leadership: The Carter Administration and the Crisis of Confidence," *Presidential Studies Quarterly* 16 (1986), p. 643.

74. Sheldon Goldman, "Judicial Appointments and the Presidential Agenda," in Paul Brace, with Christine B. Harrington and Gary King, eds., *The Presidency and American Politics* (New York: New York University Press, 1989), p. 33.

75. Walter F. Murphy, "Reagan's Judicial Strategy," in Larry Berman, ed. *Looking Back on the Reagan Presidency* (Baltimore: The Johns Hopkins University Press, 1990), p. 219.

76. Steven Markman, "Memorandum for Attorney General Meese: A Comparison of Judicial Selection Procedures," as quoted in David M. O'Brien, "The Reagan Judges: His Most Enduring Legacy?" in Charles O. Jones, ed., *The Reagan Legacy* (Chatham, NJ: Chatham House, 1988), p. 97.

77. Murphy, "Reagan's Judicial Strategy," p. 219.

78. Sheldon Goldman, "Judicial Appointments and the Presidential Agenda," p. 19.

79. Robert H. Birkby, "The Courts: 40 More Years?" in Michael Nelson, ed., *The Elections of 1984* (Washington, DC: CQ Press, 1984), p. 242.

80. Murphy, *Looking Back on the Reagan Presidency*, p. 219.

81. Ibid.

82. Bruce Fein, quoted by Aric Press and Ann McDaniel, "Judging the Judges," *Newsweek*, 14 October 1985, p. 73.

83. Cohen, "Conservatives Step up Efforts to Promote Reagan-Minded Judges to the U.S. Bench," *National Journal*, July 6, 1985, p. 1560.

84. *Congressional Quarterly Weekly Report*, September 7, 1985, p. 1759.

85. This point has been made by Wallace Earl Walker and Michael R. Reopel, "Strategies for Governance: Transition and Domestic Policymaking in the Reagan Administration," *Presidential Studies Quarterly* 16 (Fall 1986), p. 744.

86. Ibid.

87. Kernell defines "going public" as "a class of activities in which presidents engage as they promote themselves and their policies before the American public." Samuel Kernell, *Going Public: New Strategies of Presidential Leadership* (Washington, DC: CQ Press, 1986), p. 198. Also see Hedrick Smith, "Again, President Is Drawing Conservatives' Ire," *New York Times,* January 13, 1982; Howell Raines, "Reagan Runs a Reverse, Collides with Right Wing," *New York Times,* August 15, 1985; Hedrick Smith, "Reagan Bid Reopens Rift with Right," *New York Times,* February 19, 1983, p. 7; and Adam Clymer, "Fire and Brimstone," *New York Times,* March 19, 1983, p. 11.

88. Walker and Reopel, "Strategies for Governance: Transition and Domestic Policymaking in the Reagan Administration," p. 741.

89. Reagan's general philosophy on civil rights is well captured by William Bradford Reynolds, chief of the Justice Department's Civil Rights Division, who stated "There's growing awareness that the agencies that enforce civil rights laws have been overly intrusive." See M. Wines, "Administration Says It Merely Seeks a 'Better Way' to Enforce Civil Rights," *National Journal* 27 (March 1982), p. 536.

90. Schwartz, *Packing the Courts*, p. 18.

91. Reagan had maintained a hard-line antiabortion stance for some time. As governor of California, he had refused to sign the state's 1967 abortion reform statute until the provision for abortion in the case of fetal abnormality was deleted. See Tatalovich and Daynes, *The Politics of Abortion*, p. 228.

92. See Laura B. Weiss, "1980 Presidential Campaign: Abortion Question Poses Constant Concern" *Congressional Quarterly Weekly Report*, March 15, 1980, p. 734.

93. *Reagan for President, "Abortion,"* undated as reprinted in Jeff Fishel, *Presidents and Promises* (Washington, DC: CQ Press, 1985), p. 125.

94. Johnson, *National Party Platforms of 1980*, p. 183; and/or "1980 Republican Platform Text," *Congressional Quarterly Weekly Report*, July 19, 1980, p. 2,043.

95. See *Congressional Quarterly Weekly Report* 38, no. 2046 (1980) and Gary W. Fowler, "Judicial Selection under Reagan and Carter: A Comparison of Their Initial Recommendation Procedures," *Judicature* 67 (1984), p. 267.

96. David O'Brien, *Storm Center* (New York: W.W. Norton and Company, 1986), p. 41.

97. As quoted by Schwartz, *Packing the Courts*, p. 18.

98. As quoted by Rodney Hyman, Betty Sarvis, and Joy Walker Bonar in *The Abortion Question* (New York: Columbia University Press, 1987), p. 130.

99. Michael Nelson editor, *The Elections of 1984* (Washington, DC: CQ Press, 1984), p. 22.

100. *Los Angeles Times*, June 2, 1986, pp. 1–17.

101. *Thornburgh v. American College of Obstetricians and Gynecologists*, 54 U.S.L.W. 4618 (1986), 4621, 4625.

102. See Charles Fried, *Order and Law: Arguing the Reagan Revolution—A Firsthand Account* (New York: Simon and Schuster, 1991), pp. 33–36; and Hyman et al., *The Abortion Question*, 1987, p. 130.

103. For insightful and detailed discussions on the *Thornburgh* brief, see both Lincoln Caplan, *The Tenth Justice: The Solicitor General and the Rule of Law* (New York: Vintage Books, 1987), Chapter 10, "The Abortion Brief," pp. 135–154; and Charles Fried *Law and Order*, pp. 33–36.

104. Caplan, *The Tenth Justice,* p. 140.

105. *New York Times*, April 22, 1984, E5. Also Robert H. Birkby, "The Courts: 40 More Years?" in Michael Nelson, ed., *The Elections of 1984* (Washington, DC: CQ Press, 1984), p. 246.

106. *Washington Post*, February 19, 1980.

107. Ibid.

108. Schwartz, *Packing the Courts*, p. 24.

109. On September 10, 1985, the Helms school prayer court-stripping bill was also defeated.

110. Elder Witt, *A Different Justice: Reagan and the Supreme Court* (Washington, DC: CQ Press, 1986), p. 119.

111. *Reagan for President, "Affirmative Action,"* as reprinted in Jeff Fishel, *Presidents and Promises* (Washington, DC: CQ Press, 1985), p. 125.

112. Previously OFCCP's guidelines were any federal contractor with fifty or more employees and contracts worth $50,000.

113. See *Congressional Quarterly Weekly Report*, 1981, "Affirmative Action Assailed in Congress: Administration" 39, no. 37, September, pp. 1749–1753.

114. Ibid.

115. Reagan's first Solicitor General Rex E. Lee argued the administration's case opposing affirmative action in the joint claims, *Firefighters Local Union No. 1784 v. Stotts*, and *Memphis Fire Department v. Stotts* (467 U.S. 561, 1984). In sum, in 1981, a federal judge had ordered the Memphis fire department to implement "budget-dictated" layoffs by dismissing senior white firefighters; thus enabling more recently hired African-Americans to keep their jobs. The appeals court upheld the order against the city and the Reagan administration backed the city when the issue was appealed to the Supreme

Court. Assistant Attorney General for Civil Rights William Bradford Reynolds joined Lee in the administration's friend of the court brief. Essentially, the *amicus* brief argued that the lower court judge's action was illegal; that is, affirmative action plans are unconstitutional when they are adopted to benefit any persons or groups who were not themselves the victims of discrimination.

116. Witt, *A Different Justice*, p. 126.

117. See the *New York Times*, February 17, 1983.

118. *United Steel Workers of America v. Weber* 443 U.S. 193 (1979).

119. Ronald Brownstein and Nina Easton, *Reagan's Ruling Class: Portraits of the President's Top 100 Officials*, (Washington, DC: The Presidential Accountability Group, 1982), p. 401.

120. Schwartz, *Packing the Courts*, p. 186.

121. *New York Times*, October 3, 1982.

122. Michael Preston, "Affirmative Action Policy: Can It Survive the Reaganites?" in Michael Combs and John Gruhl, eds., *Affirmative Action: Theory, Analysis, and Prospects* (Jefferson, NC: McFarland and Company, 1986), pp. 165–167.

123. Reynolds remark is quoted in *Hearings before the U.S. Senate Judiciary Committee on the Nomination of William Bradford Reynolds to Be Attorney General*, 1985, 99th Congress, 1st session, p. 961.

124. GOP Platform, in *Congressional Record* (daily edition), September 2, 1976, p. H9475.

125. Johnson, *National Party Platforms of 1980*, p. 183.

126. *Reagan for President, "Busing,"* as reprinted in Fishel, *Presidents and Promises*, p. 125.

127. Johnson, *National Party Platforms of 1980*, p. 184.

128. Fishel, *Presidents and Promises*, p. 159.

129. Bullock and Lamb, *Implementation of Civil Rights Policies*, p. 60.

130. For a brief summary of Reynolds' attacks on Supreme Court decisions, see Schwartz, *Packing the Courts*, pp. 182–184.

131. *Hearings before the U.S. Senate Judiciary Committee on the Nomination of William Bradford Reynolds to Be Attorney General*, 1985, 99th Congress, 1st session, p. 961.

132. Schwartz, *Packing the Courts*, p. 183.

133. S. Puro, "The United States as Amicus Curiae," in S. Ulmer, ed., *Courts, Law, and Judicial Processes* (New York: Free Press, 1971), pp. 224–226; and generally Robert Scigliano, "The Presidency and the Judiciary," in M. Nelson, ed., *Presidency and the Political Systems* (Washington, DC: CQ Press, 1984).

134. For example, see Steven A. Shull, *The President and Civil Rights Policy: Leadership and Change* (Westport, CT: Greenwood Press, 1989), p. 98.

135. See Johnson, *National Party Platforms of 1980*, p. 198.

136. Reagan staunchly opposed the bill initially, threatening to a veto if the "pretty extreme" House bill became law. See Amaker, *Civil Rights and the Reagan Administration,* note 36, p. 155. Also, see *Congressional Quarterly Weekly Report*, May 8, 1982, p. 1041; Fishel, *Presidents and Promises*, p. 168; also Nadine Cohodas, "Voting Rights Extension Cleared for President Reagan," *Congressional Quarterly Weekly Report*, June 26, 1982, pp. 1503–1504.

137. Indeed, at a speech before the American Bar Association, Reagan not only took undue credit for getting the bill passed but for the Justice Department's "vigorous enforcement" of the act also. See Amaker, *Civil Rights and the Reagan Administration*, pp.

143–146.

138. These plans were later invalidated in the Federal Courts. For discussion see *Hearings Before the U.S. Senate Judiciary Committee on the Nomination of William Bradford Reynolds to Be Attorney General*, 1985, 99th Congress, 1st session, pp. 268, 376, 449.

139. Lacovara, "The Wrong Way to Pick Judges," *New York Times* (October 3, 1986), p. A35.

140. Table 3.11, Chapter 3.

141. For a more in-depth study of the socioeconomic, political, and other characteristics of Reagan's appointees see Sheldon Goldman "Reagan's Judicial Legacy: Completing the Puzzle and Summing Up," *Judicature* 72 (1989), pp. 318–330.

142. For a thorough, and at times heated debate on the Reagan administration's record on appointing women and minorities, see "The Performance of the Reagan Administration in Nominating Women and Minorities to the Federal Bench," Hearing before the Committee on the Judiciary, United States Senate, 100th Congress, second session, February 2, 1988, serial No. J-100-47 (Washington, DC: Government Printing Office, 1990).

143. David M. O'Brien, "The Reagan Judges," p. 76.

144. Goldman, "Reagan's Judicial Legacy: Completing the Puzzle and Summing Up," p. 323.

145Telephone interview with Bruce Fein, December 10, 1986, as quoted in O'Brien, *Judicial Roulette*, p. 25.

146. Witt, *A Different Justice*, p. 100.

147. See Bruce Fein, "A 'Reagan' Court would Overturn Past Errors," *Human Events* (July 6, 1983).

148. Johnson, *National Party Platforms of 1980*, p. 203.

149. Sheldon Goldman, "Reaganizing the Judiciary: The First Term Appointments," *Judicature* 68 (April/May 1985), p. 334.

150. O'Brien, *Judicial Roulette*, p. 60.

151. James P. Pfiffner, "White House Staff Versus the Cabinet: Centripetal and Centrifugal Roles," *Presidential Studies Quarterly* (Fall 1986), pp. 680–681. See Hugh Heclo, "One Executive Branch of Many?" in Anthony King, ed., *Both Ends of the Avenue* (Washington, DC: American Enterprise for Public Policy Research, 1984), pp. 26–58.

152. O'Brien, "The Reagan Judges: His Most Enduring Legacy?" in *The Reagan Legacy: Promise and Performance*, p. 66.

153. Interview with Bruce Fein, December 10, 1986, as quoted in O'Brien, *Judicial Roulette*, p. 61, which quotes the Office of Legal Policy, "Myths and Reality–Reagan Administration Judicial Selection," October 31, 1986, in an unpublished memorandum obtained from Deputy Assistant Attorney General Steve Matthews.

154. See G. Fowler, "A Comparison of Initial Recommendation Procedures: Judicial Selection under Reagan and Carter," *Yale Law and Policy Review* 1 (1983), p. 270.

155. The *Congressional Quarterly Service* reported in September 1985 that the ABA Committee at times gave the names of potential nominees to liberal groups so that groups like the NAACP could do its own investigations.

156. See Goldman, "Reaganizing the Judiciary," pp. 313, 315–16; and Stephen J. Markman, "Judicial Selection: The Reagan Years," in Abraham et al., *Judicial Selection: Merit, Ideology, and Politics*, pp. 33–47.

157. Of course this centralization was also useful in negotiating with Republican representatives as the Reagan administration continued the policy of consulting about judicial vacancies with Republican representatives from states for which there was no Re-

publican senator. See Walter F. Murphy, "Reagan's Judicial Strategy," in Larry Berman, ed., *Looking Back on the Reagan Presidency* (Baltimore: The Johns Hopkins University Press, 1990), p. 33, note 24.

158. See Goldman, "Reaganizing the Judiciary," p. 315.

159. Presidential Counselor Fred Fielding quoted on National Public Radio, "All Things Considered," August 28, 1985 and reprinted in O'Brien, "The Reagan Judges: His Most Enduring Legacy?" p. 68.

160. O'Brien, *Judicial Roulette*, p. 61.

161. Statement at panel on Reagan's Judges, Conference of Alliance for Justice," Washington, DC, February 12, 1987, as quoted in O'Brien, *Judicial Roulette*, p. 61.

162. As quoted in "Conservatives Pressing to Reshape Judiciary," *Congressional Quarterly Weekly Report*, September 7, 1985, p. 1759. E. Meese, address before the Palm Beach County Bar Association, February 10, 1986; and interviews with Department of Justice officials Terry Eastland (September 26, 1986), Dwight Rabuse (October 28, 1986), and Steve Matthews (October 28, 1986).

163. See "Justice under Reagan," *U.S. News and World Report*, October 14, 1985, p. 65.

164. O'Brien, *Judicial Roulette*, p. 62.

165. Schwartz, *Packing the Courts*, p. 100.

166. Lacovara, "The Wrong Way to Pick Judges," *New York Times,* October 3, 1986, p. A35.

167. Address by Ed Meese before the Palm Beach County Bar Association, February 10, 1986:6, as quoted in O'Brien, *Judicial Roulette*, p. 63.

168. Schwartz, *Packing the Courts*, p. 76.

169. *Congressional Quarterly Weekly Report*, August 25, 1984, p. 2110.

170. Reagan, Message to the National Convention of the Knights of Columbus, August 5, 1986. As quoted in O'Brien, "The Reagan Judges: His Most Enduring Legacy?" in *The Reagan Legacy: Promise and Performance*, p. 62.

171. Markman, "A Comparison of Judicial Selection Procedures," p. 34, as quoted in O'Brien, "The Reagan Judges: His Most Enduring Legacy?" in *The Reagan Legacy: Promise and Performance*, p. 67. For a sympathetic description of Reagan's judicial selection process, see also Stephen J. Markman, "Judicial Selection: The Reagan Years," in Abraham, *Judicial Selection: Merit, Ideology and Politics,* pp. 33–48.

172. "Meese's Agenda for Ensuring the Reagan Legacy," *Los Angeles Times*, "Opinion," September 28, 1986.

173. Schwartz, *Packing the Courts*, p. 75.

174. See discussion in Chapter 3, this volume.

175. For a case study on the failed Bork nomination, see Kevin L. Lyles, "The Bork Nomination and Black Americans: A Case Study," in Lucius Barker and Mack Jones, *African-Americans and the American Political System* (Englewood Cliffs, NJ: Prentice-Hall, 1994), pp. 133–172.

176. Stephen J. Markman, "Judicial Selection: the Reagan Years," in Abraham, *Judicial Selection: Merit, Ideology, and Politics*, p. 38.

177. A Friend of the Constitution, "Congress, the President, and Judicial Selection: Lessons from the Reagan Years." This is an article written by an anonymous high-ranking official in the Reagan administration and included in Abraham, *Judicial Selection: Merit, Ideology, and Politics*, pp. 54–55. *A Friend of the Constitution* was the pseudonym chosen by Chief Justice John Marshall for his defense of *McCulloch v. Maryland* [17 U. S. (4 Wheat.) 316, 4 L. Ed. 579] in the newspapers of Virginia in 1819.

This source hereafter cited as "Friend of the Constitution."

178. Friend of the Constitution, "Congress, the President, and Judicial Selection: Lessons from the Reagan Years," in Abraham, *Judicial Selection: Merit, Ideology, and Politics*, p. 55.

179. Ibid.

180. Ibid., p. 56.

181. Ibid., p. 57.

182. Quoted in David M. O'Brien, "The Reagan Judges: His Most Enduring Legacy?" in Jones, *The Reagan Legacy: Promise and Performance*, p. 67. Also see Henry J. Abraham, "Beneficial Advice or Presumptuous Veto? The ABA's Committee on Federal Judiciary Revisited," in Abraham, *Judicial Selection: Merit, Ideology, and Politics*, p. 67; Interviews with Philip A. Lacovara (October 28, 1986), John Lane (December 3, 1986), and several former members of the ABA Committee on the Federal Judiciary, as quoted in O'Brien, *Judicial Roulette*, p. 61; and also, P. Lacovara, "The Wrong Way to Pick Judges," *The New York Times*, October 3, 1986, p. A35.

183. See Abraham, "Beneficial Advice or Presumptuous Veto?," p. 67.

184. Harold Chase, *Federal Judges: The Appointing Process* (Minneapolis: University of Minnesota Press, 1972), p. 179.

185. Office of Legal Policy, *Myths and Realities—Reagan Administration Judicial Selection*, December 29, 1987, p. 7.

186. Telephone interview with Bruce Fein (December 10, 1986), as quoted in O'Brien, *Judicial Roulette*, 1988, p. 92.

187. See the *Washington Post*, August 21, 1988, C6. For example, "The ABA has come to have a virtual veto power before a nomination is made as well as great influence on the Senate during the confirmation process. The significance of its imprimatur is so great that even now a split vote by the ABA on the level of a candidate's qualification can be used against him as it was in the case of Judge Bork."

188. See Goldman, "Reaganizing the Judiciary"; and Goldman, "Reagan's Judicial Appointments at Mid-Term: Shaping the Bench in his Own Image," *Judicature* 66 (1983), p. 335.

189. Abraham, *Judicial Selection: Merit, Ideology, and Politics*, p. xviii.

190. David Whitman, "Are Reagan's New Judges Really Closet Moderates?" *Washington Post*, August 9, 1987, C1.

191. Testimony of Herman Schwartz, U.S. Congress, Senate, *Confirmation Hearings on Federal Appointments: Hearings before the Committee on the Judiciary*, 1985, 99th Congress, 1st session, pt. 2 (Washington, DC: Government Printing Office, 1985), p. 449.

192. *Congressional Quarterly Weekly Report*, January 15, 1983, pp. 83–85.

193. *New York Times*, April 22, 1984, E5.

194. O'Brien, *Judicial Roulette*, p. 46.

195. "The Reagan Judiciary and Environmental Policy: The Impact of Appointments to the Federal Courts of Appeals," *Boston College Environmental Affairs Law Review* 18 (Summer 1991), p. 706.

6   Presidential Agendas and Judicial Appointments: From Bush Republicans to Clinton Democrats, 1988–1996

INTRODUCTION

In line with their immediate predecessors, the administrations of Bush and Clinton (first term) also demonstrated attempts to pack the district courts with nominees who would reflect their preferred judicial philosophy. Like presidents Carter and Reagan before them, reviews of Bush and Clinton show that they too were directly involved in the selection and nomination processes. And, as we shall see, this involvement also brought about dramatic and significant changes in the nature and character of the federal judiciary.

GEORGE W. BUSH

> I strongly believe that federal judges should be appointed on the basis of personal and professional qualifications. I am firmly committed to appointing judges who are dedicated to interpreting the law as it exists, rather than legislating from the bench. I also remain committed to appointing to the bench the best qualified candidates we can find—regardless of race and gender.[1]

The election of George Bush on November 8, 1988 followed eight years of President Reagan's unprecedented involvement in staffing the federal district courts along ideological lines. Bush's presidential leadership style, however, lacked the passionate ideological commitment of Reagan,[2] and consequently, Bush approached district court judge nominations with less intensity. Overall, Bush's vision, as summarized at the beginning of his presidency, was "to preside over a calm period of national growth, cooperation, and renewal; to manage world affairs with skill and subtlety; and to achieve maximum ends with minimalist means and modest rhetoric."[3]

Hints of Bush's position with regard to judicial selection were made clear during his 1988 presidential campaign. Bush stated he was "firmly committed to appointing judges who are dedicated to interpreting the law as it exists, rather than legislating from the bench."[4] And, it was not long after taking office that it became clear that conservatives expected Bush to continue to honor Reagan's promise of transforming the federal courts through the appointment power.[5] The policy of appointing conservatives to the courts "was the greatest priority of conservatives who followed George Bush's election," said Clint Bolick, leader of a conservative group that monitors judicial appointments.[6] "It's a very tasty morsel he gives to the rightwingers," said one federal judge regarding Bush's efforts to appoint conservative judges.[7]

Senator Orrin G. Hatch (R-UT), for instance, said of the contrast between Reagan and Bush, "Ronald Reagan knew his greatest legacy was going to be the federal courts. I think George Bush thinks the courts are important, but [a conservative dominance] is already there." Hatch maintained that Reagan had already "tapped" the better-known candidates: "All the conservative law professors have been gobbled up. When Reagan succeeded Democratic President Jimmy Carter, he had a ready pool of high-profile conservative lawyers."[8]

Next, we turn to a review of President Bush's views regarding the issue areas with which this study is concerned.

Abortion

In 1987 when Vice President of the United States George Bush wrote in his autobiography, *Looking Forward*:

I oppose abortion, except in cases of rape, incest, or when the life of the mother is at stake. Reagan and I both disapproved of the Supreme Court ruling in *Roe v. Wade*; we agreed that some form of constitutional amendment was needed to overturn the decision.[9]

And, during his 1988 presidential campaign, Bush repeatedly said he opposed abortion generally, but would make exceptions if the life of the woman were endangered or if the pregnancy resulted from rape or incest. However, after becoming president, Bush consistently opposed federal funding of *any* abortion except when needed to save the life of the woman.[10]

Bush also supported and defended the GOP platform plank calling for a constitutional amendment to ban abortions and his opposition to abortion remained a clear policy objective throughout his tenure as president. For example, although Congress passed numerous bills to allow federal funding of abortions for rape and incest victims and to permit the District of Columbia to use local tax funds to pay for abortions, President Bush vetoed all of the measures. Additionally, Bush even opposed and threatened to veto legislation allowing the use of tissue from aborted fetuses for research.[11] In a letter to Congress, Bush stated directly, "I will veto any legislation that weakens current or existing regulations."[12]

More specifically, for example, in January of 1989, Bush (1) stated that *Roe v. Wade* was "wrong and should be overturned"; (2) defined abortion as an issue of "moral gravity," resting on principles and faith that assert and affirm that human life in all forms must be respected; and (3) stated his position that "when it comes to abortion, there's a better way: the way of adoption, the way of life."[13]

Later that year, at a press conference in June of 1989, Bush said, "I am firmly positioned in favor of overturning *Roe v. Wade* and that's my position, and I'm not going to change that position."[14] President Bush not only wanted the Supreme Court to overturn *Roe v. Wade*,[15] but also wanted to pass a "human life" amendment to the Constitution that would permanently make abortion illegal except in cases of incest, rape, and a threat to the mother's well being.

The following year, speaking at a March for Life Rally in 1990, Bush remarked that the pro-life movement "reminds us all in government that Americans from all walks of life are committed to preserving the sanctity of human life."[16] In 1991, Bush stated once again that abortion "fundamentally contradicts the values of America," values that demand respect for human life as "sacrosanct and beyond question."[17]

The Bush administration also continued the practice of barring abortion counseling at federally funded clinics citing—as the Reagan administration had done in the 1980—Title X of the Public Health Service Act of 1970.[18] And, Charles Fried, solicitor general under the Reagan administration (1985–1989), was called back by the Bush administration to present its argument for overruling *Roe* in a friend-of-the-Court argument in the *Webster* case[19]—essentially the same argument made by Fried for the Reagan administration (see Chapter 5).[20]

Fried began his argument for the Bush administration as follows:

Today the United States asks this Court to reconsider and overrule its decision in *Roe v. Wade*. At the outset, I would like to make quite clear how limited that submission is. First, we are not asking the Court to unravel the fabric of unenumerated and privacy rights which this Court has woven together. . . . Rather, we are asking the Court to pull this one thread.[21]

Evidence suggests clearly that the Bush administration was concerned about abortion when selecting judges. The Bush administration "may not ask the potential nominee (yes or no, do you support abortion) but they know the answer," explained George Kassouf of the Alliance for Justice, a group active in leading the fight against confirmation of some the most conservative Reagan and Bush nominees.[22] It is also clear that the abortion issue was key to many other Bush appointments as well. For example, after President Bush nominated Dr. Antonia Novello to be surgeon general, White House press secretary Marlin Fitzwater assured reporters that Novello "supports the president's policies" on abortion. Fitzwater continued when asked whether the Bush administration was using abortion as a "litmus test" for appointments, "You can call it whatever you want—but the fact is, yes, anybody who is coming into a policymaking position, we'll ask what their beliefs are and whether they can support our policy."[23]

Throughout his term as president, and leading into the 1992 campaign, Bush defended his belief that life begins at conception. In addressing antiabortion demonstrators gathered in Washington in 1992 to mark the anniversary of the *Roe v. Wade* decision, Bush said that "from the moment the miracle of life occurs, human beings must cherish life, must hold it in awe, must preserve, protect and defend it."[24]

Religious Liberty

Overall, President Bush, like President Reagan, favored a decreased separation between church and state. In a March 22, 1989 speech, for example, Bush stated, "I very openly advocate prayer in the schools. I am not going to change my mind about it. I'm absolutely convinced that it is right."[25] Bush, like President Reagan before him, also supported both a constitutional amendment to restore voluntary school prayer and tuition tax credits (the voucher system) for parents who send their children to private and/or religious schools. Accordingly, said Bush in a January 29, 1990 speech, "I will not see the option of religious-based child care restricted or eliminated."[26]

Bush's solicitor general also joined the school board in *Lee v. Weisman*[27] as an amicus curiae, arguing in support of allowing prayers at formal graduation exercises. In *Weisman*, Bush's Justice Department also asked the Supreme Court to overturn its 1971 precedent (*Lemon v. Kurtzman*)[28] that established a three-part test for determining whether a governmental action amounts to the establishment of religion.[29] The Supreme Court, however, in a 5–4 decision, held that official prayer at a public school graduation violated the constitutional separation of church and state. Afterward, Bush expressed his dissatisfaction with the decision, stating that, "[T]he Court has unnecessarily cast away the venerable and proper American tradition of non-sectarian prayer at public celebrations."[30]

Affirmative Action

President Bush, who as a candidate for the Senate in 1964 and then opposed the 1964 Civil Rights Act, believed that affirmative action was inconsistent with "traditional American values."[31] As such, President Bush in general showed little support for legislation seeking to redress past (or present) discriminatory patterns through affirmative action statutes.[32] Bush denounced the use of statistical information as rigid quota formulas and supported a Department of Justice rationale of "color blind" enforcement of civil rights laws. President Bush's policy objective with regard to affirmative action was to "put the power in the hands of the people."[33] And, although Bush did sign the Civil Rights Act of 1991, he vetoed an earlier 1990 version labeling it a "quota bill."[34] Consider, however, that it is in just such cases—when Congress acts to undo Supreme

Court rulings as it did with the Civil Rights Act of 1991—that these new laws will sooner or later return to the lower courts to be interpreted. For background on the 1990 and 1991 legislation see the following summary.

The Civil Rights Act of 1990 and 1991

The Civil Rights Act of 1990 was introduced to reverse a series of civil rights decisions issued by the Supreme Court during its 1988–1989 term, as well as some other conservative civil rights decisions that the Court had issued since 1985, that eroded equal employment opportunities for minorities and women.[35] President Bush, however, consistently warned that he would not sign any law that might lead to hiring quotas. "I want to sign a civil rights bill," said Bush at a White House Rose Garden ceremony on May 17, 1990, "but I will not sign a quota bill."[36] Bush wrote to key senators on October 16, 1990, before their vote that he believed the 1990 bill would cause business to adopt hiring and promotion quotas. Bush wrote, "It will also foster divisiveness and litigation rather than conciliation and do more to promote legal fees than civil rights. If the bill is presented to me, I will be compelled to veto it."[37] Despite Bush's warning, the 1990 bill passed the Senate, 65–34, on July 18, 1990, and the House, 227–157, on August 3, 1990. And, as promised, on October 22, President Bush vetoed the 1990 legislation after a battle with Democratic sponsors over whether the 1990 bill would establish quotas for minorities and women and thereby discriminate against whites[38]—even though the bill explicitly forbade quotas.[39]

The Senate failed to override the president's veto by only one vote, thus marking the first defeat for a civil rights bill since the Eisenhower administration. In addition to Bush's opposition to quotas, the president's proposal also set lower limits on damages than the vetoed bill passed by Congress.[40]

After the Senate failed to override Bush's veto, Ralph G. Neas, executive director of the Leadership Conference on Civil Rights, stated "George Bush is a Ronald Reagan in sheep's clothing. While his style and rhetoric may differ, his substantive civil rights policies are just as deadly to those who are the victims of job discrimination."[41]

About four months later, in January of 1991, the Civil Rights Act of 1991 was introduced in the House and passed in June of 1991 after numerous compromises were reached between President Bush and Senate Republicans who supported the legislation.[42] Bush eventually gave his endorsement to the compromise bill at a news conference held on October 25, 1991, stating the new agreement "does not resort to quotas. . . . I wanted a non-quota civil rights bill that I could sign. And assuming there are no changes in the bill as agreed to last night . . . I will enthusiastically sign this bill," said Bush.[43] The Civil Rights Act of 1991 was signed into law by Bush on November 21, 1991.[44]

In sum, the Civil Rights Act of 1991 overruled many of the conservative decisions of the Rehnquist Court's 1988–1989 term, as well as some earlier and later decisions.[45]

School Desegregation

President Bush repeatedly called himself the "education president." And, continuing the legacy of President Reagan, school desegregation remained under attack during the Bush administration. As under Reagan, the Bush Justice Department continued to substitute voluntary desegregation plans despite the resegregation caused by many such plans.[46] Calling his plans "freedom of choice," President Bush generally favored court orders to halt desegregation efforts, especially when busing was involved. Bush also, in a signed message to Congress transmitting the Educational Excellence Act of 1989, supported the creation of a Magnet Schools of Excellence program that would support the "establishment, expansion, or enhancement of magnet schools *without regard to the presence of desegregation plans*" (emphasis added).[47] The act did promise, however, that no magnet school would be supported under this program if the "award itself" would result in segregation or impede the process of desegregation.[48] Even so, however, Bush had little success negotiating agreements with Congress and his school choice initiative was not passed.

In yet another example, the Department of Education under the Bush administration announced that it would withdraw federal funds from universities with special scholarships that the department held were "racially discriminatory." This new policy toward minority scholarships, however, was quickly withdrawn for further study under pressure from the White House. "The Bush administration even threatened to use *Brown* [1954] as a source of legal authority for invalidating minority scholarship programs as a species of unconstitutional affirmative action."[49]

Voting/Elections

Although both major parties have been slow to support legislation that would increase the low levels of participation in American elections, it should be noted that George Bush vetoed the "motor voter" bill in 1992 to prevent, in his view, "corruption of the voting process." On July 20, 1992, during a campaign visit to California, President Bush was asked: "Mr. President, was the primary reason that you vetoed the motor voter bill the fact that it would increase the number of poor and young voters in which you have gotten little strength? If not, can we have a brief explanation?" Bush responded:

No, that had nothing to do with the veto of the bill. States have the right to set their own registration; everybody has a way to register. It has nothing to do with the poor and the young. Frankly, I think we're going to do very well with the young, and hopefully, with the poor. What it has to do though, is with guarding against corruption of the voting process, and that's why I vetoed it.[50]

SELECTION, SCREENING, AND NOMINATION UNDER BUSH

The Federal Judgeship Act of 1990 created seventy-four additional district court judgeships, but President Bush, unlike President Reagan, did not set out initially to remold the federal judiciary. Although Bush spoke generally about seeking conservative judges who would not "legislate from the bench," he did not often elaborate on what that specifically meant.[51]

In his directives to senators, however, Bush indicated he was searching for "qualified judicial conservatives." Said Bush, "by 'qualified' candidates, I mean *not only* persons who have the training, intellect, character, and temperament to be excellent judges, *but also* persons who understand the separation of powers and the judicial role within our constitutional system and who are committed to interpreting the law and not legislating from the bench" (emphasis added).[52] In short, Bush wanted nominees whose judicial philosophy favored government's interests over an individual's.

Patrick J. Leahy (D-VT), a member of the Senate Judiciary Committee, said, "I get far less of a sense in the Bush administration that there's a litmus test and an interest in symbolic appointments, as there was under Reagan."[53] As late as 1990, midway through the Bush administration, numerous scholars admitted it was "difficult to discern a pattern in Bush's judges beyond that they are conservatives, defined by a narrow reading of the Constitution and favoring of government interest over individual rights."[54] Bruce Fein, a former associate deputy attorney general under Reagan who had helped to screen nominations, said in 1990 that "none of Bush's nominations makes a philosophical statement."[55]

Highlighting the first two years of the Bush administration was the terribly slow and deliberate pace at which nominations were made. During his first year in office, for example, Bush put just fifteen judges on the bench, the fewest of any president in a single year since John F. Kennedy in 1963. There were fifty-nine vacancies at the start of 1990, many of which had existed since the first half of 1989.[56] As described by political scientist Sheldon Goldman in 1990, "[T]he Justice Department and administration have been moving excruciatingly slowly . . . it's like paralysis. My general impression," stated Goldman, "is that there is a lack of focus and that they are torn between different imperatives. The Reagan administration [unlike Bush] knew what it wanted and went out and got it."[57] Consider the complex and controversial issue of nomination delay.

Initial Delays: Confirmations with All Deliberate Speed

Concern for the Bush administration's unprecedented delays in making judicial nominations were sounded from both sides of the aisle. "It seems to me like [the Bush administration] ought to think in terms of only having a window of two years to make a real impact on the judiciary," stated Sen. Charles Grassley (R-IA). "And that impact over the next two years can be felt for the next twenty years."[58] In a polite, yet poignant, exchange between Senate Judiciary Committee Chairman Joseph Biden (D-DE) and Senator Orrin Hatch (R-UT) at a November 1990 Judiciary Committee meeting, Biden cautiously called attention to the few nominations coming to the Senate during the same year that Congress would consider whether or not to authorize additional federal judgeships to handle record high caseloads. "I am not casting aspersions," continued Biden, "I am not suggesting that it would be moved any faster. I do just point out where we are with regard to judicial nominations." Senator Hatch interjected: "I will cast aspersions. I think it is abominable, because we can't handle the caseloads in most of the areas now."[59]

Consider also, for example, during debate in 1990 on a judgeship bill (HR 5316) to increase the number of district court judges, House Judiciary Committee Chairman Jack Brooks (D-TX), directly criticized President Bush for moving too slowly to fill existing judicial vacancies. Said Brooks, "It's clear that these new judgeships could do nothing to ease the court's caseload unless the president acts decisively to fill these [existing] vacancies and make nominations for these new positions."[60] Similarly, Senator Alan Simpson (R-WY) expressed displeasure with the Bush administration's delays. "We fought like dogs," said Simpson, "to get a drug bill. You can talk about gun control and guns and education and rehabilitation and capital punishment, but all that pales before the action of having a defendant appear in court for a trial—and they can't appear in court for a trial if there is not a judge on the bench. It is absolutely absurd."[61]

In defense of the Bush administration's slow pace in filling vacancies, Attorney General Dick Thornburgh—who was appointed at the end of the Reagan administration in August of 1988—reassured the Judicial Conference of the United States during the fall of 1988 that while "the process has been slow, it was going forward, and progress is being made." Thornburgh explained further that delays should be attributed to the "political nature of the process."[62] "Politics is, essentially, public debate in microcosm played out in a game that combines the intricacies of chess and the audacity of old-fashioned hardball, with vacancies left in limbo by complex stalling maneuvers designed to put the administration in checkmate, and with nominees knocked out of the game after being hit with a few too many well-placed bean balls. . . . It remains a reality of the judicial nomination process that these are the rules of the game as it is currently being played."[63]

One of the ironies of Thornburgh's comments, however, as discussed below under "Bush and the Senate," is that a substantial number of Bush's nominations were delayed by Republican senators.

Two of the most important innovations during the Reagan era—the President's Committee on Federal Judicial Selection,[64] and the systematic screening of all potential nominees to the federal bench—were maintained by the Bush administration.[65] Initially, judicial selection under Bush was shared by the office of the attorney general, Richard Thornburgh,[66] and the White House-based President's Committee on Federal Judicial Selection, chaired by the White House counsel. Essentially, the chain of command was from the president to the White House counsel to the attorney general. This screening process generally included extensive personal interviews in the Department of Justice (by Barbara Drake, deputy assistant attorney general, 1991–1992) and careful screening by the White House counsel's office.

The White House and the Attorney General

The White House Counsel's office was the center for the philosophical screening of candidates. White House Counsel C. Boyden Gray, for example, left little doubt that the Bush administration's desire was to appoint judges with a "conservative philosophy."[67] Procedurally, however, it was Associate White House Counsel Lee Liberman (a former clerk for Supreme Court Justice Scalia) who was usually responsible for screening candidates, including evaluating the judicial opinions of nominees if candidates had judicial records.

The Department of Justice also continued the unpopular practice of requesting multiple names from senators for judicial nominees—a practice that President Reagan had tried to enforce. Despite opposition from senators, Murray G. Dickman, assistant attorney general, explained that Justice Department officials "believe the best nominee [would] emerge if there is a pool of candidates from which to choose."[68] Notable also was the departure of the Attorney General Dick Thornburgh in August of 1991 to campaign for a Senate vacancy in Pennsylvania, created by the death of Senator John Heinz and to be filled by special election.[69] Significantly, Thornburgh's assistant, Murray Dickman, who had focused on the political aspects of the judicial selection, left with Thornburgh, leaving Barbara Drake, deputy assistant attorney general in the Justice Department's Civil Rights Division to take on Dickman's responsibilities. In total, Drake, who had until Dickman's departure only assisted with judicial selection by evaluating the professional qualifications and acting as a liaison between the Justice Department and the ABA's Standing Committee on Federal Judiciary, then added Dickman's political and administrative responsibilities to her full time work in the Civil Rights Division.[70]

The result of these added responsibilities clearly created a significant burden on Drake and, at first, nominations were made slowly. This additional responsibility was made even greater by the seventy-four additional district court judgeships created by the Federal Judgeship Act of 1990. Drake, however, by 1992 acted with unprecedented speed on judicial nominees. In 1992, for example, the Senate Judiciary Committee cleared a record number of appointments for a presidential election year, with fifty-three confirmations to the district courts.[71] In fact, of the 142 district court nominations made during the last two years of the Bush administration, ninety were made under Drake's supervision. At the same time, however, there were also a record number of nominations for which the committee took no action, including forty-two district court appointments.[72]

It is also important to note that the seemingly amicable relationship of shared decision making between the White House counsel's office with the Justice Department regarding judicial selection marked the first time in history that women played major roles in the judicial selection process. And, as evidenced in the following section that profiles Bush's appointees, Lee Liberman's and Barbara Drake's key positions in the White House and the Justice Department may have increased the chances of female judicial candidates (especially in the wake of the Thomas-Hill hearings that contributed to Bush appointing a higher proportion of women to the federal bench than Carter's heretofore unprecedented proportion; see Table 3.11.

Bush and the ABA

When attempting to deflect criticisms for moving too slowly to fill vacancies, Justice Department spokesman David Runkel cited what he termed a "fairly protracted and public disagreement with the ABA on their involvement."[73]

Bush, Thornburgh, and the ABA[74]

Initially, Attorney General Dick Thornburgh wanted to bring in conservative Republican Robert B. Fiske, Jr. to be deputy attorney general in charge of judicial selection. Right-wing Republicans, however, objected to Fiske because he had been chairman of the ABA Standing Committee on Federal Judiciary. Mostly, these objections centered around perceptions that the ABA improperly used political or ideological criteria to assess nominees' qualifications, especially since four committee members had voted Robert Bork "not qualified" for the Supreme Court. In part, to soften opposition to Fiske, Thornburgh asked the ABA to refrain from considering political or ideological views when rating nominees. In response, the ABA maintained that it did not consider such views. This response was unsatisfactory to Thornburgh, who declared that the administration would no longer consult with the ABA until it disavowed considering political or ideological views when rating nominees. Eventually, the ABA complied and added to its rules: "[P]olitical or ideological philosophy are not considered."[75]

Members of the Senate Judiciary Committee were also dissatisfied with the ABA's role in rating nominees and on June 2, 1989 held a formal hearing to debate the ABA committee's role.[76] It was at this meeting that in deference to the concerns of the Senate Judiciary Committee and the attorney general the ABA reported that it would eliminate the "exceptionally well qualified" ratings, leaving only "well qualified," "qualified," and "not qualified."[77] In spite of these concessions from the ABA, key Republicans still opposed Fiske and on July 6, 1989, Fiske asked that his name be withdrawn.[78] It was after the withdrawal of Fiske that judicial selection was officially centered in the attorney general's office and Murray Dickman, assistant to the attorney general, was charged with coordinating judicial selection in the Justice Department.

In short, some conservatives charged that the ABA was screening political philosophy, but the dispute was resolved in June 1990 after ABA officials said that the Standing Committee on Federal Judiciary would refuse to consider political philosophy in its evaluation. Additionally, as discussed previously in Chapter 3 and above, it was during the Bush administration that ABA Standing Committee dropped its "exceptionally well qualified" so that "well qualified" became its highest rating.

Eventually, district court judge nominees did make it to the ABA and the ABA averaged about two months in giving its evaluation of them.[79] The majority received a unanimous "well qualified" rating and Bush did not nominate any candidates who received a "not qualified" rating. In fact, in comparison, the Bush appointees received the highest ABA ratings of any administration's appointees until Clinton (see Table 3.11).

Bush and the Senate Judiciary Committee: Nominations Stalled Again

Highlighting the tensions between the White House and Democrats on the Senate Judiciary Committee was the issue of judiciary committee access to FBI reports on judicial nominees. After all, many believe it was the leaking to the press of Anita Hill's judiciary committee affidavit (including allegations of sexual harassment against Clarence Thomas) that led to the hearing on charges of sexual harassment.[80] Afterward, President Bush attempted to tighten the reins on FBI reports and demanded that only designated committee members be allowed to read them. President Bush said, in a speech on October 24, 1991:

I have ordered that the FBI reports be carried directly to committee chairmen and any members designated by the chairmen. The members will read the reports immediately in the presence of the agent, and return them. No FBI reports will stay on Capitol Hill. And furthermore, members only will have access to these reports.[81]

However, the move to restrict access to FBI reports backfired on the president. The Senate Judiciary Committee on November 21, 1991 rebuffed President Bush's new FBI policy with a unanimous, bipartisan resolution calling for reinstated access to the FBI reports. Senate Judiciary Committee chairman Joseph Biden threatened that the committee would therefore have to supplement the FBI reports with its own investigatory personnel at a cost of millions of dollars annually and refused to move *on any* nominations until these new investigatory personnel were functioning. Consequently, many of Bush's confirmations, especially lower court confirmations that had already received lower priority during the Thomas-Hill hearings, were effectively delayed yet again.[82] Eventually, Bush softened his position and agreed to restore FBI report access to committee members and staff under stricter security. However, by the time the matter was resolved and the Thomas confirmation hearings ended, thus allowing the Senate Judiciary Committee to resume more attention to the lower courts, Bush was running for reelection.[83] Clearly, at this late date, Democrats especially might have been willing to hold up appointments awaiting the outcome of the presidential election.[84]

Additionally, several of Bush's nominees were also criticized for belonging to clubs that had discriminatory membership policies. According to a report from the "People for the American Way," a group that scrutinizes judicial candidates, "Twelve nominees reported that they resigned from these clubs prior to their nomination, while others cited changes in the clubs' policies. The remaining handful ultimately resigned their club memberships after tough questioning from the Senate Judiciary Committee." In August 1990, prior to Bush's 1991 attempt to restrict the committee's access to FBI reports, the Senate Judiciary Committee unanimously adopted a resolution saying that it is inappropriate for nominees or potential nominees to belong to discriminatory clubs "unless such persons are actively engaged in bona fide efforts to eliminate the discriminatory practices."[85]

Bush also experienced confirmation problems due to partisan infighting and senatorial courtesy. Early in 1991, for example, two district court nominees' appointments in Alabama and Arkansas were stalled due to infighting between Republican Senator James Jeffords of Vermont and the Bush administration.[86] Essentially, the issue was whether Jeffords would be allowed to determine the federal district judgeship nominee (Fred I. Parker) for his state. That is, because the White House refused to nominate Parker, Jeffords' candidate, Jeffords decided to block the Senate approval of the Alabama and Arkansas nominees (whom the Senate Judiciary Committee had already approved). "If we do not receive what I consider satisfactory reconciliation of this confrontation," said Jeffords, "I intend to put a hold on all new judgeships that are to be confirmed by this body until such time as that prerogative [senatorial courtesy] has been re-established."[87] It has been noted however, that while initially threatening to "hold all new judgeships," after pressure from colleagues, Jeffords decided to block only two—Edwin L. Nelson, nominated to the Northern District of Alabama, and Susan W. Wright, for the Eastern and Western Districts of Arkansas. Significantly, of all the states represented by the eight nominees brought to the floor during the Parker controversy, only Alabama and Arkansas had two Democratic senators.[88] Consider, for example, Jeffords' reply to criticisms raised by Senator Howell Heflin (D-AL) as to why the Alabama and Arkansas nominees had been "arbitrarily singled out": "It hurts me to have to do this, but I hope that my distinguished colleague [Heflin], who I know is a judge, recognizes the prerogative of the Senate is extremely important. I know of no other way I can impress upon this body and impress upon the White House [my support for the Parker appointment] without taking this action, as much as it grieves me."[89]

Despite the fact that the two judges blocked appeared to have been partisan decisions, Democrats still held to their overall support for senatorial courtesy. For example, Democratic Senate Judiciary Committee Chairman Biden used the floor dispute over Jeffords' actions for an opportunity to chastise the Bush administration and support senatorial prerogative: "Unlike five bureaucrats in the White House subjecting nominees to litmus tests or any other tests, the home-state senators know better the quality of the people in their states, and they know those in the bar and the bench who are going to be recommending yes or no on particular nominees. . . . Unless the administration has consulted with, discussed with, and had the input of the senators from the states from which these judges originate, they will have a great deal of difficulty moving through the committee."[90]

Other key Democrats as well made sure that the blame for moving slowly on judicial appointments be attributed to the Republicans. For example, then Senate Majority Leader George Mitchell (D-ME), in response to Jeffords' (and other GOP members) intentions to hold up confirmations, noted for the record: "I am merely making a point: Constantly statements are being made about the pace of nominations, and I just want the record to be complete that a substantial number of these nominations are being blocked by Republican senators."[91]

On balance, although the Federal Judgeship Act of 1990 that created seventy-four new district court judges took effect on December 1, 1990, it took fifteen months or more to select only twelve nominees to fill a handful of these new positions. According to the Administrative Office of the U.S. Courts, in 1992, it took an average of 385 days from the day of the vacancy until a nomination was made by the Bush administration.[92] Despite such longer periods of time required for nomination, however, many judicial scholars generally agree that "more often than not, President Bush had his way in making judicial selections."[93]

The Bush Appointments: A Profile

They [Bush aides] are just really comfortable with the good old boy network. They [the nominees] are the people who they would see back at their social clubs or who they hang around with, the wealthy people they grew up with.[94]

As stated earlier, the "Judgeships Act" of 1990 gave President Bush seventy-four new district court positions. And, despite President Bush's slow start in appointing district court judges, during his one term he did in fact eventually appoint 148 district court judges—mostly male (80 percent), white (90 percent),[95] and with an individual net worth of $500,000+ (60 percent). In fact, about one-third reported their wealth at more than $1 million. Also, as indicated earlier in Chapter 3 (see Table 3.11), about 90 percent were Republicans,[96] 60 percent reported past party activism, and a record number of them were recruited from large law firms. Like Carter and Reagan before him, a greater number of Bush's appointees had previous judicial experience than had prosecutorial experience. In fact, judicial selection under President Bush utilized a "farm team" approach; Bush showed a preference for recruiting state judges and federal magistrates[97] for district court openings in greater proportions than previous administrations. In doing so, Bush was often able to review a candidate's proven track record before nomination.[98] Promoting from within the judiciary "sounds as if it's the right thing to do—it's meritorious on its face," said Howard M. Metzenbaum (D-OH, and member of the Senate Judiciary Committee), "[B]ut it provides for inbreeding, more of the same kind of people."[99]

Regarding diversity, as indicated in Table 3.11, about one in five of Bush's district court appointees were women (about 20 percent), breaking Carter's heretofore unprecedented record of 14.4 percent. In raw numbers, however, both Carter and Bush appointed twenty-nine women. As explained by one analyst, "[I]t is likely that in at least a few instances, Republican senators were convinced of the political importance of finding qualified women, particularly in light of the Clarence Thomas-Anita Hill hearings."[100] However, pressure to appoint more racial minorities was apparently not as compelling. Bush appointed proportionally more African-Americans than Reagan but far fewer than Carter; specifically, 6.8 percent (10) for Bush compared to 13.9 percent (28) for Carter.

Bush's proportion of Latino appointees dropped below both the Reagan and Carter records, and, for the first time since the Nixon administration, no Asian-Americans were appointed.

Overall, however, differences between Bush's and Reagan's nominees are few. Sheldon Goldman concluded, for instance, that Bush not only "sought to transform the federal judiciary," but also "has made the federal bench far more conservative than when Reagan took office."[101] Nearly one-third of Bush's judicial appointees had worked for the Reagan administration. As characterized by Clint Bolick, director of the Landmark Legal Foundation Center for Civil Rights, "[T]his is one area that conservatives have to be pleased with the Bush administration, from a quality and a philosophical standpoint."[102] Similarly, President Reagan's former attorney general, Edwin Meese, surmised that the Bush administration officials "have done an excellent job . . . the results are the same as in the Reagan administration."[103]

Consider also, for example, an evaluation of the Reagan-Bush appointees by Judge Stephen Reinhardt, a Ninth Circuit Carter appointee. "Since Reagan and Bush appointees began to dominate the court," Reinhardt says, "it has become more and more likely for civil cases to be thrown out because of missed filing deadlines. . . . You file a day late, your case is dismissed. . . . I'm not saying all Bush appointees are for these things, and all Carter appointees are against them, but in the current climate [1992], these kinds of measures are far more acceptable than they once were." Reinhardt also states that the Reagan-Bush dominated courts have issued more unpublished opinions and cut both oral argument time and the permitted length of briefs. [104]

For the most part, Bush's nominations to the federal courts generally, including his 1990 appointment of David Souter to the Supreme Court, occurred without notable opposition from either the public or Democratic senators.[105] However, the one exception to the generally noncontroversial Bush nominees was the Supreme Court confirmation of Justice Clarence Thomas on October 15, 1991.[106] In fact, Thomas' narrow 52–48 confirmation was perhaps the most significant and consequential event involving the judiciary during the Bush administration and certainly did not comport with the president's "kinder and gentler" politics. Unlike David Souter, who had published no scholarly articles, Thomas had written and spoken extensively in support of the "Right's" social agenda. And, despite President Bush's claim that the Thomas appointment had "nothing to do with race," it is obvious that race was clearly a factor in Bush's assessment that Thomas was the "best-qualified" to succeed the retiring Justice Thurgood Marshall.[107]

Clearly, issues raised in the Thomas confirmation can provide a richer understanding of judicial selection during the Bush administration as well as add to our overall assessment of the role of the courts in the political process. With respect to the Thomas battle, for example, political scientist Sheldon Goldman found that there are "hints" in the record to support the notion that senators who strongly backed Thomas suffered some fallout with the Senate Judiciary Committee with respect to district court nominees. For example, Senator John Danforth (R-MO), who personally vouched and led the fight for the Thomas nomination, found that only three of seven Missouri district court nominees were confirmed.[108] In another example, Senator Alfonse D'Amato (R-NY), saw only five of twelve New York district courts nominees confirmed.[109] Overall, fallout from the Thomas-Hill debacle exacerbated tensions between the White House and the Senate Judiciary Committee and seems to have adversely impacted Bush's success in gaining confirmation for his district court appointees.

BILL CLINTON: THE FIRST TERM

President Clinton's 1992 victory over incumbent President Bush not only signaled a return of the Democratic party to the White House but also the chance to appoint federal judges by a Democratic administration for the first time in twelve years. During the 1992 presidential election campaign, Clinton was quick to criticize the Bush administration's judicial appointments, noting a "sharp decline in the selection of women and minority judges, at the very time when more and more qualified women and minority candidates were reaching the time of their lives when they could serve as judges."[110] Though apparently unaware of Bush's unprecedented proportion of women appointees, Clinton's statements clearly signaled his belief that more women and minorities should be appointed to the federal courts and that, if elected, he would work to that end. Also, during the 1992 presidential campaign, Clinton promised to appoint "men and women of unquestioned intellect, judicial temperament, broad experience and a demonstrated concern for, and commitment to, the individual rights protected by our Constitution, including the right to privacy."[111] More specifically, during his 1992 presidential campaign, Clinton "promised to reshape the character of the federal courts, reversing the trend to the right under the Reagan and Bush Administrations."[112]

Clinton's election did in fact end twelve years of Republican-controlled appointments to the federal courts and right-wing conservatives were swift to respond. For example, Clinton's 1992 election win was met immediately with the formation of the Free Congress Foundation's "Judicial Selection Monitoring Project." The monitoring project uses high-tech media and communication (including a cable television station) to coordinate right-wing groups to contest Democratic nominees to the federal courts.[113] "I don't feel we have much of a choice," said Marianne Lombardi, the project's deputy director. "They're going to load up the courts with liberals and activists. We can't just stand by and let them do it."[114] Failed Supreme Court nominee Robert Bork was an immediate and vocal supporter of the Judicial Selection Monitoring Project. "The judicial selection monitoring project is so vitally important to our nation's future," wrote Bork in a fund-raising letter to potential donors to the project dated just days after the 1992 election, "that, even before the first Clinton nominee is named, conservatives must organize and prepare to meet the coming challenge."[115]

Expectations were high among many pro-choice and pro-church/state separation advocates following Clinton's 1992 election to the presidency. Clinton's opposition to tax credits for sectarian schools and his "freedom of conscience" stance on abortion led Edd Doer, executive director of Americans for Religious Liberty, in 1993 to predict that "Congress will at last pass, and President Clinton will sign, the Religious Freedom Restoration Act,"[116] and, "Congress will pass, and President Clinton will sign, the Freedom of Choice Act to protect abortion rights from adverse state action."[117]

Next I turn to a review of Clinton's policy positions regarding the five key policy issues with which this study is concerned.

Abortion

In the 1992 Clinton-Gore campaign treatise, *Putting People First*,[118] Clinton promised to sign the Freedom of Choice Act: "Our government has no right to interfere with the difficult and intensely personal decisions women must sometimes make regarding abortion." Clinton promised to "urge" Congress to repeal the Hyde Amendment and expressed opposition to "any federal attempt to limit access to abortion" through a mandatory waiting period or requirement of parental or spousal consent.[119] Clinton also called for measures to protect against "radical demonstrators who illegally block health clinics."[120] And, indeed, one of Clinton's first acts—January 22, 1993—was to lift the executive orders banning abortion counseling in federally funded family planning clinics and the use of fetal tissue for medical research.[121]

All in all, during his first term, President Clinton fostered a climate more favorable to the pro-choice agenda than the previous pro-life Bush administration. But at times Clinton sent mixed signals. In January of 1993, for example, President Clinton signed four executive orders on abortion-related issues and stated: "Our goal should be to protect individual freedom, while fostering responsible decision-making, an approach that seeks to protect the right to choose, while reducing the number of abortions."[122]

However, Clinton certainly did not look to lead a pro-choice charge. Clinton, for example, did not lobby the House of Representatives when, in July of 1993, it considered—and passed by eighty-five votes—the Hyde Amendment banning government-financed abortions. Moreover, Clinton "made no effort to broker the dispute that derailed the Freedom of Choice Act" (also summer 1993).[123] When asked about his lack of visibility on these issues, Clinton aid George Stephanopoulos explained simply, that Clinton "was not asked."[124]

A key abortion issue that came to the forefront of the debate during Clinton's first term was the congressional attempt to ban "partial-birth" abortions.[125] Significantly, the partial-birth ban marked the first time the Senate passed a measure to restrict a specific abortion method. Prior to its passing the House and Senate, President Clinton made clear his plans to veto the bill. Having "studied and prayed about this issue . . . for many months," Clinton stated that partial-birth abortions must be available to protect the "health" of the mother. A White House statement said the ban was unconstitutional as written and that the bill would have to include an exception for both the life and health of the woman for Clinton to sign it.[126] Specifically, in a February 28, 1996 letter to longtime abortion opponent Rep. Henry Hyde (R-IL), Clinton again outlined his concerns, saying the bill would not "meet the constitutional requirements in *Roe* and the decisions that have followed it, to provide protection for both the life and health of the mother in any laws regulating abortion."[127]

As expected, Clinton's veto threat drew immediate criticism. The bill's sponsor, Rep. Charles T. Canady (R-FL), warned that if Clinton vetoes this bill "he will demonstrate that he is an extremist on the issue of abortion." And, as one observer put it, "pro-life activists want to use this against Mr. Clinton in the campaign." The Clinton camp responded by threatening to claim that Bob Dole wanted to appoint conservative judges who would "criminalize abortion." "They know that judges cannot criminalize abortion. In fact, as Mr. Clinton's veto proves, today in this country even legislators cannot criminalize abortion."[128]

Clinton's proposed veto also drew criticism from the Catholic hierarchy. For example, Cardinal Joseph Bernadin of Chicago declared that a Clinton veto would send a "very disturbing message to which persons of good will must give serious consideration as they cast their ballots in November."[129]

Nonetheless, and despite biting criticisms from abortion opponents, President Clinton vetoed the partial-birth abortion ban. In an April 10, 1996 message to Congress vetoing the bill (HR 1833), Clinton stated:

I have always believed that the decision to have an abortion generally should be between a woman, her doctor, her conscience, and her God. I cannot sign HR 1833, as passed, because it fails to protect women in such dire circumstances—because by treating doctors who perform the procedure . . . as criminals, the bill poses a serious harm to women. This bill . . . violates the constitutional command that any law regulating abortion protect both the life and the health of the woman.[130]

Following Clinton's partial-birth message, abortion proponents and others, including the American Civil Liberties Union (ACLU), were quick to praise the President's veto.[131]

Clinton's appointment of Justice Ruth Bader Ginsburg to the Supreme Court, who supports a woman's right to choose (although framed in equal protection terms instead of *Roe v. Wade*),[132] reflected well his judicial expectation on this issue, at least at the Supreme Court level. Others have suggested, however, that "Clinton has declined to impose a pro-choice litmus test on nominees to the federal district court judgeships."[133]

Religious Liberty

During the 1992 presidential campaign and throughout his first term, Clinton often discussed broad issues related to religion and its role in American society.

For example, Clinton's chief strategist, James Carville, described a Clinton campaign speech at Notre Dame University on September 11, 1992 as a "defining speech," revealing Clinton as an "unabashed Christian."[134] Clinton noted "my faith is a source of pride to me . . . if elected, I will be the first president to graduate from a Catholic college."[135] And Clinton used his acceptance speech at the Democratic National Convention to explain his conception of the relation between religion and politics. Scripture says, stated Clinton, that "our eyes have not yet seen, nor our ears heard, what we can build." However, despite his stated strong personal religious beliefs, Clinton opposed tax credits for sectarian schools, but supported the Religious Freedom Restoration Act (RFRA), calling it "a very important issue to me, personally," before it was enacted in November of 1993.[136]

On several occasions, President Clinton also publicly praised Stephen Carter's book, *The Culture of Disbelief: How American Law and Politics Trivialize Religious Devotion*, which argues that American society too often treats people of religious conviction as oddities in political life. Clinton, referring to Carter's book at a meeting with religious leaders in August 1993, stated that "people should not have to shed their religious beliefs before entering the public square."[137] Reiterating a theme in Carter's book, President Clinton stated forthrightly that freedom of religion should not mean "freedom from religion," or that "those of us who live by faith shouldn't frankly admit that we are animated by that faith, that we try to live by it—and that it affects what we feel, what we think, and what we do."[138]

Although President Clinton did not support a school prayer amendment during his first term, he nonetheless supported the notion of school prayer.[139] In July 1995, for instance, Clinton traveled to James Madison High School in the Washington suburb of Vienna, Virginia to give a forty-five-minute speech devoted to the proposition that public schools are not required to be "religious free zones." Afterward, Clinton also released a memorandum he previously sent to Attorney General Janet Reno and Education Secretary Richard Riley, which explored about two dozen specific ways in which public schools "might accommodate, or at least allow," what Clinton called "religious expression."[140] Essentially this memo suggested that there might be some constitutionally acceptable forms of religious expression "that need not be left at the schoolhouse door." Even more, the memo suggested that "generally, students may pray in a nondisruptive manner when not engaged in school activities or instruction."[141]

On balance, Clinton's support for school prayer is clear. "Some Americans have been denied the right to express their religion," Clinton said, "and that has to stop. It is crucial that government does not dictate or demand specific religious views, but equally crucial that government doesn't prevent the expression of specific religious views."[142]

Clinton and Civil Rights: An Overview

President Clinton's record on civil rights in general is somewhat difficult to label. Upon entering office in January 1993, Clinton appointed more women and minority-group members to cabinet and other high-level positions than any other president. Clinton became the first president to support an end to bias against homosexuals in the military, and he stepped up enforcement of fair housing laws and defended the government's affirmative action role, declaring in a July 1995 speech that his goal was to "mend it, not end it." And, as discussed below, among Clinton's judicial appointments are historic numbers of minorities and women to the federal district courts. As one *New York Times* columnist put it in 1996, "In his nearly four years in office, President Clinton has amassed a civil rights record rivaling that of any president in the last 30 years."[143] "If you look at his overall record, both in the appointments he's made and the policies he's pursued," said Wade Henderson, executive director of the liberal-oriented Leadership Conference on Civil Rights, "his record stands with the best of recent presidents, with the possible exception of Lyndon Johnson."[144]

On the other hand, conservatives continued to criticize Clinton's appointments throughout his first term. "Philosophically, I think they are straight, pro-preference liberals on these issues," said Linda Chavez, president of the Center for Equal Opportunity, a conservative group. "They interpret affirmative action to mean having double standards, having different rules according to race, with attention to the bottom line, according to numbers. There's not a whole lot of difference between the way the Clinton people enforce the law and the way the Carter people did."[145]

However, while key conservatives continued to complain about Clinton being too liberal, some liberal groups also maintained that he has not done enough to combat the Reagan-Bush legacy. Many have noted his reneging on a pledge to remove the ban on homosexuals in the military, his signing of a welfare bill that some civil rights advocates say will throw at least a million children into poverty,[146] and Clinton was especially criticized for his withdrawal of his nomination of University of Pennsylvania law professor Lani Guinier in 1993 to head the Justice Department's Civil Rights Division.

In short, Guinier had been a classmate of both Clinton and his wife Hillary at Yale Law School. Many felt that because of her reputation with the NAACP Legal Defense Fund, Guinier seemed an appropriate selection for assistant attorney general for civil rights. However, Guinier's academic writings supporting "cumulative voting" and "proportional representation" created strong reaction from opponents who labeled her a "Quota Queen." Clinton withdrew Guinier's nomination a month later without letting her appear before the Senate Judiciary Committee, and, despite a warning issued at a Congressional Black Caucus press conference by Representative Kweisi Mfume that the president "risked losing 40 very important votes if he refused to stand by Guinier."[147]

According to Stephanopoulos, the White House mishandled the nomination by not thoroughly reviewing Guinier's published work before the nomination. Ultimately, Clinton admitted that he was not aware that his own policies on equal opportunity and political equality contradicted some of Guinier's.[148]

Affirmative Action

Affirmative action has been good for America. . . . We should reaffirm the principle of affirmative action and fix the practices. We should have a simple slogan: Mend it, but don't end it.[149]

After his first-term election in 1992, Clinton assembled a cabinet that included four African-Americans, three women and two Latinos. Some, like Attorney General Janet Reno or Commerce Secretary Ron Brown, were given jobs historically reserved for white men. And, as detailed below, Clinton's district court appointees included higher percentages of women and minorities than for any previous presidents.

In defining his administration's position, President Clinton made it clear that he was against quotas: "I'm against quotas—I'm against giving anybody any kind of preference for something they're not qualified for," Clinton said. "But, because I still believe that there is some discrimination and that not everybody has an opportunity to prove they are qualified, I favor the right kind of affirmative action."[150]

However, in 1995, reportedly worried about the mounting political challenges to affirmative action programs (including attacks from Senator Bob Dole, then Senate majority leader and eventual 1996 Republican party nominee),[151] Clinton sought to redefine his administration's position on affirmative action. In short, Clinton called a group of House Democrats to the White House and told them the administration would be conducting an "urgent review" of all federal affirmative action programs.[152] Clinton also asked Vice President Gore to study ways the government can target contracts to businesses that set up shop and hire people in severely distressed communities—urban or rural.[153]

And, after a review that took five months, Clinton did decide to defend affirmative action. In a high profile speech at the National Archives on July 19, 1995, Clinton, drawing on a 100-page report, admitted that though his administration's review indicated that some programs may need to be changed or eliminated, "there is still a need for affirmative action." Although Clinton did not outline specific changes, he nonetheless directed all departments and agencies to eliminate any program that "creates a quota, creates preferences for unqualified individuals, creates reverse discrimination or continues even after its equal opportunity purposes have been achieved." "When affirmative action is done right," said Clinton, "it is flexible, it is fair, and it works." [154] Clinton concluded:

Let me be clear, affirmative action has been good for America. Affirmative action has not always been perfect, and affirmative action should not go on forever. [I]t should be retired when its job is done. I am resolved that that day will come. But the evidence suggests, indeed screams, that that day has not come. The job of ending discrimination in this country is not over. . . . Based on the evidence . . . we should reaffirm the principle of affirmative action and fix the practices. We should have a simple slogan: Mend it, but don't end it.[155]

In sum, President Clinton tried to extend the application of affirmative action to include women, the disabled, and poor whites. And, despite the moderate tone of Clinton's positions, some liberals also were put more at ease by Clinton's speech. For example, a November 1995 ABA press release praised President Clinton, stating that the president "defends affirmative action as 'good for America,' and supports the concept of providing a 'helping hand' to those 'who historically have been excluded' from the old-boy networks."[156] "As the president demonstrated in affirmative action, just the use of the bully pulpit can change the debate," said Charles Kamasaki, senior vice president with the National Council of La Raza, a Latino advocacy group. "We were in a free fall on affirmative action until the time the president made his speech. And almost since that time, from a policy perspective, the Republicans have been on the defensive."[157]

On balance, during his first term, Clinton was able to play both sides of the fence. As one commentator put it, Clinton has defended affirmative action and racially earmarked federal jobs to the make the government "look more like America," with the full knowledge that such programs will be found unconstitutional in the courts. "So he waits until they're forcibly dismantled by the court, and plays factional politics until they go."[158]

Presidential policy objectives are also demonstrated by the arguments their solicitors general bring to the court by way of amicus briefs. The difference between the Bush and Clinton presidencies is strikingly evident. Drew S. Days III, Clinton's solicitor general, rewrote several amicus briefs that had been filed by Bush's solicitor general for cases heard by the Supreme Court during the 1993–1994 term. In one case, for example, Days argued that the Civil Rights Act of 1991 should be applied retroactively whereas the Bush administration had earlier argued that it should not be.[159]

Overall, it is clear that President Clinton practiced, even if he did not preach, affirmative action when selecting federal judges (see discussion below). Clinton stated:

I have always practiced it [affirmative action]. Look at my appointments to the federal bench, ones which, I might add, I've been regularly attacked for trying to achieve diversity. . . . I have made an extra effort to look for qualified candidates who could serve with distinction and make a contribution to this country and make the federal bench reflective of the American population. I did not do it with any quota system in mind, and I have not guaranteed anybody a job. I have made an extra effort to do that.[160]

School Desegregation

"I [Clinton] graduated from a segregated high school seven years after President Eisenhower integrated Little Rock Central High School. . . . My experiences with discrimination are rooted in the South and the legacy slavery left."[161]

For the most part, during his first term President Clinton avoided discussion of school desegregation. The Clinton administration's initiatives in education instead centered around new intergovernmental relationships between individual states and the federal government.[162] These policies, including Goals 2000, deal generally with such matters as curriculum, assessment, professional development, teacher education, materials, and so on; they are, however, generally silent as to the continuing dilemma of unequal educational opportunities. As reported by a former member of the K–12 Education Task Force of the Clinton/Gore Transition Team, Clinton's "education policy is predicated on systemic state reform" and the development of national standards.[163]

Clinton's affirmative action speech at the National Archives on July 19, 1995 did, however, include a vague endorsement for the value of diversity, if not school desegregation per se. "Now college presidents will tell you," said the president, "that the education their schools offer actually benefits from diversity; colleges where young people get their education and make personal and professional contacts that will shape their lives. If their colleges look like the world they're going to live and work in, and they learn from all different kinds of people things they can't learn in books, our systems of higher education are stronger."[164]

Overall, though President Clinton held to the view that eliminating discrimination and racism are a "never-ending job, here and around the world,"[165] it is clear that Clinton did not consider school desegregation to be a priority in his first term.

Voting/Election

When President Kennedy barely carried my home state in 1960, the poll tax system was still alive and well there.

—Bill Clinton (1995)[166]

In a 1988 speech, President Clinton called for a review of several initiatives to reduce what he termed "cumbersome and outdated administrative impediments standing in the way of voting rights," including, election-day registration, registration by mail, and registration by state agencies, including "motor voter" registration.[167] And, in 1993, after signing the motor-voter law, Clinton was able to proclaim "today we celebrate our noble tradition by signing into law our newest civil rights law, the National Voter Registration Act of 1993, which all of us know and love as 'motor voter.' The principle behind the legislation is clear: Voting should be about discerning the will of the majority not about testing the administrative capacity of a citizen."[168]

Generally, President Clinton maintained a supportive stance toward voting rights and elections. For example, following the Supreme Court's 1995 decision in *Miller v. Johnson*,[169] invalidating a Georgia redistricting plan that created additional majority-minority districts, Clinton released a statement condemning the Court's action.

The decision is a setback in the struggle to ensure that all Americans participate fully in the electoral process and it threatens to undermine the promise of the Voting Rights Act. . . . My administration remains committed to full enforcement of the Voting Rights Act. We will continue to ensure that minority citizens in racially polarized areas have an effective remedy against unlawful dilution of their votes and against impairment of their ability to participate in the electoral process. . . . While the ruling in the Georgia case is unfortunate, I am gratified that the court's statements and actions in all its voting rights cases today make clear that race properly may be considered in the drawing of legislative districts. . . . We will not let this decision turn back the clock. We will not abandon those citizens who look to the Voting Rights Act to protect their constitutional rights.[170]

SELECTION, SCREENING, AND NOMINATION UNDER CLINTON

The Setting: Clinton's Opportunity

During his 1992 campaign for the presidency, then-Governor Clinton made note of the fact that judicial appointments were deeply political and gave some indication of his desire to appoint a more diverse bench if elected:

The judicial appointment and approval process has become more politicized than ever before, and this can contribute to substantial delays in filling vacancies on the federal bench. It is my hope, however, that by concentrating on the merits of judicial appointees, I will be able to work with the Senate to fill vacancies as expeditiously as possible. . . .

As a former professor of constitutional law, I will be very careful to select . . . only those with unquestionably good judgment, excellent educational backgrounds, and wide-ranging experiences. I also believe it is important that the federal judiciary represent society as a whole, and I am willing to make sure that all qualified candidates are given due consideration.[171]

However, after winning the 1992 election, Clinton spoke more ambiguously about what he wanted to accomplish with his judicial appointments. As one analyst put it: "The Clinton administration doesn't know yet what kind of people it wants on the bench. This is the dilemma of being a new liberal or an old liberal. This is the internal debate that has characterized this administration."[172]

When President Clinton took office in 1993, Republican appointees outnumbered Democrats by more than two to one; that is, the last two presidents had picked 70 percent of the judges then sitting in the federal courts. Yet eighty-five district court positions were vacant on the day Clinton was elected. President Clinton, like President Bush, was also initially slow to make appointments. Five months after taking office, for example, Clinton had not filled even one of the 123 vacancies—15 percent—on the federal appellate and district court bench.

Initial Delays. Just as delays at the beginning of the Bush presidency worried many Republicans, similar delays worried key Democrats and others at the beginning of the Clinton administration as well. "If Mr. Clinton fails to move quickly," said Nan Aron of the liberal Alliance for Justice, "a conservative-dominated bench may frustrate his ambitious agenda."[173] There was also concern expressed by key members of the Senate Judiciary Committee. Senate Judiciary Committee Chairman Joseph Biden (D-DE), expressed his concern at a June 1993 hearing: "It is disappointing," said Biden, "that we are sitting here in the middle of June with not a single judicial nomination having been sent to this committee."[174]

In addressing these concerns, Clinton's first White House counsel, Bernard Nussbaum, pointed to the eighty-eight-day Supreme Court search (Clinton announced his selection of U.S. Court of Appeals Judge Ruth Bader Ginsburg to replace retiring Supreme Court Justice Byron White, on June 14, 1993) as having taken top priority.[175] Following White's announcement that he would retire at the end of the term, Clinton himself indicated that "he would move deliberately and extensively to consider a wide variety of potential candidates."[176] Nussbaum also pointed to the administration's difficulties in getting key people in place to handle judicial selection. For instance, the official designated to oversee judicial selection at the Justice Department did not conclude her confirmation hearings until the middle of June due to delay caused in part by concern over her past membership in an all-white country club.[177]

Concerns about delay were also voiced from sitting district court judges. "You'd think [the Clinton administration] would want to get going" stated Texas U.S. District Court Judge Lucius Bunton, a Carter appointee. Bunton, concluded "[I]t's kind of frustrating out here," noting that pending vacancies were "exacerbating delays in civil trials that stretch to three years or more."[178] Thomas Platt, chief judge of the Eastern District of New York indicated in May of 1994 he had a backlog of more than 1,200 civil cases, compared with the national average of 410 combined civil and criminal cases. "Among the New York Judges," said Judge Platt, "I am not atypical," adding that, "the old maxim—justice delayed is justice denied—still remains true today."[179]

Furthermore, reports early on during the Clinton administration also indicated that Clinton's personal, though sporadic, participation in discussions about lower court appointments also slowed the selection process. Clinton's desire to be personally involved in approving judges was something his Republican predecessors left entirely to aides.[180] These same reports suggest too that Senate Democrats, who would by tradition make recommendations to a Democratic president, were simply "out of practice" given the three past Republican terms, and thus were slow to send candidates' names to the White House.[181] Critics of Clinton's slow progress on judicial section also pointed to the president's unhurried appointment of Janet Reno as attorney general and also charged the FBI and the ABA with "dragging out their own detailed reviews," a charge those organizations denied.[182] Whatever the reason, it is clear that judicial nominations are taking longer in modern times. In 1979, for example, it took the White House and Congress an average of 292 days to fill a vacancy; by the 1990s, it was taking an average of 804 days.[183]

Despite these initial delays, however, evidence below indicates that Clinton did give judicial selection considerable attention.

Clinton's First Term Appointments: 1993–1996

I have appointed more women and minorities to the federal bench than any other president, more than the last two combined.

—Remarks by President Clinton, July 19, 1995.[184]

A profile of President Clinton's first term district court appointments reveals that Clinton appointed 169 district court judges—mostly male (69.8 percent) and mostly white (72.2 percent). But Clinton's overall proportion of white males (47.3 percent) was well below any previous administration (see Table 3.11, Chapter 3). In fact, the overall number of women appointed to the district courts during Clinton's first term (both on terms of proportion as well as in raw numbers, 30.2 percent and fifty-one respectively) was the largest number of women appointed in history for any administration. See Figure 6.1.

Figure 6.1
Percentage of Female Appointees to the District Courts, 1960–1996

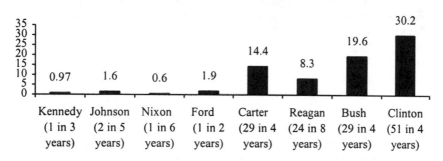

	Kennedy (1 in 3 years)	Johnson (2 in 5 years)	Nixon (1 in 6 years)	Ford (1 in 2 years)	Carter (29 in 4 years)	Reagan (24 in 8 years)	Bush (29 in 4 years)	Clinton (51 in 4 years)
	0.97	1.6	0.6	1.9	14.4	8.3	19.6	30.2

President Clinton's appointments of racial minorities was also significant. During only his first two years in office, Clinton appointed a historic proportion of African-Americans (twenty-seven)—eleven more than the total number of Bush and Reagan African-American appointees combined twelve-year record of sixteen, and, only one less than Carter's four-year record of twenty-eight. Overall, Clinton appointed thirty-three African-Americans to the district courts during his first term (Table 3.11). Clinton appointee, Judge Vanessa Gilmore, for example, a thirty-seven-year-old African-American female appointed to the Southern District of Texas in 1994, was then the youngest sitting federal judge in the nation.[185] Clinton also appointed eleven (6.5 percent) Latino judges (the second highest percentage after Carter), two Asian-American judges, and the first Native American federal judge, Billy Michael Burrage of Oklahoma (see Table 3.11).[186] Additionally, Clinton also appointed the "first openly gay federal judge."[187] In all, Clinton's proportion of white male appointees during his first term marked the first time in history that a *majority* of a president's district courts appointees were not white males. It is also noteworthy that Clinton's appointees have the highest ABA ratings compared to all previous administrations examined (Table 3.11).[188] "I have appointed at this point in my tenure [1995] more judges to the federal bench who were women or members of racial minorities than my three predecessors combined, I believe," said Clinton. "My judges have the highest ratings, on average, from the American Bar Association of any of the last four Presidents."[189]

Also, as indicated in Table 3.11, about 90 percent of Clinton's appointees were Democrats and 54 percent reported past party activism. Clinton's appointees also show a nearly equal proportion of millionaires as for Bush appointees. Like presidents Carter, Reagan, and Bush, before him, a greater number of Clinton's appointees had previous judicial experience than had prosecutorial experience. In fact, Clinton's appointees surpassed all these past presidents' records with nearly 50 percent coming from the judiciary. Thus, like Bush before him, President Clinton continued the trend of promoting from within the federal judiciary, making judicial experience the single most dominant experiential variable.[190]

Procedurally, in 1993 President Clinton assigned judicial selection to the Justice Department's Office of Policy Development and on April 29, 1993 he nominated Eleanor D. Acheson to head the office as assistant attorney general. However, until Acheson was confirmed on August 2, judicial selection was temporarily housed in the Office of the White House Counsel under the direction of Ronald A. Klain, associate White House counsel.[191] After Acheson was confirmed as assistant attorney general, Klain moved to the Justice Department and Victoria L. Radd became associate White House counsel in charge of judicial selection. Radd concentrated on judicial selection during 1994 and commented in a 1994 interview that she worked closely with Assistant Attorney General Acheson and other Office of Policy Development officials.[192] In addition to Acheson, in the Office of Policy Development Deputy Attorney General Peter Erichsen worked full-time on judicial selection with as many as fifteen other part-time people in the Justice Department.[193]

Published reports indicate that candidates for the district courts came from recommendations by Democratic senators, or in the absence of a Democratic senator, from the Democratic members of the House of Representatives or other high-ranking Democratic Party officials.[194] Acheson's deputy, Erichsen, was appointed chair of a Justice Department judicial selection committee that met regularly to consider the *professional* qualifications of the candidates.

At the Justice Department, "each judicial candidate was assigned to a Justice Department lawyer who took responsibility for gathering and analyzing the relevant materials, including . . . an analysis of his or her judicial record," and coordinated each candidate's visit to the Justice Department, where typically six staff members interviewed the candidate.[195] According to Acheson, in advance of a candidate's visit to Washington, extensive background information is gathered and "in excess of 60 telephone calls are typically made to various individuals who have interacted professionally with the candidate." About 10 percent of those interviewed, stated Acheson, are eliminated from further consideration.[196]

While the Justice Department committee met regularly to consider the *professional* qualifications of candidates, the Office of the White House Counsel committee considered the *politics*, including an assessment of potential political difficulties that might arise during confirmation. In fact, the counsel's office, reportedly "sounded out" Republican senators and worked closely with Senator Orrin Hatch, the ranking Republican on the Senate Judiciary Committee during the 103rd Congress (Hatch later became chair during the 104th Congress).[197]

Each week Clinton's joint White House-Justice Department "Judicial Selection Group" met to consider which candidates would be presented to President Clinton himself for consideration.[198] From the White House team, the committee was chaired by the White House counsel,[199] and included associate White House counsel Victoria Radd (again, she replaced Ronald Klain who moved to the Justice Department); Deputy White House Counsel Joel Klein (replaced by James Castello); deputy Bruce R. Lindsey; a representative of the Office of Legislative Affairs, the vice president's counsel, and, the deputy chief of staff for the First Lady who is also an assistant to the president. From the Justice Department team, the joint committee included Assistant Attorney General Acheson, her deputy Peter Erichsen,[200] another deputy Roslyn Mazer, and counselor and chief of staff in the Civil Rights Division, Susan Liss (also a former deputy). Reports also indicate that Attorney General Janet Reno was an ex officio member but "typically did not attend meetings."

On balance, judicial selection during Clinton's first term was generally highlighted by the close interaction between the Office of the White House Counsel and the Justice Department's Office of Policy Development. Again, the Justice Department focused on the professional qualifications while the White House handled the politics. According to Acheson, the White House "made a determined effort not to screen nominees ideologically" following President Clinton's comments to Democratic senators that there was to be no ideological screening. [201] For President Clinton, said Acheson, intellectual ability and judicial temperament were of paramount importance as well as understanding the role of the district courts to follow precedent.[202] As indicated by John Quinn, the Clinton White House counsel, "Our mission is not to counteract the conservative appointments of the Reagan and Bush years." Rather, Quinn continued, "this president is a moderate, who brings mainstream, Main Street values to the job of selecting judges."[203] In another instance, Acheson, stated, "we know that many people expected us to do the mirror-image of what the Republicans had done, that is, fill the courts with young liberal and progressive candidates in order to bring the courts back from their lunge to the right."[204] However, according to Acheson, "the administration rejects candidates with ideological agendas and stresses diversity without sacrificing quality."[205] But not all welcomed the administration's position. For example, Nan Aron, the head of the Alliance for Justice, a coalition of liberal groups that monitors court appointments, said that,

"While the administration deserves much credit for both the excellence and diversity of its judicial appointments, it is clearly disappointing that the president failed to address the issue of correcting the imbalance of the courts from the previous Republican presidents."[206]

To be sure, Clinton was careful in attempts to avoid controversial labels. For instance, his choice of Ruth Bader Ginsburg for the Supreme Court signaled clearly his moderation and centrist approach to judicial nominations. Regarding his appointment of Ginsburg, Clinton said, "Ruth Bader Ginsburg cannot be called a liberal or a conservative, she has proved herself too thoughtful for such labels."[207]

It should also be pointed out that under Clinton judicial selection was placed for the first time under offices headed by women: a female assistant attorney general, Eleanor Acheson; an office in a Justice Department under the leadership of a woman for the first time, Attorney General Janet Reno; and; under the direction of an assistant White House counsel—also a woman—Victoria L. Radd.

Overall, the Democratic-controlled 103rd Congress was generally hospitable to President Clinton's nominees—107 district court judges were confirmed out of 118 nominated (about 91 percent). And, the Senate confirmed 99 percent of Clinton's judges without even a roll call vote.[208] On the other hand, the Republican-controlled 104th Congress was less accommodating—sixty-two district court judges were confirmed out of eighty-five nominated (about 73 percent).[209]

Clinton, Judicial Selection, and the 104th Congress

As a result of the November 1994 midterm elections, the Republican party took control of both houses of Congress. In fact, the 1994 midterm elections marked the first time since 1946 that the Republican party took control of both houses of Congress during a Democratic presidency.

As indicated above, during the first two years of the Clinton administration, the judicial selection process was run by officials from the Justice Department and the White House counsel's office. But after the Republicans gained control of Congress in 1994, the process was taken over in part by Clinton's top political aides, including Harold Ickes, a deputy chief of staff, and George Stephanopoulos, a senior adviser. In the several months after that switch, the administration's aversion to any kind of controversy reached new levels. In fact, the Clinton administration earned a reputation for avoiding confirmation battles altogether. Assistant Attorney General Acheson confirmed this point saying that "We've steered clear of a few people who might have been fabulous judges but who would have provoked a fight that we were likely to lose."[210] Acheson stated directly:

There are a couple of cases in which we decided that even if we thought we had a shot at winning a fight . . . that it was not worth the time and resources . . . because these fights go for months, and during that period it is very difficult to concentrate. . . . It's not that we doubt that people would be excellent if you could ever get them into the position. It's a question . . . of at what cost?[211]

Consider, for example, the new White House team speedily dropped the proposed nominations of Judith McConnell and Samuel Paz to Federal District Court seats in California. Ms. McConnell, a veteran state court judge, had awarded custody of a sixteen-year-old boy to his father's male partner after his father's death because the mother had been declared unfit. Police organizations said they would oppose the nomination of Paz because he was a lawyer who specialized in bringing abuse suits against the police. Perhaps one of the more stunning examples of White House efforts to avoid controversy involved Peter Edelman, who with his wife, Marian Wright Edelman, are longtime friends of the Clintons.[212] Clinton first signaled that he would nominate Peter Edelman, a law professor at Georgetown University, to an appeals court seat and then to a lesser seat on the district court. But, after conservatives voiced their opposition, Clinton abandoned Edelman's nomination altogether.[213]

Consider also that in 1995 and 1996 there was a significant increase in white appointees and a dramatic decline in the appointment of African-Americans to the district courts. In fact, the proportion of white males appointed by Clinton increased by 50 percent in the latter half of his first term.[214]

At the same time, during the 104th Congress, the Clinton administration continued its collaborative relationship with Republican Senate Judiciary Committee chair, Senator Orrin Hatch. Assistant Attorney General Acheson described the value of consulting with Senator Hatch: "It is just a better way of doing business. . . . He [Hatch] gives good advice and a good sense of what's going to work and what's not going to work."[215] Consider the response of Senator Hatch in a November 1995 interview. Senator Hatch was asked: "What is your view of the quality of judicial nominees your committee has processed this Congress? What has been the practice for determining who gets a hearing and what are the prospects for judicial nominees as we approach 1996?" Hatch responded:

I believe that the Judiciary Committee has processed many worthy nominees during this Congress. The administration has worked to consult with me on many nominees. The White House and Justice Department officials in charge of judicial selection communicate with me and with my staff on a regular basis. I trust that this effective working relationship will continue. In general, we schedule nominees for hearings as soon as their background and legal checks are completed. As a result, I have moved nominees at an equitable pace.[216]

Traditionally, senators from the party that does not control the White House have historically tried to stall judicial nominations during a campaign year in hopes that their party's candidate might inherit filling any leftover vacancies. Indeed, published research supports the fact that presidential terms experience a "significant decline in confirmation rate in the fourth year." [217] In fact, confirmation rates decline year by year into the president's term. The end of the first term of the Clinton presidency was no different. In November of 1995, for example, Senate controversy—in part over the stalled confirmation of Associate Attorney General Merrick Garland for a seat on the United States Court of Appeals for the District of Columbia[218]—on judicial nominations had generated enough partisan gridlock to prevent any nominee from having been confirmed since early that summer (1995).[219] Regarding the stalled Garland appointment, Senator Charles Grassley (R-IA) and majority leader Senator Bob Dole (R-KS) (the eventual Republican party presidential nominee in 1996 who had the final decision on whether to place the nomination before the full Senate) both insisted that their opposition was not partisan but argued that the circuit court already had too many judges and they were attempting to save additional costs to the taxpayers.[220]

Nor did other Republican senators want any confirmations in 1996. For example, for the first six months of the 1996 election year, political infighting among senators prevented confirmation of a single federal judge. However, in July 1996, Trent Lott (R-MS), the new Senate majority leader who took over upon the resignation of Bob Dole, was able to persuade his Senate colleagues to unanimously approve the nominations of three district court judges (one for Missouri, one for Louisiana, and one for Colorado).[221] Before the vote, minority leader Tom Daschle (D-SD) said he and Lott had been trying to "find a way to take action on as many as 23 judicial nominations that had been endorsed by the Senate Judiciary Committee." "He has given me his assurance that we will attempt—all we can do is attempt—to work through this list of 23 judges that are on the calendar," said Daschle. "This [the three] is the first down payment." [222]

The ABA. Relations with the ABA during the second half of Clinton's first term remained good. However, during his 1996 campaign for the White House, Republican presidential nominee Bob Dole repeatedly attacked the ABA for its "liberal" leanings and stated that, if elected, he would end "its highly influential role in the selection process."[223] Similarly, Thomas L. Jipping, Director of the Free Congress Foundation's Judicial Selection Monitoring Project[224]—a "New Right" organization formed to monitor Clinton's appointments and to mobilize grassroots opposition, stated that:

The fact that 82% of the ABA federal judiciary committee's political donors are Democratic Party contributors is the latest evidence that the ABA has shed its pretense as a non-partisan professional association. The ABA is an increasingly political interest group and should no longer enjoy a special role, almost a veto power, in the judicial selection process.

The ABA predictably wants to protect its uniquely powerful role in the judicial selection process, but it cannot deny the facts. Thousands of lawyers and judges have in recent years quit their membership because the ABA itself has become increasingly political and increasingly liberal.[225]

But, ABA President Roberta Cooper Ramo brushed aside such charges. When asked about some of the problems or issues the committee faced, Ramo replied:

At our mid-year meeting, we had a superb day-long program on the federal judicial nomination process and the qualities we need to be looking for in federal judges who will be sitting in the next century. For the program, we had Republicans and Democrats, people who had been in the White Houses since the Kennedy Administration, people who had worked for the Senate Judiciary Committee, and Supreme Court reporters. At the end of the day, everyone agreed that, with probably one exception, the process works very well. And the exception was that it seemed to take too long, particularly for the district judge slots, where often we have people left hanging for over a year.

It is not the ABA committee that takes long. We do our work in 30 days unless there is a problem, in which case we notify everybody and occasionally it takes another 30 days. I think the ABA committee works superbly. Although people raise questions from time to time, I cannot imagine that the American public does not want to know how the profession views a judicial nominee who will have lifetime tenure on the federal bench. I believe the committee behaves in a fair way and that the reporting is appropriate. It is appropriate to look at the committee's criteria from time to time.[226]

On balance, judicial selection remained a common issue for Clinton's 1996 reelection campaign. In an April 19, 1996 speech to the American Society of Newspaper Editors, Republican candidate Bob Dole charged that Clinton was promoting "an all star team of liberal leniency" and that Clinton's re-election "could lock in liberal judicial activism for the next generation."[227] In that same speech, Dole proposed removing the ABA from its role in reviewing potential judicial appointees because "they have become another blatantly liberal advocacy group."[228] Early in the 1996 campaign, White House Counsel Jack Quinn, writing in the *Wall Street Journal*, defended Clinton's appointees against attacks that they were soft on crime compared to appointees of presidents Reagan and Bush.[229] And, just three months before Clinton's November 1996 reelection for a second term, Senator Orrin Hatch, said that "whoever was elected president this November would have an awesome opportunity to name new federal judges."[230]

Again, during the second session of the 104th Congress there were sixty-two district court judges confirmed, bringing Clinton's total number to 169. However, just about three weeks before the November 1996 election, the Administrative Office of the U.S. Courts reported forty-four vacancies on the district courts with no (0) nominees pending.[231] Altogether, in recent times, a president can expect about fifty federal judgeships to open up annually as a result of deaths, retirements, and moves to senior status. Thus, by the end of Clinton's second term (in 2001), Clinton judges may well dominate the federal courts. In fact, several projections are that Clinton will appoint more federal judges than any other president in history. More specifically, it is projected that Clinton will appoint about 354, or 58 percent, of the total number of district court judges.[232]

And, some indication of the Clinton's views on judicial selection and the kind of judges he will appoint during his second term can be gleaned from his written responses to questions posed by the American Judicature Society (AJS) during the 1996 election campaign:

AJS: How do you plan to facilitate filling the federal judgeships that currently stand vacant?

Clinton: When I took office nearly four years ago, there were approximately 115 vacancies in the federal judiciary. Since that time, more than 150 judges have retired from active service. By focusing on nominating individuals of unquestioned excellence, rather than basing selections on rigid adherence to a strict ideological agenda, my administration has filled over 200 judgeships, more than either of my immediate predecessors. Each of these appointments received strong, and unusually overwhelming, bipartisan support.

Although at the beginning of the year we had reduced the number of judicial vacancies to less than 50, the lowest level in quite some time, I was deeply disappointed by the unprecedented slowdown in confirmations that occurred in the Senate during 1996. During the last session of Congress, the Senate confirmed only 17 judges—the lowest election year total in over two decades. In contrast, the average number of confirmations in the last four presidential election years was almost 54 judges, three times the number confirmed in 1996. As problematic, the Senate failed to confirm a single nominee to the courts of appeals during the second session, the first time a session of Congress has ended in this fashion in over 40 years.

As a result, the number of judicial vacancies has climbed steadily during the course of the year and now stands at around 65. With another 15 judges who have already expressed their intention to retire before the end of the year and scores more who are eligible, we could quite easily find the number of judicial vacancies approaching 100 by the time the next president is inaugurated in January 1997. Hopefully, with the help of a renewed sense of cooperation after the election, I will be able to work with the Senate, much as I did in 1993, 1994, and 1995, to fill these vacancies in an expeditious fashion.

AJS: What characteristics will you look for in a prospective federal judge?

Clinton: As I have over the last four years, I intend to select individuals with outstanding capabilities and a broad array of professional experience and individuals who reflect the incredible diversity of our nation. I made a similar pledge four years ago when I provided my views on judicial selection at the invitation of the American Judicature Society, and we have been tremendously successful in achieving these goals during my first term in office.

First, with regard to professional competence, fully 68 percent of my appointments have received the highest rating of "well-qualified" from the American Bar Association, the only nonpartisan organization that officially evaluates judicial candidates. That is the highest percentage of "well-qualified" nominees of any president since the ABA began providing its evaluations in 1952 at the invitation of President Eisenhower. Second, my administration has been able to set extraordinarily high standards while simultaneously achieving an unprecedented degree of diversity. Over 50 percent of my appointments have been women and minorities, the highest percentage in history. In a second term, I hope to build on and improve the record of achievement we have established thus far.[233]

Of course, it remains to be seen, however, just how successful President Clinton will be with regard to judicial selection during his second term—a term that began with the Republican party in control of both houses of the 105th Congress.[234]

Clinton, Judicial Selection, and the 105th Congress

The 1996 election not only resulted in Republican control of both houses of Congress, but also marked the first time in American history that a Democratic president was elected with a Republican Congress. Just hours after President Clinton's 1996 reelection win, Senate majority leader Trent Lott warned Clinton that the GOP majority would "resist with every fiber of our being" if Clinton "names the kind of federal judges who would overturn this week's election results with next year's court decisions."[235] Consider also the words and tone of Senate Judiciary Committee Chairman Orrin Hatch, in an address to the Federalist Society on November 15, 1996, regarding judicial selection.

If President Clinton is permitted to use the next four years to fill our courts with liberal activists, the damage to our Constitution, the rule of law, and our very right to democratic self-government will be irreparable literally for decades to come. The stakes are nothing less than this. . . .

I plan to stand firm and exercise the advise and consent power . . . to ensure that President Clinton does not pack the judiciary with liberal activists who will make mincemeat of our Constitution and laws. . . .

Should President Clinton nominate judges whose records demonstrate that they will be judicial activists who twist the law to impose their own policy preferences rather than apply the law as it is enacted, I will oppose them. [C]onducting a fair confirmation process most assuredly does not mean granting the President carte blanche in filling the federal judiciary. It is as simple as this: Those nominees who are, or will be, judicial activists should not be nominated by the president or confirmed by the Senate, and I personally will do my best to see to it that they are not.[236]

A few months later, on February 3, 1997, the Judicial Selection Monitoring Project delivered a copy of the Senator Hatch's pledge to not confirm any "nominees who are, or will be, judicial activists" to each U.S. Senator and asked each senator to sign it.[237]

Along side Senator Hatch, early in 1997 Senator John Ashcroft (R-MO) spearheaded a series of Senate Judiciary Committee hearings on "judicial activism." Senator Ashcroft began his public campaign with a March 1997 speech when he referred to "renegade judges, a robed, contemptuous intellectual elite" and the problem of "judicial despotism."[238] Later, during a June 11, 1997 Senate Judiciary Committee hearing, Ashcroft softened his attack, claiming his criticism of judicial activism was not aimed at Democratic appointees. Said Ashcroft:

I am committed to trying to eliminate judicial activism without regard to whether my party appointed the judges or whether I like the outcome in a particular case as a policy matter.[239]

Some Senate Democrats, however, have claimed that the Hatch-Ashcroft crusade against judicial activism is simply a smoke screen to block Clinton's second term nominees. "They don't' like the fact that Clinton is president and has the power to appoint federal judges," said Senator Dick Durbin (D-IL), a member of the judiciary committee. "They're out to stop these nominees, and any excuse will do."[240] Just two months after the Senate Judiciary Committee hearings on judicial activism began, Attorney General Janet Reno devoted an entire speech to this issue. As reported, Attorney General Reno, speaking in San Francisco on August 5, 1997, to the American Bar Association at its annual meeting, charged Senate Republicans with an "unprecedented slowdown" in confirming judges and with threatening "judicial independence."[241]

On balance, it is assured that Clinton's second term should provide unparalleled opportunities for making appointments to the federal courts as well as perhaps equally unparalleled partisan opposition to such appointments.

CONCLUSION

Having laid out the presidential expectation profiles in chapters 4, 5, and 6, I next turn to an analysis of the extent to which particular presidents have been able to promote their policy objectives via their judicial appointments to the federal district courts in Chapter 7.

NOTES

1. George Bush, "Candidates State Positions on Federal Judicial Selection," *Judicature* 72 (1988), p. 77.

2. See Kerry Mullins and Aaron Wildavsky, "The Procedural Presidency of George Bush," *Political Science Quarterly* 107 (1992), pp. 46, 51; and Colin Campbell, S.J. and Bert A. Rockman, eds., *The Bush Presidency: First Appraisals* (Chatham, NJ: Chatham House Publishers, 1991).

3. See Mark Davis, "Writing for a President Indifferent to Speeches," *Los Angeles Times*, 17 January 1993; and Lance Blakesley, *Presidential Leadership: From Eisenhower to Clinton* (Chicago: Nelson-Hall Publishers, 1995).

4. Bush, "Candidates State Positions on Federal Judicial Selection," p. 77.

5. Mark Silverstein, *Judicious Choices: The Politics of Supreme Court Confirmations* (New York: W. W. Norton and Company, 1994), p. 124.

6. Quoted in Neil A. Lewis, "Selection of Conservative Judges Guards Part of Bush Legacy," *New York Times*, July 1, 1992, p. A13.

7. Ibid.

8. Joan Biskupic, "Bush's Nominees Lack Baggage That Reagan's Often Carried," *Congressional Quarterly*, September 22, 1990, p. 3019.

9. George Bush, *Looking Forward* (Garden City, NY: Doubleday, 1987), p. 207.

10. For discussion, see "Congress Puts Bush on Spot over Funding on Abortion," *Congressional Quarterly Weekly Report* 47, October 14, 1989, pp. 2708–2711.

11. For discussion, see "Fetal Research Splits Abortions Foes, May Mean First Bush Veto Override," 50 *Congressional Quarterly Weekly Report*, May 23, 1992, pp. 1454–1455.

12. "Bush Insists He Won't Allow Easing of Abortion Bans," 49 *Congressional Quarterly Weekly Report*, June 8, 1991, p. 1504. See also, "Steadfast Veto Threats From Bush . . . ," 49 *Congressional Quarterly Weekly Report*, December 14, 1991, p. 3642.

13. *Public Papers of the Presidents of the United States*, Federal Register Division, National Archives and Records Service (Washington, DC: Government Printing Office, 1/23/89). Cited hereafter as *Public Papers of the Presidents.*

14. *Public Papers of the Presidents*, 6/27/89.

15. Bush's opportunity came in the case of *Planned Parenthood of Southeastern Pennsylvania v. Casey*, 505 U.S. 833 (1992), but the Supreme Court, 5–4, affirmed a right to abortion.

16. *Public Papers of the Presidents*, 4/30/90.

17. *Public Papers of the Presidents*, 4/3/91

18. A five-justice majority of the Supreme Court upheld this interpretation of Title X in *Rust v. Sullivan*, 500 U.S. 173 (1991).

19. *Webster v. Reproductive Health Services*, 492 U.S. 490 (1989).

20. Charles Fried, *Order and Law: Arguing the Reagan Revolution—A Firsthand Account* (New York: Simon and Schuster, 1991), pp. 20, 75–76, 85–87. See also, See Marian Faux, *Crusaders: Voices from the Abortion Front* (New York: Birch Lane Press, 1990), p. 42; and Tony Mauro, "In the Eye of the Abortion Storm," *USA Today*, April 26, 1989.

21. The oral argument is reprinted in the *New York Times*, April 27, 1989, p. B12, col. 1.

22. Tony Mauro, "High Stakes, Low Courts," *The Washington Monthly* 16 (July-August 1996), p. 20.

23. "Abortion Continues to Shape Hill Plans, Bush Policies," 47 *Congressional Quarterly Weekly Report*, November 4, 1989, pp. 2953–2954.

24. *Congressional Quarterly Weekly Report*, January 25, 1992, p. 170.

25. *Public Papers of the Presidents*, 3/22/89.

26. *Public Papers of the Presidents*, 1/29/90.

27. *Lee v. Weisman*, 505 U.S. 577 (1992).

28. *Lemon v. Kurtzman*, 403 U.S. 602 (1971).

29. In *Lee v. Weisman*, the Supreme Court voted 5–4 to prohibit official prayer at high school graduation ceremonies, ruling that under such circumstances, students who objected to such prayers might nonetheless feel induced to conform. Just two years later, in *Joint School District No. 241 v. Harris* (1995), the Supreme Court vacated as moot a lower court's ruling that student-initiated prayers at graduation ceremonies are unconstitutional but offered no explanation or guidelines.

30. *Congressional Quarterly Weekly Report*, June 27, 1992, p. 1884.

31. See "Merit, Heart, Will—and Affirmative Action," *Newsday*, June 4, 1991, p. 56.

32. For an argument that President Bush throughout his career sought to exploit racial divisiveness in his political activities, see Thomas Edsall and Mary Edsall, *Chain Reaction: The Impact of Race, Rights and Taxes on American Politics* (New York: W. W. Norton and Company, 1991).

33. *Public Papers of the Presidents*, 5/17/90.

34. For a thorough examination of the shifting patterns of partisan voting and leadership in Congress as well as President Bush's shifting positions, see Mark Stern, "Party Alignments and Civil Rights: Then and Now," *Presidential Studies Quarterly* 25 (1995), pp. 413–427.

35. The overturned decisions included, for example, *Patterson v. McClean Credit Union* (491 U.S. 164 [1989]) in which the Supreme Court ruled that the 1866 Civil Rights Act did not protect employees from blatant race discrimination once they have been hired; *Wards Cove Packing Co., Inc. v. Atonio* (490 U.S. 642 [1989]), in which the Supreme Court overturned an earlier ruling, *Griggs v. Duke Power Company* (402 U.S. 424 [1971]), and shifted the burden to employees of proving that an employer's hiring practices were discriminatory; and *Martin v. Wilks* (490 U.S. 755 [1989]), in which the Supreme Court allowed white firefighters to challenge an affirmative action settlement that had been in effect for eight years. See Eskridge, "Reneging on History? Playing the Court/Congress/President Civil Rights Game," *California Law Review* 79 (1991), pp. 613–617.

36. "Bush Shifts on Job-Rights Bill, but Differences Remain," 48 *Congressional Quarterly Weekly Report*, May 19, 1990, p. 1563.

37. "Expected Bush Veto Looming over Civil Rights Measure," 48 *Congressional Quarterly Weekly Report*, October 20, 1990, p. 3519.

38. For a discussion of these "last-second" negotiations over the bill, including the enlistment of former Transportation Secretary William T. Coleman called in by the White House on October 19, see "Expected Bush Veto Looming over Civil Rights Measure," p. 3518.

39. For the text accompanying President Bush's October 22 veto of the civil rights bill (S 2104), see "Bush Vetoes Rights Bill, Objects to 'Quotas,'" 48 *Congressional Quarterly Weekly Report*, October 27, 1990, p. 3654. See also *New York Times*, October 23, 1990.

40. For a discussion on Bush's veto of the 1990 bill, see Stephen L. Wasby, "Epilogue," in Ronald J. Fiscus, Stephen L. Wasby, eds., *The Affirmative Action Controversy* (Durham: Duke University Press, 1992), pp. 122–126.

41. "Expected Bush Veto Looming over Civil Rights Measure," p. 3519.

42. Bush, nonetheless, continued to vigorously attack the measure well into 1991, denouncing it as a quota bill. The House of Representatives passed the revised 1991 bill, 273–158, knowing that members might be subjects of a racial scare advertising about whites losing jobs to blacks like that used by Senator Jesse Helms (R-NC) in his 1990 campaign. See *New York Times,* May 31, June 6, 1991.

43. *New York Times*, October 26, 1991.

44. See The Civil Rights Act of 1991, by the Committee of Federal Legislation, reported in the *Record of the Association of the Bar of the City of New York* 48 (1993), pp. 75–124.

45. See, for example, *Congressional Quarterly Almanac 1991* (Washington, DC: CQ Press, 1992), 251–261; Richard L. Alfred and Thomas A. Knowlton, "Civil Rights Act Will Encourage Federal Claims: The Civil Rights Act of 1991," *Massachusetts Lawyers Weekly,* December 9, 1991, p. 5; David Broder, "Bush's Favorite Victim," *Washington Post*, June 9, 1991, p. D7; William Raspberry, "Bush, Civil Rights and the Specter of David Duke," *Washington Post*, October 30, 1991, p. A23; William Schneider, "For Danforth & Co., An Uncivil Snub," *National Journal*, July 6, 1991, p. 1716.

46. See Gary Orfield, "The Growth of Segregation in American Schools: Changing Patterns of Segregation and Poverty Since 1968" (Prepared for the National School

Board Association, 1993)

47. *Weekly Compilation of Presidential Documents*, Government Printing Office, Washington, DC: April 5, 1989, pp. 482–485.

48. *Public Papers of the Presidents*, 5/12/89.

49. See Cooper, "Race-Based Student Aid: Practice and Policy; U.S. Providing $100 Million in Minority Scholarships While Proposing to Restrict Colleges," *Washington Post*, December 26, 1991, p. A21.

50. *Weekly Compilation of Presidential Documents*, Government Printing Office, Washington, DC: July 20, 1992, p. 1280.

51. Joan Biskupic, "Bush's Nominees Lack Baggage That Reagan's Often Carried," *Congressional Quarterly*, September 22, 1990, p. 3019.

52. *Congressional Quarterly*, January 19, 1991, p. 171

53. Biskupic, "Bush's Nominees Lack Baggage That Reagan's Often Carried," p. 3019.

54. Ibid., p. 3020.

55. Joan Biskupic, "Bush Lags in Appointments to the Federal Judiciary," *Congressional Quarterly*, January 6, 1990, p. 42.

56. Biskupic, "Bush's Nominees Lack Baggage That Reagan's Often Carried," p. 3019.

57. Biskupic, "Bush Lags in Appointments to the Federal Judiciary," p. 38.

58. Ibid.

59. Ibid.

60. Kenneth Jost, "Beefing up the Bench," *Congressional Quarterly*, September 22, 1990, p. 3019.

61. Biskupic, "Bush Lags in Appointments to the Federal Judiciary," p. 42.

62. Ibid., p. 38.

63. Ibid., p. 42.

64. This committee met weekly at the White House, was chaired by White House Counsel C. Boyden Gray, and included Assistant Attorney General Murray Dickman (until his departure and then Deputy Assistant Attorney General Barbara Drake), Assistant White House Counsel Lee Liberman, the attorney general, the assistant to the president for personnel, the assistant to the president for legislative affairs, and the White House chief of staff. See Sheldon Goldman, "The Bush Imprint on the Judiciary: Carrying on the Tradition," *Judicature* 74, (1991), pp. 295–296.

65. Silverstein, *Judicious Choices*, p. 124.

66. Thornburg terminated the Justice Department's Office of Legal Policy, led by an assistant attorney general, that handled judicial selection during the Reagan administration.

67. Interview with Carl Stern, NBC Nightly News, October 5, 1992. An account of an interview with Gray noted that the "President is looking for judges who are not activists. Mr. Gray also said that if Mr. Bush is reelected, he would continue to name judges with a conservative philosophy." Neil Lewis, "Biden Warns Bush on Supreme Court Nominations," *New York Times*, June 26, 1992, p. B-8.

68. Joan Biskupic, "Senators Demonstrate They Prefer to Judge Nominees for Themselves," *Congressional Quarterly*, January 6, 1990, p. 40.

69. Attorney General Thornburgh was replaced by William Barr, a close friend of C. Boyden Gray. See David Johnston, "New Attorney General Shifts Department's Focus," *New York Times*, March 3, 1992, p. A-17.

70. As reported, Drake had three full-time assistants and one secretary to help with ju-

dicial selection. About ten other DOJ officials assisted with the interviewing but Drake herself had the task of dealing with senators, the nominees themselves, interest groups, and the ABA. See Goldman, "Bush's Judicial Legacy: The Final Imprint," p. 285.

71. Ibid., p. 284.

72. Ibid. As assessed by Sheldon Goldman, the controversial nominations "fell by the wayside, and others without strong backing from Democratic senators had rough going. On the other hand, nominees for the district courts in states of the Republican members of the Senate Judiciary were all confirmed."

73. Biskupic, "Bush Lags in Appointments to the Federal Judiciary," p. 38.

74. The majority of the information proved in this box is taken from a account of the Fiske-ABA controversy by Goldman, "The Bush Imprint on the Judiciary: Carrying on the Tradition," pp. 295–296.

75. Marianne Lavelle, ". . . And the Role of the ABA," *National Law Journal*, August 6, 1990, p. 43.

76. "ABA's Role under Scrutiny in High Court, Senate," 47 *Congressional Quarterly Weekly Report*, April 22, 1989, pp. 896–898.

77. "Justice Department and ABA Settle Their Differences," 47 *Congressional Quarterly Weekly Report*, June 3, 1989, p. 1327.

78. See Wines, "Thornburgh Abandons Choice for Top Justice Post," *New York Times*, July 7, 1989, pp. A-1, A-11.

79. Goldman, "Bush's Judicial Legacy: The Final Imprint," p. 285.

80. *Congressional Quarterly Weekly Report*, 1991, pp. 2948, 3031.

81. *The DOJ Alert* 15 (November, 1991); See also, *New York Times*, February, 5, 1992.

82. See David Johnston, "New Rules Stall U.S. Confirmations," *New York Times*, January 20, 1992, pp. A-12.

83. As explained by Sheldon Goldman, "Traditionally, minimal confirmation activity occurs during presidential election years, especially when the Senate is controlled by one party and the White House by another." "Bush's Judicial Legacy: The Final Imprint," p. 284.

84. Lewis, "Waiting for Clinton, Democrats Hold up Court Confirmations," *New York Times*, September 1, 1992, pp. A-1, B-6.

85. *Congressional Quarterly*, January 19, 1991, p. 174.

86. It remains unclear exactly what the Bush administration's specific objections were to Jeffords' choice of Fred I. Parker, who had been deputy attorney general when Jeffords was state attorney general in 1969–1973. Murray Dickman, assistant attorney general, explained only that after interviewing Parker, officials had decided that he was not acceptable. Dickman, refusing to elaborate on why Parker was unacceptable, did mention concern, however, that Parker had once belonged to an all-male club and that the Senate may view that as a problem. See Joan Biskupic, "Senators Demonstrate They Prefer to Judge Nominees for Themselves," *Congressional Quarterly Weekly Report*, January 6, 1990, pp. 40–41.

87. Joan Biskupic, "Senators Demonstrate They Prefer," p. 40.

88. Ibid.

89. Ibid., p. 41.

90. Joan Biskupic, "Senators Demonstrate They Prefer," p. 40.

91. Ibid.

92. *The Third Branch*, vol. 24, November 5, 1992.

93. See, Robert Carp, Donald Songer, C. K. Rowland, Ronald Stidham, and Lisa

Richey-Tracy, "The Voting Behavior of Judges Appointed by President Bush," *Judicature* 76 (1993), p. 301. These authors cite additional evidence for Bush's clout in the fact that only one of his thirty-six vetoes was overridden by the Congress as a whole. "Even when he was 10 percentage points behind Bill Clinton in the polls and the economy was in shambles," they state, "Bush was able to exert considerable clout with much of Congress."

94. Senator Patrick J. Leahy of Vermont, as quoted in *Congressional Quarterly*, January 19, 1991, p. 173.

95. Although Bush's record on appointing minorities and women is poor, he is on record as having written to then Senate Minority Leader Bob Dole (R-KS) on November 30, 1991, noting the role of Republican senators in choosing district court candidates and asking for more qualified female and minority recommendations. Clearly, the data show that for whatever reasons, Dole was not responsive to Bush's request. Regarding the lack of minority Bush appointees, former Michigan Supreme Court Justice Dennis W. Archer, chairman of the ABA's Commission on Opportunities for Minorities in the Profession, explained it in terms of partisanship: "It is not accurate to say that the applicant pool doesn't exist, it is more correct to say that [Bush officials] do not seek minority or women applicants, and it is clear that Democrats need not apply." *Congressional Quarterly*, January 19, 1991, p. 172.

96. However, Bush appointees included an unprecedented proportion of Independents, 6.1 percent, President Clinton's first-term appointments, however, included an even higher proportion of Independents, 7.5 percent. See Table 3.11, Chapter 3.

97. See Christopher E. Smith, "Former U.S. Magistrates as District Judges: The Possibilities and Consequences of Promotion within the Federal Judiciary," *Judicature* 73 (1990), p. 268.

98. See "Bush Treads Well Worn Path in Building Federal Bench," *Congressional Quarterly*, January 18, 1992, p. 111; and "How the Candidates Stand on Legal Issues," *L.A. Daily Journal*, 11/4/88.

99. See "Bush Treads Well Worn Path in Building Federal Bench," p. 111.

100. Goldman, "Bush's Judicial Legacy: The Final Imprint," p. 290.

101. Ibid., pp. 282, 296.

102. *Congressional Quarterly*, January 19, 1991, p. 174.

103. Ibid., p. 171.

104. Tony Mauro, "High Stakes, Low Courts," 16 *The Washington Monthly*, July-August, 1996, pp. 17–18.

105. According to Senate Judiciary Committee member Senator Paul Simon, Souter was "as blank a slate as anyone ever offered by a President for a seat on the Court." Paul Simon, *Advice and Consent: Clarence Thomas, Robert Bork, and the Intriguing History of the Supreme Court's Nomination Battles* (Washington, DC.: National Press Books, 1992), p. 76.

106. Thomas was previously nominated and subsequently appointed to the U.S. Court of Appeals for the District of Columbia by President Bush in 1990.

107. For a discussion on the politics of the Bush strategy in the selection of Thomas, see Silverstein, *Judicious Choices,* pp. 99–100, 157, 163–164. At the least, the Thomas confirmation highlights attempts by modern presidents to pack the courts with ideologues—no matter the political price and irrespective of the nominee's qualifications. Many studies have chronicled and analyzed the Thomas confirmation. See for example, Timothy Phelps and Helen Winternitz, *Capitol Games* (New York: Hyperion, 1992); Simon, *Advice and Consent*; and Robert Chrisman and Robert L. Allen, eds., *Court of*

Appeal: The Black Community Speaks out on the Racial and Sexual Politics of Clarence Thomas vs. Anita Hill (New York: Ballentine, 1992). See also an essay by Lucius J. Barker and Kevin L. Lyles, published in the professional newsletter of the National Conference of Black Political Scientists (1992).

108. Goldman, "Bush's Judicial Legacy: The Final Imprint," p. 285.

109. Ibid.

110. Bill Clinton, "Judiciary Suffers Racial, Sexual Lack of Balance," *National Law Journal* (November 2, 1992), p. 15.

111. Ibid.

112. Labaton, "President's Judicial Appointments: Diverse, But Well in the Mainstream," *New York Times,* October 17, 1994, p. A15.

113. As of this writing, detailed monthly reports, *The Judicial Selection Monitor*, are available from the Judicial Selection Monitoring Project web site at [http:\www.fcref.org/jsmp.htm].

114. Lombardi is quoted in Ruth Shalit, "Borking Back," *New Republic,* May 17, 1993, p. 20.

115. See Neil A. Lewis, "Conservatives Set for fight on Judicial Nominees," *New York Times*, November 13, 1992, p. B16.

116. An act designed to reverse the Supreme Court's 5–4 *Smith* ruling downgrading free-exercise-of religion claims against state action.

117. See Edd Doerr, "Church and State: Good News So Far," *The Humanist* 53 (January/February 1993), pp. 8–9.

118. *Putting People First.*

119. Fred Barnes, "Bush II," *The New Republic* 209 (October 11, 1993), p. 12.

120. *Putting People First.* For example, Attorney General Janet Reno testified on Capitol Hill in favor of legislation protecting abortion clinics by requiring stiff federal penalties for protesters who block the entrances to such clinics.

121. *Congressional Quarterly Weekly Report*, July 3, 1993, p. 1737.

122. Barnes, "Bush II," p. 10. One of President Clinton's first executive orders permitted women and dependents of members of the military to obtain abortions at overseas facilities, so long as the women paid for the procedure. The Republican-dominated House, however, repudiated Clinton's order and included in the fiscal 1996 defense authorization (HR 1530) the renewed ban on abortions at overseas bases. For discussion and legislative debate, see "Abortion Curb Approved," 53 *Congressional Quarterly Weekly Report*, June 17, 1995, p. 1758.

123. For an unflattering discussion of Clinton's role on these points, see Barnes, "Bush II," pp. 10–12.

124. Ibid., p. 10.

125. The bill would make it a federal crime, punishable by fines and up to two years in prison, for a doctor to perform a partial-birth abortion, unless it was necessary to save the life of the woman. The *Los Angeles Times* graphically described the partial-birth procedure: "[A] physician extracts a fetus feet first from the womb and through the birth canal until all but its head is exposed. Then tips of surgical scissors are thrust into the base of the fetus's skull, a suction catheter is inserted through the opening, and the brain is removed before completing the abortion." For discussion, see "Against Infanticide," *National Review*, April 22, 1996, pp. 19–20.

126. Colette Fraley, "Senate Votes to Ban Procedure Despite Veto Threat," 53 *Congressional Quarterly Weekly Report*, December 9, 1995, p. 3738.

127. "Late-Term Procedure Bill Heads to Clinton for Expected Veto," 54 *Congres-*

sional Quarterly Weekly Report, March 30, 1996, pp. 885–886.

128. See "Respectful Dissents: Tom's Dissent: Judgeships and the Ballot Box," for NET: Political News Talk Network, at [http://net.fcref.org/comm/LNcomm/ln040896. htm]. April 29, 1996.

129. For this response and other responses to Clinton's proposed veto from the Catholic hierarchy, see "Against Infanticide," pp. 19–20.

130. For the complete text of President Clinton's April 10, 1996 message to Congress vetoing HR 1833, see 54 *Congressional Quarterly Weekly Report*, April 13, 1996, p. 1009. See also, *New York Times*, April 11, 1996, p. A1.

131. See the ACLU press release, "ACLU Lauds Presidential Veto of Bill Banning Abortion Technique" released Thursday, April 11, 1996 [http://www.aclu.org/news/ n041196.html]

132. Ruth Bader Ginsburg, "Some Thoughts on Autonomy and Equality in Relation to *Roe v. Wade*," *North Carolina Law Review* 63 (1985), p. 382.

133. Barnes, "Bush II," p. 10.

134. See Fred Barnes, "The New Covenant," *The New Republic* 207 (November 9, 1992), pp. 32–33.

135. Ibid., p. 32.

136. The RFRA was a legislative response to the Supreme Court's 1990 decision in *Employment Division, Department of Human Resources of Oregon v. Alfred L. Smith*, where the Rehnquist Court continued its restrictive view of the free exercise guarantee when it considered a state's enforcement of its criminal laws against the sacramental use of the drug peyote (494 U.S. 872 [1990]).

137. For a discussion of Clinton's praise of Carter's book, see Terry Eastland, "Religion, Politics and the Clintons," *Commentary* 97 (January 1994), pp. 40–43.

138. Ibid., p. 43.

139. While taking questions from the press in 1994, Clinton was asked his views on a proposal by Speaker Newt Gingrich (R-GA), who called for hearing on a constitutional amendment to restore prayer to public schools. President Clinton responded, "I want to reserve judgment, I want to see the specifics." "I'll be glad to discuss it," said Clinton. However, soon afterward the White House backed away from Clinton's statement saying the administration preferred a legislative approach rather than a constitutional amendment. See "School Prayer Issue Picking up Speed," 52 *Congressional Quarterly Weekly Report*, November 19, 1994, p. 3353.

140. For discussion on this memo, see an editorial in *America* 173 (September 23, 1995), p. 3.

141. Ibid.

142. Robert Marshall Wells and Holly Idelson, "Clinton Acts on Prayer Issue," 53 *Congressional Quarterly Weekly Report*, July 15, 1995, p. 2075.

143. Steven A. Holmes, "The Clinton Record: Civil Rights, Clinton Steers a Bumpy Course," *New York Times* October 20, 1996. [http://www.nytimes.com/web/docsroot/ library/politics/civil-rights-exclusive.html]

144. Ibid.

145. Ibid.

146. Ibid.

147. For a very concise summary of the Guinier episode, see Karen Branan, "Lani Guinier: The Anatomy of a Betrayal," 4 *Ms.*, September/October 1993, pp. 50–57. See also John Broker and Paul Richter, "Cronies: Clinton Draws Heavily on Friends for Jobs," *Los Angeles Times*, 7 June 1993, Sec. A. President Clinton noted, for example,

that "Lani analyzed the weakness of the present remedies available under the Voting Rights Act—and many of her analyses I agree with—but seemed to be arguing for principals of proportional representation in minority veto as general remedies that I think are inappropriate as general remedies and antidemocratic views difficult to defend." See Karen Ashlin, et al., *Public Papers of the Presidents of the Presidents: William Judge. Clinton.* 2 vols. (Washington, DC: Government Printing Office, 1993), p. 809. As an interesting aside, consider Karen Branan's observation following Clinton's decision to withdraw Guinier's nomination: "After she'd been left twisting in the wind, Clinton sat at a lavish dinner party in the White House and told his guests something so bizarre it still resonates: 'I just love her,' he said. 'If she called me and told me she needed $5,000, I'd take it from my account and send it to her no questions asked.' As one observer remarked 'He [Clinton] was treating her like a welfare queen—read Quota Queen—looking for a handout. It had the instant effect of putting her in a subservient position and him in a position of great generosity" (Branan, "Lani Guinier: The Anatomy of a Betrayal," p. 57).

148. Branan, "Lani Guinier: The Anatomy of a Betrayal," pp. 50–57.

149. From the remarks delivered by President Clinton at the National Archives on July 19, 1995, and as reprinted in the *Congressional Digest* 75 (June-July 1996), p. 168.

150. Transcript of Presidential Debate, the *New York Times*, October 17, 1996. See Holmes, "The Clinton Record," [http://www.nytimes.com/web/docsroot/library/politics/civil-rights-exclusive.html].

151. Ibid.

152. For a first-hand account of the Clinton White House review of affirmative action, see Christopher Edley, Jr., *Not All Black and White* (New York: Hill and Wang, 1996). As reported therein, Edley, the point man for the Clinton White House, "had extensive discussions with President Clinton and other administration officials, weighing all the relevant legal and social-science evidence, public-policy developments, and private practices."

153. American Bar Association press release, "Is it the Beginning of the End for Affirmative Action?" November 7, 1995 [http://www.abanet.org/media/nov95/action.html].

154. President Clinton at the National Archives on July 19, 1995 as reprinted in the *Congressional Digest* 75 (June-July 1996), pp. 166–168. See also, Holmes, "The Clinton Record," [http://www.nytimes.com/web/docsroot/library/politics/civil-rights-exclusive.html]. Administration officials professed that Clinton had reached his decision out of principle; critics said it was "political pandering." As explained by Holmes, "amid the assertions over the reasons behind Clinton's decision, one major event does stand out. On June 12, 1995, the Supreme Court, in a 5-to-4 ruling in *Adarand Constructors Inc. v. Pena*, upheld federal affirmative action programs but said steps had to be taken to ensure that programs were justified and that their implementation did not run roughshod over the rights of whites. While civil rights groups initially bemoaned the High Court's decision, it soon became clear that the decision carried an enormous political silver lining for the administration. In effect, the justices had said, mend it but don't end it. As a result, the decision allowed the administration to modify affirmative action programs in ways that pre-empted the criticisms raised by Republicans while fending off liberals by saying that changes were mandated by the Supreme Court." "It set the outer bounds," Stephanopoulos said, "because it was harder for the opponents of affirmative action to argue with doing away with it when a conservative Supreme Court had not ruled it illegal." For discussion on the Clinton administration's response to the *Adarand* decision, see Edley, *Not All Black and White*, pp. 63–73.

155. Ibid. See also, "Clinton Comes to the Defense of Affirmative Action," 53 *Congressional Quarterly Weekly Report,* July 22, 1995, p. 2194. For significant excerpts from the official White House transcript of President Clinton's July 19 address on affirmative action, see 53 *Congressional Quarterly Weekly Report,* July 22, 1995, pp. 2208 2209.

156. American Bar Association press release, "Is it the Beginning of the End for Affirmative Action?" November 7, 1995 [http://www.abanet.org/media/nov95/action.html].

157. Holmes, "The Clinton Record," October 20, 1996 [http://www.nytimes.com/web/docsroot/library/politics/civil-rights-exclusive.html].

158. "The Race Gap," *The New Republic,* August 14, 1995, p. 7.

159. William H. Freivogel, "Ginsburg May Alter Balance in Key Civil Rights Cases," *St. Louis Post-Dispatch,* October 3, 1993, p. 1B.

160. *Congressional Quarterly Weekly Report,* 1995, p. 352.

161. The White House, Office of the Press Secretary, July 19, 1995. Remarks by the President on Affirmative Action, The Rotunda, National Archives, [http://gort.ucsd.edu/docs/presafir.html].

162. See Susan H. Fuhrman, "Clinton's Educational Policy and Intergovernmental Relations in the 1990s," *Publius* 24 (Summer 1994), pp. 83–97.

163. Ibid.

164. President Clinton at the National Archives on July 19, 1995 as reprinted in the *Congressional Digest* 75 (June-July 1996), p. 167.

165. *Los Angeles Times,* 6/11/96.

166. The White House, Office of the Press Secretary, July 19, 1995. Remarks by President Clinton on Affirmative Action, The Rotunda, National Archives, [http://gort.ucsd.edu/docs/presafir.html].

167. Bill Clinton, "State Initiatives to Increase Voter Participation," in Karen McGill and William L. Taylor, eds., *Voting Rights in America* (Washington, DC: Leadership Conference Education Fund Joint Center for Political and Economic Studies, 1992), pp. 143–151.

168. Ashlin et al., *Public Papers of the Presidents,* p. 707.

169. *Miller v. Johnson* (115 S. Ct. 2475 [1995]).

170. The White House, Office of the Press Secretary, Statement by President Clinton released on June 29, 1995.

171. Joshua Lazerson, "Bill Clinton States Positions on the Federal Judiciary," *Judicature* 76 (August-September, 1992), pp. 97, 100.

172. Michael Krauss, a professor at George Mason University School of Law. As quoted in Zehren, "Justice Delayed," note 76.

173. Paul M. Barrett, "Chance to Alter Conservative Judiciary Beckons, but Seats on Federal Benches Remain Unfilled," *Wall Street Journal,* June 28, 1993, p. A16.

174. Ibid.

175. Ibid. President Clinton had only been in office about two months when Byron White, the only Democrat then remaining on the Supreme Court, announced his retirement.

176. See, e.g., *New York Times,* May 9, 1993, p. 22; *New York Times,* June 15, 1993, p. A22.

177. Barrett, "Chance to Alter," p. A16.

178. Ibid.

179. Charles V. Zehren, "Justice Delayed by Empty Benches; Clinton Falls Short on a Promise to Fill Scores of Judgeships," *Newsday* (Nassau and Suffolk Edition), May 28,

1994, p. A08.

180. Bob Woodward, in his book *The Agenda: Inside the Clinton White House*, discusses Clinton's reluctance to terminate debate in order to make crucial decisions (New York: Simon and Schuster, 1994). One this point, For example, Lloyd Bensten, Clinton's secretary of the treasury, once described Clinton as the "meetingest fellow he'd ever seen" (Woodward, p. 328).

181. Barrett, "Chance to Alter," p. A16.

182. Zehren, "Justice Delayed," note 177.

183. Ibid., note 76.

184. The White House, Office of the Press Secretary, July 19, 1995. Remarks by the President on Affirmative Action, The Rotunda, National Archives.

185. "Faces of Today's Black Woman," *Ebony*, March 1997, p. 98.

186. Sheldon Goldman and Matthew D. Saranson, "Clinton's Nontraditional Judges: Creating a More Representative Bench," *Judicature* 78 (September-October 1994), pp. 68–73.

187. According to the "Alliance for Justice Judicial Selection Project Annual Report 1994," in May 6, 1994, Deborah Batts, "an open lesbian, quietly became the first openly gay person to be appointed to the federal courts." A graduate of Radcliffe College and Harvard Law School, Batts practiced law for six years with Cravath, Swaine & Moore, then became an assistant U.S. attorney, and later an associate professor at Fordham University School of Law. "Confirmed to the district court for the Southern District of New York, her sexual orientation was not raised at all during her confirmation hearing" [http://essential.org/afj/jsprep.html].

188. However, the Clinton proportion of those rejected by the ABA was also the highest since the Kennedy administration. See Goldman's "Judicial Selection under Clinton," p. 285.

189. *Congressional Quarterly Weekly Report*, 1995, p. 461.

190. Smith, "Former U.S. Magistrates as District Judges," p. 268.

191. Klain was a former Senate Judiciary Committee chief counsel and he worked closely with Senate Judiciary Committee Chairman Joseph Biden.

192. Personal interview with Radd by political scientist, Sheldon Goldman, University of Massachusetts at Amherst, on December 21, 1994, cited in "Judicial Selection under Clinton: A Midterm Examination," *Judicature* 78 (May-June, 1995), p. 278.

193. This description of the process is provided by Sheldon Goldman who (1) recounts a presentation given by Assistant Attorney General Eleanor Acheson at the Southern Political Science Association annual meeting, November 6, 1994 in Atlanta Georgia; (2) also interviewed Acheson following her presentation; as well as (3) conducted telephone interviews with Victoria Radd on December 21, 1994; and (4) with Peter Erichsen, April 6, 1995. These accounts are summarized in Goldman's "Judicial Selection under Clinton," p. 278.

194. Sheldon Goldman and Elliot Slotnick, "Clinton's First Term Judiciary: Many Bridges to Cross," *Judicature* 80 (May–June, 1997), pp. 254–255.

195. Ibid., Goldman interviews.

196. Ibid.

197. Goldman and Slotnick, "Clinton's First Term Judiciary," p. 255.

198. Procedurally, as reported, Clinton receives a memo from the White House counsel's office suggesting nominees. Clinton himself will sometimes suggest names or ask for more names.

199. The White House counsel was Bernard Nussbaum until April 5, 1994; Lloyd N.

Cutler, who served from April 5 through September 1994; and Abner J. Mikva since October 1, 1994.

200. Deputy Erichsen worked full-time on judicial selection for the Department of Justice until moving to the Office of White House Counsel in 1996 where he coordinated judicial selection efforts for the remainder of the 104th Congress.

201. Goldman's "Judicial Selection under Clinton," p. 279.

202. Ibid.; Acheson's presentation at the Southern Political Science Association meetings in 1994.

203. Neil Lewis, "Clinton Legacy: Moderate Judge Appointments," *New York Times*, August 1, 1996, A-1, p. 20. A recent study by Donald Songer, Robert A. Carp, and Ronald Stidham suggests also that "Clinton's judges are decidedly less liberal than other modern Democratic Presidents." In fact, this study concluded that the "ideological fingerprints" of Clinton's judges "most resemble those of judges selected by President Ford." See "The Voting Behavior of President Clinton's Judicial Appointees" *Judicature* 80 (July-August 1996), pp. 16–20.

204. Neil Lewis, "Clinton Legacy," p. 20.

205. Ted Gest, "Disorder in the Courts?," *U.S. News and Word Report*, February 12, 1996.

206. Neil Lewis, "Clinton Legacy," p. 20.

207. Holly Idelson, "Clinton's Choice of Ginsburg Signals Moderation," *Congressional Quarterly*, June 19, 1993, p. 1369.

208. Judicial Selection Monitoring Project, "Largest Coalition in History of Oppose Judicial Activism," January 23, 1997 [http://www.fcref.org/jsmp/oppose.htm], p 1.

209. See generally, Goldman and Slotnick, "Clinton's First Term Judiciary," pp. 254–273.

210. Terry Eastland, "If Clinton Wins, Here's What the Courts Will Look Like," *Wall Street Journal*, February, 28, 1996, p. A-21.

211. Goldman and Slotnick, "Clinton's First Term Judiciary," p. 257.

212. Hillary Clinton is on record explaining how her life was "turned around by Edelman." Ms. Clinton stated, for example, "I owe much of what I believe and much of what I am as an adult . . . to my friend and mentor, Marion Wright Edelman. She has helped me give direction and shape to my life." See "Hillary Clinton Reveals Black College Grad Helped Direct and Shape Her Career," *Jet* 83 (October 26, 1992), p. 6.

213. Neil Lewis, "Clinton Legacy: Moderate Judge Appointments," *New York Times*, August 1, 1996, A-1, p. 20.

214. These figures are provided by Goldman and Slotnick, "Clinton's First Term Judiciary," p. 260.

215. Ibid., p. 256.

216. *The Third Branch*, "An Interview with Senator Orrin Hatch on Courts, Legislation, and Judicial Nominees," [http://www.uscourts.gov/ttb/nov95/hatch. htm], November 1995.

217. Garland W. Allison, "Delay in Senate Confirmation of Federal Judicial Nominees," *Judicature* 80 (1996), pp. 8–15, esp. Table 4, p.11.

218. Merrick was eventually approved by the Senate in 1997, 76–23. See Judicial Selection Monitoring Project, "Role Call Votes," [http://www.fcref.org/jsmp/rollcall. htm], pp. 1-3.

219. For a summary of the surrounding controversy, see Neil Lewis, "Partisan Gridlock Blocks Confirmations of Federal Judges," *New York Times*, November 29, 1995.

220. Ibid.

221. Roger K. Lowe, "Senate Compromise May Allow Confirmation of Federal Judges," *The Columbus Dispatch*, July 14, 1996, p. 3B.

222. Ibid. As of November 1996, the Clinton confirmation count remained at 204, compared to 189 for President Bush, and, 164 for President Reagan in his first term.

223. Price, "Rating Those Who Rate Judges," *Investor's Business Daily*, June 17, 1996, p. A1; and Neil Lewis, "Senator's Question Bar Association's Role in Selecting Judges," *New York Times*, May 22, 1996, p. A14.

224. See W. John Moore, "Judges on the Left! Hold that Line," *National Journal*, April 22, 1993, p. 1246.

225. Press release by the NET: Political News Talk Network, "ABA Partisan, Evidence Shows," [http://net.fcref.org/press/release6.htm], April 29, 1996. See also the *Washington Post*, April 29, 1996.

226. "An Interview with the President of the American Bar Association Roberta Cooper Ramo, The Third Branch," March 1996 [http://www.uscourts.gov/ttb/mar96ttb/ramos.htm].

227. Katharine Seelye, "Dole Criticizes Court Nominees," *New York Times*, April 20, 1996, p. 1.

228. *The Judicial Selection Monitor*, September 1996 [http://www.fcref.org/jsmp/monitor/ september96.htm], p.4.

229. Clint Bolick at the Institute for Justice released a study in April 1996 charging that Clinton's U.S. Court of Appeals judges for the Fourth Circuit vote for criminal defendants about 90 percent of the time while non-Clinton judges vote for criminal defendants just 40 percent of the time. For commentary on this point and Quinn's comments, see "Respectful Dissents: Tom's Dissent: Judgeships and the Ballot Box," for NET: Political News Talk Network [http://net.fcref.org/comm/LNcomm/ln040896.htm], April 29, 1996.

230. Lewis, "Clinton Legacy, " p. 20.

231. "The Vacancy List for Article III Judgeships," U.S. Federal Courts' Home Page maintained by the Administrative Office of the U.S. Courts [http://www.uscourts.gov/vacancies/index.html].

232. *The Judicial Selection Monitor*, November 1996 [http://www.fcref.org/jsmp/monitor/november96.htm]. See also Eastland, "If Clinton Wins," p. A-21. Eastland predicts about 350 district court judges.

233. See "Presidential Candidates Respond to AJS Questions about the Justice System," [http://homepage.interaccess.com/~ajs/President.html].

234. As of this writing, the Congress had failed to act on the Judicial Conference's request for additional judgeships. The conference submitted a "draft bill" creating twenty new temporary courts of appeals judgeships and five temporary district court judgeships. The conference had also asked Congress to convert five existing temporary judgeships to permanent status and the extend the expiration date for six temporary judgeships.

235. *The Judicial Selection Monitor*, November 1996, [http://www.fcref.org/jsmp/monitor/november96.htm].

236. Ibid.

237. See *Judicial Selection Monitoring Project*, "The Hatch Pledge," [http://www.fcref.org/jsmp/adopt/hatch.htm], pp. 1–2. As of May 18, 1997, only eight senators had signed Hatch's pledge.

238 *St. Louis Post-Dispatch*, "Ashcroft Hearings Targeting Judicial Activism but Critics Say Eliminating Liberal Judges is Main Goal," June 13, 1997.

239. Ibid. See also, Thomas L. Jipping, "The Danger of More Activist Judges," in the *Washington Times*, January 28, 1997, and as available at [http://www.fcref.org/jsmp/oped/012897.htm].

240. *St. Louis Post-Dispatch*, June 13, 1997.

241. See Thomas L. Jipping, "Face the Facts Miss Reno," in the *Washington Times*, August 7, 1997, and as available at [http://www.fcref.org/jsmp/oped/080797.htm].

7 Presidential Expectation and Judicial Performance

The Constitution is what the judges say it is.[1]

INTRODUCTION

In this chapter, I discuss the extent to which district court judges have supported the policy objectives of their appointing presidents by reviewing and comparing these judges' significant decisions (the SDCC data) with the corresponding judges' appointing presidents' policy objectives.[2] Specifically, I examine the nexus between what presidents want the "law" (Constitution and statutes) to mean, and what judges in fact say the "law" means. This comparative analysis allows us to discern more clearly the extent to which these determinations comport with the expectations of the appointing presidents and the efficacy of their varied selection politics.

For this part of the analysis, the expectation profiles developed in the previous chapters are grouped into combinations of several general subjective categories; specifically, "high," "moderate," and "low-no" priority, and, "high," "moderate" and "low-no" expectation. The high priority rating is used when the given president expressed a direct and specific policy preference—for example, President Reagan's explicit promise to "bring prayer back into the classroom." Similarly, what I term high expectation issues are also those issues on which a given president expressed an explicit desire to appoint judges they believed shared and would promote policy preferences similar to their own (on that specific issue). Again, an example would be President Reagan's specific promise to overturn *Roe v. Wade* and to appoint antiabortion judges who shared this view.

The *second* profile category, moderate priority issues, are those where a president expressed moderate, but not strong and deep, concern about an issue—for example, President Ford's limited and sporadic attention to voting rights guarantees. Likewise, a moderate-expectation issue is one where the president and/or his administration did not directly (or explicitly) attempt to select judges to promote either side of the policy issue.

The *third* category, low-no priority, are policy issues about which a given president, for whatever reason, expressed little or no policy preference; thus, it is inappropriate to construct a presidential profile on these issues. For example, the abortion question is assigned a low-no priority rating for Kennedy and Johnson. And, of course, a low-no expectation rating likewise reflects a policy area that a given president did not overtly consider in the politics and process of judicial selection.

Before detailing the policy performance ratios for each president, let us briefly review the policy selection procedures explained earlier. To begin, I reviewed common agenda items (issues) for all eight presidents and selected five generally concomitant issues for analysis in the expectation profiles: abortion rights, religious liberty, affirmative action, school desegregation, and voting rights. All or most of these issues cut across the administrations of each of the presidents involved. However, one must keep in mind that each policy area is not equally relevant for each president. For example, the SDCC data reveal that the abortion issue was not a salient policy question before the federal district courts in the early sixties for Kennedy and Johnson. See Appendix B, Table B.2. It is also important to recall that not every president exhibited expectations for their federal appointments on any or all issues.

Nonetheless, in order to provide a uniform, comparative basis for analysis across all eight presidential administrations, an expectation-performance discussion is offered for each president on each issue. Indeed, irrespective of a given president's lack of an explicit articulated policy goal or expectation, the fact remains that his judges nevertheless will inevitably decide significant cases in that particular area. That such instances do exist, allows us to draw conclusions with respect to the expectation/performance thesis and provides insight and perspectives on policy inclinations of a given president's judicial appointments.

Caution must be exercised, however, when analyzing the judicial performance data tables. The small number of cases in many cells—especially for more recent presidential administrations—prevents more than simply presenting the available support scores and describing the general trends.

A Note on Recent Presidential Administrations. Given the lag period between appointment to the bench and the opportunity for a president's appointees to decide a representative number of significant cases, it is too soon at the time of this writing to fully assess the long-term policy support patterns of presidents Reagan, Bush, and, especially, Clinton. That is, quantitative analysis of significant decisions of recent presidents' appointees' are hindered by the substantial interval between a president's election and the time when their appointees' judicial decisions are published in sufficient number.[3] Moreover, analysis using the SDCC data is even more hindered than "all case" approaches for quantitative analysis since it includes not all cases printed, but, only the "significant" cases. For these reasons, the modest findings for recent presidents represent only a small descriptive prelude to the body of law and policy these judges will eventually contribute. And that body of law may enhance, or retard, these presidents' policy objectives.

The Presidential Profiles: A Review

John Kennedy, 1960–1996. President Kennedy's presidential-expectation profile suggests only one high priority/high expectation issue: religious liberty. Affirmative action is assigned high priority but moderate expectation, and both school desegregation and voting rights issues represent moderate priority/moderate expectation issue areas. Because abortion was not yet a national political issue, it is assigned low-no priority/low-no expectation status given its relative nonexistence as a policy concern for the Kennedy administration.

Consistent with the current literature on President Kennedy's positions on civil rights, the expectation profiles regarding school desegregation and voting rights suggest a less than convincing commitment by Kennedy to the realization of these more controversial and specific policy goals. As detailed in Chapter 4, Kennedy avoided pushing for school desegregation as well as increased voting rights, fearing that such activity might jeopardize his other policy objectives. Therefore, both school desegregation and voting rights are assigned moderate priority status. And, of course, given Kennedy's willingness to appoint segregationist district court judges, I likewise assign a moderate expectation rating for these issues. Voting rights and school desegregation decisions have accounted for the highest proportions of Kennedy's judges' significant opinions across the five policy areas to date, about 38 percent and 31 percent, respectively (see Figure 7.1).

Figure 7.1
Significant Opinions: Kennedy's Appointees

Lyndon Johnson, 1964–1996. The expectation profile for President Johnson suggests essentially three high priority/high expectation issue areas: affirmative action, school desegregation, and voting rights. These three represent policy/issue areas about which Johnson expressed a direct and forceful concern. On the other hand, both abortion and religious liberty were low-no priority and low-no expectation issues for the Johnson administration. Notice also that voting rights decisions have accounted for the highest proportion, almost 35 percent, of all Johnson's judges' significant opinions across the five policy areas to date (see Figure 7.2).

Figure 7.2
Significant Opinions: Johnson's Appointees

Religious Liberty 19.52%

Abortion 8.09%

School Desegregation 26.67%

Affirmative Action 10.95%

Voting Rights 34.77%

Richard Nixon, 1969–1996. President Nixon's 1968 presidential campaign set the stage for a transformation in the politics of judicial appointments. This transformation was clearly evidenced in Nixon's campaign pledge to appoint strict constructionists—conservative judges who were clearly committed to judicial self-restraint.

The Nixon expectation profile generated two high priority/high expectation issues: abortion and school desegregation; one high priority/moderate expectation issue: affirmative action; and one low-no priority and low-no expectation issue: voting rights. Religious liberty issues were of little or no priority or expectation concern for the Nixon administration. Ironically, as graphically depicted in Figure 7.3, religious liberty opinions account for the largest proportion, about 30 percent, of the significant opinions reported for Nixon appointees across all five of the policy categories.

Figure 7.3
Significant Opinions: Nixon's Appointees

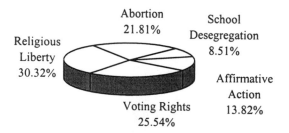

Abortion 21.81%

School Desegregation 8.51%

Religious Liberty 30.32%

Affirmative Action 13.82%

Voting Rights 25.54%

Gerald Ford, 1974–1996. Judicial selection for President Ford was less than a "front burner" concern. The Ford profile, as reviewed in Chapter 4, revealed only one high priority/high expectation issue: school desegregation. Both abortion rights and voting rights were assigned moderate priority/moderate expectation status. Religious liberty and affirmative action issues were not found to be central to the Ford agenda; if anything, they were almost nonexistent. Thus, these issue areas were viewed as being of low-no priority/low-no expectation concern to the Ford administration. Religious liberty decisions have accounted for the highest proportion, about 41 percent, of all Ford's judges' significant opinions across the five policy areas to date (see Figure 7.4).

Figure 7.4
Significant Opinions: Ford's Appointees

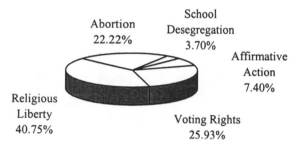

James Carter, 1977–1996. President Carter's presidential policy objective profile revealed only one high priority/high expectation issue: affirmative action (see Chapter 6). Abortion rights were clearly a high priority issue on the Carter agenda, given the repeated and focused attention on the issue. Carter's positions on abortion rights, however, were most often confusing and unclear. That is, even though abortion was seemingly a high priority issue for the Carter administration generally, the president never provided clear leadership or specific goal objectives. Thus, in the absence of an articulated policy direction or goal, one would have to have low-no expectations as to their implementation or support. School desegregation is rated moderate priority/moderate expectation, and, for comparative purposes, I assign both religious liberty and voting rights low-no priority/low-no expectation status, given Carter's almost complete lack of articulated policy views on these issues. Nonetheless, despite religious liberty being a nonissue in Carter's selection politics, as represented in Figure 7.5, Carter appointees rendered more significant opinions concerning issues of religious liberty than in any one of the other four policy areas under review. Indeed, religious liberty cases represent just over 40 percent of the total number of significant cases for Carter appointees.

Ronald Reagan, 1981–1996. The analysis presented in Chapter 5 suggests that all five policy areas were high priority/high expectation issue areas for President Reagan, both in terms of general policy formation and leadership goals (see Chapter 5). And the president's views were specifically reflected in the administration's procedures for the selection, nomination, and appointment of district court judges. Indeed, as discussed earlier, the Reagan administration influenced greatly the outer bounds of the issue areas selected for this study. In sum, the presidential policy objective profile (PPOP) for President Reagan revealed all five of the issue areas as being high priority/high expectation issue areas: abortion rights, religious liberty, affirmative action, school desegregation, and voting rights. To date, religious liberty decisions have accounted for the highest proportion, nearly 35 percent, of all Reagan's judges' significant opinions across the five policy areas to date (see Figure 7.6).

Figure 7.5
Significant Opinions: Carter Appointees

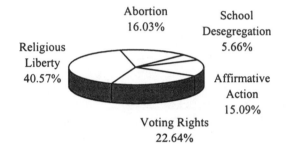

Abortion 16.03%

School Desegregation 5.66%

Religious Liberty 40.57%

Affirmative Action 15.09%

Voting Rights 22.64%

Figure 7.6
Significant Opinions: Reagan's Appointees

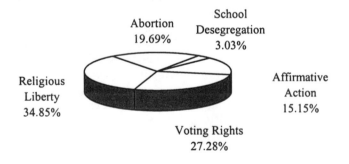

Abortion 19.69%

School Desegregation 3.03%

Religious Liberty 34.85%

Affirmative Action 15.15%

Voting Rights 27.28%

George Bush, 1988–1996. As detailed in Chapter 6, President Bush also was directly involved in the selection and nomination processes. And, although Bush approached district court judges' nominations with less intensity than Reagan, he continued the existing policy of appointing to the courts conservative judges favoring government interests over individual rights.

President Bush clearly opposed abortion and evidence suggests that the Bush administration considered a candidate's position on the matter when selecting judges; therefore, abortion was assigned to the high priority/high expectation category. Bush also supported both a constitutional amendment to restore voluntary school prayer and tuition tax credits (high priority), but there is little evidence to prove that the issue of religious liberty was a litmus test for Bush district court judge nominees (i.e., its ranking of moderate to low expectation). The analysis in Chapter 6 similarly suggests that President Bush did not support affirmative action, school desegregation plans, nor the motor-voter bill. However, there is little evidence to support the position that nominees were specifically selected or rejected along these lines. Therefore, Bush might generally be said to have given each of these three issues areas moderate priority and moderate expectation.

Bill Clinton (First Term), 1992–1996. President Clinton was especially careful to avoid any charges of appointing ideologues to the federal bench and specifically demanded that there was to be no ideological screening of nominees (Chapter 6). Regarding abortion, President Clinton promised to appoint judges committed to individual rights, "including the right to privacy." This statement, along with his veto of the partial-birth abortion ban, suggests a relatively high priority, but moderate expectation for the abortion issue.

On the one hand, Clinton opposed tax credits for sectarian schools and opposed a school prayer amendment; however, on the other hand, he supported the Religious Freedom Restoration Act and generally supports school prayer. Therefore, Clinton's religious liberty profile is labeled moderate priority and moderate expectation.

Clinton's record on civil rights in general is somewhat difficult to label. Clinton's stance on affirmative action ("mend it but don't end it"), school desegregation, and voting rights certainly have been labeled moderate by most observers. Therefore, Clinton might best be characterized as having given moderate priority and moderate-low expectation, to these three issues.

Next, I turn to a comparative analysis for each policy issue area across each administration. These tables present the expectation/performance support scores for each of the eight presidential appointment cohorts in the five policy issues areas.

Judicial Performance

Abortion. As detailed in Chapter 4, for President Kennedy the reproduction issue was more focused on birth control than abortion; for example, Kennedy did support increased research to improve fertility control. Overall, however, the abortion issue was not a significant feature in Kennedy's expectation profile; thus, it is assigned to the low-no priority/low-no expectation category.

Nonetheless, as indicated in Table 7.1, Kennedy appointees have written twelve significant abortion opinions and a majority of these (7–5) favored the pro-choice position. Thus, although abortion was not a primary issue in judicial selection during the Kennedy administration, Kennedy appointees have more often than not adopted and promoted the pro-choice position of the Democratic party.

For President Johnson, the abortion issue was not a significant policy nor judicial expectation issue. Nonetheless, observe in Table 7.1 that Johnson's district court appointees have been nearly unanimous, 94 percent (17–1), in their pro-choice performance.

In the absence of a well-articulated or defined presidential expectation profile, these decisions clearly reflect the overall liberal character of Johnson's appointees and signal the overall congruence of their decisions with the pro-choice stance of the Democratic party.

Table 7.1
A Comparison of Significant Abortion Rights Opinions for the Appointees of Presidents Kennedy through Clinton, 1960–1996

Appointing President	Pro-Choice Opinions	Antiabortion Opinions
John Kennedy[d] 1961–1996 (35 yrs.)	58.3% (7)	41.6% (5)
Lyndon Johnson[d] 1963–1996 (33 yrs.)	94.4% (17)	5.5% (1)
Richard Nixon[a] 1968–1996 (28 yrs.)	82.9% (34)	17.0%* (7)
Gerald Ford[c] 1972–1996 (24 yrs.)	100% (6)	—
James Carter[b] 1976–1996 (20 yrs.)	76.4% (13)	23.5% (4)
Ronald Reagan[a] 1980–1996 (16 yrs.)	46.1% (6)	53.8%* (7)
George Bush[a] 1988–1996 (8 yrs.)	—	100%* (1)
Bill Clinton[e] 1992–1996 (4 yrs.)	100%* (2)	—
Total	85	25

*Clearly stated presidential policy objective.
[a]High priority/high expectation issue.
[b]High priority/low-no expectation issue.
[c]Moderate priority/moderate expectation issue.
[d]Low-no priority/low-no expectation issue.
[e]High priority/moderate expectation.

President Nixon's intense antiabortion position was repeatedly based on the assertion that the unborn have rights—rights that must be recognized by law. However, not only was this right not recognized by three of his four Supreme Court appointments in the landmark *Roe v. Wade* decision, but it was also *not* supported by an overwhelming majority of his district court appointees. Table 7.1 shows that Nixon's district court appointees rendered forty-one significant opinions and the overwhelming majority of these opinions, about 83 percent, were pro-choice. The ratio of pro-choice opinions to antiabortion opinions was 34–7, plainly an instance of judicial performance running contrary to presidential designs. Thus, on the abortion issue, Nixon appointees have thus far bucked both the president's and the antiabortion (or pro-life) stance of the Republican party.

President Ford, like Nixon, personally opposed abortion. However, President Ford was less direct in his opposition, stating he would "support but not seek" a "states' rights" amendment. The SDCC data (see Table 7.1), indicate that Ford's appointees rendered six significant abortion opinions, and all six (100 percent) were pro-choice opinions. This result is clearly *not* in line with President Ford's overall expectation profile.

As discussed in Chapter 5, President Carter vacillated on the abortion question in an apparent attempt to appease both pro-choice and pro-life advocates. He opposed, for example, a constitutional amendment to overturn *Roe v. Wade*. On the other hand, however, he also opposed federal funding for abortions. Overall, however, the SDCC data suggest that Carter's judges' expectation/performance ratios are reflective and congruent with the controlling legal doctrines (e.g., *Roe v. Wade*), and with the pro-choice stance of the Democratic party.

Specifically, Carter appointees rendered seventeen significant abortion decisions. And, although Carter's personal preference and policy expectation were not always clear, his judicial appointees have thus far promoted the Democratic party line. The SDCC data, summarized in Table 7.1, indicates that just over 76 percent of Carter's appointees' significant decisions have upheld the pro-choice stance, a ratio of 13–4. Thus, in the absence of clear presidential policy positions, Carter's judges have thus far reflected dominant legal trends.

In contrast to President Carter, President Reagan's policy position, as well as judicial expectations, on abortion issues were strikingly clear. Reagan, promising only to appoint antiabortion judges, stated directly that the "national tragedy of abortion . . . must end" (see Chapter 5). To date, Reagan's judges have penned thirteen significant abortion opinions that have thus far adopted the antiabortion position at a near-even ratio of 7–6, which is at face value a relatively insignificant ratio (see Table 7.1). However, it *is* strongly significant that the performance of Reagan's judges marks the *first* instance, especially since abortion became a key issue, that any president's judges rendered proportionally more antiabortion than pro-choice opinions. As a matter of fact, it marks the first instance where the expectation/performance ratios have been close to supporting the pro-life position; for example, even presidents Nixon's and Ford's appointees (fellow Republicans) heavily favored the pro-choice position: 82.9 percent and 100 percent respectively.

The opportunity for President Bush—who continued the previous Reagan administration's attack on abortion rights—to promote his antiabortion stance by way of his district court appointments has thus far been somewhat limited. To date, Bush's appointees have penned only one significant decision, and significantly, this one opinion is an antiabortion decision. On the contrary, President Clinton's judges, whose decisions are also limited as of yet, have penned just two significant abortion opinions. Both of these two opinions support President Clinton's pro-choice stance (see Table 7.1).

Religious Liberty. Religious liberty issues were of major concern to President Kennedy. As detailed in Chapter 4, Kennedy reaffirmed, both during the 1960 campaign and after the election, his strong belief "in an America where the separation of church and state [was] absolute." Kennedy's direct and frequently articulated stance against church-state entanglement was clearly a major concern to him and his administration. And, even though the president did not expressly select judges in accordance with this stance, the SDCC data reveal that Kennedy's appointees have rendered thirty significant opinions involving religious freedom and over half (about 57 percent) of these opinions promoted his position. Though not an overwhelming difference, the Democratic party line as well as the Kennedy stance has been nonetheless supported.

Issues of religious liberty, like the abortion issue, were not of central interest in the Johnson presidency—particularly not so regarding the selection of district court judges. And issues of religious liberty, school prayer, and church-state relations were not as strongly supported as the abortion issue by Johnson's appointees.

As indicated in Table 7.2, Johnson's judges have rendered forty-three separate significant opinions on religious liberty issues. These opinions supported the liberal or "increased separation" position in 60 percent of the cases—a ratio of 26–17.

Similarly, religious liberty was not a key issue area for President Nixon, nor was it discussed significantly in the process of judicial selection. Nonetheless, Nixon's appointees have decided significant religious liberty cases and the SDCC data reveal that these Nixon appointees have leaned slightly toward the liberal stance. Specifically, Nixon's judges have rendered fifty-seven significant religious liberty opinions (see Table 7.2). Ironically, these religious liberty opinions account for the largest number, nearly 30 percent, of significant opinions reported thus far for Nixon appointees across all five of the selected policy categories. See Figure 7.2. In sum, the SDCC data reveal that a ratio of 31–26, or 57 percent, of these opinions favor the increased separation of church and state and related religious liberty issues.

The Ford administration expressed little concern and gave little priority to issues of religious liberty. The SDCC data reveal that Ford's appointees may be credited with eleven significant religious liberty opinions. Ironically, like Nixon, Ford judges rendered more opinions dealing with issues of religious liberty, a nonissue on his agenda, than in any of the other four policy areas under review. Moreover, the SDCC analysis reveals that 63.6 percent, or seven of eleven, of these opinions promoted a "pro" school prayer (or decreased separation between church and state) position (see Table 7.2). Thus, despite the absence of a well-articulated presidential agenda, Ford's appointees once again have promoted the Republican party stance on church-state issues.

Religious liberty was mostly a nonissue for the Carter administration. This was especially true regarding his selection of federal judges. Nonetheless, as represented in Figure 7.3, Carter appointees rendered more significant opinions concerning issues of religious liberty, 40 percent, than in any one of the other four policy areas under review. As indicated in Table 7.2, Carter appointees have rendered forty-three significant religious liberty decisions and almost 63 percent of these opinions served to increase the separation between church and state, a ratio of 27–16.

Table 7.2
A Comparison of Significant Religious Liberty Opinions for the Appointees of Presidents Kennedy through Clinton, 1960–1996

Appointing President	Decreased Separation	Increased Separation
John Kennedy[a] 1961–1996 (35 yrs.)	43.3% (13)	56.6%* (17)
Lyndon Johnson[b] 1963–1996 (33 yrs.)	39.5% (17)	60.4% (26)
Richard Nixon[b] 1968–1996 (28 yrs.)	45.6% (26)	54.3% (31)
Gerald Ford[b] 1972–1996 (24 yrs.)	63.6% (7)	36.3% (4)
James Carter[b] 1976–1996 (20 yrs.)	37.2% (16)	62.7% (27)
Ronald Reagan[a] 1980–1996 (16 yrs.)	65.2%* (15)	34.7% (8)
George Bush[c] 1988–1996 (8 yrs.)	33.3% (1)	66.6% (2)
Bill Clinton[d] 1992–1996 (4 yrs.)	100% (1)	—
Total	96	115

*Clearly stated presidential policy objective.
[a]High priority/high expectation issue.
[b]Low-no priority/low-no expectation issue.
[c]High priority/moderate to low expectation issue.
[d]Moderate priority/moderate expectation issue.

Similar to the abortion question, President Reagan's positions regarding issues of religious liberty and the separation between church and state were direct and frequent (see Chapter 5). In fact, Reagan's support went so far as to present to Congress a constitutional amendment to permit voluntary and vocal prayer in pubic schools. Interestingly, however, our findings indicate that this stance has not been as strongly shared and promoted by Reagan's judicial appointees.

Specifically, Reagan's judges have thus far authored twenty-three significant decisions regarding issues of religious liberty (see Table 7.2). At a ratio of 15–8, 65 percent of these opinions supported a decreased separation between church and state. Although the frequency of opinions is smaller than the numbers for most previous presidents under review, the Reagan performance ratio does indicate more support for lowering the wall of separation between church and state than is indicated for any previous president.

The current SDCC data for presidents Bush and Clinton are comparatively limited. In the first instance, for President Bush, who openly advocated prayer in the schools, the issue of religious liberty was important but was not given the kind of high priority it assumed under the Reagan administration. To date, Bush's appointees have rendered just three significant cases, a 2–1 ratio favoring increased separation between church and state. In the second instance, President Clinton's judges have thus far rendered only one significant religious liberty opinion—a single opinion favoring a decreased separation between church and state and in line with Clinton's pro-school prayer position, albeit a single case (see Table 7.2).

Affirmative Action. The PPOP analysis in Chapter 4 indicated that affirmative action was a high priority/moderate expectation issue for the Kennedy administration. It was Kennedy who issued Executive Order No. 10925 requiring in part that contractors "take *affirmative action* to ensure that participants are employed . . . without regard to their race, creed, color or national origin" (see Chapter 4). Even though Kennedy's appointees have rendered few (six) significant affirmative action opinions (see Table 7.3), the SDCC data reveal that those opinions compare at a 4–2 ratio favoring affirmative action policies (66 percent).

But, it was the executive orders of Lyndon Johnson that put the "teeth" in affirmative action. Thus, it is not surprising that the significant opinions written by Johnson appointees similarly reflect a commitment to affirmative action. As shown in Table 7.3, Johnson's appointees rendered twenty-four significant affirmative action opinions and about 79 percent of these supported affirmative action polices and programs, a ratio of 19–5. Clearly, President Johnson's strong support of affirmative action has been reflected in the significant decisions written by his district court appointments.

The expectation profile for President Nixon suggests high priority, but only moderate support, for affirmative action by the Nixon administration. This support was said to have gone from "lukewarm to cold" because Nixon did not follow up on many of his initial efforts (see Chapter 4). Nixon's appointees have rendered twenty-six significant district court opinions on affirmative action matters to date and 54 percent of these opinions support the pro-affirmative action position, a ratio of 14–12 (see Table 7.3). Taking into account the vacillating nature of Nixon's expectation profile, the near-even split between pro- and antiaffirmative action opinions is not unexpected.

Next, the SDCC data generated only two significant opinions for Ford appointees, one enhancing and one restricting affirmative action policies (see Table 7.3). Thus, Ford's assigned low-no expectation position regarding affirmative action has yielded much the same result, in other words, low-no significant performance pattern to date.

By contrast, for President Carter, the enhancement and enforcement of affirmative action policies were among the most articulated and overriding policy objectives of his administration (see Chapter 5). This position was also expressed in Carter's unprecedented number of appointments of both African-American, Latino, and women judges to the district courts (see Table 3.11). The SDCC data reveal that Carter appointees have decided sixteen significant affirmative action opinions and the overwhelming majority (almost 88 percent) have supported affirmative action polices—a support ratio of 14–2 (see Table 7.3).

Table 7.3
A Comparison of Significant Affirmative Action Opinions for the Appointees of Presidents Kennedy through Clinton, 1960–1996

Appointing President	Support	Oppose
John Kennedy[b] 1961–1996 (35 yrs.)	66.6% (4)	33.3% (2)
Lyndon Johnson[a] 1963–1996 (33 yrs.)	79.1%* (19)	20.8% (5)
Richard Nixon[b] 1968–1996 (28 yrs.)	53.8% (14)	46.1% (12)
Gerald Ford[c] 1972–1996 (24 yrs.)	50% (1)	50% (1)
James Carter[a] 1976–1996 (20 yrs.)	87.5%* (14)	12.5% (2)
Ronald Reagan[a] 1980–1996 (16 yrs.)	40% (4)	60%* (6)
George Bush[b] 1988–1996 (8 yrs.)	—	—
Bill Clinton[b] 1992–1996 (4 yrs.)	—	—
Total	56	28

*Clearly stated presidential policy objective.
[a]High priority/high expectation issue.
[b]High priority/moderate expectation issue.
[c]Low-no priority/low-no expectation issue.

Similarly, but in contrast, President Reagan firmly and actively opposed affirmative action—more so than any other president under review. For example, his actions through William Bradford Reynolds to overturn the *Weber* decision, as well as his stated desire to appoint judges who shared his same disdain for affirmative action (including quotas and set-asides, etc.), all indicate a strong high priority/high expectation profile for President Reagan (see Chapter 5). To date, Reagan's appointees have penned ten significant affirmative action opinions and four of these have supported affirmative action programs/policies while six have opposed such programs/polices (see Table 7.3). Though not as strong as Reagan's position, thus far the performance of Reagan's judges has mirrored his policy expectations. Specifically, Reagan's judges' performance mark the *only* instance to date for any president under review that the proportion of antiaffirmative action opinions is *greater* in number than those in support.[4]

Finally, and to date, there are no significant affirmative action cases reported in the SDCC data for either President Bush or President Clinton. As explained earlier, this is primarily due to the recentness of their administrations plus the lag period between appointment to the bench and the opportunity for a president's appointees to decide a representative number of significant cases.

School Desegregation. Although reluctant to press for broad substantive school desegregation measures, President Kennedy's federalizing of the Mississippi National Guard during the Meredith crisis carried both a substantive and symbolic message of support for this issue (see Chapter 4). And, as evidenced in Table 7.4, this message was heard by Kennedy's district court appointees. Given the forty-eight significant school desegregation opinions written by Kennedy appointees, the SDCC data reveal that nearly 65 percent supported school desegregation, a ratio of 31–17.

Table 7.4
A Comparison of Significant School Desegregation Opinions for the Appointees of Presidents Kennedy through Clinton, 1960–1996

Appointing President	Restrict	Enhance
John Kennedy[b] 1961–1996 (35 yrs.)	35.4% (17)	64.5% (31)
Lyndon Johnson[a] 1963–1996 (33 yrs.)	37.5% (21)	62.5%* (35)
Richard Nixon[a] 1968–1996 (28 yrs.)	37.5%* (6)	62.5% (10)
Gerald Ford[a] 1972–1996 (24 yrs.)	100% (1)	—
James Carter[b] 1976–1996 (20 yrs.)	16.6% (1)	83.3% (5)
Ronald Reagan[a] 1980–1996 (16 yrs.)	100%* (2)	—
George Bush[b] 1988–1996 (8 yrs.)	—	—
Bill Clinton[c] 1992–1996 (4 yrs.)	—	—
Total	48	81

*Clearly stated presidential policy objective.
[a]High priority/high expectation issue.
[b]Moderate priority/moderate expectation issue.
[c]Moderate priority/moderate-low expectation issue.

It was not until the 1964 Civil Rights Act that Congress, through the persistent efforts of President Johnson and civil rights leaders, fully endorsed school desegregation. And this endorsement has thus far been shared and promoted by a majority of Johnson's district court appointees. Johnson's district court appointees addressed the issue of school desegregation in fifty-six significant opinions (see Table 7.4) and about 63 percent of these, or a ratio of 35–21, enhanced school desegregation efforts. Consequently, again President Johnson has thus far achieved measured success in promoting his high priority expectation issues.

For the Nixon administration, school desegregation was also an especially high priority/high expectation issue. An essential element of Nixon's Southern strategy was to "impede desegregation efforts." These efforts, discussed at length in Chapter 3, included pursuing antibusing legislation, redirecting the enforcement efforts of the Department of Justice and HEW; and "making judicial appointments calculated to reduce what he perceived to be excessive intrusions by federal courts into state and local matters." But, the SDCC data reveal that Nixon's judges' significant district court school desegregation opinions have not supported this position.

Specifically, Nixon's appointees have penned sixteen significant school desegregation decisions and the majority, 62.5 percent, of these opinions favored school desegregation policies at a 10–6 ratio (Table 7.4). Thus, despite Nixon's expressed and direct attempts to appoint judges who shared his opposition to forced school desegregation, the majority of significant district court opinions rendered by his appointees to date have not supported that view.

It is also interesting to note from Table 7.4 that, despite President Nixon's ardent attack on school desegregation, the proportions of his judges rendering significant antidesegregation opinions are almost identical to those of both Kennedy and Johnson appointees: 37.5 percent, 35.4 percent, and 37.5 percent, respectively.

Similar to President Nixon before him, President Ford also actively sought to retard school desegregation. This was reflected especially through Ford's adamant opposition to busing. However, proportional to his overall comparative dearth of district court appointees, only once to date has a Ford appointee rendered a significant opinion on this issue (see Table 7.4). Nonetheless, this one opinion represents the only instance where the antidesegregation opinion(s) of a particular administration's judges' outnumber the pro-desegregation opinion(s), albeit a single case.

School desegregation was not an administrative priority for the Carter presidency (see Chapter 4). President Carter, as one political scientist put it, "sent Congress neither positive nor negative proposals; he said nothing about the issue."[5] This lack of presidential guidance and policy direction, however, is *not* reflected in the SDCC data analysis for Carter. On the contrary, the SDCC data indicate that Carter's appointees have rendered six significant school desegregation decisions to date and, as indicated in Table 7.4, five of these, (83 percent) favored increased efforts to desegregate public schools. In sum, despite his moderate priority/moderate expectation profile stance, Carter's judges have thus far reflected a strong pro-desegregation performance record.

Ronald Reagan's opposition to both school desegregation and busing have been well chronicled (see Chapter 4). However, the frequency of significant school desegregation opinions diminished rather drastically by the middle to late 1980s (see Appendix B, Table B.2).[6] Accordingly, the SDCC data reveal that only two significant school desegregation opinions were rendered by Reagan appointees to date. Nonetheless, observe in Table 7.4 that both these opinions opposed/restricted school desegregation efforts. And, as with affirmative action, Reagan's judges' performance patterns mark the only instances where the proportion of anti-school desegregation opinions out number those in support (again, albeit only two opinions).

To date, there are no significant school desegregation cases reported in the SDCC data for either President Bush or President Clinton.

Voting Rights. As detailed in Chapter 4, Kennedy was reluctant to speak out against the intimidation of African-American voters; his administration's commitment to protecting voting rights was marginal at best. Moreover, Kennedy knowingly appointed district court judges whose anti-civil rights views were well known to both his administration and the Justice Department (see Chapter 4).

The SDCC data reveal that Kennedy's lackluster support for civil rights has been endorsed in the majority of significant voting rights opinions penned by Kennedy's district court appointees. Rather than promoting increased voting rights, a ratio of 32–26, or 55 percent, of Kennedy's appointees have decided against voting rights guarantees (Table 7.5).

In contrast to Kennedy, voting rights were of special concern for the Johnson administration, who "inextricably linked the power of the federal government with the goals of [Martin Luther] King and others to civil rights" (see Chapter 4). And once again, the president's strong views have been reflected in the judicial performance of his district court appointees. As indicated in Table 7.5, judges appointed by Johnson have rendered seventy-four significant voting rights opinions. These seventy-four opinions, as discussed earlier in this chapter, account for the highest proportion, 33.6 percent, of all Johnson's judges' significant opinions across the five policy areas (See Figure 7.1).

More importantly, well over half (nearly 64 percent) of these opinions enhanced voting rights. Thus, overall Johnson's appointees have promoted, rather than restricted, voting rights issues at a ratio of 47–27 (see Table 7.5).

Nixon's expectation profile provides data consistent with the generally accepted view that under the Nixon administration, voting rights guarantees were only casually enforced (Chapter 4). Nixon's Southern strategy included reducing federal pressure on that region and removing key features of the voting rights acts. But this was not a primary policy objective of the administration. Hence, again the issue receives a moderate priority/moderate expectation rating. To date, Nixon's appointees have rendered forty-eight significant voting rights opinions. As indicated in Table 7.5, a simple majority of these, 58.3 percent, have, however, *enhanced* voting rights guarantees. Again, the SDCC data are incongruous with Nixon's policy expectations.

Notwithstanding Ford's 1975 signing of the extension of the Voting Rights Act, voting rights were also of only moderate-priority/moderate expectation concern to him. As one scholar summarized, Ford "did not make vigorous enforcement of the Act one of his highest priorities." Therefore, his expectations were tenuous at best. Ford's appointees have penned seven significant voting rights opinions and, as summarized in Table 7.5, these cases restricted the guarantees of voting rights at a 4–3 ratio.

Table 7.5
A Comparison of Significant Voting Rights Opinions for the Appointees of Presidents Kennedy through Clinton, 1960–1996

Appointing President	Extend	Restrict
John Kennedy[b] 1961–1996 (35 yrs.)	44.8% (26)	55.1% (32)
Lyndon Johnson[a] 1963–1996 (33 yrs.)	63.5%* (47)	36.4% (27)
Richard Nixon[b] 1968–1996 (28 yrs.)	58.3% (28)	41.6% (20)
Gerald Ford[b] 1972–1996 (24 yrs.)	42.8% (3)	57.1% (4)
James Carter[c] 1976–1996 (20 yrs.)	79.1% (19)	20.8% (5)
Ronald Reagan[a] 1980–1996 (16 yrs.)	38.8% (7)	61.1%* (11)
George Bush[b] 1988–1996 (8 yrs.)	50% (1)	50% (1)
Bill Clinton[d] 1992–1996 (4 yrs.)	100% (1)	—
Total	132	100

*Clearly stated presidential policy objective.
[a]High priority/high expectation issue.
[b]Moderate priority/moderate expectation issue.
[c]Low-no priority/low-no expectation issue.
[d]Moderate priority/moderate-low expectation issue.

Similar to his reluctance to confront questions of religious liberty, Carter also often avoided addressing voting rights concerns directly. This was especially the case with regard to the selection and nomination of district court judges. Nonetheless, Carter appointees have rendered twenty-four significant voting rights opinions to date and about 79 percent of these extended guarantees of voting rights. These opinions (see Table 7.5) are generally in line with the perceived liberal and/or Democratic party stance at a ratio of 19–5.[7]

The SDCC data reveal that President Reagan's judges' positions on voting rights have thus far been consistent with his overall assault on civil rights. Reagan's appointees may be credited with eighteen significant voting rights opinions and, as indicated in Table 7.5, these significant opinions restrict guarantees of voting rights at a ratio of 11–7. Though yet another close ratio, still the balance to date swings in Reagan's favor.

President Bush's appointees have to date rendered only two significant voting rights opinions, one supporting and one restricting voting rights guarantees. President Clinton's appointees are thus far credited with only one significant opinion supporting voting rights guarantees (see Table 7.5). These preliminary findings for President Reagan are highly suggestive, given the reality that his conservative court-packing campaign did not really get under way until mid-1985.[8] Thus, the pattern of relationships between these recent presidents and their respective judges' performance is yet in its infant stages. President Reagan, during his eight-year tenure, appointed about half of the lower bench, and President Clinton stands to do the same. Thus, these presidents' appointees have the potential to influence significant policy outcomes well into the twenty-first century.

Chapter Summary

The basic task of this chapter has been to demonstrate the proportional frequency in which judges have rendered significant district court opinions supporting or opposing their appointing president's legal policy positions. The most obvious finding is that in all but two instances, when presidents have expressed an overt policy objective (i.e., high priority/high expectation), they have achieved strong measures of proportional success. The documented exceptions to this general finding include Nixon's lack of success regarding issues of abortion and school desegregation.[9] The SDCC analysis also suggests that lower federal court judges are not totally constrained by strict higher court guidelines and have been free to vote their own policy proclivities.

The next chapter, Chapter 8, examines whether and to what extent African-American and Latino judges might differ from their white male cohorts utilizing these judges' responses to issues raised in the National District Court Judge Survey (NDJS).

NOTES

1. Chief Justice Charles Evan Hughes, Speech at Elmira, New York (May 3, 1907), as quoted by Robert Bork in *The Tempting of America: The Political Seduction of the Law* (New York: The Free Press, 1990), p. 176.

2. For a more detailed discussion of the "significant case" approach, as well as an overview of the frequencies and nature of the cases selected, see Appendix B in this volume.

3. For example, other recent exploratory studies on the voting behavior of President Clinton's judicial appointees reveal that "even near the end of Clinton's four-year term, the number of his appointees' published decisions is rather modest." See Ronald Stidham, Robert A. Carp and Donald Songer, "The Voting Behavior of President Clinton's Judicial Appointees," *Judicature* 80 (1996), p. 16.

4. Also, as evidenced in Table 7.3, the two highest proportions in support of affirma-

tive action are those of presidents Johnson and Carter, both of whom were initially found to merit a high priority/high expectation rating in support of the affirmative action issue.

5. Gary Orfield, *Must We Bus? Segregated Schools and National Policy* (Washington, DC: The Brookings Institution, 1978), p. 278.

6. Essentially, in addition to an increase in the number of civil rights cases now being heard at the state court level, the overall decrease in the number of school desegregation cases may also be attributed to the fact that many of these cases were initiated soon after the *Brown* decision and have, for the most part, already run the gamut of the district courts.

7. For example, the 1980 Democratic party platform did address the need to decrease the limits on campaign contributions from political action committees and to provide public financing of congressional campaigns. And, with respect to participation in the electoral process, the 1980 platform encouraged "voter participation in elections through the use of simplified procedures of registration in states that lack mail or election day registration procedures, and by resisting efforts to reduce access to bilingual ballots." See Donald Johnson, *National Party Platforms of 1980* (Urbana: University of Illinois Press, 1982), p. 67.

8. Herman Schwartz, *Packing the Courts: The Conservative Campaign to Rewrite the Constitution* (New York: Charles Scribner's Sons, 1988), p. 153.

9. Nixon's lack of success was not unexpected however. As detailed more fully in Chapter 4—and in previous analyses as well—Nixon's inability to "affect the overall philosophy of the federal bench was ultimately frustrated by the political concessions the Administration was forced to make." See David M. O'Brien, *Judicial Roulette: Report of the Twentieth Century Fund Task Force on Judicial Selection* (New York: Priority Press, 1988), p. 57. After all, during Nixon's second term the Democratic party controlled both houses of Congress, and this factor, combined with the fallout from the Watergate scandal, forced Nixon to increasingly partisan considerations in his appointments. This led him, for example, to become more acquiescent to the nominees of individual senators.

8   Does Race Make a Difference?: Perceptions and Attitudes of African-American, Latino, and White District Court Judges

For most . . . in America, regardless of status, political persuasion, or accomplishments, the moment never arrives when race can be treated as a total irrelevancy.[1]

INTRODUCTION

The previous chapters have examined the institutional role and function of the federal district courts in the political process. These analyses have also explored the contextual dynamics of the selection and confirmation processes. This chapter argues that these judges might also be viewed as "gatekeepers" of different colors. Indeed, data generated in the National District Court Judge Survey (NDJS) offer strong support that there are significant differences in how African-American, white, and Latino[2] judges view their individual and institutional role and functions in the policy process. In other words, who sits on these courts may in large measure determine what groups and interests are represented.

The NDJS is an especially useful tool in assessing differences between judges from different racial backgrounds and supplements the limited data generated in the SDCC analysis. That is, because of the relatively few significant cases written by African-American or Latino judges, in part due to the recentness of many of their appointments (especially prior to President Clinton; see Figure 8.1), the significant case methodology used in the previous chapter yields sparse results (See Appendix B, Part II). For example, between 1960 and 1996, African-American judges wrote only 2.2 percent (twenty) of the total (699) significant opinions rendered across the five policy areas. Latino judges rendered only four of these 699 significant opinions.[3]

Clearly, given the limited data base, one must be careful not to extrapolate the findings on twenty significant opinions to the overall population of African-American judges. Nonetheless, several tentative conclusions may be drawn from this point of analysis. On balance, both the fact that few African-American and Latino judges have been appointed and the small number of their significant opinions have ramifications throughout the judicial policymaking arena. This is especially the case in light of those studies suggesting that African-Americans and Latinos may view and assess political and legal issues quite differently than whites.[4] However, because judges operate in the political process—not as a matter of choice, but of function—the significant case approach is not an especially informative tool given the limited opportunities of the these judges to write significant cases. In other words, the data are limited enough to preclude much meaningful analysis (see Appendix B, Part II). What is clear, however, is that the NDJS data indicate convincingly that racial differences do seem to exist along a number of dimensions, and appear especially stark between African-American judges and their white counterparts.

Figure 8.1

Percentage of African-American, Latino, and White District Court Judges Appointed by President

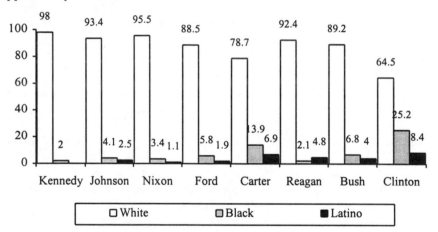

Therefore, to better observe and analyze the policy positions of African-American and Latino judges relative to white judges, next I go directly to NDJS data. To do so, a comparative description and assessment of how African-American, Latino, and white federal district court judges view various aspects of their role and function as policy actors in the American political system generally is provided. Specific attention is also given to how these judges assess the selection and appointment process. Overall, these findings provide a descriptive picture of African-American and Latino district court judges' expectations and evaluations of their the key policymaking role and function of district court judges compared to their white counterparts.

The balance of this chapter addresses these differences. Specifically, it offers a comparative assessment of how African-American, Latino, and white judges respond to various NDJS questions concerning the nature, role, and functioning of the federal district courts. In order to put this assessment in broader perspective, however, let us first take a brief look at what previous research tells us in this regard.

African-American Judges

Honorable [African-American] judges must forget the status aristocracy of the robe and remember the aristocracy of the Constitution. That precious paper which stands between him and a slave society.[5]

Increasingly, attention is being given to whether judges from different racial and ethnic backgrounds might view and perform their roles and functions differently. For example, earlier basic research suggests that African-Americans may not only participate in a strikingly different manner than do whites, but that African-Americans also view and assess political and legal issues quite differently than whites.[6] Thus, it is appropriate to assess the extent to which race may affect these judges' attitudes and values. Nonetheless, extant research focusing on African-American judges has generally been done in limited context and focused on decisional outcomes.[7] The assumption frequently made is that African-American judges might not only represent interests that differ from their white cohorts, but share varied perceptions of their roles in the political process.

Largely based on this theoretical premise, scholars have also attempted to assess the role and representational interests of African-American judges.[8] Similar in theoretical perspectives, these studies have primarily focused on the suggestion that African-American judges identify themselves as more liberal than conservative,[9] thus indicating a general tendency of African-Americans to take more liberal policy positions than whites.[10]

For example, one study reports that some 40 percent of all African-American judges consider providing substantive representation an important function of their service on the bench[11] and that approximately one-third of all African-American judges believe that providing symbolic representation (pride, inspiration, and status) is also an important function of their service on the bench.[12] For some, these studies suggest that African-American judges may better promote the interests of African-Americans, thus reducing the incidence of racism in the American legal system.[13]

The majority of these studies have focused broadly on the background and performance of African-American judges in limited context[14] and have given little to no attention to systematically or empirically examining these judges' attitudes with regard to specific issues of public policy, the courts themselves as policymaking institutions, the recruitment process, and so on.[15]

In fact, little attention has been given to the policy interests represented by African-American judges and whether or not their behavior comports with presidential policy objectives and expectations. Furthermore, those that have addressed judicial behavior have done so in specific contexts, for example, in the severity of criminal sentencing.[16]

On balance, these studies on the role and representational interests of African-American judges suggest that race is significant. They suggest that African-American judges are distinguishable from their white male cohorts in terms of interest representation. These studies, however, do not attempt to empirically and systematically analyze the attitudes and values of these judges in terms of the "presidential expectation" thesis used here. Thus, here I discuss African-American judges as part of my study of presidential policy objectives and expectations and judicial performance to determine what, if any, observable differences might be found between their attitudes and values and those of their white counterparts.

Latino Judges

Similarly, I also examine the differences between Latino judges and their white and African-American counterparts. Indeed, parallels are often drawn between the quests for political inclusion and socioeconomic mobility of African-Americans and Latinos generally.[17] However, unlike the current, though limited, scholarly treatment of African-American judges, the field remains generally bereft of any treatment of Latino district judge behavior.[18] In fact, Latinos—U.S. residents of Mexican American, Puerto Rican, Cuban, or a variety of other "Hispanic" backgrounds—have not received much attention in political science or law-related research generally.[19] Moreover, studies of Latino politics and behavior must account for differences in group identity, perceptions of discrimination, political participation, political ideology and orientation, and so on, between various Latino groups.[20]

Nonetheless, taken as a whole, most of these studies suggest that Latinos are somewhat "different" as well as "disadvantaged" both politically, socially, and economically relative to the dominant (white) groups as well as to other minority groups (e.g., African-Americans).[21] As such, given the lack of scholarly research to date, Latino judges are examined below as part of the study of presidential policy objectives and expectations and judicial performance to determine also what, if any, observable differences might be found between them and their white or African-American counterparts.

On balance, a discussion of the above matters yields theoretical as well as practical implications regarding the role of federal district court judges as policymakers in the American political system generally, as well as insights on the impact of race and political leadership in the United States. Next, I examine the extent to which African-American and Latino judges have promoted the policies of their appointing presidents.

RACE AND THE NATIONAL DISTRICT COURT JUDGE SURVEY

To address the theoretical and practical assessments outlined above, in the following section data generated from the NDJS is utilized. Again, this survey questionnaire was designed to measure these judges' perceptions and to gauge their attitudes regarding a variety of issues, including the following: their general role in making pubic policy, their perceptions and insights on various civil rights and civil liberties issues, how these judges view their colleagues, their views regarding adherence to legal precedents, and the judges' institutional relationships with the executive and legislative branches.

As indicated in Table 8.1, the racial composition of the respondents in the NDJS is nearly identical to their representation in the total judgeship population—within one percentage point. Clearly, both African-Americans and Latinos continue to be grossly underrepresented on the district courts despite their representation and increased voting strength nationally.

Table 8.1
Racial Representation in the NDJS

RACE	Population[1]	NDJS Respondents
White judges[2]	753 (93.07%)	452 (92.62%)
African-American judges	30 (3.70%)	17 (3.48%)
Latino judges	26 (3.21%)	19 (3.89%)
Total	809 (100%)	488 (100%)

1. Again, although there are only 649 authorized district courts judgeships, because senior judges were also included in the NDJS, the total number of judges surveyed was 809.
2. White judges include all non-African-American and non-Latino judges.

To further assess the extent to which African-American and Latino judges compare with their white counterparts, the NDJS data are organized under four general categories: (I) perceptions of district court judges as policymakers; (II) district court judges and judicial selection; (III) district court judges' perceptions of the court as an institution; and (IV) district court judges' perceptions on miscellaneous issues.[22]

Race and Perceptions of District Court Judges as Policymakers

The extent to which African-American and Latino judges view themselves as part of the policymaking process can tell us a great deal about their role in and impact on that process.

For example, the extent to which these judges feel obligated to promote the policy positions of their appointing presidents could constrain as well as enhance their overall political leadership roles. Consider, for example, when asked if the "decisional patterns of district court judges reflect the political values of their appointing president," almost 28 percent of white judges and 21 percent of Latino judges agreed, compared to nearly 53 percent of African-American judges (see Table 8.2, Q12). Clearly, the NDJS data reveal that African-

American judges feel that district court judges in general are more likely to reflect the political and legal values of their appointing president than either white or Latino judges.[23]

Or consider, for example, the theoretical and practical implications of Chief Justice Charles Evan Hughes' comment, "the Constitution is what the judges say it is,"[24] with respect to the NDJS respondents' perceptions. When this statement was put to them directly, nearly 71 percent of African-American judges agreed compared to only 47 percent for both white and Latino judges (Table 8.2, Q17). These results suggest at a minimum that the African-American respondents, more so than their white or Latino cohorts, take a very realistic behavioral perspective of the crucial role of individual judges in constitutional interpretation.

When asked whether "district court judges *should* make policy," similarly large majorities from each group disagreed: whites, 75 percent; African-Americans, 64 percent; and Latinos, 67 percent, respectively (Table 8.2, Q19). However, nearly a fourth (23.53 percent) of the African-American judges "agreed" that they "should make policy" compared to only 15 percent for both whites and Latinos. African-American judges also had the highest percentage of "no opinion" responses (11.76 percent), indicating some measure of support. Notice also that just over 17 percent of white judges and 10 percent of Latino judges responded "strongly disagree" compared to a 0 percent response from African-American judges. This 17 percent is significant as it represents about 136 individual white judges—nearly three times the total number of all African-American judges. Overall, these responses reflect more of an inclination for African-Americans, than for Latinos and whites, to make policy at the district court level.

When asked, "Do you feel your personal attitudes and values affect your discretionary judgments on the Court?" (Table 8.2, Q27), about 47 percent for each group admitted to "sometimes." However, as shown in Figure 8.2, just over 41 percent of the African-American judges responded "often," compared to only about 4.87 percent of white judges and about 16 percent of Latino judges, respectively. Clearly, African-American judges are far more willing to admit that their personal attitudes and values affect their discretionary judgments than are others. In fact, just over 35 percent of whites and 31 percent of Latino judges say these factors "seldom" affect their decisions on the court.

Moreover, when similarly asked, "To what extent do you feel *other* district court judges allow their personal attitudes and values to affect their discretionary judgments on the court?" (Table 8.2, Q28), nearly an equally small percentage of white judges responded "often" (7.74 percent) compared to again a much higher percentage for African-American judges (41.18 percent). Thus, the responses to both questions, Q27 and Q28, reveal that more African-American judges than Latino or white judges admit both that they sometimes allow their personal attitudes and values to affect their discretionary policymaking and, similarly, believe *other* judges do also. On the other hand, only 4.87 percent of

Table 8.2
Race and the Perceptions of District Court Judges as Policymakers

	% Strongly Agree	% Agree	% No Opinion	% Disagree	% Strongly Disagree
Q12. To a large extent, the decisional patterns of district court judges reflect the political values of their appointing president.					
White	0.88	26.77	9.51	56.42	6.19
African-American	5.88	47.06	11.76	35.29	—
Latino	—	21.05	10.53	57.89	10.53
Q13. Even if a district court judge strongly believes a particular Supreme Court decision is "wrong," the district court judge is nonetheless bound to follow such a ruling.					
White	50.88	46.46	0.22	1.55	—
African-American	17.65	70.59	—	11.76	—
Latino	26.32	73.68	—	—	—
Q17. The Constitution is what judges say it is.					
White	5.09	42.48	4.42	36.06	9.73
African-American	—	70.59	11.76	17.65	—
Latino	21.05	26.32	10.53	31.58	5.26
Q19. District court judges *should* make policy.					
White	0.44	15.49	7.74	57.96	17.26
African-American	—	23.53	11.76	64.71	—
Latino	—	15.79	10.53	57.89	10.53

	Often	Sometimes	Seldom	Never
Q27. Do you feel your personal attitudes and values affect your discretionary judgments on the court?				
White	4.87	51.33	35.62	6.19
African-American	41.18	47.06	11.76	—
Latino	15.79	47.37	31.58	5.26
Q28. To what extent do you feel other district court judges allow their personal attitudes and values to affect their discretionary judgments on the court?				
White	7.74	63.94	24.56	0.66
African-American	41.18	52.94	—	—
Latino	15.79	78.95	5.26	—

Percentages may not total 100 because "missing responses" are omitted.

whites responded "often" for themselves and just a slightly higher percentage, 7.74 percent believe others "often" do. Note, however, that although 47 percent of Latino judges admitted that they sometimes allowed their personal attitudes to affect their discretionary judgments (Q27), nearly 80 percent of Latino respondents feel that *others* do. Thus, Latino judges to a greater extent project value-laden discretionary judgments on "others," but not themselves.

Figure 8.2

Personal Attitudes and Values Affect My Discretionary Judgment

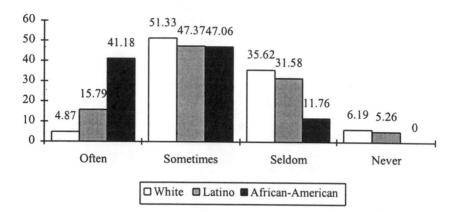

Consistent with the above evidence that African-American judges may view their task differently than do white and Latino judges, African-American judges are also marginally more willing to buck the system than white and Latino judges. Consider that when asked, "Even if a district court judge strongly believes a particular Supreme Court decision is wrong, the district court judge is nonetheless bound to follow such a ruling" (Table 8.2, Q13), a smaller percentage of African-American judges (17 percent) and Latino judges (26 percent) "strongly agreed" than white judges (50 percent). Nonetheless, if I collapse the "strongly agree" and "agree" responses, nearly 100 percent of whites and Latino judges, and 88 percent of African-American judges agreed. Significantly, however, almost 12 percent of African-American judges disagreed as compared to only about 1.5 percent of white and 0 percent of Latino judges, respectively.

Race and Judicial Selection

Because the selection, nomination, and confirmation processes are directly related to the context as well as the content of judicial policymaking it is appropriate to look at any differences along racial lines of judges' perceptions about the processes of judicial selection. The NDJS data are divided into three sections: (1) general, (2) the executive branch, and (3) the Senate.

Judicial Selection: General

When asked whether a "district court nominee's ideology is given more consideration than his/her merit qualifications" (Table 8.3, Q4), about 50 percent of the white judges, compared to about 70 percent of African-American and 73 percent of Latino judges, agreed. However, only about 6 percent of African-American judges and about 15 percent of Latino disagreed compared to about 35 percent of white judges. Thus, a much higher percentage of white judges disagree that ideology is given "more" consideration. This higher percentage of "disagreement" with the statement suggests a higher level of support for the meritocracy argument for the appointment process for whites than for either African-American or Latinos.

Table 8.3
Race and District Court Judicial Selection

	% Strongly Agree	% Agree	% No Opinion	% Disagree	% Strongly Disagree
Judicial Selection: General					
Q4. All too often, a district court nominee's ideology is given more consideration than his/her merit qualifications.					
White	7.52	41.59	11.06	35.18	3.54
African-American	11.76	58.82	23.53	5.88	—
Latino	10.53	63.16	10.53	10.53	5.26
Q5. District court judges' confirmations are way too "political."					
White	3.54	28.10	8.19	55.31	4.42
African-American	—	47.06	17.65	23.53	5.88
Latino	—	47.37	15.79	31.58	—
Q7. Partisan politics dominate and control district court appointments.					
White	8.63	55.31	6.64	26.99	1.11
African-American	11.76	76.47	—	5.88	—
Latino	15.79	63.16	5.26	10.53	5.26
Q8. Special interests are "too involved" in the selection and evaluation of district court nominees.					
White	3.32	19.69	17.26	50.88	8.19
African-American	—	41.18	17.65	41.18	—
Latino	10.53	31.58	21.05	36.84	—

Table 8.3 (continued)

	% Strongly Agree	% Agree	% No Opinion	% Disagree	% Strongly Disagree
Q11. A district court nominee's rating by the American Bar Association Standing Committee on Federal Judiciary is a fair and generally accurate measure of his/her qualifications.					
White	7.74	65.93	6.42	13.94	5.75
African-American	—	47.06	5.88	41.18	5.88
Latino	10.53	52.63	10.53	26.32	—
Q34. State and/or local government official[s] played an influential role in my Senate confirmation to the district court.					
White	4.65	21.24	12.83	36.06	23.89
African-American	17.65	29.41	17.65	23.53	11.76
Latino	10.53	5.26	15.79	42.11	26.32

Judicial Selection: The Executive Branch

	% Strongly Agree	% Agree	% No Opinion	% Disagree	% Strongly Disagree
Q1. The president exercises too much control over district court appointments.					
White	3.10	8.85	7.08	58.19	22.35
African-American	5.88	11.76	17.65	47.06	17.65
Latino	—	10.53	15.79	47.37	26.32
Q6. The Justice Department now plays too active a role in the selection and evaluation of district court nominees.					
White	14.82	32.30	15.04	33.41	4.42
African-American	29.41	41.18	5.88	23.53	—
Latino	15.79	47.37	10.53	26.32	—
Q21. In general, modern presidents have usually attempted to appoint district court judges who share their basic political values.					
White	9.29	79.42	5.97	4.65	—
African-American	17.65	76.47	5.88	—	—
Latino	5.26	78.95	15.79	—	—

Table 8.3 (continued)

	% Strongly Agree	% Agree	% No Opinion	% Disagree	% Strongly Disagree
Judicial Selection: The Senate					
Q2. The Senate *should* "rubber stamp" presidential nominees to the federal district courts.					
White	0.44	4.65	1.55	67.70	25.22
African-American	—	—	5.88	52.94	41.18
Latino	—	5.26	5.26	52.63	36.84
Q3. In practice, the Senate *does* "rubber stamp" presidential nominees to the federal district courts.					
White	0.66	25.22	5.53	59.96	7.08
African-American	17.65	41.18	11.76	29.41	—
Latino	5.26	36.84	10.53	36.84	10.53

Percentages may not total 100 because "no response" answers are omitted.

Along this same line, about 47 percent of both African-American and Latino judges responded that "district court judges' confirmations are way too political," compared to only about 32 percent for white judges (Table 8.3, Q5). Even more, on this same question, just about 59 percent of white judges disagreed that confirmations are too "political" as opposed to only about 29 percent for both African-American and Latino judges. Overall, these results suggest that both African-American and Latino judges view the confirmation process as more "politically" driven than white judges.

Pushing the issue further, the NDJS also asks the judges whether they believe that "partisan politics dominate and control district court appointments." In response, an overwhelming number (about 88 percent) of African-American judges and about 79 percent of Latino judges agreed with this statement as compared to about 64 percent for white judges (Table 8.3, Q7). Similarly, the 29 percent of white judges disagreeing is far greater than those nearly 6 percent of African-American judges and 15 percent of Latino judges disagreeing, respectively. Again, these data support a more "politicized" view of the appointment process by African-American and Latino judges than by white judges.

With regard to the role of special interests, about equal numbers of African-American and Latino judges (around 41.5 percent) split evenly when asked whether "Special interests are '*too involved*' in the selection and evaluation of district court nominees." That is, about 40 percent of each minority group agreed and about 37 percent disagreed (Table 8.3, Q8). However, only about 23 percent of white judges agreed while 59 percent of white judges disagreed. And 8.19 percent of white judges "strongly" disagreed—compared to a zero "strongly" disagree response for both African-American judges and Latino judges. Clearly, again these data suggest that white judges view the appointment process as less politicized than African-American or Latinos.

Another aspect of the confirmation process that has engendered significant scholarly attention as well as controversy in recent times is the role and influence of the ABA through its Standing Committee on Federal Judiciary. The NDJS data reveal that the controversy over the ABA committee exists along racial lines also. When asked, for example, whether a "district court nominee's rating by the American Bar Association Standing Committee on Federal Judiciary is a fair and generally accurate measure of his/her qualifications," about half, 47 percent, of African-American judges agreed as compared to much higher percentages of agreement among Latinos and whites (about 63 percent for Latino judges and almost 74 percent for white judges, Table 8.3, Q11). However, what is even more telling is that a similarly high percentage of African-American judges disagreed (about 47 percent) compared to only about 20 percent for white judges and 26 percent for Latino judges. Thus, the NDJS data suggest that African-American judges are considerably more distrusting of the ABA's ratings than are Latino and white judges.

When asked whether "state and/or local government official[s] played an influential role in my Senate confirmation to the district court," nearly half, about 47 percent, of African-American judges responded affirmatively compared to only about a quarter (26 percent) for white judges and about 16 percent for Latino judges (Table 8.3, Q34). Once again, the African-American respondents portray a more politicized view of the appointment process, as well as their political experiences in it. Of course, the lower responses by whites and Latino judges do not confirm the absence of state and local officials' influence in their appointments; they may merely indicate that whites and Latino judges are less willing to admit that these officials influenced their confirmations, if in fact they did. The higher percentage (60 percent) of whites responding that state and/or local government official[s] did not play an influential role in their confirmations is also consistent with the results discussed above (Table 8.3, Q5), indicating that just over 60 percent of white judges disagreed that confirmations are "too political" opposed to only about 30 percent for both African-American and Latino judges.

Judicial Selection: The Executive Branch

Differences between African-American, Latino, and white judges regarding the executive branch and judicial selection present a mixed picture. With regard to attitudes regarding the control of the appointment process by the president, most judges, regardless of race, feel that presidential control is not excessive. Responding to whether the "president exercises too much control over district court appointments," for example, about 12 percent of white judges, about 18 percent of African-American judges, and about 10.5 percent of Latinos agreed (Table 8.3, Q1). The NDJS data, however, reveal a bit more support for the executive in the appointment process by white judges than by African-American or Latino judges.

A clearer picture emerges when examining these judges' views on the role of the Justice Department in the selection process. A significant majority of African-American judges (about 70 percent) and Latino judges (about 63 percent) agreed that "the Justice Department now plays *too active* a role in the selection and evaluation of district court nominees." (See Table 8.3, Q6). This compares with a less than half (about 47 percent) of white judges who similarly agreed.

On balance, issues of executive influence in judicial selection, and how these judges perceive that influence, might be put into sharper perspective by the judges' responses to the question of whether "in general, modern presidents have usually attempted to appoint district court judges who share their basic political values." Overwhelmingly, about 89 percent of white judges, about 94 percent of African-American judges, and 84 percent of Latino judges all responded affirmatively to that statement (Table 8.3, Q21).

Judicial Selection: The Senate

Differences among African-American, Latino, and white judges' perceptions of the role of Senate in the selection process are intriguing. When these judges were asked if the Senate "*should* rubber stamp . . . nominees," significant majorities across all three racial groups disagreed: African-American judges, 94 percent; Latino judges, 89 percent; and white judges, 92 percent, respectively (Table 8.3, Q2). However, when asked whether in practice the Senate "*does* 'rubber stamp[s]' presidential nominations to the federal district courts," differences across racial groups is dramatic. The NDJS data reveal that a majority 59 percent of African-American judges agreed that the Senate *does* in fact rubber stamp nominations, compared to about 42 percent of Latino judges and only about 26 percent of white judges (Table 8.3, Q3). Put another way, looking at the negative (disagree) responses to this question reveals that African-American judges perceive the Senate's role in the confirmation process as much more proforma than do the vast majority of white judges, 29 percent to about 67 percent, respectively. And again, the difference between African-American and white judges is most dramatic—with Latino judges again falling between the two.

District Court Judges' Perceptions of the Court as an Institution

An assessment of the limits and capacity of federal district court judges as participants in the policymaking process also requires attention to not only these judges' perceptions of themselves as political actors but also of these judges' perceptions of the courts as political institutions.

When asked, for example, whether "overall the federal judiciary *is becoming* more 'conservative' than it was in the 1960s, 1970s, and early 1980s," an overwhelming majority, 94 percent of African-American judges, 84 percent of Latino judges, and 77 percent of white judges agreed (Table 8.4, Q18). But racial differences among the judges increased sharply when similarly asked if the

Table 8.4
District Court Judges' Perceptions of the Court as an Institution

	% Strongly Agree	% Agree	% No Opinion	% Disagree	% Strongly Disagree
Q18. Overall, the federal judiciary *is becoming* more "conservative" than it was in the 1960s, 1970s, and early 1980s.					
White	15.27	61.50	11.28	10.40	0.88
African-American	52.94	41.18	5.88	—	—
Latino	15.79	68.42	10.53	5.26	—
Q20. Overall, the federal judiciary *should* be more conservative than it was in the 1960s, 1970s, and early 1980s.					
White	6.86	28.32	25.00	31.42	7.52
African-American	—	5.88	5.88	47.06	41.18
Latino	5.26	15.79	26.32	31.58	21.05

Percentages may not total 100 because "no response" answers are omitted.

federal judiciary *should* be more conservative. An overwhelming majority, 88 percent, of African-American judges disagreed (41 percent of whom strongly disagreed). By contrast, a bare majority, 53 percent of Latino judges disagreed (21 percent of which strongly disagreed), while considerably less than half—about 39 percent of white judges—disagreed (of which only 7.52 percent strongly disagreed). See Table 8.4, Q20, and Figure 8.3.

Figure 8.3
"The Federal Judiciary *Should* Be More Conservative"

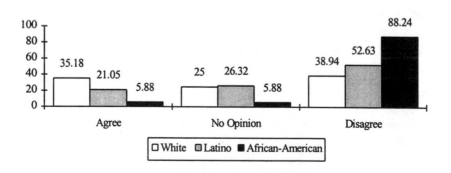

Clearly, African-American judges as a group are not deterred in their views by popular notions and empirical realities, suggesting that the federal judiciary is in fact "more conservative."[25] Indeed, this analysis suggests that African-American judges see a leadership role for the federal judiciary that is apparently quite different from their fellow judges, particularly white judges.

District Court Judges' Perceptions on Race, Class, and Related Issues

How district court judges exercise their policymaking role and function might also be conditioned by their individual and collective perceptions of particular salient issues that continue to generate sharp controversy and discussion in American politics and society.

For example, when the judges were asked to indicate the extent to which "Blacks have made considerable progress in securing civil rights," an over-whelming 90 percent of white judges agreed—of whom 11.06 percent strongly agreed (Table 8.5, Q22). Similarly, a strong majority of Latino judges, about 68 percent, also agreed. In stark contrast, however, less than half, 47 percent, of African-American judges agreed and there were no (0 percent) strongly agree responses. Even more dramatic is that over half of the African-American judges responding, 53 percent, did not agree that blacks had made considerable progress, while only about 21 percent of Latino judges and even fewer white judges (7 percent) think likewise (see Figure 8.4). At a minimum, these responses alone suggest that with respect to civil rights, African-American judges are far less willing to accept popular notions that the civil rights struggle is over—indeed, over half disagree that there has been considerable progress.

Table 8.5
District Court Judges' Perceptions on Race, Poverty, and Related Issues

	% Strongly Agree	% Agree	% No Opinion	% Disagree	% Strongly Disagree
Q22. Blacks have made considerable progress in securing civil rights.					
White	11.06	79.20	1.33	5.53	1.11
African-American	—	47.06	—	47.06	5.88
Latino	5.26	63.16	10.53	15.79	5.26
Q23. Black litigants are treated fairly in the justice system.					
White	11.73	71.46	4.42	9.07	0.88
African-American	—	17.65	5.88	52.94	17.65
Latino	10.53	52.63	10.53	15.79	5.26

Table 8.5 (continued)

	% Strongly Agree	% Agree	% No Opinion	% Disagree	% Strongly Disagree
Q24. Poor litigants are treated fairly in the courts.					
White	9.07	71.90	3.76	12.61	0.88
African-American	—	23.53	5.88	64.71	5.88
Latino	10.53	52.63	21.05	15.79	—
Q25. More women and minority judges would *improve* the overall quality of the district courts.					
White	6.19	30.31	26.11	29.65	5.53
African-American	64.71	35.29	—	—	—
Latino	21.05	36.84	26.32	15.79	—

Q35. Would you say that the government is pretty much run by a few big interests looking out for themselves or that it is run for the benefit of all the people?	A few big interests	All the people	Do not know/ not sure
White	17.92	46.02	26.99
African-American	47.06	—	47.06
Latino	5.26	42.11	36.84

Q26. How would you characterize your judicial beliefs?	Liberal	Moderate	Conserva- tive	Other
White	7.74	63.27	19.91	7.96
African-American	29.41	52.94	—	17.65
Latino	10.53	63.16	15.79	10.53

Percentages may not total 100 because "no response" answers are omitted.

These data lend some support to both the scholarly literature suggesting the courts are not the best forum for long lasting policy change[26] as well as studies challenging the tangible and lasting benefits to African-Americans as a result of the formal civil rights movement and the plethora of legal battles over the last few decades—including such noted cases as *Brown v. Board of Education*.[27]

Consider also that when asked whether "Black litigants are treated fairly in the justice system," it is evident once that again race matters. As indicated in Figure 8.5, the racial polarization is equally clear. For example, while over 83 percent of white judges and some 63 percent of Latino judges agreed that blacks are treated fairly in the justice system, only about 18 percent of African-American judges agreed (Table 8.5, Q23.) Put another way, a majority of African-American judges disagreed (71 percent), of which 18 percent disagreed strongly with the notion that black litigants are treated fairly. In stark contrast, only about 10 percent of white judges and about 21 percent of Latino judges likewise disagreed. Nonetheless, consider for example, that in response to Q23 ("Black litigants are treated fairly in the justice system,") Judge 662 (a white judge and Reagan appointee) wrote the unsolicited comment in the margin "I believe Black litigants generally are treated fairly in the federal courts. I have serious doubts about some state courts." Further, these results lend empirical support to existing hypotheses that African-American judges may better promote the interests of African-Americans, thus reducing the incidence of racism in the American legal system.[28]

Figure 8.4
"Blacks Have Made Considerable Progress in Securing Civil Rights"

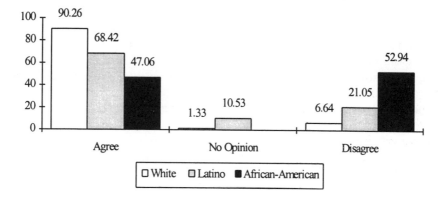

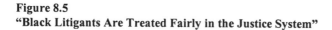

Figure 8.5
"Black Litigants Are Treated Fairly in the Justice System"

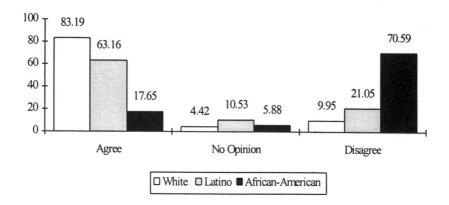

Evidence of racial polarization between African-American judges and white judges remains similarly strong for responses to race-neutral questions as well. When judges were asked whether "poor litigants are treated fairly in the courts," 81 percent of white judges agreed, including a 9 percent strongly agree response; a majority of Latino judges also agreed (about 63 percent). In sharp contrast, less than one-fourth of African-American judges agreed with this view (24 percent). In fact, about 71 percent of African-American judges responded that the poor *are not* treated fairly in court while only 13 percent of white judges think so. Conversely, 13 percent of white judges disagreed that the poor are treated fairly in court compared to just over 70 percent of African-American judges (Table 8.5, Q24). Notice too, that while Latinos are generally overrepresented in the lower socioeconomic class in the United States,[29] Latino judges once again tend to more closely mirror the white judges' attitudes, remaining somewhat in between the more polarized black/white responses (see Figure 8.6).

On this issue, the NDJS findings take on added significance in light of decades of commentary, theories, and empirical research that describe African-Americans and Latinos as disproportionately disadvantaged due to poverty.[30] More specifically, for decades commentators have noted that poor people suffer from discriminatory treatment in the criminal justice system. In his classic study of race relations in the 1940s, for example, Gunnar Myrdal documented many detrimental consequences for poor people drawn into the criminal court system. Myrdal observed that "[t]he American bond and bail system works automatically against the poor classes" and that when state prison systems need money, "the inclination is to fine Negroes and poor whites to reduce the burden of cost of the legal system."[31] In 1967, for example, while working for the President's Commission on Law Enforcement and Administration of Justice, Patricia Wald, later to become a United States Court of Appeals judge, wrote that "[t]he poor are arrested more often, convicted more frequently, sentenced more harshly, rehabilitated less successfully than the rest of society."[32] Still other theorists have posited that: "The lower class person is (1) more likely to be scrutinized and therefore to be observed in any violation of the law, (2) more likely to be arrested if discovered under suspicious circumstances, (3) more likely to spend time between arrest and trial in jail, (4) more likely to come to trial, (5) more likely to be found guilty, and (6) if found guilty more likely to receive harsh punishment."[33]

At bottom, the judges' responses to questions regarding the treatment of African-American litigants and the poor in the courts tell us that, in addition to the institutional limits and capacity of the courts to bring about fundamental policy change, African-American judges, more so than white and Latino judges, characterize the justice system as being unfairly biased against other African-Americans and the poor.

In this regard, many have argued that one way to combat institutional biases is to diversify the institutions' policymaking membership—often requiring affirmative action policies and practices. And clearly this was the order of the day for both the Carter and Clinton administrations (see Chapters 5 and 6) who made (and are making) unprecedented attempts to diversify the federal bench. Nonetheless, as indicated in Table 8.5 (Q25), when asked whether "more women and minority judges would *improve* the overall quality of the district courts," all (100 percent) African-American judges agreed, including 65 percent who strongly agreed. This compares to about 36 percent of white judges (only 6 percent of whom strongly agreed). Note also that about 35 percent of white judges *disagreed* that more women and minority judges would improve the district courts (see Figure 8.7). Regarding Latino judges, just over one half (58 percent), agreed that more women and minorities would improve the judiciary; however, about 26 percent also selected the no opinion response. These findings suggest directly that African-American judges themselves view both racial and gender diversity to be high priorities on improving the overall quality of the courts. It should also be noted that more white judges disagreed (35 percent) than agreed (30 percent) that more women and minority judges would *improve* the overall quality of the district courts.

Figure 8.6
"Poor Litigants Are Treated Fairly in the Courts"

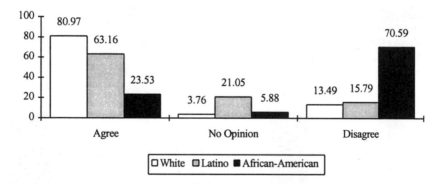

To gauge more general notions about how these judges view the political system overall, each judge was asked "would you say that the government is pretty much run by a few big interests looking out for themselves or that it is run for the benefit of all the people?" As indicated in Table 8.5 (Q35), and depicted in Figure 8.8, again race matters.

What is strikingly clear from Figure 8.8 is that African-American judges' and white judges' views on who runs the government are very dissimilar. It is also clear once again that Latino judges' views on this issue mirror those of white judges far more than African-American judges. For example, white judges (at 46 percent) and Latino judges (at 42 percent) selected "all the people," compared to 0 percent, for African-American judges. In fact, African-American judges were evenly split between "a few big interests," and "undecided." Put another way, African-American judges and white judges are inversely related to each other on this issue. Again, the NDJS data demonstrate the empirical reality of the fundamental black/white differences between federal district court judges' perceptions and the more middle ground position for Latino judges.

Figure 8.7
"More Women and Minority Judges Would *Improve* the Overall Quality of the District Courts"

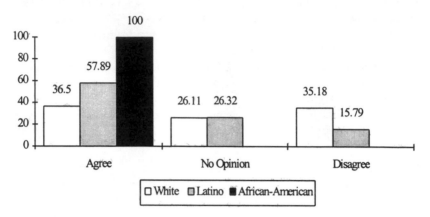

Figure 8.8
Who Runs the Government?

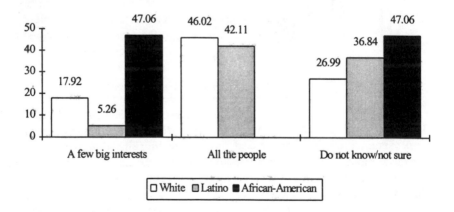

Finally, the NDJS data also reveal the scholarly limitations, and give pause to rethink the use of commonly used labels such as liberal or conservative when describing district court judges—especially when distinguishing judges by race. Despite the empirical evidence discussed above that reveals the depth of polarization between African-American and white judges on various issues, including the value of diversity in the courts and the fair treatment of blacks or poor litigants in the justice system, when these same judges were asked to characterize their judicial beliefs, only 20 percent of whites selected conservative and about 71 percent selected liberal and moderate. See Table 8.5, Q26.

Figure 8.9
Liberal, Moderate, or Conservative

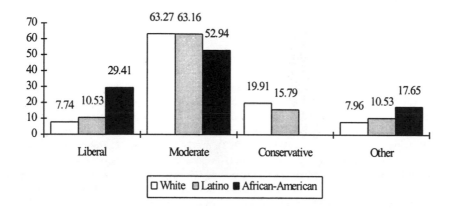

CONCLUSIONS

In this chapter, I provided a comparative description and assessment of how African-American, Latino, and white federal district court judges view various aspects of their role and function as policy actors in the American political system generally. Specific attention was also given to how these judges assess the selection and appointment process.

On balance, the NDJS data support and enhance extant studies suggesting that African-American judges might view and assess political and legal issues quite differently from whites. Overall, the NDJS data provide a polarized picture of African-American, and, to some extent, Latino district court judges regarding their expectations and evaluations of their key policymaking role and functions compared to that of their white counterparts.

Overall, however, the potential policymaking and impact of this racial polarization is tempered by the limits and capacity of courts as governing institutions in the political process. Thus, for example, although a majority of African-American judges disagree that "Black litigants are treated fairly in the justice system," the question remains how these judges might be able to work within the limits and capacity of the judicial system to change the overall treatment of African-Americans within the system. Essentially, it must be remembered that the judiciary remains very much a part of the existing political-social order. That is, the policymaking potential of federal courts in large measure rests on whether particular presidents wish to use their judicial appointments to bring about such change.

In sum, this chapter has provided a descriptive picture of African-American and Latino district court judges' expectations and evaluations of their key policymaking role and function compared to the perceptions of their white counterparts. As such, this analysis extends the extant studies on African-American judges and contributes to laying a new foundation for further study of Latino judges.

NOTES

1. Ellis Cose, *The Rage of a Privileged Class* (New York, NY: HarperCollins Publishers, 1993), p. 28.

2. There remains considerable debate within scholarly literature regarding the use of the term "Hispanic" that is now used by the U.S. Census Bureau. Throughout this study, and especially in this chapter, I use the term "Latino," although the term "Hispanic" is perhaps more widely used. See Rodney E. Hero, *Latinos and the U.S. Political System* (Philadelphia: Temple University Press, 1992), pp. 2–3. See also, Carlos Muñoz, *Youth, Identity, Power: The Chicano Movement* (New York: Verso, 1989); Rodolfo Acuña, *Occupied America: A History of Chinos*, 3rd ed. (New York: Harper and Row, 1988); and Martha E. Gimenez, "Latin/Hispanic—Who Needs a Name? The Case Against a Standardized Terminology," *International Journal of Heath Services* 19, no. 3 (1989), pp. 557–571. In general, this debate suggests that the term Hispanic acts as a form of stereotyping by masking the diversity within and between Latino groups and overemphasizing the Spanish and European aspects of the Latino political experience while deemphasizing the Latino New World experience in the Americas—particularly the experience of conquest by the United States (see Margarita Melville, "Hispanics: Race, Class, or Ethnicity?" *Journal of Ethnic Studies* 16 (1988), pp. 67–83.

3. Detailed in Appendix B, Part II in this volume, specifically, these data support those who find that African-American judges do indeed tend, more than their white cohorts, to promote minority interests—especially on issues like affirmative action, school desegregation, and voting rights. But given the relatively small number of "significant cases" decided to date by African-American judges, it might be suggested that this potential for policy change is not being met with the personnel to effect it. This limitation is even more evident with regard to Latino judges.

4. See, for example, Katherine Tate, *From Protests to Politics: The New Black Voters in American Elections* (Cambridge: Harvard University Press, 1993); Lee Sigelman and Susan Welch, *Black American's Views of Racial Inequality: The Dream Deferred* (New York: Cambridge University Press, 1991); Susan Welch and Michael Combs, "Interracial Differences in Opinions on Public Issues in the 1970s," *Western Journal of Black Studies* 7 (1983), pp. 136–141; and Howard Schuman, with Charlotte Steeh and Lawrence Bobo, *Racial Attitudes in America: Trends and Interpretations* (Cambridge: Harvard University Press, 1985).

5. Bruce Wright, "A Black Brood on Black Judges," *Judicature* 57 (1973), p. 23.

6. Sidney Verba and Norman H. Nie, *Participation in America* (Chicago: University of Chicago Press, 1972), esp. chapter 10.

7. Susan Welch with Michael Combs and John Gruhl, "Do Black Judges Make a Difference?" *American Journal of Political Science* 32 (1988), pp. 126–136.

8. For example, Beverly B. Cook, "Black Representation in the Third Branch," *Black Law Journal* 1 (1971), p. 260; Thomas Uhlman, "Race, Recruitment, and Representation: Background Differences between Black and White Trial Court Judges," *Western Political Quarterly*, 30 (1977), pp. 457–470; Thomas G. Walker and Deborah J. Barrow, "The Diversification of the Federal Bench: Policy and Process Ramifications," *Journal of Politics* 47 (1985), pp. 596–617; Welch, Combs, and Gruhl, "Do Black Judges Make a Difference?" p. 126.

9. Michael David Smith, *Race versus the Robe: The Dilemma of Black Judges* (New York: National University Publications, 1983).

10. Susan Welch and Michael W. Combs, "Interracial Differences in Opinions on Public Issues in the 1970's," *Western Journal of Black Studies* 7 (1983), pp. 136–141; Richard Seltzer and Robert Smith, "Race and Ideology," *Phylon* 46, (1985), pp. 98–105. However, this view has come under fire lately: see Mack Jones, "The Political Thought of the New Black Conservative: An Analysis, Explanation and Interpretation," in Franklin D. Jones and Michael O. Adams, eds., *Readings in American Political Issues* (Dubuque, IA: Kendall Hunt, 1987), pp. 23–49.

11. Smith, *Race versus the Robe*; See also Welch, Combs, and Gruhl, "Do Black Judges Make a Difference?" p. 126; Hanna Pitkin, *The Concept of Representation* (Cambridge: Harvard University Press, 1967); and Frederick Mosher, *Democracy and the Public Service* (New York: Oxford University Press, 1968).

12. Smith, *Race versus the Robe*.

13. George W. Crockett, "Racism in the Courts," *Journal of Public Law* 20 (1970), pp. 285–288.

14. Cook, "Black Representation in the Third Branch"; Uhlman, "Race, Recruitment, and Representation"; Smith, *Race Versus the Robe*; and Elliot Slotnick, "The Paths to the Federal Bench: Gender, Race, and Judicial Recruitment Variation," *Judicature* 67 (1984), pp. 371–388.

15. Thomas Uhlman, "Black Elite Decision Making: The Case of Trial Judges," *American Journal of Political Science* 22 (1978), pp. 884–895; Jon Gottschall, "Carter's Judicial Appointments: The Influence of Affirmative Action and Merit Selection on Voting on the U.S. Court of Appeals," *Judicature* 67 (1983), pp. 165–173; and Walker and Barrow, "The Diversification of the Federal Bench," pp. 596–617. For example, Walker and Barrow, looking at a sample of Carter's appointments to the district courts, reported no significant variance between black and white judges in numerous categories of cases. In contrast, Gottschall, looking at Carter's appointments to the appellate courts found that African-American judges tended to support the rights of criminal defendants substantially more than whites; however, there were no significant differences reported in race or sex discrimination cases.

16. Uhlman, "Black Elite Decision Making"; Gottschall, "Carter's Judicial Appointments"; and Welch, Combs, and Gruhl, "Do Black Judges Make a Difference?"

17. See Rufus P. Browning, Dale Marshall, and David Tabb, *Protest Is Not Enough: The Struggle of Blacks and Hispanics for Equality in Urban Politics* (Berkeley, CA: University of California Press, 1984); Paula McClain and Joseph Stewart, Jr., *Can We All Get Along?* (Boulder, CO: Westview Press, 1995); Hero, *Latinos and the U.S. Political System*; and Andrew Hacker, *Two Nations: Black and White, Separate, Hostile, Unequal* (New York: Ballantine Books, 1992).

18. For example, see Frank Torres, "To Have and Have Not: Hispanics in the New York Federal Judiciary," *New York State Bar Journal* (January 1991), pp. 45–47.

19. Hero, *Latinos and the U.S. Political System*, p. 1; Manuel Avalos, "A Report to the Executive Council of the Western Political Science Association," Salt Lake City, Utah, unpublished, 1989; Ernest Wilson, "Why Political Scientists Don't Study Black Politics but Historians and Sociologists Do," *PS: Political Science and Politics* 18 (1985), pp. 600–606; Benjamin Barber, "The Nature of Contemporary Political Science: A Roundtable Discussion," *PS: Political Science and Politics* 23 (March 1990), p. 40.

20. Hero, *Latinos and the U.S. Political System*; and, McClain and Stewart, *Can We All Get Along?*

21. Hero, *Latinos and the U.S. Political System*, p. 8.

22. Unless otherwise stated, I collapse "strongly agree" with "agree" and I collapse "strongly disagree" with "disagree."

23. Note that the wording of this question assumes that district court judges have some perceptions of their appointing president's policy expectations.

24. Speech at Elmira, New York, May 3, 1907, as quoted by Robert Bork in *The Tempting of America: The Political Seduction of the Law* (New York: The Free Press, 1990), p. 176.

25. See, for example, Gerald N. Rosenberg, *The Hollow Hope* (Chicago: The University of Chicago Press, 1991).

26. For example, Robert Dahl, "Decision-Making in a Democracy: The Supreme Court as a National Policy-Maker," *Journal of Public Law* 6 (1957), pp. 279–295; Donald Horowitz, *The Courts and Social Policy* (Washington, DC: The Brookings Institution, 1977).

27. Lucius J. Barker and Mack Jones, *African-Americans and the American Political System* (Englewood Cliffs, NJ: Prentice-Hall, 1994), esp. Chapter 5; Alphonso Pinkney, *The Myth of Black Progress* (Cambridge: Cambridge University Press, 1985).

28. See, for example, Bruce Wright, *Black Robes, White Justice* (Secaucus, NJ: Lyles Stuart, Inc., 1987).

29. See Frank D. Bean and Marta Tienda, *The Hispanic Population of the United States* (New York: Russell Sage Foundation, 1987); Hero, *Latinos and the U.S. Political System*; and, McClain and Stewart, *Can We All Get Along?*

30. For example, William Wilson, *The Truly Disadvantaged* (Chicago: The University of Chicago Press, 1987); Andrew Hacker, *Two Nations: Black and White, Separate, Hostile, Unequal* (New York: Ballantine, 1992).

31. Gunnar Myrdal, *An American Dilemma: The Negro Problem and Modern Democracy* (New York: Harper and Row, 1944), pp. 548–549.

32. Patricia Wald, "Poverty and Criminal Justice," Appendix C in Task Force on the Administration of Justice, Task Force Report: The Courts (Washington, DC: Government Printing Office, 1967), p. 151.

33. William J. Chambliss, *Crime and the Legal Process* (New York: McGraw-Hill, 1969), p. 86.

9   Does Gender Make a Difference?: Perceptions and Attitudes of Female District Court Judges

Times are changing. The president made that clear by appointing me, and just last week, naming five other women to Article III courts. . . . Justice Sandra Day O'Connor recently quoted Minnesota Supreme Court Justice Jeanne Coyne, who was asked: Do women judges decide cases differently by virtue of being a woman? Justice Coyne replied that, in her experience, "a wise old man and a wise old woman reach the same conclusion."

I agree, but I also have no doubt that women, like persons of different racial groups and ethnic origins, contribute . . . a "distinctive medley of views influenced by differences in biology, cultural impact, and life experience."

A system of justice will be richer for diversity of background and experience. It will be poorer, in terms of appreciating what is at stake and the impact of its judgments, if all of its members are cast from the same mold.

—Ruth Bader Ginsburg, remarks following her inauguration as an associate justice of the U.S. Supreme Court, August 10, 1993[1]

INTRODUCTION

In line with the above remarks of Justice Ginsburg, this chapter offers a comparative assessment of how female and male federal district court judges view various aspects related to the nature and role of their courts in the policy system. In addition, specific attention is given to how these judges assess the judicial appointment and selection processes, as well as their own role and function as policy actors.

This assessment, just as in the previous chapter, is based on data gained from the NDJS. Overall, the findings provide a descriptive picture as to whether and to what extent differences exist between male and female district court judges. Both the assessment and findings, just as in the previous discussion on race (Chapter 8), might prove better understood when placed in the overall context of the extant research in this area.

WHY GENDER? WHAT EXTANT RESEARCH SUGGESTS

For several decades, analyses exploring the behavior of women decision makers in American politics, including studies focusing on female members of Congress,[2] views of female political party leaders,[3] female civil servants,[4] and female state legislators[5] have failed to reveal largely significant differences based on gender. A common explanation in early research for this lack of expected difference (that women tend to make policy decisions only marginally different than men) has been tokenism.[6] More recent research, however, has tied differences between male and female officeholders to an individuals' commitment to feminist ideology,[7] membership in women's supportive networks,[8] and, the proportion of women officeholders in various specific settings.[9]

However, few studies have attempted to empirically address whether female judges might behave differently from male judges because of methodological problems inherent in studying the small number of women judges.[10] Judge Burnita Mathews, appointed to the D.C. District Court in 1949, was the first woman appointed to a federal district court. However, only four women had been appointed to the district courts and two women to the federal courts of appeals when President Jimmy Carter reformed the judicial selection process in 1977.[11] Fortunately, over the last decade, in addition to increasing the number of women justices on the Supreme Court from one to two, the number of women judges on other federal and state courts has also more than doubled.[12] Thus, a minimally sufficient number of women now sit on the federal district courts (121 as of 1994) to pursue a study of their voting behavior as well as their shared attitudes and values (see Table 3.11).[13]

Given this increase in the numbers of female judges, studies of judicial behavior have also begun to examine the extent to which women might bring both a different perspective and a different decision making pattern to the court. Feminist jurisprudence includes a variety of perspectives;[14] however, most feminist legal theory supports the notion that the presence of professional women in the legal system creates the potential for a significant impact on the policymaking activity of the courts.[15]

Extant studies on gender-specific issues provide some support for the notion that female judges might bring different perspectives and decisionmaking patterns to the courts. For example, one study found that female judges exhibited more feminist attitudes on women's issues (such as marital name change) than did male judges.[16] Another study found a weak relationship between the presence of female state supreme court justices and sex discrimination rulings.[17] And, it has also been found that the presence of female state supreme court justices increases the proportion of favorable alimony and property settlement decisions.[18]

When looking at policy areas that are not gender specific, research has also yielded mixed findings. For example, studies on the sentencing patterns of urban trial judges reveal no significant differences between male and female judges and attribute this lack of "difference" to tokenism.[19] Yet, in another study based on a small sample of twenty-four Carter-appointed district court judges, researchers found: (1) no gender based differences in criminal rights decisions; but (2) that female judges were less likely than male judges to support personal liberties claims and the position of racial minorities; and (3) that male judges are less likely than female judges to support government policy in economic regulation cases.[20] On the other hand, studies of female judges on the U.S. courts of appeals did not find any significant differences between voting behavior of male and female judges.[21]

More recently, a 1993 study examining the voting behavior of female circuit court judges in employment discrimination, criminal procedural rights, and obscenity cases found gender differences in two of the three subject areas.[22] Specifically, statistically significant differences were found between male and female judges in employment discrimination cases and criminal procedural rights cases, but in obscenity cases no significant differences were found. Despite these results, the authors do not totally ascribe these differences solely to a unique feminine voice. They suggest, for example, that their findings could be partly explained by female judges' sensitivity to certain types of claims by virtue of their gender-based life experiences.

On balance, studies of the role and representational interests of female judges suggest that gender is significant—that female judges are distinguishable from their male cohorts in terms of interest representation. These studies have not, however, examined interest representation in terms of an attempt to empirically and systematically assess how these judges compare with their male cohorts in the context of presidential expectation and judicial performance.[23] However, because of the relatively few significant cases written by female district court judges, in part due to the recentness of many of their appointments, the significant case methodology used in previous chapters yields sparse results (see Appendix B, Part II). For example, between 1960 and 1996, female district court judges wrote only about 2 percent (eighteen) of the total (699) significant opinions generated in the SDCC data (see Appendix B). A majority (eleven) of these opinions were written by Carter appointees, and, as detailed in Appendix B, tend to support pro-civil rights/liberties interests as well as the pro-choice position. However, general conclusions, given the limited number of cases generated by the SDCC data, are limited.

At most, the SDCC data suggest that female judges do indeed tend, more than their male cohorts, to promote minority interests—especially on issues like affirmative action, school desegregation, and voting rights. But given the relatively small number of "significant cases" decided to date by female judges, it is too early to form broad generalizations about these findings.

Therefore, just as with the issue of race (examined in Chapter 8), again it is helpful to turn the NDJS data to better discern and analyze differences that might exist between the policy positions and attitudes of female district court judges and their male cohorts.

THE GENDER GAP, OR, SHE SAID, HE SAID

The NDJS, as discussed earlier, was designed to measure the perceptions, attitudes, and values of federal district court judges on a variety of issues. These include the general role of district court judges in the policy process; their perceptions and insights on various civil rights and civil liberties issues; how they view their colleagues; their views regarding adherence to legal precedents; and their institutional relationships and interactions with the executive and legislative branches.[24]

The gender makeup of the population of judges is approximately 90 percent male and about 10 percent female.[25] However, male judges responded to the NDJS at a rate of nearly 62 percent, while female judges responded at a much lower rate of 42 percent (see Appendix A). Nonetheless, although the NDJS respondents represent the "male perspective" slightly more than their representation among all district court judges in the survey population, as indicated in Table 9.1, the gender distribution of the NDJS data closely reflects the actual distribution among all district court judges.

Table 9.1
Gender Representation in the NDJS

Gender	Population*	NDJS Respondents
Male	739 (91.3%)	458 (93.3%)
Female	70 (8.7%)	30 (6.1%)
Total	809 (100%)	488 100%

*Again, although there are only 649 authorized district courts judgeships, because senior judges were also included in the NDJS, the total number of judges surveyed was 809.

This chapter is organized to examine the distinctions between male and female judges, if any, that might be drawn from the NDJS data. The discussion is organized under four general categories: (I) perceptions of district court judges as policymakers; (II) district court judges and judicial selection; (III) district court judges' perceptions of the court as a institution; and (IV) district court judges' perceptions on race, poverty and related issues.[26]

I. Gender and Perceptions of District Court Judges as Policymakers

The extent to which female judges view themselves as part of the policymaking process might tell us a great deal about their representative role and impact on that process. More generally, it could add to ongoing research on the role of female judges in the overall study of women and political leadership.

Certainly, the extent to which female judges differ from their male colleagues with regard to their commitment to promoting the policy positions of their appointing presidents could affect the overall nature and status of their political leadership. But, when asked whether the "decisional patterns of district court judges reflect the political values of their appointing president," there were similar percentages of agreement between female and male judges, 23.3 percent and 28.6 percent, respectively. By contrast, however, the NDJS data reveal that male judges are somewhat more inclined than female judges to "disagree" with these sentiments (62.5 percent to 54.2 percent, respectively), and that nearly three times as many female judges (23.3 percent) chose the no opinion response as compared to only 8.7 percent for male judges who did so (see Table 9.2, Q12).

With regard to willingness to buck the system, the NDJS data reveals no significant difference between female and male judges. When asked "even if a district court judge strongly believes a particular Supreme Court decision is 'wrong,' the district court judge is nonetheless bound to follow such a ruling" nearly all judges, both women and men, agreed.[27] See Table 9.2, Q13.

The NDJS data also reveal limited (minimal) distinction (+/- 8–10 percent) between female and male judges with regard to their responses to Chief Justice Charles Evan Hughes' comment, "the Constitution is what the judges say it is." When this statement was put to them directly, about 40 percent of female judges agreed compared to 49 percent of male judges. Conversely, about 53 percent of female judges disagreed compared to 43 percent of male judges (Table 9.2, Q17).

Limited difference based on gender is also revealed by the judges' responses to the statement, "district court judges *should* make policy." Although the percentage of males responding "strongly disagree" is about 10 percent higher than for female judges, when these categories are collapsed almost equal percentages may be said to have agreed and disagreed (see Table 9.2, Q19).

Nearly equal numbers of male and female judges responded "sometimes" (51 percent and 53 percent, respectively), when they were asked "do you feel your personal attitudes and values affect your discretionary judgments on the court?" (Table 9.2, Q27). However, the percentage of female judges responding "often" was double the percentage for males; i.e., 13.3 percent to 6.1 percent, respectively. See Figure 9.1.

When this question was worded to ask "to what extent do you feel other district court judges allow their personal attitudes and values to affect their discretionary judgments on the court?" (Table 9.2, Q28), a similar pattern (as in Q27 above) was found. Again, the percentage of judges responding "sometimes," "seldom," or "never" are about equal; however, the percentage of female judges responding "often" (16.7 percent) is about double the percentage for males (8.7 percent).

Table 9.2
Gender* and Perceptions of District Court Judges as Policymakers

	% Strongly Agree	% Agree	% No Opinion	% Disagree	% Strongly Disagree
Q12. To a large extent, the decisional patterns of district court judges reflect the political values of their appointing president.					
Female	—	23.3	23.3	43.3	10.0
Male	1.1	27.5	8.7	56.6	5.9
Q13. Even if a district court judge strongly believes a particular Supreme Court decision is "wrong," the district court judge is nonetheless bound to follow such a ruling.					
Female	53.3	46.7	—	—	—
Male	48.5	48.5	.2	.2	
Q17. The Constitution is what the judges say it is.					
Female	6.7	33.3	3.3	40.0	13.3
Male	5.5	43.4	5.0	34.9	9.0
Q19. District court judges *should* make policy.					
Female	—	10.0	6.7	76.7	6.7
Male	.4	16.2	8.1	57.0	17.0
Q27. Do you feel your personal attitudes and values affect your discretionary judgments on the court?	Often	Sometimes	Seldom	Never	
Female	13.3	53.3	26.7	6.7	
Male	6.1	50.9	35.2	5.9	
Q28. To what extent do you feel other district court judges allow their personal attitudes and values to affect their discretionary judgments on the court?					
Female	16.7	63.3	20.0	—	
Male	8.7	64.2	23.1	.7	

Percentages may not total 100 because "missing responses" are omitted.
Female (N = 30).
Male (N = 458).
*For all questions regarding gender, controlling for race would account for less than a 2% difference; i.e., 29 of the 30 females responding were white females.

Figure 9.1
Personal Attitudes and Values Affect My Discretionary Judgment

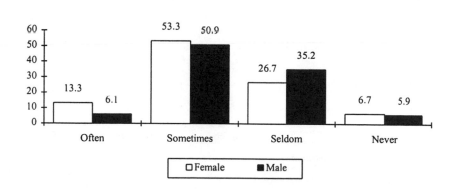

II. District Court Judges, Gender, and Judicial Selection

Because the selection, nomination, and confirmation processes are directly related to the context as well as the content of judicial policymaking, it is appropriate to examine any differences among gender regarding perceptions about the processes of judicial selection. The following NDJS data are divided into three categories: (a) general; (b) the executive branch; and (c) the Senate.

A. Judicial Selection: General

Consider, for example, that when asked whether a "district court nominee's ideology is given more consideration than his/her merit qualifications," nearly equal percentages of female (46.6 percent) and male (51.1 percent) judges agreed (Table 9.3, Q4). And, when similarly asked whether "[D]istrict court judges' confirmations are way too political," again there were only slight differences between the female and male judges (Table 9.3, Q5). For instance, about the same percentages for each agreed; a slighter higher percentage of male judges (58.3 percent) disagreed than female judges (46.7 percent); and. the no opinion response for female judges was again about twice that for males (16.7 percent to 8.3, percent respectively).

In another example, when asked whether "partisan politics dominate and control district court appointments" (Q7), the percentage of male judges agreeing was about 10 percent higher than for females (66 percent compared to 56.7 percent). On the same question, 30 percent of females disagreed compared to slightly fewer males, 26.8 percent, and the "no opinion" response for females doubled that for males (see Table 9.3, Q7).

When asked whether "special interests are '*too involved*' in the selection and evaluation of district court nominees," similar percentages (about a 4 percent difference) of female and male judges agreed and disagreed (See Table 9.3, Q8). Similarly, NDJS responses regarding the role of the ABA in the confirmation process did not reveal notable distinctions between female and male perceptions of that committee's role. For example, when asked if "a district court nominee's rating by the American Bar Association Standing Committee on Federal Judiciary is a fair and generally accurate measure of his/her qualifications," about 67 percent of females agreed compared to about 73 percent for males. About 20 percent of both males and females disagreed and, again, the no opinion response for female judges is about twice the percentage for males (see Table 9.3, Q11).

Table 9.3
Gender and Judicial Selection

	% Strongly Agree	% Agree	% No Opinion	% Disagree	% Strongly Disagree
A. Judicial Selection: General					
Q4. All too often, a district court nominee's ideology is given more consideration than his/her merit qualifications.					
Female	13.3	33.3	13.3	33.3	3.3
Male	7.4	43.7	11.4	33.2	3.5
Q5. District court judges' confirmations are way too "political."					
Female	—	36.7	16.7	46.7	—
Male	3.5	29.0	8.3	53.7	4.6
Q7. Partisan politics dominate and control district court appointments.					
Female	6.7	50.0	13.3	30.0	—
Male	9.2	56.8	5.9	25.3	1.3
Q8. Special interests are "*too involved*" in the selection and evaluation of district court nominees.					
Female	6.7	23.3	16.7	46.7	6.7
Male	3.3	20.7	17.5	50.2	7.6
Q11. A district court nominee's rating by the American Bar Association Standing Committee on Federal Judiciary is a fair and generally accurate measure of his/her qualifications.					
Female	3.3	63.3	13.3	16.7	3.3
Male	7.9	64.8	6.1	15.3	5.7
Q34. State and/or local government official(s) played an influential role in my Senate confirmation to the District Court.					
Female	6.7	23.3	20.0	16.7	33.3
Male	5.2	20.7	12.7	37.1	22.9

Table 9.3 (continued)

	% Strongly Agree	% Agree	% No Opinion	% Disagree	% Strongly Disagree
B. Judicial Selection: The Executive					
Q21. In general, modern presidents have usually attempted to appoint district court judges who share their basic political values.					
Female	20.0	63.3	10.0	6.7	—
Male	8.7	80.3	6.1	4.1	.2
Q1. The president exercises too much control over district court appointments.					
Female	3.3	6.7	10.0	60.0	20.0
Male	3.1	9.2	7.6	57.2	22.5
Q6. The Justice Department now plays too active a role in the selection and evaluation of district court nominees.					
Female	30.0	36.7	16.7	13.3	3.3
Male	14.4	33.0	14.4	34.1	4.1
C. Judicial Selection: The Senate					
Q2. The Senate *should* "rubber stamp" presidential nominees to the federal district courts.					
Female	—	10.0	3.3	60.0	26.7
Male	.4	4.1	1.7	67.0	26.2
Q3. In practice, the Senate *does* "rubber stamp" presidential nominees to the federal district courts.					
Female	3.3	36.7	3.3	50.0	6.7
Male	1.3	25.5	6.1	58.5	7.0

Percentages may not total 100 because "no response" answers are omitted.

The final NDJS question asked in the general selection category was whether "state and/or local government official(s) played an influential role in my Senate confirmation to the District Court." Again, as indicated in Table 9.3, Q34, there is limited difference between the percentages of female and male judges responding to this question. Female judges disagreed at a rate about 10 percent less than male judges and agreed at a rate about 4 percent higher. The female no opinion response was again somewhat higher than for males, 20 percent compared to only about 13 percent.

Overall, the NDJS data on the general selection process suggest little difference between female and male judges on these questions concerning the politicized nature of the appointment process. One point that may be noted, however, is the higher percentage of female judges selecting the no opinion response.[28]

B. *Judicial Selection: The Executive Branch*

First, issues of presidential influence in judicial selection, and how male and female district court judges perceive that influence, might be put into clearer perspective by the judges' responses to the question: "In general, modern presidents have usually attempted to appoint district court judges who share their basic political values." Overwhelmingly, about 83 percent of female judges, and about 89 percent of male judges responded affirmatively to the statement (Table 9.3, Q21). Notice also, that 20 percent of female judges, compared to 8.7 percent of male judges, responded "strongly agree."

In addition, as indicated in Chapter 2, about 80 percent of all NDJS respondents disagreed that the "president exercises too much control over district court appointments." Differences across gender on this question account for less than a 3 percent difference for each response option between male and female judges (Table 9.3, Q1). However, the NDJS data reveal somewhat greater distinction regarding differences between male and female judges' views on the role of the Department of Justice in the selection process. When asked, for example, whether "the Justice Department now plays too active a role in the selection and evaluation of district court nominees," 66.7 percent of female judges agreed compared to 47.4 percent for male judges (Table 9.3, Q6). Similarly, about 17 percent of female judges disagreed, compared to over double that percentage (38.2 percent) for male judges (see Figure 9.2).

Figure 9.2
The Justice Department Now Plays Too Active a Role in the Selection Process

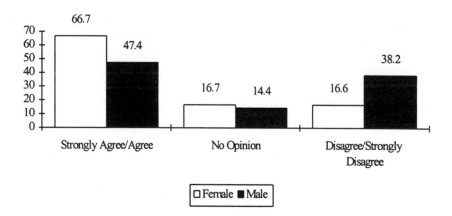

On balance, while like percentages of male and female judges overwhelmingly recognize that presidents attempt to appoint judges who share their basic political values (Q21) and do not agree that the president exercises too much control over such appointments (Q1), female judges appear far less supportive the role of the Justice Department in that process (Q6).[29]

C. Judicial Selection: The Senate

Differences between female and male district court judges' perceptions of the role of Senate in the selection process are intriguing. When asked, for example, if the Senate *should* "rubber stamp" . . . nominees," a slightly higher percentage of female judges (10 percent) agreed as compared to a smaller percentage of male judges (4.5 percent). Even so, a significant majority of both female and male judges disagreed that the Senate *should* rubber stamp nominees, 86.7 percent and 93.2 percent, respectively (Table 9.3, Q2). However, when asked whether in practice the Senate "*does* rubber stamp[s] presidential nominations to the federal district courts," a considerably higher percentage of female judges agreed (40 percent) compared to male judges (26.8 percent); double the percentage of male to female judges responded "no opinion"; 65.5 percent of male judges disagreed compared to 56.7 percent of female judges (Table 9.3, Q3). These differences, while not as dramatic as differences along racial lines,[30] do suggest that female judges might perceive the Senate's role in the confirmation process as somewhat more pro-forma than do male judges.

III. District Court Judges, Gender, and Perceptions of the Courts as Institutions

This section suggests that an assessment of the limits and capacity of federal district courts as participants in the policymaking process focus attention on both these judges' views of themselves as policy actors as well as their attitudes about courts as policy institutions.

This policy dimension, as discussed in Chapter 2, is reflected in the fact that about 80 percent of all judges agreed that the federal judiciary "is becoming more 'conservative' than it was in the 1960s, 1970s, and early 1980s" (Q18). And, as indicated in Table 9.4, 70 percent of female judges responding supported this notion compared to 78 percent of male judges responding. However, double the percentage (20 percent) of female judges selected no opinion than did male judges (10 percent). Moreover, when asked "if the federal judiciary *should* be more conservative," very little difference (+/- 4 percent) is reported between female and male respondents choosing the "agree" or "disagree" options (see Table 9.4, Q20).

With regard to the public image of the courts as institutions, consider also that when asked whether controversial Supreme Court nomination battles, "like those of Robert Bork and Clarence Thomas, have harmed the overall public image of the federal judiciary," there is almost no difference between the male and female respondents. Moreover, it is interesting to note that despite the staunch opposition by numerous women's groups to the Supreme Court nomination of Robert Bork,[31] as well as the allegations of sexual harassment surrounding the confirmation of Clarence Thomas, both female and male judges assess the damage to the federal judiciary about equally (see Figure 9.3).

Table 9.4
District Court Judges' Perceptions of the Court As an Institution

	% Strongly Agree	% Agree	% No Opinion	% Disagree	% Strongly Disagree
Q18. Overall, the federal judiciary *is becoming* more "conservative" than it was in the 1960s, 1970s, and early 1980s.					
Female	10.0	60.0	20.0	10.0	—
Male	17.0	61.1	10.5	9.8	.9
Q20. Overall, the federal judiciary *should* be more conservative than it was in the 1960s, 1970s, and early 1980s.					
Female	—	30.0	30.0	26.7	13.3
Male	7.0	26.9	24.0	32.3	9.0
Q9. Controversial Supreme Court nomination battles, like those of Robert Bork and Clarence Thomas, have harmed the overall public image of the federal judiciary.					
Female	26.7	50.0	—	20.0	3.3
Male	25.1	51.3	4.4	16.4	2.4

Percentages may not total 100 because "no response" answers are omitted.

Figure 9.3
Nomination Battles Like Robert Bork and Clarence Thomas, Have Harmed the Overall Public Image of the Federal Judiciary

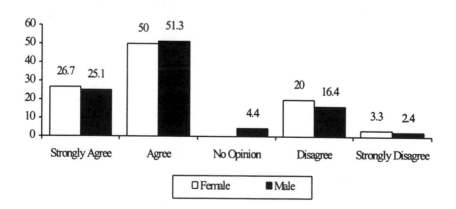

IV. Gender, Judges, and Perceptions of Race, Poverty, and Other Issues

The extent to which district court judges perform their policymaking function is also conditioned by their individual and collective perceptions of the nature and severity of key controversial issues that, sooner or later, reach the judiciary. This final section of questions addresses several of these key concerns.

Limited difference (about 10 percent) between female and male responses was revealed when these judges were asked if they agreed that "one of the special and unique functions of the federal judiciary is to protect minority rights against the majority" (Table 9.5, Q31). About 70 percent of female judges agreed compared to about 81 percent of male judges who agreed. Several other NDJS questions address issues of minority rights. For example, with regard to questions concerning the continuing dilemma of race in America, when the judges were asked to indicate the extent to which they felt "Blacks have made considerable progress in securing civil rights," a smaller percentage (80 percent) of female judges agreed compared to 88.4 percent for male judges (Table 9.5, Q22). Recall from Chapter 7 that less than half, 47.06 percent, of African-American judges agreed with that statement. However, despite dissimilar views on the extent to which African-Americans have made civil rights progress, some evidence suggests that female judges are more willing to recognize unfair treatment of African-Americans in the criminal justice system than are male judges. For example, as depicted in Figure 9.4, when asked whether "Black litigants are treated fairly in the justice system," 66.6 percent of female judges agreed compared to 81 percent for male judges (Table 9.5, Q23).

Table 9.5
District Court Judges' Perceptions on Miscellaneous Issues

	% Strongly Agree	% Agree	% No Opinion	% Disagree	% Strongly Disagree
Q31. One of the special and unique functions of the federal judiciary is to protect minority rights against the majority.					
Female	26.7	43.3	10.0	16.7	3.3
Male	25.1	55.5	5.7	11.1	.4
Q22. Blacks have made considerable progress in securing civil rights.					
Female	10.0	70.0	3.3	10.0	3.3
Male	10.5	77.9	1.5	7.2	1.3
Q23. Black litigants are treated fairly in the justice system.					
Female	13.3	53.3	6.7	23.3	3.3
Male	11.1	69.9	4.6	10.0	1.5

Table 9.5 (continued)

	% Strongly Agree	% Agree	% No Opinion	% Disagree	% Strongly Disagree
Q24. Poor litigants are treated fairly in the courts.					
Female	10.0	50.0	10.0	26.7	—
Male	8.7	70.7	4.1	13.8	1.1
Q25. More women and minority judges would *improve* the overall quality of the district courts.					
Female	23.3	30.0	33.3	6.7	3.3
Male	7.9	30.8	24.7	29.5	5.2

	A Few Big Interests	All the People	Do Not Know/ Unsure
Q35. Would you say that the government is pretty much run by a few big interests looking out for themselves or that it is run for the benefit of all the people?			
Female judges	40.0	23.3	33.3
Male	17.0	45.6	27.7

Percentages may not total 100 because "no response" answers are omitted.

Figure 9.4
"Black Litigants Are Treated Fairly in the Justice System"

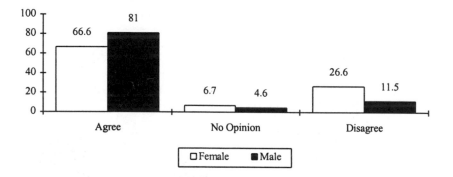

Differences between female and male judges are stronger yet concerning the treatment of poor litigants. When judges were asked whether "poor litigants are treated fairly in the courts," 60 percent of female judges agreed, compared to almost 80 percent for male judges (Table 9.5, Q24). Again, utilizing data presented in Chapter 7, recall that nearly 70 percent of African-American judges disagreed with this statement compared to 12.7 percent for white males, 15.8 percent for Latino males, and 24.1 percent for white female[32] judges (see Figure

9.5).

Figure 9.5
Gender, Race, and the Poor

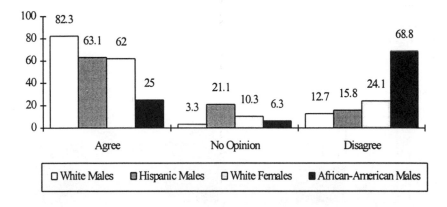

In addition to issues concerning the treatment of African-Americans and the poor, the NDJS data also asked whether "more women and minority judges would *improve* the overall quality of the district courts." As indicated in Table 9.5 (Q25), male judges are almost evenly spilt on this issue: 38.7 percent agree and 34.7 percent disagree. However, it should be noted that only 10 percent of all female judges responding disagreed with this belief, compared to almost 35 percent of responding males who disagreed (see Figure 9.6).

Figure 9.6
"More Women and Minority Judges"

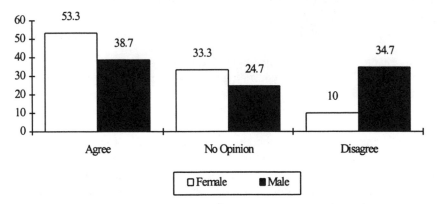

Lastly, to gauge more general notions about how female and male judges might view the political system overall, each judge was asked, "would you say that the government is pretty much run by a few big interests looking out for themselves or that it is run for the benefit of all the people?" As indicated in Table 9.5 (Q35), and depicted in Figure 9.7, it is this question that reveals one of the most dramatic differences between male and female judges' perceptions regarding the political system.

Figure 9.7
Who Runs the Government?

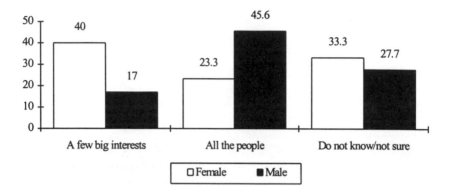

What is strikingly clear from Figure 9.7 is that the percentage of female judges who believe that the government is run by "a few big interests" is more than double that for male judges. Likewise, the percentage of males choosing "all the people" more than doubles the percentage of female judges adopting this view. Here, more so than for any previous question, the NDJS data suggest the empirical reality of any fundamental "male/female" differences between federal district court judges' perceptions of government and politics.

CHAPTER SUMMARY

This chapter provided a comparative description and assessment of how female and male federal district court judges view various aspects of their role and function as policy actors in the American political system generally. Specific attention was also given to how these judges assess the selection and appointment process.

Overall, the NDJS data on the general selection and appointment processes suggest little difference between female and male judges. More significant differences were found regarding issues of race and poverty and the most dramatic findings involved women judges' more general beliefs about the political system, specifically, how the government is run "by a few big interests."

Overall, the limited SDCC results (Appendix B) and the NDJS data analysis complement existing studies that provide limited support for the thesis that female judges bring a different perspective to the bench. However, for the most part, like previous studies, for many reasons this analysis does not support gender-specific generalizations. These reasons, discussed at length in previous works,[33] include first, that the psychological and legal theories regarding differences between men and women may be wrong; that is, the theory that women and men approach and resolve moral and legal problems differently is incorrect.[34] Second, it is possible that voting behavior (SDCC data) and the questions asked in the NDJS are not the most appropriate tools for determining the difference between male and female judges. It could be also that more survey questions regarding gender-related issues may have revealed greater differences. Third, as explained by Sue Davis and others, it could be that "differences among men and women are neutralized by the very nature of law and the legal process."[35] More specifically, it could be that because female judges are a small minority of newcomers to the bench, they are especially careful to maintain reputations as team players. This rationale might help to explain the much higher percentages of "no opinion" responses by female judges than for male judges for many of the NDJS questions.

Yet a fourth explanation put forth to partially explain the minor differences revealed in studies of male and female judges' decision making tendencies concerns the law school experience. Because women judges attended law schools controlled by and large by men, those women who were best socialized are thought more likely to succeed, and thus, less likely to exhibit the differences attributed to women by feminist theory.[36]

Overall, the combined voting behavior (SDCC) and survey (NDJS) findings comport with the general findings of previous studies that collectively offer little empirical support for the theory that female judges will speak with a unique voice. Nonetheless, female judges are clearly making a distinctive contribution to our legal system. As such, only future research—when data for voting behavior has increased and survey data focusing more directly on gender-related issues as well as female judge socialization is generated—will make it possible to more accurately assess the nature and extent of women's impact on the legal system.

NOTES

1. See Justice Ginsburg's remarks, as reprinted in *Judicature* 77 (November-December, 1993), p. 126.

2. See, for example, Shelah G. Leader, "The Policy Impact of Elected Women Officials," in Joseph Cooper and Louis Maisel, eds., *The Impact of the Electoral Process* (Beverly Hills: Sage Publications, 1977), p. 265–285; Kathleen Frankovic, "Sex and Voting in the U.S. House of Representatives," *American Political Quarterly* 5 (1977), pp. 315–331; Freida Gehlen, "Women Members of Congress: A Distinctive Role," in Marianne Githens and Jewel L. Prestage, eds., *A Portrait of Marginality* (New York:

McKay, 1977); or Susan Welch, "Are Women More Liberal Than Men in the U.S. Congress?" *Legislative Studies Quarterly* 10 (1985), pp. 125–134.

3. Edmund Constantini and Kenneth H. Craik, "Women as Politicians: The Social Background, Personality and Careers of Female Party Leaders," *Journal of Social Issues* 28 (1972), pp. 217–236.

4. Frank J. Thompson, "Civil Servants and the Deprived: Sociopolitical and Occupational Explanations of Attitudes Towards Minority Hiring," *American Journal of Political Science* 22 (1978), pp. 325–347.

5. Sue Thomas and Susan Welch, "The Impact of Gender on Activities and Priorities of State Legislators," *Western Political Quarterly* 44 (1991), pp. 445–456.

6. Marianne Githens and Jewel Prestage, *A Portrait of Marginality* (New York: McKay, 1977); Beverly B. Cook, "Women Judges and Public Policy in Sex Integration," in D. W. Steward, ed., *Women in Local Politics* (Metuchen, NJ: Scarecrow Press, 1980), pp. 130–148; Beverly B. Cook, "Will Women Judges Make a Difference in Women's Legal Rights? A Prediction of Attitudes and Simulated Behavior," in Margherita Rendal and Georgina Ainsworth, eds., *Women, Power and Political Systems* (London: Croom Helm, 1980), pp. 216–239; Rosabeth Moss Kanter, *Men and Women in Corporations* (New York: Basic Books, 1993).

7. Susan J. Carroll and Taylor, "Gender Differences in Policy Priorities of U.S. State Legislators," paper presented at the 1989 meeting of the American Political Science Association, Atlanta (cited in Elaine Martin, "The Representative Role of Women Judges," *Judicature* 77 (1993), p. 166.

8. In "The Representative Role of Women Judges," Elaine Martin examines "off-the-bench and collective behavior" by women judges. Martin, using survey data rather then voting behavior, asks what part personal commitment to representing women's interests may play in the role orientations of women judges. Focusing on members of the National Association of Women Judges (NAWJ), Martin finds that the organization acts as a support group to promote a representative role for its members; that NAWJ members are more likely than nonmembers to support the notion of representative roles for women judges, and that many individual members of the NAWJ actively seek to play a representative role in their communities. This representative perspective is most apparent with respect to women attorneys, but is not limited to that. Martin's findings suggest that the representative role envisioned by women judges includes "both the notion of 'standing for' women, and the notion of 'acting for' women's perspectives." Martin finds little support among women judges for the notion that women have a "different voice" and no support for the idea of "tokenistic" behavior. Martin concludes that the representative role seen for women judges by the NAWJ members is "relatively moderate and in keeping with the general conservatism of the profession." See also, Susan J. Carroll, *Women as Candidates in American Politics* (Bloomington: Indiana University Press, 1985).

9. See summary and discussion by Martin, "The Representative Role of Women Judges," p. 166.

10. Elaine Martin argues that these methodological problems persist despite increases in the number of women judges. "Women Judges: Making a Difference," 6 *Women's Rights L. Rep.* 66 (1991).

11. See Larry Berkson and Susan Carbon, *The United States Circuit Judge Nominating Commissions: Its Members, Procedures and Candidates* (Chicago: American Judicature Society, 1980); Elaine Martin, "Women on the Federal Bench: A Comparative Profile," *Judicature* 65 (1982), pp. 307–313; and "Gender and Judicial Selection: A Comparison of the Reagan and Carter Administrations," *Judicature* 71 (1987), pp. 136–

142; Beverly B. Cook, "Women as Judges," *Women in the Judicial Process* (Washington, D.C.: The American Political Science Association, 1988).

12. See Elaine Martin, "Women on the Bench: A Different Voice?" *Judicature* 77 (1993), pp. 126–127. Cynthia Fuchs Epstein cites the National Center for State Courts that in 1993 there were approximately 2,300 women judges are on the bench, nearly four times the 1980 number. However, the center includes administrative law judges in this list, so the 1980 and 1993 numbers are not directly comparable.

13. "The ABA estimates that 20 percent of the legal profession is female. Most female lawyers work in private firms, yet only 6 percent of all partners are women; 25 percent of associates are women." Joan Biskupic, "Bush Boosts Bench Strength of Conservative Judges," *Congressional Quarterly Weekly Report*, January 19, 1991, p. 172.

14. For example, see Leslie Friedman Goldstein, "Can This Marriage Be Saved? Feminist Public Policy and Feminist Jurisprudence," in Leslie Goldstein, ed., *Feminist Jurisprudence: the Difference Debate* (Savage, MD: Rowman and Littlefield, 1992); Cass R. Sunstein, "Feminism and Legal Theory," *Harvard Law Review* 101 (1988), pp. 826–848; Gayle Binion, "The Nature of Feminist Jurisprudence," *Judicature* 77 (1993).

15. The work of psychologist Carol Gilligan is often cited as providing a source of feminist legal theory as well as empirical support for this claim. See Carol Gilligan, *In a Different Voice: Psychological Theory and Women's Development* (Cambridge: Harvard University Press, 1982). A case in point, an analysis by Suzanna Sherry, of the decision making of Justice Sandra Day O'Connor, drawing on Gilligan's work, concluded that in fact O'Connor's decisions manifest "feminine jurisprudence." See Suzanna Sherry, "Civic Virtue and the Feminine Voice in Constitutional Adjudication," *Virginia Law Review* 72 (1968), pp. 543–615.

16. Beverly B. Cook, "Will Women Judges Make a Difference in Women's Legal Rights? A Prediction of Attitudes and Simulated Behavior," in Margherita Rendal and Georgina Ainsworth, eds., *Women, Power and Political Systems* (New York: St. Martin's Press, 1980). See also, Elaine Martin, "Differences in Men and Women Judges: Perspectives on Gender," *Journal of Political Science* 17 (1989), pp. 74–85.

17. See Gerald S. Gryski with Eleanor C. Main and William J. Dixon, "Models of State High Court Decision Making in Sex Discrimination Cases," *Journal of Politics* 48 (1986), pp. 143–155. See also, David W. Allen and Diane E. Wall, "The Behavior of Women State Supreme Court Justices: Are They Tokens or Outsiders?" *Justice System Journal* 12 (1987), pp. 232–245.

18. David W. Allen, *Conditions and Consequences of Women on State Courts of Last Resort*, unpublished Ph.D. dissertation, University of Wisconsin-Milwaukee, 1988.

19. Herbert Kritzner and Thomas M. Uhlman, "Sisterhood in the Courtroom: Sex of Judge and Defendant in Criminal Case Disposition," *Social Science Journal* 14 (1977), pp. 77–88; John Gruhl, Susan Welch, and Cassia Spohn, "Women as Policy Makers: The Case of Trial Judges," *American Journal of Political Science* 25 (1981), pp. 308–322.

20. Thomas G. Walker and Deborah J. Barrow, "The Diversification of the Federal Bench: Policy and Process Ramifications," *Journal of Politics* 47(2) (1985), Table 1, p. 605.

21. See, for example, Sue Davis, "The Impact of President Carter's Judicial Selection Reforms: A Voting Analysis of the United States Courts of Appeals," *American Politics Quarterly* 14 (1986), pp. 320-344; Jon Gottschall, "Carter's Judicial Appointments: The Influence of Affirmative Action and Merit Selection in Voting on the U.S. Courts of Appeals," *Judicature* 67 (1983), pp. 165–173.

22. See Sue Davis, Susan Haire, and Donald R. Songer, "Voting Behavior and Gender on the Courts of Appeals," *Judicature* 77 (1995), p. 267.

23. Sue Davis, Susan Haire, and Donald R. Songer, do, however, provide analysis that provides a control for party of the appointing president. See "Voting Behavior and Gender," p. 132.

24. For example, Cynthia Fuchs Epstein's recent study focusing on female lawyers concludes that women have been an extraordinary force for change in the legal profession, especially in the last few decades. However, because the legal system implicitly devalues female litigants and fails to accord them equal justice, Epstein concludes that the solution seems to lie in heightened participation of women in decision making roles. Cynthia Fuchs Epstein, *Women in Law* (Champaign: University of Illinois Press, 1993).

25. At the time of this writing, however, President Clinton was steadily increasing the percentage of female district court judges at an unprecedented rate.

26 Unless otherwise stated, I collapse "strongly agree" with "agree" and I collapse "strongly disagree" with "disagree."

27. Recall that very little difference was found between white and Latino (both about 100 percent), and African-American (88 percent) judges in Chapter 7 on this question either; i.e., nearly all agree..

28. However, the difference between the "no response" rates for male and female judges would only change their respective agree or disagree percentages about 8 percent or less.

29. While any attempt to explain this difference from the available data is purely speculative, one might consider that perhaps female judges feel more highly scrutinized by the DOJ in the evaluation process. Should this be the case, a perceived higher level of scrutiny might also account for female judges' higher no opinion response rates for other questions as well.

30. Reported in Chapter 7, differences across racial groups for this question are dramatic. The NDJS data reveal that a majority (58.83 percent) of African-American judges agreed that the Senate *does* in fact rubber stamp nominations, compared to only about 42 percent of Latino judges and only about 26 percent of white judges. Put another way, a look at the negative ("disagree") responses to this question reveals that African-American judges perceive the Senate's role in the confirmation process as much more pro-forma than do the vast majority of white judges, 30 percent to about 67 percent, respectively. And again, the difference between African-American and white judges is most dramatic—with Latino judges again between the two.

31. For a detailed case study on the failed Supreme Court nomination of Robert Bork, see Kevin L. Lyles, "The Bork Nomination and Black America: A Case Study," in Lucius Barker and Mack Jones, *African-Americans and the American Political System* (Englewood Cliffs, NJ: Prentice-Hall, 1994), pp. 133-160.

32. Only one African-American female judge responded to the NDJS. Her response, "strongly disagree," accounts for the difference in all females disagreeing (26.6 percent) and the percentage for white females, 24.1 percent (Figure 9.5). Some discussion and survey data, however, on African-American female judges is provided by Jewel L. Prestage, "Black Women Judges: An Examination of Their Socio-Economic, Educational and Political Backgrounds and Judicial Placement," in Franklin D. Jones and Michael O. Adams, eds., *Readings in American Political Issues* (Dubuque, IA: Kendall/Hunt, 1987), pp. 324–344.

33. A very good summary of the reasons for the less than dramatic differences between male and female judges' voting behavior is provided in Davis, Haire, and Songer, "Voting Behavior and Gender."

34. Cynthia Epstein, *Deceptive Distinctions: Sex, Gender, and the Social Order* (New Haven, CT: Yale University Press and New York: Russell Sage Foundation, 1988).

35. Davis, Haire, and Songer, "Voting Behavior and Gender," p. 133

36. Ibid.

10 The Gatekeepers: Conclusions

INTRODUCTION

This book has examined the interaction of law and politics in the federal district courts. My primary findings allow us to delineate more precisely the nature and effect of the various linkages between law and politics in our constitutional governing system. Particularly, the findings shed light on the role and function of federal district courts in the judicial hierarchy and in the policy process generally. This study also examines the relative role of the president in judicial selection, namely presidential attempts to achieve executive policy goals through the judicial performance of their district court nominees.

The analysis also demonstrates vividly that federal district court judges themselves hold a wide variety of views and perspectives on how they view their role and the basic interactive nature of law and politics in our governing system. As such, the findings illuminate and reinforce several key lessons that may be discerned from this study of the federal district courts.

LESSONS

1. BOTH THE SYSTEMIC AND INSTITUTIONAL ROLE AND FUNCTION OF THE UNITED STATES DISTRICT COURTS PLACE THEM SQUARELY IN THE POLICYMAKING PROCESS.

The analysis throughout this volume reveals, in many instances, that federal district court judges play important roles and hold the balance in decisions on the principal issues of the day, including: abortion, court-ordered busing, affirmative action, school prayer, and religious freedoms. Thus, district courts, like the U.S. Supreme Court, invariably become involved, as Jack Peltason states it, in major policy and political battles—"not as a matter of choice but of function."[1] And, the manner in which these interest conflicts are resolved holds significant consequences for "who gets what, when, and how" in the policy process.

In many instances, however, this important policy role of courts, especially lower trial courts, continues to be obscured by those who espouse more formalized views of the role of courts and law. For example, William Bradford Reynolds analogizes the role of the judge to that of an umpire: "Rather the job of a judge," he said, "is much like that of an umpire or referee: simply to call the balls and strikes; not undertake to rewrite the rule books."[2] However, what Reynolds fails to explain, and what this analysis highlights, is that when a baseball pitch *appears* to graze the corner of home plate, umpires exercise discretion when calling balls and strikes. Judges exercise similar discretion. Thus, the umpire (or judge) can clearly influence, even determine, the outcome of the game.

2. EXPANDED JURISDICTION, INCREASED CASELOADS, AND THE SHEER NUMBERS OF DISTRICT COURT JUDGES, SERVE TO FURTHER ENHANCE THE KEY POLICYMAKING POTENTIAL OF THE DISTRICT COURTS.

The district courts are currently the only trial courts in the federal judicial system with original jurisdiction that is, in part, exclusive and, in part, concurrent with that of state courts and that of the U.S. Supreme Court. Adjudicating both civil and criminal cases, the district courts are the "workhorses" of the national court system. These trial courts dispose of cases and controversies under the plethora of federal law stemming from the Constitution, from laws made in pursuance of it, and from treaties of the United States. Thus, these expanded jurisdictional boundaries serve to increase the potential policy areas that presidents may hope to affect through judicial appointments.

Additionally, the steadily increasing number of civil filings, particularly in cases involving federal questions, also highlights the salient position and function of the federal district judge. Federal district court judges not only apply and/or interpret the law, but also impede or promote the policy positions of their appointing presidents. And it is this potential for judges to decide issues of salient public policy that leads presidents to nominate candidates whom they estimate might share and promote policy preferences similar to their own. Theoretically, it follows then that the increased jurisdiction, caseload, and the sheer number of sitting judges serve to further enhance the key policymaking roles and potential that these lower court judges already possess.

These factors all contribute to the increasing policymaking potential of district court judges and operate to intensify the interests of presidents, politicians, and others in the selection, nomination, and appointment of these judges.

3. THE PRESIDENT CAN PLAY A KEY ROLE, BUT, DOES NOT ENJOY

UNFETTERED DISCRETION IN THE SELECTION AND SCREENING OF DISTRICT COURT JUDGE NOMINEES.

This analysis highlights both the numbers of individuals, interests, and institutions involved in the nomination and screening of district court judges and the increasing interdependence of these participants in the selection process. Particularly, this study illuminates the roles and influence of the White House, the Justice Department, and the Senate Judiciary Committee in the dynamics of judicial selection. Even so, with few exceptions, the entire process remains one of relatively low visibility. This analysis demonstrates, for example, that partisan politics often play a pivotal role in district court judicial appointments; in other words, the outcomes of national, state, and even local elections may determine who occupies the federal bench.

Indeed, the findings reveal that the selection, screening, nomination procedures, and guidelines of federal district court judge selection are tailored by each individual presidential administration, and at times result in shifts of power, procedure, and participants.

While, for example, the *formal* (constitutional) methods of selection have not changed, other participants also share the president's appointing power. These include the nominating commissions, executive committees on judicial selection, the ABA, the FBI, the attorneys general and other Justice Department officials, and both state and local as well as federal elected officials (especially home-state senators via the operation of senatorial courtesy). No single scenario controls all appointments.

4. HOW PRESIDENTS ARE INVOLVED IN THE SELECTION PROCESS, AS WELL AS THE EXTENT TO WHICH THEY ARTICULATE SPECIFIC POLICY POSITIONS, LARGELY DETERMINES THEIR SUCCESS IN PROMOTING POLICY OBJECTIVES VIA THEIR JUDICIAL APPOINTMENTS.

Factors that influence presidential success in the confirmation process include the following: (1) the nominee's rating by the ABA; (2) the standing of the president and the year of the president's term in which nominations are made; (3) the political party of the Senate majority; (4) whether there is a Senate Judiciary Committee member from the nominee's home state; and (5) the party of the senators from the nominee's state. On balance, the myriad of political and legal forces continually at work in the nation, coupled with increased scrutiny of appointments and confirmations generally guarantee potentially powerful opposition to nominees whose history and/or personal characteristics and ideologies stray too far from the mainstream.

The extent to which an individual president might be able to promote and achieve policy goals through judicial appointments is determined in part by many factors, including the following: (1) the individual president's ideological commitment and personal philosophy regarding judicial appointments; (2) the extent to which a president is involved in the selection and screening processes; (3) a given president's opportunity in terms of vacancies available; (4) the individual president's political clout generally throughout the entire political landscape; and (5) the existing state of the law that might leave more or less discretion for lower court involvement in policymaking. Overall, presidents have achieved measurable success in most instances where they have expressed strong and direct policy preferences on specific issues and were also directly involved in the appointment processes.

5. THE "SIGNIFICANT DISTRICT COURT CASE" (SDCC) DATA ILLUMINATE VIVIDLY THE DISCRETIONARY POLICYMAKING ROLE OF DISTRICT COURT JUDGES. IN THE OVERWHELMING MAJORITY OF DISTRICT COURT CASES, HOWEVER, POLICY DETERMINATIONS RESULT FROM MECHANICALLY FITTING THE FACTS OF A GIVEN CASE TO THE LEGAL CONSTRAINTS FOUND IN PRECEDENT, STATUTE, AND CONSTITUTIONAL LAW.

My review of significant cases across the five policy areas suggests that there are indeed important instances where judges' attitudes and values may influence their decisions; in these instances, judges may practice discretionary policymaking. These significant cases portend and fashion the legal framework within which current and future policy battles are fought. And, it is just in such instances (significant cases), that presidents hope to promote their policy agendas via the selection and appointment processes and where individual judges' personal attitudes and values may influence their decision making.

However, district court judges are not merely "executive agents" in the judicial policymaking arena through which presidents may promote their policy agendas. No matter how much presidents try to "pack" the courts, the rule of law and the institutional nature and function of the district courts make it difficult for district court judges to routinely act as pawns in presidential schemes to seek fundamental policy change via the appointment process. Certainly, judges and judicial policymaking in the overwhelming majority of cases are constrained by the rule of law; policymaking C. Herman Pritchett has termed "mechanical jurisprudence,"[3] where "a government of laws, not men," seem to dominate decision making.

6. RACE AND GENDER CAN MAKE A DIFFERENCE IN JUDICIAL POLICYMAKING.

This analysis has provided special focus to determine the extent to which African-American, Latino, district court judges and/or female judges might represent interests that differ from their white male cohorts even if appointed by the same president.

Specifically, data from the National District Court Survey (NDJS) support the extant body of research that suggests that African-American judges, and to a lesser extent female judges, might tend, more than their white male cohorts, to promote minority interests—especially on issues like affirmative action, school desegregation, and voting rights.

But given the relatively few number of African-American, Latino, and female judges, it may be suggested that this potential for policy change is not being met with the personnel to effect it. Clearly of course, this depends squarely on whether appointing presidents wish to bring about such change.

Therefore, and because white males make up about 75 percent of all current district courts judges overall, diversity in the federal bench remains a key issue in analyses of the federal district courts and in assessments of American politics generally. After all, an important rationale for promoting diversity in the federal bench is not just because some might believe a newly integrated federal bench will more frequently operate to guarantee minority or women's rights and/or exercise its discretion in a way that is somehow more "fair." Promoting diversity on the federal courts also is required to sustain the legitimacy and integrity of the courts themselves in a democratic system. If we are to continue to expect all the people (especially minorities and women) to have confidence in the fairness of the judiciary and respect and abide by its rulings, then it remains critical that these groups believe that their voices, policy interests, and perspectives, are being taken into account in the judicial decision making process.

7. INDIVIDUALS AND GROUPS SEEKING MAJOR POLICY CHANGE SHOULD PAY CLOSE ATTENTION TO JUDICIAL SELECTION, FOR WHO SITS ON THE COURTS TENDS TO DETERMINE WHAT COMES OUT OF THE COURTS.

Another conclusion that may be drawn from this analysis is that electoral and partisan politics dominate judicial appointments. Not only do the outcomes of presidential elections largely determine who occupies the federal bench, but also the standing and position (e.g., popularity) of a president may well determine his ability to pack the court with his appointees despite the institutionalized checks of the Senate, the ABA, and so on.

Thus, increased attention must be focused on the district courts, particularly by interests that seek to promote and protect their civil rights and liberties. Groups must remember that important legal battles begin not with the opening argument at trial, but rather with a recommendation from the attorney general or a given senator as to whom should be appointed to the federal bench.

For these reasons, the composition of the lower federal courts could increasingly prove to be a salient issue in future campaigns for the presidency and in given Senate races as well. And, because the Supreme Court seems inclined to hear far fewer cases, especially in recent years, these lower federal courts could, in effect, become the courts of last resort for a plethora of highly controversial issues.

A FINAL WORD

My study focuses attention on the nature and role of federal district courts in American politics and society. It suggests vividly the increasing importance and potential of these courts in the formulation and implementation of public policy. In particular, this study shows, for example, that presidents who have achieved much success in particular policy areas are those who expressed clear policy preferences on specific issues and actively recruited judges who share those views. As a result, the overall role and authority of our federal district courts, when exercised by judges so selected, point up clearly the potential presidents have to use the judiciary in attempts to promote and achieve their policy objectives.

Moreover, this analysis underscores the reality that judges, however selected, are clearly involved in interest conflict and are thus part of the political process and group struggle, not by choice but by function. It becomes important then, as this study suggests, to consider the judicial values and perspectives shared among and between judges of different racial backgrounds, as well as differences between male and female judges. These factors might well determine policy outcomes in judicial decision making

Finally, this volume indicates clearly that although the Reagan, Bush, and Clinton (first term) administrations have ended, because of the systemic nature of judicial policymaking and the life tenure of judicial appointments, the impact of judges appointed by these presidents will undoubtedly be felt well into the next century. Thus, judicial scholars, as well as those writing about the American policymaking process generally, would do well to include increased attention to the federal district courts as key actors—gatekeepers—in the political-legal process. In large measure, they do indeed determine what comes into and what gets out of the federal judicial system.

NOTES

1. Jack Peltason, *Federal Courts in the Political Process* (Garden City, NY: Doubleday, 1955), p. 3.

2. William Bradford Reynolds, "Adjudication as Politics by Other Means: The Corruption of the Senate's and Consent Function in Judicial Confirmations," in Henry J. Abraham, with Griffin B. Bell, Charles E. Grassley, Eugene W. Hickok, Jr., John W. Kern III, Stephen J. Markman, and William Bradford Reynolds, eds., *Judicial Selection: Merit, Ideology, and Politics* (Washington, DC: National Legal Center for the Public Interest, 1990), p. 22.

3. The notion of "mechanical jurisprudence" was developed some time ago and should be attributed to C. Herman Pritchett, "The Development of Judicial Research," in Joel B. Grossman and Joseph Tanenhaus, eds., *Frontiers of Judicial Research* (New York: John Wiley and Sons, 1969), pp. 27–33.

Appendix A: The National District Court Judge Survey (NDJS)

BRIEF METHODS AND PROCEDURES

NDJS data utilized in this study were collected using a mail survey question-naire sent to all federal district court judges (including senior judges) listed in the *Judicial Staff Directory*.[1] Two waves of survey questionnaires were mailed; the first in April 1992, and the second in July 1993 (N=809). For the first wave, two attempts were made to contact each judge. The initial attempt included mailing the four-page survey with cover letter to each judge listed in the 1992 *Judicial Staff Directory*. Second, a postcard reminder was mailed to each judge (not yet responding) ten days after the initial mailing. The identical procedures were followed for the second wave, using the 1993 *Judicial Staff Directory* for the judges who had not yet responded and to include new appointments to the bench.

THE SURVEY POPULATION AND THE RESPONDENTS: SELECTED INDEPENDENT VARIABLES

Of the 809 surveys mailed, 491 (60.6 percent) responded. Overall the char-acteristics of those judges who responded closely mirror the survey population. Consider the following characteristics:

Position/Status

As indicated in Table A.1, associate judges accounted for approximately 63 percent of the survey population of judges and made up about 60 percent of the respondents. Senior judges made up 25 percent (206) of the survey population and 27 percent (135) of the respondents. Finally, chief judges made up 11 per-cent (90) of the survey population and 12 percent (60) of the respondents. In each instance, the respondents closely reflect the survey population.

Table A.1
Judicial Position/Status

Position	Survey population	Respondents
Associate judges	513 (.634)	293 (.597)
Senior judges	206 (.255)	135 (.274)
Chief judges	90 (.111)	60 (.122)
Unknown*	—	3 (.006)
Total	809 (100%)	491 (100%)

*Three judges elected to cut the reference number from the survey making it impossible to attribute any independent variable characteristics to these judges.

Age

The average age of the survey population closely mirror the ages of the respondents. As indicated in Figure A.1, the age distribution among the respondents is proportionally representative of the age of the survey population.

Figure A.1
Age

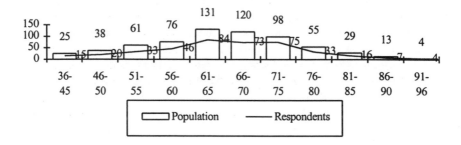

Race

Detailed in Table A.2, the racial composition of the respondents closely reflects the racial composition of the survey population, for example, the court at the time of the survey was as a whole 96 percent white, 3.7 percent African-American, and 3.2 percent Latino. The respondents are 96 percent white, 3.4 percent African-American, and 3.8 percent Latino.

Gender

The gender makeup of the survey population of judges was approximately 91 percent male and about 9 percent female. However, male judges responded at a rate of nearly 62 percent while female judges responded at a much lower rate of

42 percent. As a result, the respondent data represent the "male perspective" slightly more than their true representation in the survey population (93 percent compared to 91 percent). See Table A.3.

Table A.2
Race

Race	Race of judges in survey population	Race of respondents
White	753 (93.07%)	452 (92.05%)
African-American	30 (3.70%)	17 (3.46%)
Latino	26 (3.21%)	19 (3.86%)
Unknown	—	3 (.06%)
Total	809 (100%)	491 100%

Table A.3
Gender

Gender	Gender of judges in the survey population	Gender of respondents
Male	739 (.913)	458 (.933)
Female	70 (.087)	30 (.061)
Unknown	—	3 (.006)
Total	809 (100%)	491 100%

APPOINTING PRESIDENT

Lastly, the respondents also very closely mirror the distribution of judges by appointing president in the survey population. See Table A.4 below.

Table A.4
Appointing President

Appointing president	Representation in the survey population	Representation among the respondents
Truman	4 (.005)	2 (.004)
Eisenhower	12 (.015)	9 (.018)
Kennedy	24 (.029)	12 (.024)
Johnson	63 (.078)	41 (.084)
Nixon	100 (.124)	62 (.126)
Ford	32 (.039)	20 (.041)
Carter	178 (.220)	111 (.226)
Reagan	252 (.311)	153 (.312)
Bush	144 (.178)	78 (.159)
Unknown		3 (.006)
Total	809 (100%)	491 100%

Here is a copy of the official NDJS questionnaire:

District Court Judge Questionnaire

1. The president exercises too much control over district court appointments.

Strongly Agree	Agree	No Opinion	Disagree	Strongly Disagree
☐	☐	☐	☐	☐

2. The Senate *should* "rubber stamp" presidential nominations to the federal district courts.

Strongly Agree	Agree	No Opinion	Disagree	Strongly Disagree
☐	☐	☐	☐	☐

3. In practice, the Senate *does* "rubber stamp" presidential nominations to the federal district courts.

Strongly Agree	Agree	No Opinion	Disagree	Strongly Disagree
☐	☐	☐	☐	☐

4. All too often, a district court nominee's ideology is given more consideration than his/her merit qualifications.

Strongly Agree	Agree	No Opinion	Disagree	Strongly Disagree
☐	☐	☐	☐	☐

5. District court judge confirmations are way too "political."

Strongly Agree	Agree	No Opinion	Disagree	Strongly Disagree
☐	☐	☐	☐	☐

6. The Justice Department now plays *too active* a role in the selection and evaluation of district court nominees.

Strongly Agree	Agree	No Opinion	Disagree	Strongly Disagree
☐	☐	☐	☐	☐

7. Partisan politics dominate and control district court appointments.

Strongly Agree	Agree	No Opinion	Disagree	Strongly Disagree
☐	☐	☐	☐	☐

8. Special interests are "too involved" in the selection and evaluation of district court nominees.

Strongly Agree	Agree	No Opinion	Disagree	Strongly Disagree
☐	☐	☐	☐	☐

9. Controversial Supreme Court nomination battles, like those of Robert Bork and Clarence Thomas, have harmed the overall public image of the federal judiciary.

Strongly Agree	Agree	No Opinion	Disagree	Strongly Disagree
☐	☐	☐	☐	☐

10. While interpreting and applying the law, district court judges *make* policy.

Strongly Agree	Agree	No Opinion	Disagree	Strongly Disagree
☐	☐	☐	☐	☐

11. A district court nominee's rating by the American Bar Association Standing Committee on Federal Judiciary is a *fair and generally accurate* measure of his/her qualifications.

Strongly Agree	Agree	No Opinion	Disagree	Strongly Disagree
☐	☐	☐	☐	☐

12. To a large extent, the decisional patterns of district court judges reflect the political values of their appointing presidents.

Strongly Agree	Agree	No Opinion	Disagree	Strongly Disagree
☐	☐	☐	☐	☐

13. Even if a district court judge strongly believes a particular Supreme Court decision is "wrong," the district court judge is nonetheless bound to follow such a ruling.

Strongly Agree	Agree	No Opinion	Disagree	Strongly Disagree
☐	☐	☐	☐	☐

14. Given their role in judicial review and statutory interpretation, district court judges are involved in the policy process, regardless of their judicial philosophy.

Strongly Agree	Agree	No Opinion	Disagree	Strongly Disagree
☐	☐	☐	☐	☐

15. To what extent do *you* make public policy?

A Lot	Occasionally	Seldom	Never
☐	☐	☐	☐

16. Most of the time district court judges interpret the law; however, on occasion they *should* make the law.

Strongly Agree	Agree	No Opinion	Disagree	Strongly Disagree
☐	☐	☐	☐	☐

17. "The Constitution is what the judges say it is."

Strongly Agree	Agree	No Opinion	Disagree	Strongly Disagree
☐	☐	☐	☐	☐

18. Overall, the federal judiciary *is becoming* more "conservative" than it was in the 1960s, 1970s, and early 1980s.

Strongly Agree	Agree	No Opinion	Disagree	Strongly Disagree
☐	☐	☐	☐	☐

19. District court judges *should* make public policy.

Strongly Agree	Agree	No Opinion	Disagree	Strongly Disagree
☐	☐	☐	☐	☐

20. Overall, the federal judiciary *should* be more "conservative" than it was in the 1960s, 1970s, and early 1980s.

Strongly Agree	Agree	No Opinion	Disagree	Strongly Disagree
☐	☐	☐	☐	☐

21. In general, modern presidents have usually attempted to appoint district court judges who share their basic political values.

Strongly Agree	Agree	No Opinion	Disagree	Strongly Disagree
☐	☐	☐	☐	☐

22. Blacks have made considerable progress in securing civil rights.

Strongly Agree	Agree	No Opinion	Disagree	Strongly Disagree
☐	☐	☐	☐	☐

23. Black litigants are treated fairly in the justice system.

Strongly Agree	Agree	No Opinion	Disagree	Strongly Disagree
☐	☐	☐	☐	☐

24. Poor litigants are treated fairly in the courts.

Strongly Agree	Agree	No Opinion	Disagree	Strongly Disagree
☐	☐	☐	☐	☐

25. More women and minority judges would *improve* the overall quality of the district courts.

Strongly Agree	Agree	No Opinion	Disagree	Strongly Disagree
☐	☐	☐	☐	☐

26. How would you characterize your judicial beliefs?

Liberal	Moderate	Conservative	Other
☐	☐	☐	☐

27. Do you feel your personal attitudes and values affect your discretionary judgments on the court?

Often	Sometimes	Seldom	Never
☐	☐	☐	☐

28. To what extent do you feel *other* district court judges allow their personal attitudes and values to effect their discretionary judgments on the court?

Often	Sometimes	Seldom	Never
☐	☐	☐	☐

29. How much did "politics" play a role in *your* nomination and confirmation to the district court.

A lot	Some	Very Little	None
☐	☐	☐	☐

30. Generally, it has been the judiciary, more so than the president or the Congress, that has led the fight for minority rights.

Strongly Agree	Agree	No Opinion	Disagree	Strongly Disagree
☐	☐	☐	☐	☐

31. One of the special and unique functions of the federal judiciary is to protect minority rights against the majority.

Strongly Agree	Agree	No Opinion	Disagree	Strongly Disagree
☐	☐	☐	☐	☐

32. Generally, I consider myself to be a:

Republican	Democrat	Independent	Other
☐	☐	☐	☐

33. In what area of law do you feel you have written your most significant case decision(s) as a district court judge?

Criminal Justice ☐   *Labor and Economic Regulation* ☐
Civil Rights and Liberties ☐   *Other:* _____

34. State and/or local government official[s] played an influential role in my Senate confirmation to the district court.

Strongly Agree	Agree	No Opinion	Disagree	Strongly Disagree
☐	☐	☐	☐	☐

35. Would you say the government is pretty much run by a few big interests looking out for themselves or that it is run for the benefit of all the people?

A few big interests   All the people   Do not know/ unsure

☐   ☐   ☐

36. Before becoming a judge, how would you characterize your past participation in politics?

Very active   Active   Occasional   Never

☐   ☐   ☐   ☐

37. Over the next year, may we contact you regarding a personal interview for our study?

Feel free to contact me   Not sure   Please do not attempt to arrange an interview

☐   ☐   ☐

NOTE

1. *Judicial Staff Directory* (Mount Vernon, VA: Staff Directories, Ltd., 1992, 1993).

Appendix B: The Significant District Court Case Data (SDCC)

PART I

General Methodological Review and Data Summary

The "significant district court case" data (SDCC) was compiled utilizing the Bureau of National Affairs' publication, *U.S. Law Week*. *U.S. Law Week*, a well-recognized and independent source, publishes a weekly "Digests of Significant Opinions Not Yet Generally Reported." Specifically, the data were obtained by going page by page through the weekly "Digests of Significant Opinions Not Yet Generally Reported in *U.S. Law Week*.[1] The SDCC data therefore consist of *all* significant cases published between July 1960 and December 1996, across the five policy areas.[2]

This procedure allows for an assessment of the substantive/qualitative policy implications of a manageable number of *significant* cases representative of federal district court policymaking. As stated in Chapter 1, this has been the widely accepted practice among political scientists and others in studying judicial politics and policymaking. For example, case books and treaties on constitutional law and civil liberties do not, and need not, include abstracts of every case the Supreme Court decides. On the contrary, these works include only the "significant" cases, those that signal new or important judicial positions (e.g., doctrinal developments) in important policy conflicts. Clearly, the "significant case" approach can also prove useful in analyzing the policymaking activities of federal district courts as well.

Thus, in contrast to earlier studies, the significant case approach used in this analysis provides an innovative departure from the more often used vote counting methodologies utilizing the "all case" or "all published case" approaches. The significant case approach, then, provides an excellent context in which to view how presidents fare in attempts to achieve their policy objectives through their judicial appointments.

Some Additional Methodological Concerns

First, the SDCC analysis is *limited to full, written, published significant opinions*. However, published opinions generally account for less than ten percent of the 250,000 plus cases filed each year in the district courts.[3] District court judges are not obligated to pen full opinions or to submit their opinions for publication. Although prudence, professionalism, historical tradition, and procedure dictate that any case of reasonable magnitude would be given written treatment, there still remains the chance that a "significant" case was not afforded a full written opinion. As such, the analysis in Chapter 7 is guided by the assumption that district court judges generally follow their federal judicial circuit's publication criteria. These criteria, developed in accord with the Judicial Conference of the United States' 1964 directives, established that federal district court judges *should* publish only those opinions that are of "general precedential value."[4]

In the main, however, researchers examining published and unpublished decisions have "discovered no widespread 'hiding' of law declaring opinions—that is, opinions that clearly broke new ground on important issues."[5] A study of fifth circuit appellate cases found that only rarely unpublished cases contained precedential value.[6] However, more recent studies have suggested that unpublished district court decisions may at times contain precedential information, such as important public policy issues.[7] Donald Songer, for example, reports that in some district court cases without published opinions the "judges faced a choice situation which permitted them discretion to make decisions consistent with their personal values and policy preferences."[8]

On balance, and with deference to the many well-respected judicial scholars that have argued that "final published court opinions tell only a small part of the story of any given case because they do not consider all the nuances of the case and how the judge ruled on various motions made throughout the trial," this book adopts Kenneth Dolbeare's position (who relied on the *Federal Supplement* in his classic study of federal trial courts and urban public policy a quarter of a century ago), that "no practical alternate exists."[9] Thus, lacking consistent evidence to the contrary, this analysis comports with scholars concluding that district judges follow both their federal judicial circuit's publication criteria, and the Judicial Conference's directives, publishing only those opinions in which the legal question extends further that the dispute at hand—opinions that "create law."

Second, the *dismissal of cases* is another factor that plagues studies on judicial policymaking. Clearly, focusing on cases in which judicial decisions are made obscures the reality that inaction or the refusal to adjudicate a petitioners' claim is in effect judicial policymaking. Judges may influence policy outcomes by simply refusing to hear or by dismissing a case. Thus, the analysis here and conclusions regarding expectation/performance are limited to describing the instances where federal district court judges "decided to decide."[10]

Third, that *courts are not self-starters* is another systemic factor that should be considered. This factor, of course, grows out of the very nature and operation of the judicial process itself. Indeed, a judge's opportunities to make policy are influenced to a large extent by the sociopolitical climate. Judges can only promote or retard the policy objectives of their appointing president if the respective cases and controversies are brought to the bar by outside litigants. Thus, judges and judicial decisions, as potential vehicles for social and political policymaking, are circumscribed by the number and nature of the cases brought to the court.

Case Frequencies and Summary Observations

As indicated in Table B.1, the SDCC collection and coding procedures generated 766 significant district court case opinions for judges appointed by presidents Kennedy through Clinton across the five policy areas over the approximately thirty-six-year period.[11] The individual totals of reported significant opinions range from as few as four for President Clinton (in about three years), to as many as 215 for President Johnson (in about thirty-three years) as of December 1996 (Table B.1).

Table B.1
Significant Cases, 1960–1996

	District court judges appointed	Significant opinions reported 1960–1996
Kennedy (1960–1996)	103	154
Johnson (1963–1996)	122	215
Nixon (1968–1996)	179	188
Ford (1972–1996)	52	27
Carter (1976–1996)	202	106
Reagan (1980–1996)	290	66
Bush (1988–1996)	148	6
Clinton (1992–1996)	169*	4
Total	1203	766

*Appointees confirmed as of the 104th Congress (1996).

PART II

Race, Gender, and the SDCC Data

African-American Judges

Indicated in Table B.2, between 1960 and 1996, a total of eighty-eight African-Americans were appointed to the district courts, and thirty-three (37.5 percent) of these were Clinton appointees. See Table 3.11 also.

These eighty-eight African-American judges represent about 7 percent of the total 1,265 appointments made between 1960 and 1996. However, these eighty-eight African-American judges have thus far written only 2.7 percent (twenty-one) of the total (766) significant opinions rendered across the five policy areas (1960–1996). See Table B.2.

Table B.2
Number of African-American District Court Judges and Their Significant Opinions, 1960–1996

Appointing president	Total appointments	African-American appointments	Total significant opinions	Significant opinions by African-American judges
Kennedy	103	3	154	1 (<1%)
Johnson	122	5	215	9 (4.1%)
Nixon	179	6	188	1 (<1%)
Ford	52	3	27	—
Carter	202	28	106	9 (8.4%)
Reagan	290	6	66	—
Bush	148	10	6	1 (16%)
Clinton*	169	33	4	—
Totals	1265	88 (6.9%)	766	21

*Appointees confirmed as of the 104th Congress (1996).

As indicated in Table B.3, President Kennedy's 154 significant opinions include only one opinion by an African-American judge: an opinion restricting voting rights guarantees. Johnson's judges' nine significant opinions are evenly split on issues of religious liberty (one each); have supported affirmative action policies 4–1 (80 percent); and reported are three significant opinions supporting voting rights guarantees.

There is only one opinion reported for a Nixon female appointee—an opinion supporting a decreased separation between church and state. However, Carter's twenty-eight African-American district court judges have thus far produced nine significant opinions: a ratio of 3–1 supporting increased separation between church and state, a 2–1 ratio supporting abortion rights, one pro-affirmative action opinion, and one opinion extending voting rights guarantees (Table B.3).

Neither President Ford's nor Reagan's African-American appointees have thus far rendered *any* significant district court opinions across the five policy areas. And, though one opinion is recorded promoting voting rights for a Bush appointee, given the few cases to date, it is too soon to draw any tentative conclusions for President Bush's and Clinton's African-American appointees.[12] This limitation is even more evident with regard to Latino judges.

Table B.3
Judicial Performance: African-American Judges: 1960–1996

	K*	J	N	F	Ca	R	B	Cl
Abortion								
pro-abortion rights	–	–	–	–	2	–	–	–
antiabortion rights	–	–	–	–	1	–	–	–
Religious Liberty								
decrease separation	–	1	1	–	1	–	–	–
increase separation	–	1	–	–	3	–	–	–
Affirmative Action								
support	–	3	–	–	1	–	–	–
oppose	–	1	–	–	–	–	–	–
School Desegregation								
enhance	–	–	–	–	–	–	–	–
restrict	–	–	–	–	–	–	–	–
Voting Rights								
extend	–	3	–	–	1	–	1	–
restrict	1	–	–	–	–	–	–	–
Total	1	9	1	–	9	–	–	–

*K = Kennedy, J = Johnson, N = Nixon, F = Ford, Ca = Carter, R = Reagan, B = Bush, Cl = Clinton.

The SDCC and Latino Judges

As indicated in Table B.4, between 1960 and 1996, only fifty-one Latinos were appointed to the district courts. See Table 3.11 also.

Table B.4
Number of Latino District Court Judges and Their Significant Opinions, 1960–1996

Appointing president	Total appointments	Latino appointments	Total significant opinions	Significant opinions by Latino judges
Kennedy	103	–	154	–
Johnson	122	3	215	2 (< 1%)
Nixon	179	2	188	–
Ford	52	1	27	–
Carter	202	14	106	3 (2.8%)
Reagan	290	14	66	–
Bush	148	6	6	–
Clinton	169*	11	4	–
Totals	1265	51 (4%)	766	5 (< 1%)

*Appointees confirmed as of the 104th Congress (1996).

These fifty-one Latino judges represent just 4 percent of the total 1,265 appointments made between 1960 and 1996. However, only five significant cases written by Latino judges have been reported to date, less than 1 percent of all significant cases reported. Two of these five opinions were written by Johnson's appointees and both support increased separation between church and state. The remaining three were written by Carter appointees—one opinion supporting electoral rights, and one increasing and one decreasing the separation between church and state.

The SDCC and Female Judges

Detailed in Chapter 3 (Table 3.11), and in Table B.5 below, relatively few women (138) have been appointed to the federal district courts.

Table B.5
Number of Female District Court Judges and Their Significant Opinions, 1960–1996

Appointing President	Total appointments	Female appointments	Total significant opinions	Significant opinions by female judges
Kennedy	103	1	154	1
Johnson	122	2	215	4
Nixon	179	1	188	–
Ford	52	1	27	–
Carter	202	29	106	12
Reagan	290	24	66	5
Bush	148	29	6	1
Clinton*	169	51	4	1
Totals	1265	138 (11%)	766	24 (3.1%)

*Appointees confirmed as of the 104th Congress (1996).

And, as shown in Table B.5, female judges' significant opinions account for only about 3 percent (twenty-four) of the total 766 significant opinions rendered across the five policy areas for the thirty-six-year period.

Specifically, President Kennedy's judges' opinions include one opinion by a female judge, an opinion promoting increased voting rights guarantees (Table B.6). President Johnson's female appointees have penned four significant opinions: one of these opinions supports a decreased separation between church and state; one opinion supports school desegregation efforts; and the remaining two extend voting rights guarantees.

Most significant opinions by female judges to date have been written by Carter appointees. For example, as detailed in Table B.6, President Carter's three reported significant abortion decisions by female judges unanimously support the pro-choice stance. Likewise, Carter's female judges have also adopted the increased separation (e.g., anti-school prayer, etc.) position at a ratio of 5–1, and, rendered two significant opinions favoring increased voting rights guarantees.

The reported significant cases for President Reagan's female judges present somewhat of a mixed bag. These cases include two opinions supporting an increased separation between church and state; one opinion opposing affirmative action; and one opinion supporting voting rights guarantees. To date there is one significant case promoting a decreased separation between church and state for a female Bush appointee and one significant pro-choice opinions for a female Clinton appointee (see Table B.6).

Table B.6
Judicial Performance: Female Judges: 1960–1996

	K*	J	N	F	Ca	R	B	Cl
Abortion								
pro-abortion rights	–	–	–	–	3	–	–	1
anti-abortion rights	–	–	–	–	–	–	–	–
Religious Liberty								
decrease separation	–	1	–	–	2	–	–	–
increase separation	–	–	–	–	5	2	1	–
Affirmative Action								
support	–	–	–	–	–	–	–	–
oppose	–	–	–	–	–	1	–	–
School Desegregation								
enhance	–	1	–	–	–	–	–	–
restrict	–	–	–	–	–	–	–	–
Voting Rights								
extend	1	2	–	–	2	1	–	–
restrict	–	–	–	–	–	1	–	–
Totals	1	4	–	–	12	5	1	1

*K = Kennedy, J = Johnson, N = Nixon, F = Ford, Ca = Carter, R = Reagan, B = Bush, Cl = Clinton.

On balance, given the relatively small number of African-American, Latino, and female appointees, coupled with equally small numbers of reported significant cases, the SDCC data remain limited in their utility to assess the policy support patterns of these groups of judges. Therefore, again it is helpful to turn the NDJS data (see Chapters 8 and 9) to better discuss and analyze differences that might exist between these judges.

NOTES

1. Others too have used a page-by-page review of *U.S. Law Week* for data compilation. See H. W. Perry, *Deciding to Decide: Agenda Setting in the United States Supreme Court* (Cambridge: Harvard University Press, 1991), p. 180.

2. Unlike other previous research efforts, e.g., the Carp and Rowland's pathbreaking 1985 study, I elected to *include* rather than exclude significant decisions by the three-judge district courts. Therefore, in instances where *U.S. Law Week* reported significant three-judge district court decisions, I examined *each* of the judges' positions, reasoning, and holding and reported each separately.

3. Allan D. Vestal, "Publishing District Court Opinions in the 1970's," *Loyola Law Review* 4 (1970–1971), pp. 185–220.

4. Administrative Office of the U.S. Courts, 1964. The Judicial Conference of the

United States approved these criteria for each judicial circuit in the 1970s and agreed not to impose a general set of criteria for all circuits to follow in determining "precedential" cases. Thus, each circuit's guidelines differ in specificity, criteria for defining "precedential," and in the presumption for or against publication.

5. See William L. Reynolds and William M. Richman, "An Evaluation of Publication in the U.S. Courts of Appeals: The Price of Reform," *University of Chicago Law Review* 48 (1981), p. 608.

6. Philip Schuchman and Alan Gelfand, "The Use of Local Rule 21 in the Fifth Circuit: Can Judges Select Cases of No Precedential Value?" *Emory Law Journal* 29 (1980), pp. 194–230.

7. For example, see Lauren K. Robel, "The Myth of the Disposable Opinion: Unpublished Opinions and Government Litigants in the United States Courts of Appeals," *Michigan Law Review* 87 (1989), pp. 940–962; Peter Jan Honigsberg and James Dikel, "Unfairness in Access to and Citation of Unpublished Federal Court Decisions," *Golden Gate University Law Review* 18 (1988), pp. 277–299; Pamela Foa, "A Snake in the Path of the Law: The 7th Circuit's Non-Publication Rule," *University of Pittsburgh Law Review* (1977), pp. 309–340; Donald R. Songer, "Criteria for Publication and Opinions in the U.S. Courts of Appeals: Formal Rules versus Empirical Reality," *Judicature* 73 (1990), pp. 307–313; and Donald R. Songer, "Nonpublication in the United States District Courts: Official Criteria vs. Inferences from Appellate Review," *Journal of Politics* 50 (1988), pp. 206–215.

8. Songer, "Nonpublication of the United States District Courts," pp. 212–213.

9. Kenneth Dolbeare, "The Federal District Courts and Urban Public Policy: An Explanatory Study (1960–1967)," in Joel B. Grossman and Joseph Tanenhaus, eds., *Frontiers of Judicial Research* (New York: Wiley, 1969), p. 387.

10. For a contemporary discussion on the matter of granting certiorari and judicial agenda setting, see H. W. Perry, *Deciding to Decide: Agenda Setting in the United States Supreme Court* (Cambridge: Harvard University Press, 1991).

11. Each *U.S. Law Week* volume begins July 1 and ends the following calendar year on June 30. Thus I started the selection procedures with June 1960 (cases before would be outside my presidential focus) and surveyed all those cases reported through the last available *weekly* publication at the time of collection; i.e., December 1996. More specifically, the SDCC data include every weekly edition published between June 1, 1960 and December 1996—approximately thirty-six years.

12. For example, Susan Welch and Michael Combs, "Interracial Differences in Opinions on Public Issues in the 1970s," *Western Journal of Black Studies* 7 (1983), pp. 136–141.

Selected Bibliography

Abraham, Henry J. 1988. "The Reagan Judges: His Most Enduring Legacy?" In Charles O. Jones, ed., *The Reagan Legacy: Promise and Performance*. Chatham, NJ: Chatham House Publishers.

Abraham, Henry J., with Griffin B. Bell, Charles E. Grassley, Eugene W. Hickok, Jr., John W. Kern III and Stephen J. Markman, and William Bradford Reynolds, eds. 1990. *Judicial Selection: Merit, Ideology, and Politics*. Washington, DC: National Legal Center for the Public Interest.

Abraham, Henry J. 1992. *Justices and Presidents: A Political History of Appointments to the Supreme Court*. 3rd ed. New York: Oxford University Press.

Abraham, Henry J. 1993. *The Judicial Process*. 6th ed. New York: Oxford University Press.

Allison, Garland W. 1996. "Delay in Senate Confirmation of Federal Judicial Nominees." *Judicature* 80, pp. 8–15.

Alumbaugh, Steve, and C. K. Rowland. 1990. "The Links between Platform Based Appointment Criteria and Trial Judges' Abortion Judgments." *Judicature* 74, pp. 153–162.

Alumbaugh, Steve and F. Torres. 1991. "To Have and to Have Not: Hispanics in the New York Federal Judiciary." *New York State Bar Journal* 63, January.

Amaker, Norman C. 1988. *Civil Rights and the Reagan Administration*. Washington, DC: The Urban Institute Press.

American Bar Association. 1991. *Standing Committee on Federal Judiciary: How It Is and How It Works*. Chicago: American Bar Association.

Aranda, Benjamin. 1997. *Directory of the Hispanic Judges of the United States of America*. Unpublished directory prepared by the American Bar Association, Judicial Administration Division, Task Force on Opportunities for Minorities, and, the Hispanic National Bar Association Judicial Council.

Barber, James David. 1985. *The Presidential Character: Predicting Performance in the White House*. Englewood Cliffs, NJ: Prentice-Hall.

Barker, Lucius J. 1967. "Third Parties in Litigation: A Systemic View of the Judicial Function." *Journal of Politics* 29, pp. 41–69.

Barnes, Catherine. 1983. *Journey from Jim Crow: The Desegregation of Southern Transit*. New York: Columbia University Press.

Barrow, Deborah J., Gerard S. Gryski, and Gary Zuk. 1992. "Blacks, Hispanics, Women and the Federal Bench: The Dynamics of Representation." Paper presented at the Annual Meeting of the Midwest Political Science Association, April 1992.

Barrow, Deborah J., and Gary Zuk. 1990. "An Institutional Analysis of Turnover in the Lower Federal Courts, 1990–1987." *Journal of Politics* 52, pp. 457–475.

Bartals, John R. 1989. "United States District Courts En Banc—Resolving the Ambiguities." *Judicature* 73, pp. 40–42.

Bass, Harold F. 1991. "Presidential Party Leadership and Party Reform: Lyndon B. Johnson and the MFDP Controversy." *Presidential Studies Quarterly* 21 (Winter), pp. 85–101.

Bauer, Carl M. 1977. *John F. Kennedy and the Second Reconstruction*. New York: Columbia University Press.

Baum, Lawrence. 1995. *The Supreme Court*. Washington, DC: CQ Press.

Bell, Derrick. 1987. *And We Are Not Saved: The Elusive Quest for Racial Equality*. New York: Basic Books.

Benokraitis, Nijole V., and Joe R. Feagin. 1978. *Affirmative Action and Equal Opportunity: Action, Inaction, Reaction*. Boulder, CO: Westview Press.

Berkson, Larry. 1980. "Judicial Selection in the United States: A Special Report." *Judicature* 64.

Berkson, Larry, with Scott Beller and Michele Girmaldi. 1980. *Judicial Selection in the United States: A Compendium of Provision*. Chicago: American Judicature Society.

Berkson, Larry, and Susan Carbon. 1980. *The United States Circuit Judge Nominating Commissions: Its Members, Procedures and Candidates*. Chicago: American Judicature Society.

Berman, Larry. 1990. *Looking Back on the Reagan Presidency*. Baltimore: The Johns Hopkins University Press.

Bickel, Alexander M. 1986. *The Least Dangerous Branch: The Supreme Court at the Bar of Politics*. 2nd ed. New Haven: Yale University Press.

Birkby, Robert H. 1983. *The Court and Public Policy*. Washington, DC: CQ Press.

Bitzner, Lloyd, and Theodore Rueter. 1980. *Carter vs. Ford*. Madison: The University of Wisconsin Press.

Blakesley, Lance. 1995. *Presidential Leadership: From Eisenhower to Clinton*. Chicago: Nelson-Hall Publishers.

Blanearte, James E. 1994. "Latino Partner's Perspective on the Need for More Latino Lawyers." *Chicano Latino Law Review* 14, pp. 176–178.

Bork, Robert H. 1972. *Constitutionality of the President's Busing Proposals*. Washington, DC: Government Printing Office.

Bork, Robert H. 1990. *The Tempting of America: The Political Seduction of the Law*. New York: The Free Press.

Bornet, Vaughn Davis. 1983. *The Presidency of Lyndon B. Johnson*. Lawrence: University Press of Kansas.

Brace, Paul, with Christine B. Harrington and Gary King, eds. 1989. *The Presidency and American Politics*. New York: New York University Press.

Brigham, John. 1987. *The Cult of the Robe*. Philadelphia: Temple University Press.

Brownstein, Ronald, and Nina Easton. 1982. *Reagan's Ruling Class: Portraits of the President's Top 100 Officials*. Washington, DC: The Presidential Accountability Group.

Bullock, Charles S. III, and Charles M. Lamb, eds. 1984. *Implementation of Civil Rights Policy*. Monterey, CA: Brooks/Cole Publishing.

Burke, Robert F. 1984. *The Eisenhower Administration and Black Civil Rights*. Knoxville: The University of Tennessee Press.

Burner, David. 1988. *John F. Kennedy and a New Generation*. Boston: Little, Brown and Company.

Bush, George. 1987. *Looking Forward*. Garden City, NY: Doubleday.

Bush, George. 1988. "Candidates State Positions on Federal Judicial Selection." *Judicature* 72, p. 77.

Califano, Joseph A., Jr. 1981. *Governing America: An Insider's Report from the White House and the Cabinet*. New York: Simon and Schuster.

Canon, Bradley C. 1972. "The Impact of Formal Selection Processes on the Characteristics of Judges—Reconsidered." *Law and Society Review* 13, pp. 579–593.

Caplan, Lincoln. 1987. *The Tenth Justice: The Solicitor General and the Rule of Law*. New York: Vintage Books.

Carbon, Susan B., and Larry C. Berkson. 1980. *Judicial Retention Elections in the United States*. Chicago: American Judicature Society.

Carp, Robert A., and C. K. Rowland. 1983. *Policymaking and Politics in the Federal District Courts*. Knoxville: The University of Tennessee Press.

Carp, Robert A., Donald Songer, C. K. Rowland, Ronald Stidham, and Lisa Richey-Tracy. 1993. "The Voting Behavior of Judges Appointed by President Bush." *Judicature* 76, pp. 298–302.

Carp, Robert A., and Ronald Stidham. 1996. *Judicial Process in America*. 3rd ed. Washington, DC: CQ Press.

Carp, Robert A., and Russell Wheeler. 1972. "Sink or Swim: The Socialization of a Federal District Judge." *Journal of Politics* 21, pp. 359–393.

Carroll, Susan J., and Barbara Geiger-Parker. 1983. *Women Appointed to the Carter Administration: A Comparison with Men*. New Brunswick, NJ: Rutgers University Center for the American Woman and Politics.

Carter, Jimmy. 1982. *Keeping Faith: Memoirs of a President*. New York: Bantam Books.

Casper, Johnathon. 1976. "The Supreme Court and National Policy Making." *American Political Science Review* 70, pp. 50–63.

Chase, Harold W. 1972. *Federal Judges: The Appointing Process*. Minneapolis: University of Minnesota Press.

Chayes, Abram. 1976. "The Role of the Judge in Public Law Litigation." *Harvard Law Review* 89, pp. 1281–1316.

Chinn, Nancy, and Larry Berkson. 1980. *Literature on Judicial Selection*. Chicago: American Judicature Society.

Choper, Jesse. 1980. *Judicial Review and the National Political Process*. Chicago: University of Chicago Press.

Clark, David S. 1981. "Adjudication to Administration: A Statistical Analysis of Federal District Courts in the Twentieth Century." *Southern California Law Review* 55, pp. 69–152.

Combs, Michael W., and John Gruhl, eds. 1986. *Affirmative Action: Theory, Analysis, and Prospects*. Jefferson, NC: McFarland.

Congressional Quarterly Almanac, various issues, 1960–1997.

Congressional Quarterly Weekly Report, various issues, 1960–1997.

Cook, Beverly B. 1971. "Black Representation in the Third Branch." *Black Law Journal* 1, pp. 260–279.

Cook, Beverly B. 1971. "The Socialization of New Federal Judges: Impact on District Court Business." *Washington University Law Quarterly* (Spring), pp. 253–279.

Cook, Beverly B. 1973. "Sentencing Behavior of Federal Judges: Draft Cases, 1972." *University of Cincinnati Law Review* 42, pp. 597–663.

Cook, Beverly B. 1977. "Public Opinion and Federal Judicial Policy." 21 *American Journal of Political Science* 21, pp. 567–600.

Cook, Beverly B. 1980. "Will Women Judges Make a Difference in Women's Legal Rights? A Prediction of Attitudes and Simulated Behavior." In Margherita Rendal and Georgina Ainsworth, eds. *Women, Power and Political Systems*. New York: St. Martin's Press.

Cook, Beverly B. 1980. "Women Judges and Public Policy in Sex Integration." In D. W. Steward, ed. *Women in Local Politics*. Metuchen, NJ: Scarecrow Press, pp. 130–148.

Cooper, Phillip J. 1988. *Hard Judicial Choices: Federal District Court Judges and State and Local Officials*. New York: Oxford University Press.

Crockett, George W. 1970. "Racism in the Courts." *Journal of Public Law* 20, pp. 285–288.

Dahl, Robert. 1957. "Decision-Making in a Democracy: The Supreme Court as a National Policy-Maker." *Journal of Public Law* 6, pp. 279–295.

Davis, Abraham L. 1989. *Blacks in the Federal Judiciary*. Bristol, IN: Wyndham Hall Press.

Dolbeare, Kenneth. 1969. "The Federal District Courts and Urban Public Policy: An Exploratory Study (1960–1967)." In Joel B. Grossman and Joseph Tanenhaus, eds. *Frontiers of Judicial Research*. New York: Wiley, pp. 373–404.

Ducat, Craig R., and Robert L. Dudley. 1989. "Federal District Judges and Presidential Power during the Postwar Era." *Journal of Politics* 51, pp. 98–118.

Dudley, Robert, and Craig Ducat. 1986. "Federal District Judges and Presidential Power: A Multivariate Analysis." Paper presented at the Annual Meeting of the American Political Science Association, Washington, DC, August.

Early, Stephen T., Jr. 1977. *Constitutional Courts of the United States*. Totowa, NJ: Littlefield, Adams and Co.

Edley, Christopher, Jr. 1996. *Not All Black and White*. New York: Hill and Wang.

Ely, John Hart. 1980. *Democracy and Distrust: A Theory of Judicial Review*. Cambridge: Harvard University Press.

Epstein, Cynthia Fuchs. 1993. *Women in Law*. Champaign: University of Illinois Press.

Faux, Marian. 1990. *Crusaders: Voices from the Abortion Front*. New York: Birch Lane Press.

Fein, Bruce. 1983. "A 'Reagan' Court Would Overturn Past Errors." *Human Events* (July 6).

Fish, Peter. 1973. *The Politics of Federal Judicial Administration*. Princeton: Princeton University Press.

Fish, Peter. 1979. "Evaluating the Black Judicial Applicant." *Judicature* 62, pp. 495–501.

Fish, Peter. 1979. "Merit Selection and Politics." *Wake Forest Law Review* 15, pp. 635–654.

Fishel, Jeff. 1985. *Presidents and Promises: From Campaign Pledge to Presidential Performance*. Washington, DC: CQ Press.

Flanders, Steven (Project Director). 1977. *Case Management and Court Management in the United States District Courts*. Washington, DC: Government Printing Office.

Foa, Pamela. 1977. "A Snake in the Path of the Law: The 7th Circuit's Non-Publication

Rule." *University of Pittsburgh Law Review,* pp. 309–340.

Ford, Gerald R. 1979. *A Time to Heal.* New York: Harper and Row.

Ford, Gerald R. 1985. "Attorney General Edward H. Levi." *University of Chicago Law Review* 52, p. 284.

Fowler, W. Gary. 1983. "A Comparison of Initial Recommendation Procedures: Judicial Selection under Reagan and Carter." *Yale Law and Policy Review* 1, p. 299.

Franklin, Charles H., and Liane Kosaki. 1989. "Republican Schoolmaster: The U.S. Supreme Court, Public Opinion, and Abortion." *American Political Science Review* 83, pp. 751–771.

Franklin, John Hope, and Genna Rae McNeil, eds. 1995. *African-Americans and the Living Constitution.* Washington, DC: Smithsonian Institution Press.

Freedman, M. 1986. *Assembly-Line Approval: A Common Cause Study of Senate Confirmation of Federal Judges.* Washington, DC: Common Cause, January.

Fried, Charles. 1991. *Order and Law: Arguing the Reagan Revolution—A Firsthand Account.* New York: Simon and Schuster.

Galanter, Marc. 1974. "Why the Haves' Come Out Ahead: Speculations on the Limits of Legal Change." *Law and Society Review* 9, pp. 95–160.

Gazell, James A. 1983. "Federal District Court Caseloads in the Burger Era: Rearguard Tactics to a Losing War?" *Southwestern University Law Review,* pp. 699–722.

Gibson, James L. 1980. "Environmental Constraints on the Behavior of Judges: A Representational Model of Judicial Decision Making." *Law and Society Review* 14, pp. 343–370.

Githens, Marianne, and Jewel Prestage. 1977. *A Portrait of Marginality.* New York: McKay.

Goldman, Sheldon. 1965. "Characteristics of Eisenhower and Kennedy Appointees to the Lower Federal Bench." *Western Political Quarterly* 18 (December), pp. 755–762.

Goldman, Sheldon. 1972. "Johnson and Nixon Appointees to the Lower Federal Courts: Some Socio-Political Perspectives." *Journal of Politics* 34, pp. 934–943.

Goldman, Sheldon. 1974. "Judicial Backgrounds, Recruitment, and the Party Variable: The Case of the Johnson and Nixon Appointees to the United States District and Appeals Courts." *Arizona State Law Journal* 2, pp. 211–222.

Goldman, Sheldon. 1979. "Should There Be Affirmative Action for the Judiciary?" *Judicature,* 62, p.488–492.

Goldman, Sheldon. 1981. "Carter's Judicial Appointments: A Lasting Legacy." *Judicature* 64, pp. 344–355.

Goldman, Sheldon. 1982. "Judicial Selection and the Qualities that Make a 'Good' Judge." *Annals of the American Academy of Social and Political Science* 462, pp. 112–124.

Goldman, Sheldon. 1987. "Reagan's Second Term Judicial Appointments: The Battle at Midway." *Judicature* 70, pp. 324–339.

Goldman, Sheldon. 1989. "Judicial Appointments and the Presidential Agenda." In Paul Brace, Christine B. Harrington, and Gary King, eds. *The Presidency in American Politics.* New York: New York University Press.

Goldman, Sheldon. 1989. "Reagan and Meese Remake the Judiciary." In Sheldon Goldman and Austin Sarat, eds. *American Court Systems,* 2nd ed. New York: Longman, pp. 307–322.

Goldman, Sheldon. 1989. "Reagan's Judicial Legacy: Completing the Puzzle and Summing Up." *Judicature* 72, pp. 318–330.

Goldman, Sheldon. 1991. "The Bush Imprint on the Judiciary: Carrying on a Tradition."

Judicature 74, pp. 294–306.

Goldman, Sheldon. 1991. "Federal Judicial Selection." In John B. Gates and Charles A. Johnson, eds. *The American Courts: A Critical Assessment.* Washington, DC: CQ Press.

Goldman, Sheldon. 1993. "Bush's Judicial Legacy: The Final Imprint," *Judicature* 76 (April–May), pp. 282–297.

Goldman, Sheldon. 1995. "Judicial Selection under Clinton: A Midterm Examination," *Judicature* 78 (May–June), pp. 276–291.

Goldman, Sheldon, and Thomas Jahnige. 1976. *The Federal Courts as a Political System.* 2nd ed. New York: Harper and Row.

Goldman, Sheldon, and Matthew D. Saranson. 1994. "Clinton's Nontraditional Judges: Creating a More Representative Bench." *Judicature* 78 (September–October), pp. 68–73.

Goldman, Sheldon and Elliot Slotnick. 1997. "Clinton's First Term Judiciary: Many Bridges to Cross," *Judicature* 80 (May–June 1997), pp. 254–273.

Gottschall, Jon. 1986. "The Senate's Role in Judicial Appointments." Judicature 70, p. 52.

Goulden, Joseph C. 1974. *The Benchwarmers.* New York: Weybright and Talley.

Graham, Barbara Luck. 1990. "Judicial Recruitment and Racial Diversity on State Courts: An Overview." *Judicature* 74, pp. 28–34.

Graham, Hugh Davis. 1992. *Civil Rights and the Presidency: Race and Gender in American Politics, 1960–1972.* New York: Oxford University Press.

Grossman, Joel B. 1965. *Lawyers and Judges: The ABA and the Politics of Judicial Selection.* New York: John Wiley and Sons.

Gruhl, John, Susan Welch, and Cassia Spohn. 1981. "Women as Policy Makers: The Case of Trial Judges." *American Journal of Political Science* 25, pp. 308–322.

Guinier, Lani. 1991. "The Triumph of Tokenism: The Voting Rights Act and the Theory of Black Electoral Success." *Michigan Law Review* 89, pp. 1077–1154.

Guinier, Lani. 1994. *The Tyranny of the Majority: Fundamental Fairness in Representative Democracy.* New York: The Free Press.

Hall, Kermit L. 1979. *The Politics of Justice: Lower Federal Judicial Selection and the Second Party System, 1829–61.* Lincoln: University of Nebraska Press.

Hall, Kermit L., and Eric W. Rise. 1991. *From Local Courts to National Tribunals: The Federal District Courts of Florida, 1821–1990.* New York: Carlson Publishing.

Hamilton, Alexander, James Madison, and John Jay. 1961. *The Federalist Papers.* Introduction by Clinton Rossiter. New York: New American Library.

Hamilton, Charles V. 1965. "Southern Judges and Negro Voting Rights: The Judicial Approach to the Solution of Controversial Social Problems." *Wisconsin Law Review* 65 (Winter), pp. 72–102.

Hamilton, Charles V. 1973. *The Bench and the Ballot: Southern Federal Judges and Black Voters.* New York: Oxford University Press.

Harris, Joseph P. 1953. *The Advice and Consent of the Senate: A Study of the Confirmation of Appointees by the United States Senate.* Berkeley: University of California Press.

Harris, Richard. 1971. *Decision.* New York: E. P. Dutton.

Harvey, James C. 1971. *Civil Rights during the Kennedy Administration.* Hattiesburg: University and College Press of Mississippi.

Heck, Edward V., and Steven Shull. 1982. "Policy Preferences of Justices and Presidents: The Case of Civil Rights." *Law and Policy Quarterly* 4, pp. 327–338.

Hensley, Thomas, and Joyce Baugh. 1987. "The Impact of the 1978 Omnibus Judgeships Act." In Stuart Nagel, ed. *Research in Law and Public Policy Studies.* Greenwich, CT: JAI Press.

Hero, Rodney E. 1992. *Latinos and the U.S. Political System.* Philadelphia: Temple University Press.

Honigcborg, Peter Jan, and James Dikel. 1988. "Unfairness in Access to and Citation of Unpublished Federal Court Decisions." *Golden Gate University Law Review* 18, pp. 277–299.

Horowitz, Donald. 1977. *The Courts and Social Policy.* Washington, DC: The Brookings Institution.

Jackson, Donald Dale. 1974. *Judges.* New York: Atheneum.

Jacob, Herbert. 1986. *Law and Politics in the United States.* Boston: Little, Brown and Company.

Jaffe, Frederick S., Barbara L. Lindheim, and Philip R. Lee. 1981. *Abortion Politics: Private Morality and Public Policy.* New York: McGraw-Hill.

Johnson, Charles A. 1979. "Lower Court Reactions to Supreme Court Decisions: A Quantitative Explanation." *American Journal of Political Science* 23, pp. 792–804.

Johnson, Donald. 1982. *National Party Platforms of 1980.* Urbana: University of Illinois Press.

Jones, Augustus J. 1982. *Law, Bureaucracy, and Politics: The Implementation of Title VI of the Civil Rights Act of 1964.* Washington, DC: University Press of America.

Jones, Harry Wilmer. 1965. "The Trial Judge, Role Analysis and Profile." In Harry Jones, ed. *The Courts, the Public, and the Law Explosion.* Englewood Cliffs, NJ: Prentice-Hall.

Judicial Conference of the United States. 1983. *Judges of the United States.* 2nd ed. Washington, DC: Bicentennial Committee of the Judicial Conference of the United States.

Judicial Staff Directory. 1991, 1992, 1993, 1994, and 1995. Mount Vernon, VA: Staff Directories, Ltd.

Kantowicz, Edward R. 1986. "Reminiscences of a Fated Presidency: Themes from the Carter Memoirs." *Presidential Studies Quarterly* 16.

Kernell, Samuel. 1986. *Going Public: New Strategies of Presidential Leadership.* Washington, DC: CQ Press.

King, Anthony, ed. 1983. *Both Ends of the Avenue: The Presidency, the Executive Branch, and Congress in the 1980's.* Washington, DC: American Enterprise Institute for Public Policy Research.

Kitchin, William. 1978. *Federal District Judges: An Analysis of Judicial Perceptions.* Baltimore: Collage Press.

Kluger, Richard. 1975. *Simple Justice: The History of Brown v. Board of Education and Black America's Struggle for Equality.* New York: Random House.

Kritzer, Herbert M. 1978. "Political Correlates of the Behavior of Federal District Judges: A 'Best Case' Analysis." *Journal of Politics* 40, pp. 25–58.

Kritzer, Herbert M. 1979. "Federal Judges and Their Political Environment." *American Journal of Political Science* 23, pp. 194–207.

Kritzer, Herbert, and Thomas M. Uhlman. 1977. "Sisterhood in the Courtroom: Sex of Judge and Defendant in Criminal Case Disposition." *Social Science Journal* 14, pp. 77–88.

Lasky, Victor. 1968. *Robert F. Kennedy: The Myth and the Man.* New York: Trident Press.

Lasky, Victor. 1979. *Jimmy Carter: The Man and the Myth.* New York: R. Marek.

Latham, Earl. 1972. *J. F. Kennedy and Presidential Power.* Lexington, MA: DC Heath and Company.

Lawson, Steven F. 1976. *Black Ballots: Voting Rights in the South, 1944–1969.* New York: Columbia University Press.

Lazerson, Joshua. 1992. "Bill Clinton States Positions on the Federal Judiciary." *Judicature* 76 (August-September), pp. 97, 100.

Light, Paul Charles. 1982. *The Presidential Agenda.* Baltimore: The Johns Hopkins University Press.

Lipshutz, Robert, and Douglas B. Huron. "Achieving a More Representative Federal Judiciary." *Judicature* 62, pp. 483–485.

Lyles, Kevin, L. 1994. "The Bork Nomination and Black America: A Case Study." In Lucius Barker and Mack Jones, *African-Americans and the American Political System.* Englewood Cliffs, NJ: Prentice-Hall, pp. 131–172.

Lyles, Kevin, L. 1996. "Presidential Expectations and Judicial Performance Revisited: Law and Politics in the Federal District Courts, 1960–1992." *Presidential Studies Quarterly* 26, pp. 447–472.

Mackenzie, Calvin. 1981. *The Politics of Presidential Appointments.* New York: The Free Press.

Martin, Elaine. 1982. "Women on the Federal Bench: A Comparative Profile." *Judicature* 65, pp. 306–313.

Martin, Elaine. 1987. "Gender and Judicial Selection: A Comparison of the Reagan and Carter Administrations." *Judicature* 71, pp. 136–142.

Martin, Elaine. 1990. "Men and Women on the Bench: Viva la Difference?" *Judicature* 73, pp. 204–208.

Martin, Elaine. 1993. "The Representative Role of Women Judges." *Judicature* 77, pp. 166–173.

Mathias, Charles. "Advise and Consent: The Role of the United States Senate in the Judicial Selection Process." *University of Chicago Law Review* 54, p. 200.

McClain, Paula, and Joseph Stewart, Jr. 1995. *Can We All Get Along?* Boulder, CO: Westview Press.

McDowell, Gary. 1988. *Curbing the Courts: The Constitution and the Limits of Judicial Power.* Baton Rouge: Louisiana State University Press.

McFeeley, Neil D. 1987. *Appointment of Judges: The Johnson Presidency.* Austin: The University of Texas Press.

McLauchlan, William P. 1984. *Federal Court Caseloads.* New York: Praeger.

McMillian, Neil R. 1977. "Black Enfranchisement in Mississippi: Federal Enforcement and Black Protest in the 1960's." *Journal of Southern History* 43, pp. 351–372.

Melville, Margarita. 1988. "Hispanics: Race, Class, or Ethnicity?" *Journal of Ethnic Studies* 16, pp. 67–83.

Meredith, James. 1966. *Three Years in Mississippi.* Bloomington: Indiana University Press.

Miner, Roger J. 1997. "Advice and Consent in Theory and Practice." In David M. O'Brien, ed., *Judges on Judging.* Chatham, NJ: Chatham House Publishers.

Miranda, Christopher. 1993. *Directory of the Hispanic Judges of the United States of America.* Melville, New York: Hispanic National Bar Association.

Miroff, Bruce. 1976. *Pragmatic Illusions, the Presidential Politics of John F. Kennedy.* New York: McKay.

Monaghan, Henry Paul. "The Confirmation Process: Law or Politics?" *Harvard Law*

Review 101, p. 1203.

Morgan, Ruth P. 1970. *The President and Civil Rights: Policymaking by Executive Order*. New York: St. Martin's Press.

Murphy, Walter F. 1959. "Lower Court Checks on Supreme Court Power." *American Political Science Review* 53, pp. 1017–1034.

Murphy, Walter F. 1966. "Courts as Small Groups." *Harvard Law Review* 79, pp. 1565–1572.

Murphy, Walter F. 1990. "Reagan's Judicial Strategy." In Larry Berman, ed. *Looking Back on the Reagan Presidency*. Baltimore: The Johns Hopkins University Press.

Murphy, Walter F., and C. Herman Pritchett. 1986. *Courts, Judges and Politics: An Introduction to the Judicial Process*. 4th ed. New York: Random House.

Nagel, Stuart. 1969. *The Legal Process from a Behavioral Perspective*. Homewood, IL: Dorsey.

Navasky, Victor S. 1971. *Kennedy Justice*. New York: Atheneum.

Neff, Alan. 1981. "Breaking with Tradition: A Study of the U.S. District Court Judge Nominating Commissions." *Judicature* 64, pp. 256–278.

Neff, Alan. 1981. *Federal Judicial Selection During the Carter Administration: The United States District Judge Nominating Commissions, Their Members, Procedures and Candidates*. Chicago: American Judicature Society.

Nelson, Dorothy W. 1977. "Carter's Merit Plan: A Good First Step." *Judicature* 61, pp. 105–111.

Neustadt, Richard. 1960. *Presidential Power: The Politics of Leadership*. New York: John Wiley and Sons.

O'Brien, David M. 1988. *Judicial Roulette: Report of the Twentieth Century Fund Task Force on Judicial Selection*. New York: Priority Press.

O'Brien, David M. 1988. "The Reagan Judges: His Most Enduring Legacy?" In Charles O. Jones, ed. *The Reagan Legacy: Promise and Performance*. Chatham, NJ: Chatham House Publishers, pp. 64–101.

O'Brien, David M. 1996. *Storm Center*. New York: W. W. Norton.

Orfield, Gary. 1978. *Must We Bus? Segregated Schools and National Policy*. Washington, DC: The Brookings Institution.

Orman, John. 1987. *Comparing Presidential Behavior: Carter, Reagan, and the Macho Presidential Style*. Westport CT: Greenwood Press.

Ortiz, Carlos G. 1993. "The Case for a Hispanic-American Supreme Court Justice." *Bar Leader* 17, pp. 22–23.

Parker, Frank R. 1990. *Black Votes Count: Political Empowerment in Mississippi after 1965*. Chapel Hill: The University of North Carolina Press.

Parmet, Herbert S. 1982. *JFK: The Presidency of John Fitzgerald Kennedy*. Baltimore: Penguin.

Peltason, Jack. 1955. *Federal Courts in the Political Process*. Garden City, NY: Doubleday.

Peltason, Jack. 1961. *58 Lonely Men: Southern Federal Judges and School Desegregation*. Urbana: University of Illinois Press.

Performance of the Reagan Administration in Nominating Women and Minorities to the Federal Bench. Hearing before the Committee on the Judiciary, United States Senate, 100th Congress, Second Session, February 2, 1988, Washington, DC: Government Printing Office, 1990.

Perry, H. W. 1991. *Deciding to Decide: Agenda Setting in the United States Supreme Court*. Cambridge: Harvard University Press.

Pfiffner, James. 1986. "White House Staff versus the Cabinet: Centripetal and Centrifugal Roles." *Presidential Studies Quarterly* 16 (Fall), pp. 680–681.

Pfiffner, James P. 1988. *The Strategic Presidency: Hitting the Ground Running.* Chicago: Dorsey Press.

Pitkin, Hanna. 1967. *The Concept of Representation.* Berkeley: University of California Press.

Posner, Richard A. 1985. *The Federal Courts: Crisis and Reform.* Cambridge: Harvard University Press.

Prestage, Jewel L. 1987. "Black Women Judges: An Examination of Their Socio-Economic, Educational and Political Backgrounds and Judicial Placement." In Franklin D. Jones and Michael O. Adams, eds. *Readings in American Political Issues.* Dubuque, IA: Kendall/Hunt, pp. 324–344.

Preston, Michael B. 1986. "Affirmative Action Policy: Can It Survive the Reaganites?" In Michael W. Combs and John Gruhl, eds. *Affirmative Action: Theory, Analysis, and Prospects.* Jefferson, NC: McFarland.

Pritchett, C. Herman. 1948. *The Roosevelt Court: A Study of Judicial Votes and Values, 1937–1947.* New York: Macmillan.

Richardson, Richard J., and Kenneth N. Vines. 1970. *The Politics of the Federal Courts: Lower Courts in the United States.* Boston: Little, Brown and Company.

Robel, Lauren K. 1989. "The Myth of the Disposable Opinion: Unpublished Opinions and Government Litigants in the United States Courts of Appeals." *Michigan Law Review* 87, pp. 940–962.

Rodgers, Harrell R., and Charles S. Bullock. 1972. *Law and Social Change: Civil Rights Laws and Their Consequences.* New York: McGraw-Hill.

Rodman, Hyman, with Betty Sarvis and Joy Walker Bonar. 1987. *The Abortion Question.* New York: Columbia University Press.

Rosenbaum, Judith. 1977. "Implementing Federal Merit Selection." *Judicature* 61, pp. 125–128.

Rosenberg, Gerald N. 1991. *The Hollow Hope.* Chicago: University of Chicago Press.

Rowland, C. K. 1990. "The Links Between Platform Based Appointment Criteria and Trial Judges' Abortion Judgments." *Judicature* 74 (October-November), pp. 153–162.

Rowland, C. K., and Robert A. Carp. 1980. "A Longitudinal Study of Party Effects on Federal District Court Policy Propensities." *American Journal of Political Science* 24, pp. 291–305.

Rowland, C. K., with Robert A. Carp and Ronald Stidham. 1984. "Patterns of Presidential Influence on the Federal District Courts: An Analysis of the Appointment Process." *Presidential Studies Quarterly* 14, p. 548.

Rowland, C. K., Donald Songer, and Robert A. Carp. 1988. "Presidential Effects on Criminal Justice Policy in the Lower Federal Courts: The Reagan Judges." *Law and Society Review* 22, pp. 191–200.

Rowland, C. K., and Bridget Jeffery Todd. 1991. "Where You Stand Depends on Who Sits: Platform Promises and Judicial Gatekeeping in the Federal District Courts." *Journal of Politics* 53, pp. 175–185.

Rubin, Eva R. 1982. *Abortion, Politics and the Courts: Roe v. Wade and Its Aftermath.* Westport, CT: Greenwood Press.

Sarratt, Reed. 1966. *The Ordeal of Desegregation.* New York: Harper and Row.

Saunders, Doris E., ed. 1964. *The Kennedy Years and the Negro.* Chicago, IL: Johnson Publishing Company.

Schieffer, Bob, and Gary Paul Gates. 1989. *The Acting President.* New York: Dutton.

Schlesinger, Arthur M., Jr. 1965. *A Thousand Days, John F. Kennedy in the White House.* New York: Fawcett Crest.

Schmidhauser, John R. 1979. *Judges and Justices: The Federal Appellate Judiciary.* Boston: Little, Brown and Company.

Schubert, Glendon. 1957. *The Presidency in the Courts.* Minneapolis: University of Minnesota Press.

Schubert, Glendon. 1974. *Judicial Policy Making.* 2nd ed. Glenview, IL: Scott, Foresman.

Schuck, Peter H., Director. 1975. *The Judiciary Committees: A Study of the House and Senate Judiciary Committees.* The Ralph Nader Congress Project. New York: Grossman Publishers.

Schuman, Howard, with Charlotte Steeh and Lawrence Bobo. 1985. *Racial Attitudes in America: Trends and Interpretations.* Cambridge: Harvard University Press.

Schuman, Jerome. 1970/71. "A Black Lawyer's Study." *Howard Law Journal* 16, pp. 256–262.

Schwartz, Herman. 1988. *Packing the Courts: The Conservative Campaign to Rewrite the Constitution.* New York: Charles Scribner's Sons.

Scigliano, Robert. 1971. *The Supreme Court and the Presidency.* New York: The Free Press.

Seltzer, Richard, and Robert Smith. 1985. "Race and Ideology." *Phylon* 46, pp. 98–105.

Shartel, B. 1931. "Federal Judges—Appointment, Supervision, Removal—Some Possibilities under the Constitution," *Michigan Law Review* 28, p. 485.

Shull, Steven A. 1989. *The President and Civil Rights Policy: Leadership and Change.* Westport, CT: Greenwood Press.

Silverstein, Mark. 1994. *Judicious Choices: The Politics of Supreme Court Confirmations.* New York: W. W. Norton and Company.

Simon, Paul. 1986. "The Senate's Role in Judicial Appointments." *Judicature* 56, pp. 55–58.

Simon, Paul. 1992. *Advice and Consent: Clarence Thomas, Robert Bork and the Intriguing History of the Supreme Court's Nomination Battles.* Washington, DC: National Press Books.

Sitkoff, Harvard. 1981. *The Struggle for Black Equality.* New York: Hill and Wang.

Slotnick, Elliot. 1980. "Reforms in Judicial Selection: Will They Affect the Senate's Role? (Part I and II)." *Judicature* 64, pp. 60–73, 114–131.

Slotnick, Elliot. 1983. "The ABA Standing Committee on Federal Judiciary: A Contemporary Assessment—Parts 1 and 2." *Judicature* 66 (March), pp. 348–362, 385–393.

Slotnick, Elliot. 1983. "Overview: Judicial Selection. Lowering the Federal Bench or Raising it Higher?: Affirmative Action and Judicial Selection during the Carter Administration." *Yale Law and Policy Review* 1, pp. 270–298.

Slotnick, Elliot. 1984. "Gender, Affirmative Action, and Recruitment to the Federal Bench." *Golden Gate University Law Review* 14, pp. 519–571.

Slotnick, Elliot. 1984. "Judicial Selection Systems and Nomination Outcomes: Does the Process Make a Difference?" *American Politics Quarterly* 12, pp. 225–240.

Slotnick, Elliot. 1984. "The Paths to the Federal Bench: Gender, Race, and Judicial Recruitment Variation." *Judicature* 67, pp. 371–388.

Slotnick, Elliot. 1988. "Federal Judicial Recruitment and Selection Research: A Review Essay." *Judicature* 71, pp. 317–324.

Slotnick, Elliot. 1988. "Review Essay on Judicial Recruitment and Selection." *The Justice System Journal*, 13, pp. 109–124.

Smith, Christopher E. 1990. "Former U.S. Magistrates as District Judges: The Possibilities and Consequences of Promotion within the Federal Judiciary." *Judicature* 73, pp. 268–272.

Smith, Christopher E. 1990. *United States Magistrates in the Federal Courts: Subordinate Judges*. New York: Praeger.

Smith, Christopher E. 1992. "From U.S. Magistrates to U.S. Magistrate Judges: Developments Affecting the Federal District Court's Lower Tier of Judicial Officers." *Judicature* 75, pp. 210–215.

Smith, Christopher E. 1993. *Courts and Public Policy*. Chicago: Nelson-Hall.

Smith, Michael David. 1983. *Race versus the Robe: The Dilemma of Black Judges*. New York: National University Publications.

Sobel, Lester A. 1967. *Civil Rights, 1960–66*. New York: Facts on File.

Songer, Donald R. 1988. "Nonpublication in the United States District Courts: Official Criteria vs. Inferences from Appellate Review." *Journal of Politics* 50, pp. 206–215.

Songer, Donald R. 1990. "Criteria for Publication and Opinions in the U.S. Courts of Appeals: Formal Rules versus Empirical Reality." *Judicature* 73, pp. 307–313.

Sorensen, Theodore C. 1965. *Kennedy*. New York: Bantam Books.

Spohn, Cassia, John Gruhl, and Susan Welch. 1981–1982. "The Effect of Race on Sentencing: A Re-examination of an Unsettled Question." *Law and Society Review* 16, pp. 72–88.

Stern, Mark. 1989. "John F. Kennedy and Civil Rights: From Congress to the Presidency." *Presidential Studies Quarterly* (Fall), pp. 797–823.

Stidham, Ronald, and Robert A. Carp. 1987. "Judges, Presidents, and Policy Choices: Exploring the Linkages." *Social Science Quarterly* 68, pp. 395–404.

Stidham, Ronald, and Robert A. Carp. 1988. "Exploring Regionalism in the Federal District Courts." *Publius* 18, pp. 113–125.

Stidham, Ronald, Robert A. Carp, and C. K. Rowland. 1983. "Women's Rights before the Federal District Courts, 1971–1977." *American Politics Quarterly* 11, pp. 205–218.

Strong, Robert A. 1986. "Recapturing Leadership: The Carter Administration and the Crisis of Confidence." *Presidential Studies Quarterly* 16 (Fall).

Sundquist, James L. "Jimmy Carter as Public Administrator: An Appraisal at Mid-term." *Public Administration Review* 39, p. 3.

Surrency, Erwin C. 1967. "Federal District Court Judges and the History of Their Courts." 40 F.R.D. 139.

Surrency, Erwin C. 1987. *History of the Federal Courts*. New York: Oceana Publications.

Swerdlow, Joel L., ed. 1987. *Presidential Debates 1988 and Beyond*. Washington, DC: CQ Press.

Tatalovich, Raymond, and Byron W. Daynes. 1981. *The Politics of Abortion*. New York: Praeger.

Tate, C. Neal. 1981. "Personal Attribute Models of Voting Behavior of U.S. Supreme Court Justices: Liberalism in Civil Liberties and Economics Decisions, 1946–1978." *American Political Science Review* 75, pp. 355–368.

Tate, C. Neal. 1983. "The Methodology of Judicial Behavior Research: A Review and Critique." *Political Behavior* 5, pp. 51–82.

Tate, Katherine. 1993. *From Protests to Politics: The New Black Voters in American Election*. Cambridge: Harvard University Press.

Thernstrom, Abigail M. 1987. *Whose Votes Count? Affirmative Action and Minority*

Voting Rights. Boston: Harvard University Press.

Tolchin, Martin, and Susan Tolchin. 1971. *To the Victor: Political Patronage from the Clubhouse to the White House*. New York: Random House.

Totenberg, Nina. 1988. "The Confirmation Process and the Public: To Know or Not to Know." *Harvard Law Review* 101, p. 1213.

Tribe, Laurence. 1985. *God Save This Honorable Court*. New York: Random House.

Tydings, Joseph W. 1977. "Merit Selection for District Judges." *Judicature* 61, pp. 112–118.

Uhlman, Thomas. 1977. "Race, Recruitment, and Representation: Background Differences between Black and White Trial Court Judges." *Western Political Quarterly* 31, pp. 457–470.

Uhlman, Thomas. 1978. "Black Elite Decision Making: The Case of Trial Judges," *American Journal of Political Science* 22, pp. 884–895.

U.S. Law Week, General Law, vols. 1960–1997. Washington, DC: Bureau of National Affairs.

Verba, Sidney, and Norman H. Nie. 1972. *Participation in America*. Chicago: University of Chicago Press.

Vestal, Allan D. 1970–1971. "Publishing District Court Opinions in the 1970's." *Loyola Law Review* 4, pp. 185–220.

Vines, Kenneth N. 1964. "Federal District Court Judges and Race Relations Cases in the South." *Journal of Politics* 26, pp. 337–357.

Walker, Thomas G. 1970. "Judges in Concert: The Influence of the Group on Judicial Decision-Making." Unpublished Ph.D. dissertation, University of Kentucky.

Walker, Thomas G., and Deborah J. Barrow. 1985. "The Diversification of the Federal Bench: Policy and Process Ramifications." *Journal of Politics* 47, pp. 596–617.

Walker, Thomas G., and William E. Hulbary. 1980. "The Supreme Court Selection Process: Presidential Motivations and Judicial Performances." *Western Political Quarterly* 33, pp. 185–197.

Wasby, Stephen L., Anthony A. D'Amato, and Rosemary Metrailer. 1977. *Desegregation from Brown to Alexander*. Carbondale: Southern Illinois University Press.

Washington, Michelle. 1974. "Black Judges in White America." *The Black Law Journal*, pp. 241–245.

Welch, Susan, with Michael Combs and John Gruhl. 1988. "Do Black Judges Make a Difference?" *American Journal of Political Science* 32, pp. 126–136.

White, Theodore H. 1961. *The Making of the President 1960*. New York: Atheneum.

Windt, Theodore Otto, Jr. 1990. *Presidents and Protesters: Political Rhetoric in the 1960's*. Tuscaloosa: The University of Alabama Press.

Windt, Theodore, Jr., and Beth Ingold. 1983. *Essays in Presidential Rhetoric*. Dubuque, IA: Kendall/Hunt.

Witt, Elder. 1986. *A Different Justice: Reagan and the Supreme Court*. Washington, DC: CQ Press.

Wofford, Harris, Jr. 1980. *Of Kennedys and Kings, Making Sense of the Sixties*. New York: Farrar, Straus and Giroux.

Woodward, Bob. 1994. *The Agenda: Inside the Clinton White House*. New York: Simon and Schuster.

Wright, Bruce. 1973. "A Black Brood on Black Judges." *Judicature* 57, pp. 22–23.

Table of Selected Cases

Index

About the Author

KEVIN L. LYLES is Assistant Professor of Political Science at the University of Illinois at Chicago.

ISBN 0-275-96082-X

90000>

EAN

9 780275 960827

HARDCOVER BAR CODE